THE WORKS
AND CORRESPONDENCE OF
DAVID RICARDO

VOLUME III

PLAN OF THE EDITION

A General Index is in preparation.

THE WORKS
AND CORRESPONDENCE OF
DAVID RICARDO

EDITED BY
PIERO SRAFFA
WITH THE COLLABORATION OF
M. H. DOBB

VOLUME III

PAMPHLETS AND PAPERS
1809–1811

CAMBRIDGE
AT THE UNIVERSITY PRESS
FOR THE ROYAL ECONOMIC SOCIETY
1962

PUBLISHED BY
THE SYNDICS OF THE CAMBRIDGE UNIVERSITY PRESS

Bentley House, 200 Euston Road, London, N.W. 1
American Branch: 32 East 57th Street, New York 22, N.Y.
West African Office: P.O. Box 33, Ibadan, Nigeria

First printed 1951
Reprinted 1962

First printed in Great Britain at the University Press, Cambridge
Reprinted by offset-lithography by Bradford & Dickens, London, W.C. 1

CONTENTS OF VOLUME III

NOTES FROM RICARDO'S MANUSCRIPTS
1810–1811

APPENDIX

FACSIMILES

PREFATORY NOTE
TO VOLUMES III AND IV

THESE two volumes under the general title of 'Pamphlets and Papers' contain Ricardo's shorter writings. The division between the two volumes is chronological. Volume III has a greater unity in that it consists entirely of writings on monetary subjects of the period of the Bullion Controversy, while Volume IV is composed of miscellaneous pieces which extend over the later years of Ricardo's life. Each volume is divided into two parts, the first containing more formal writings intended for publication, the second notes and papers from Ricardo's manuscripts. It is chiefly in the second part of each volume that the new material will be found; practically all the writings in that part of Volume IV being unpublished hitherto.

As in the previous volumes, the editor's footnotes are distinguished by numerals and by being generally printed in double column. Two editorial footnotes which were too long for insertion in their proper places have been severally put in Appendices at the end of each of the two volumes. In printing from original manuscripts the spelling, punctuation and abbreviations of Ricardo have generally been followed, as specified in Section v of the Introduction to Volume II.

To each volume have been appended Tables of Corresponding Pages to facilitate the identification in the present edition of page-references by earlier writers to the previous editions of the pamphlets.

These two volumes had to a large extent been prepared before the War (as has been explained in the General Preface in Volume I) and thus they could benefit from the advice of the late Lord Keynes who read in draft the editorial matter and suggested a number of improvements. Acknowledgement is also due to Mr Frank Ricardo and to Mr C. K. Mill for generously making available MSS in their possession; to the Bibliothèque Publique et Universitaire de Genève for the loan of the MS of the *Notes on Bentham*; to Professor F. A. Hayek for finding the annotated copy of Blake's

Observations and to the Librarian of Somerville College, Oxford, for making it available; and to The Johns Hopkins Press for permission to use material first published by them. Special mention must be made of editorial assistance given by Dr Karl Bode and Mrs Barbara Lowe in preparing a number of these papers for publication.

P. S.

TRINITY COLLEGE
CAMBRIDGE
February 1951

PAMPHLETS AND PAPERS
WRITTEN FOR PUBLICATION
1809-1811

NOTE ON THE BULLION ESSAYS

RICARDO'S first appearance in print marked the beginning of what came to be known as the Bullion Controversy. It took the shape of an anonymous article on The Price of Gold published in the *Morning Chronicle* of 29 August 1809. His brother and biographer, Moses Ricardo, records how this contribution came to be published. 'The immense transactions', he says, 'which he had with the Bank of England, in the course of business, tallying with the train of studies on which he was then engaged, led Mr. Ricardo to reflect upon the subject of the currency, to endeavour to account for the difference which existed between the value of the coin and the Bank notes, and to ascertain from what cause the depreciation of the latter arose. This occupied much of his attention at the time, and formed a frequent theme of conversation with those among his acquaintances who were inclined to enter upon it. He was induced to put his thoughts upon paper, without the remotest view at the time to publication. The late Mr. Perry, proprietor of the Morning Chronicle, was one of the few friends to whom Mr. Ricardo showed his manuscript. Mr. Perry urged him to allow it to be published in the Morning Chronicle; to which, not without some reluctance, Mr. Ricardo consented'.[1]

After the Bank Restriction of 1797, the price of gold had remained for two years at its Mint parity of £3. 17s. 10½d.; it began to rise in 1799, reaching £4. 6s. 0d. in January 1801; and returned near to its normal level by 1804, remaining steady until late in

---

[1] *Annual Biography and Obituary for the Year 1824*, pp. 371–2. The passage continues: 'and it was inserted in the shape of letters under the signature of R., the first of which appeared on the 6th day of September, 1810.' This is quite incorrect, for in fact it was inserted in the shape of an article, unsigned, which appeared on 29 August 1809: the two other contributions to the *Chronicle* of 1809 were evoked by criticisms of the article after publication and could not have formed part of the original MS shown to Perry. The biographer is confusing the three contributions of 1809 with the three letters to the *Chronicle* of 1810.

1808. But in 1809 it had again risen sharply, touching £4. 12s. 10½d. on 4 July. Just as the previous period of a rising price for gold had produced a body of controversial literature, including Boyd's *Letter to Pitt* (1801), Thornton's *Paper Credit* (1802), and Lord King's *Thoughts on the Restriction of Payments* (1803), so now the increase in the price of gold which began in 1808 gave rise to the Bullion Controversy.

The publication of Ricardo's article started an extensive correspondence in the *Morning Chronicle*. His own further contributions were provoked by a letter defending the Bank of England against his criticisms, which appeared on 14 September 1809 and was signed 'A Friend to Bank Notes, but no Bank Director', whom Ricardo 'soon after found to be an intelligent friend of his own',[1] Hutches Trower. Ricardo's reply to this letter appeared on 20 September over the signature 'R.' A second letter from 'A Friend to Bank Notes', although dated 23 September, was not published till 30 October; and Ricardo's rejoinder, dated 4 November, and signed 'R.', did not appear until 23 November.[2] This concluded their controversy in public. But once they had established each other's identity, it seems that the two correspondents communicated their views to one another without waiting for the long delayed publication in the *Morning Chronicle*. Thus a private controversy arose between them concurrently with the last stage of their published letters and was carried on after their controversy in public had come to an end.

What is extant of this private controversy is printed in the present volume, after Ricardo's published letters, below, pp. 34–46. It is clear, however, that there must have been more communica-

---

[1] *Annual Biography and Obituary for 1824*, p. 372.

[2] The authorship was acknowledged in a leading article of the *Morning Chronicle* of 27 August 1810, after the publication of the Bullion Report: 'The letters of our invaluable correspondent Mr Ricardo, contributed most essentially to open the eyes of the public to the true cause of the depreciation of paper.' Ricardo's article and his two letters to the *Morning Chronicle* of 1809 were reprinted under the title *Three Letters on the Price of Gold*, by David Ricardo, ed. by J. H. Hollander, Baltimore, Johns Hopkins Press, 1903.

tions, and their probable sequence was as follows. To Trower's letter of 23 September published in the *Morning Chronicle* of 30 October, Ricardo must have replied with two papers:

(*a*) one not intended for publication and sent privately to Trower, which is not extant;

(*b*) the letter of 4 November, published in the *Morning Chronicle* of 23 November.

Trower's reply to (*a*), which was found among Trower's papers, is printed below, pp. 34–6; his reply to (*b*), consisting of the Observations mentioned by Ricardo (below, p. 43) was probably intended for publication, but was not inserted in the *Morning Chronicle*, and has not been found.

Ricardo's answer to both of these replies of Trower was found among Trower's papers and is printed below, pp. 36–46; the first part (pp. 36–43) deals with Trower's reply to (*a*) and the second (pp. 43–6) with Trower's reply to (*b*).[1]

Meanwhile Ricardo had decided to give further publicity to his views in the form of a pamphlet, *The High Price of Bullion, a Proof of the Depreciation of Bank Notes*, which was published by John Murray about a month after his last letter had appeared in the *Morning Chronicle*.[2]

---

[1] The first part of Ricardo's answer was first published by Dr Bonar under the title 'Ricardo on Currency' in *Economic Journal*, March 1896, pp. 64–9. The two extant papers of this private controversy between Trower and Ricardo were published in their entirety as Appendix A (1) and (2) to *Letters of David Ricardo to Hutches Trower and Others 1811–1823*, ed. by J. Bonar and J. H. Hollander, Oxford, 1899. Trower's paper is here printed from the MS now in the possession of Dr Bonar. Ricardo's paper is reprinted from *Letters to Trower*; the MS is now in the possession of Professor Hollander (see *The Economic Library of J. H. Hollander, Ph.D.*, privately printed, Baltimore, 1937, p. 314).

[2] There is some doubt as to the exact date of publication. Murray's advertisement in the *Morning Chronicle* of Tuesday, 26 Dec. 1809, announced 'On Thursday next will be published, The High Price of Bullion...', and Bosanquet (*Practical Observations*, p. 2) refers to it as 'published late in 1809'. However, the first advertisement under the usual heading 'This day is published' occurred in *The Times* of Saturday, 30 December; even this may have been premature, as it gave no price, whereas the practice was to

The relation of the pamphlet to the *Chronicle* contributions has been the subject of some confusion. Ricardo himself, in his Introduction to the first three editions of the pamphlet, says that 'he has thought proper to republish his sentiments on this question in a form more calculated to bring it to fair discussion'. McCulloch, however, who had not read any of the contributions to the *Chronicle*,[1] is certainly misleading in his statement that 'having subsequently collected the letters, and given them a more systematic form, Mr. Ricardo published them in a pamphlet', as it suggests that the pamphlet was little more than a reprint of the letters.[2] As Professor Hollander says,[3] 'An important consequence of McCulloch's editorial neglect has been a general acquiescence in the view that the *Chronicle* letters were planned and published in serial form,[4] and that the pamphlet on the "High Price of Bullion" was not merely a free version but an essential reproduction of the statements therein contained.' A comparison of the pamphlet with the contributions to the *Morning Chronicle* shows that, although the main points discussed in the pamphlet had been outlined in the letters, the former is by no means a mere reprint, but was almost entirely written afresh.

Nor is there any foundation for Professor Silberling's supposition that the *High Price of Bullion* was written before the contributions to the *Morning Chronicle*, indeed several years

do so on actual publication. The earliest advertisement stating the price (2*s.*) which has been found is that published in *The Times* of 3 Jan. 1810. Thus, publication may have been delayed a few days into the new year, which would agree with the date 1810 on the title-page of the pamphlet.

[1] As is shown by the fact that in his *Life and Writings of Mr. Ricardo* (1824 and later editions), he gives the date of the first contribution to the *Chronicle* as '6 September 1809', which is an attempt to reconcile the date given in the *Annual Obituary* (see above, p. 3, n. 1) with the year given in Ricardo's Introduction.

[2] *Literature of Political Economy*, 1845, p. 172. This suggestion is not contained in the account of the origin of the pamphlet given by McCulloch in the successive editions of his *Life and Writings of Mr. Ricardo*.

[3] Introduction to Ricardo's *Three Letters on the Price of Gold*, p. 4.

[4] In this misapprehension McCulloch was following the *Annual Obituary*; see above, p. 3, n. 1.

before.[1] He rests his case mainly on the assertion that the pamphlet 'refers to no political or economic events later than 1805'; but Ricardo's treatment being essentially abstract, no events apart from the Bank Restriction are referred to, either before or after 1805, other than movements of prices; most of these, notably the rise in the price of gold, the fall of silver compared with gold and the depression of the exchange, refer to the year 1809. It is true that Ricardo refers only to works written before 1804, but it by no means follows that his comments on them were written at the time of their publication. It appears that in the autumn of 1809, after the publication of his original article, Ricardo read or re-read a number of writers on the subject of currency, including Locke, Sir James Steuart, Adam Smith, Lord Liverpool and Thornton, making notes which have been found among Ricardo's papers.[2] None of these writers is mentioned in Ricardo's original article on The Price of Gold, but they are referred to both in the subsequent letters to the *Chronicle* (September and November 1809) and in the pamphlet. Indeed, certain controversial passages from these letters, directly replying to Trower's arguments, are repeated verbatim in the pamphlet,[3] which suggests that the latter was written some time between September and November 1809 (the Introduction is dated 1 December), during the final stage of, or immediately after, the controversy in the *Chronicle*.

[1] 'The tract was probably first thrown together several years before as essentially a criticism (through the eyes of Horner and Lord King) of Thornton's hesitant conclusions: it contains some evidence of Wheatley's influence, and, like Wheatley's Essay, refers to no political or economic events later than 1805. The main body of the tract was, in all probability, prepared prior to the articles in the Chronicle newspaper.' ('Financial and Monetary Policy of Great Britain during the Napoleonic Wars, II, Ricardo and the Bullion Report', in *Quarterly Journal of Economics*, May 1924, p. 423, n.) Professor Silberling's strange theory that the publication of the Bullion pamphlet was part of a bear manoeuvre on the Stock Exchange will be discussed in connection with Ricardo's business activities.

[2] These notes contain conclusive evidence (in the form of dated postmarks) of having been written in 1809, and some of them after the middle of October 1809.

[3] See below, pp. 24 and 82, and pp. 27 and 87–8.

On 1 February 1810, a month after the publication of the pamphlet, a speech by Francis Horner in the House of Commons, which led up to the appointment of the Bullion Committee, brought the Controversy to a further stage. Ricardo replied to this speech in a private letter, on 5 February,[1] in which he disputed Horner's statement that other factors besides the superabundance of the paper circulation had contributed to the high price of gold. A number of passages from this letter were embodied in the third edition, 'With Additions', of *The High Price of Bullion*, which was published early in March 1810,[2] and, apart from some alterations in arrangement (see below, pp. 67, n. 1 and 74, n. 1), they constituted almost the entire changes in this edition. Further additions were made in the fourth edition, which was published a year later (see below, p. 11).

The Bullion Committee was actually appointed by the House of Commons on 19 February 1810 'to enquire into the Cause of the High Price of Gold Bullion'. Their report was formally laid before the House on 8 June, but it was not printed till August, and extracts appeared in all the newspapers of Monday, 13 August 1810.[3]

The appearance of the Bullion Report gave rise to a great output of controversial pamphlets.[4] Ricardo's contribution at this stage consisted of three letters to the *Morning Chronicle* in September 1810.[5] The first, a review of the Report itself, appeared

[1] Below, VI, 1.
[2] Advertised in *Monthly Literary Advertiser* of 10 March 1810. The second edition, 'Corrected', which is a reprint of the first with merely verbal alterations, was first advertised in *The Times* of 28 February, but is likely to have been prepared for publication before Ricardo wrote his letter to Horner of 5 February.
[3] According to the *Morning Chronicle* of 13 August, the Report 'was delivered at a late hour last night.' The often quoted statement of Tooke, 'the Report

of the committee was printed, and presented to the House of Commons on the 20th June 1810, the day before the prorogation' (*History of Prices*, vol. IV, p. 98), is also disproved by the letter of Horner quoted below, p. 9.
[4] Ricardo annotated, more or less extensively, several of these pamphlets. His Notes on Trotter's *Principles of Currency and Exchanges* are printed below, p. 379 ff.; the remainder are merely marginal jottings, mostly illegible.
[5] Although the date of the first of these letters had been given in the

on 6 September.[1] The second, on Sinclair's pamphlet against the Report, on 18 September. The third, on Randle Jackson's speech at the Bank Court of 20 September attacking the Report on behalf of the Bank, appeared on 24 September.[2]

Since the early summer of 1810, the question of who should review the Report in the *Edinburgh Review* had been under consideration. On 16 July Horner had written to Jeffrey, the editor: 'I am just returned to town, after an absence of about ten days. The Bullion report, I am rather surprised to find, is not yet delivered from the printers; I revised the proof-sheets before I left town. I would rather do something for you myself, if you will let me know the utmost time you can allow me; rather, I mean, than trust that subject in the hands of any of your mercenary troops, one of whom was guilty of deplorable heresies in the account of a book by one Smith.[3] I will do a short article for you this time,

---

Memoir of Ricardo in the *Annual Biography and Obituary for 1824*, (see above, p. 3, n. 1), that reference has been regarded as merely a misprint for the date of the original article of 1809, and consequently the existence of the 1810 group of letters was generally overlooked until the discovery of their cuttings among Ricardo's Papers, when they were reprinted in Ricardo's *Minor Papers on the Currency Question*, Baltimore, 1932.

[1] This letter was reprinted, without acknowledgement to the *Morning Chronicle*, in *The Tradesman; or Commercial Magazine* for 1 Oct. 1810, pp. 344–50, under the title 'Observations on the Report of the Bullion Committee' and over the signature 'R.' What purported to be a sequel to it was inserted, unsigned, under the same title in the number for 1 Nov. 1810 of *The Tradesman*; this, however, was not by Ricardo, and had appeared as an anonymous

letter in the *Morning Chronicle* of 8 Sept. 1810.

[2] A few days later, on 1 October, Whishaw wrote to Horner from London: 'Your Bullion Report is, I think, very successful. It is much talked of and has made a greater impression than I expected; of which R. Jackson's speech (for which he has received or is to receive an handsome present from the Bank) and the various publications which have appeared, are the most decisive proofs. The discussion has been tolerably well kept up in the Morning Chronicle, to which Ricardo has contributed many very good observations.' (Unpublished MS in the possession of Lady Langman.)

[3] The author of the review of Thomas Smith's *Essay on the Theory of Money and the Exchange*, in the *Edinburgh Review* for October 1808, was James Mill (see Bain, *James Mill*, p. 91).

to do justice to Mr Ricardo and Mr Mushet, who called the public attention to this very important subject at the end of last year.'[1]

From a later letter it appears that the plan that Horner himself should write the Bullion article had been abandoned, that Ricardo had been approached and had refused[2] and that Malthus had finally undertaken to do it: 'Ricardo has taken such fright at the notion of writing in the Review, that I have not succeeded in that point; he prefers publishing in a separate pamphlet. Malthus has given me hopes that he will be able to scramble up an article this week; and I am very anxious to have the subject in his hands, and to engage him in the discussion, both because he agrees with me upon the fundamental principles of the doctrine, and because we have some differences, or rather difficulties which we try to solve differently, in some parts of the Theory. All I beg of you, though I have no right to ask any thing, is not to let Milne[3] lay his hands upon us.'[4]

The paper which Ricardo had in preparation, and which he was unwilling to publish as a review, was no doubt his *Reply to Mr. Bosanquet's Practical Observations on the Bullion Report*, which appeared as a separate pamphlet a month before the number of the *Edinburgh Review* containing Malthus's Bullion article. Bosanquet's 'dexterous but somewhat unfair pamphlet', as Horner described it,[5] was regarded at the time as the most effective of the criticisms published on the Bullion Report. He directed his criticisms particularly against 'Mr. Ricardo's work, not only as having been the immediate cause of the inquiry which has since taken place, under the authority of the house of commons, but as a syllabus of the Report which has been presented by the Committee'. The *Practical Observations on the Report of*

[1] *Memoirs and Correspondence of Francis Horner, M.P.*, ed. by Leonard Horner [2nd ed., with additions], Boston, 1853, vol. II, p. 24.
[2] The Notes on the Bullion Report (below, p. 347 ff.) written by Ricardo about this time may have been in connection with this proposal.

[3] Mill, whose family name was sometimes spelt Milne (Bain, *op. cit.* p. 3); cp. above, p. 9, n. 3.
[4] Horner to Jeffrey, 3 Dec. 1810. Unpublished MS in the possession of Lady Langman.
[5] Letter to J. A. Murray, 29 Nov. 1810, in *Memoirs and Correspondence of Francis Horner*, Boston, 1853, vol. II, p. 41.

the Bullion Committee, by Charles Bosanquet, was published by J. M. Richardson in the latter half of November 1810.[1] A 'Second Edition, Corrected, with a Supplement' appeared in December of the same year,[2] the *Supplement* being published also as a separate pamphlet. The body of Ricardo's *Reply* is based on the first edition, and was sent to the press before he had seen Bosanquet's second edition;[3] his Appendix being added later to deal with Bosanquet's *Supplement*.[4] The *Reply* was being printed at the end of December 1810, as it appears from a letter of Mill,[5] and it was published early in January 1811.[6]

Malthus's article appeared in the *Edinburgh Review* for February 1811, nominally as a review of the pamphlets on Bullion by Mushet, Ricardo, Blake, Huskisson and Bosanquet, and of Ricardo's *Reply to Bosanquet*.

Early in April[7] the fourth edition of Ricardo's *High Price of Bullion* was published.[8] The main body of the pamphlet contained few changes, but the Introduction was omitted, and an Appendix was added containing his observations on the *Edinburgh Review* article, and outlining his plan for bullion payments, which he later developed in *Economical and Secure Currency*.[9]

[1] The postscript to the 1st ed. is dated 14 Nov. 1810.

[2] The preface to the 2nd ed. is dated 3 Dec. 1810.

[3] See below, pp. 204 and 247.

[4] In the Library at Gatcombe there are Ricardo's copies of the 1st ed. of *Practical Observations* and of the separate *Supplement*. The former contains many comments in Ricardo's handwriting, but they are almost entirely illegible.

[5] 25 Dec. 1810, below, VI, 14. This letter accompanied the first part of the MS of Dumont's translation of Bentham's work on prices which Ricardo proceeded to read and criticise; see below, p. 259 ff.

[6] Advertised in *Monthly Literary Advertiser*, 10 Jan. 1811. The *Reply* did not go to a second edition. A slip of errata containing five entries was printed and is found in some copies. The corrections are noticed in footnotes below.

[7] Shortly before, on 21 March 1811, Ricardo took part in a General Court of the Bank of England at which the subject of the Bullion Report was raised, and spoke briefly on the price of gold; see below, V, 461–2.

[8] Advertised in *Monthly Literary Advertiser* for 10 April; the earliest advertisement in the *Morning Chronicle* did not appear till 27 April.

[9] The Appendix was also published as a separate pamphlet, see below, p. 99, n. 1.

On 7 April Malthus, referring to the Appendix, wrote to Horner: 'I have this moment been reading Mr. Ricardo's observations on the Review, but remain quite unconvinced—indeed there is no point on which I feel more sure than of the incorrectness of attributing the variations of the exchange exclusively to redundancy or deficiency of currency. I was sorry to find a small monosyllable put into the article either by Jeffrey, or by accident, which made a considerable alteration in the sense, and may have offended Mr. Ricardo in some degree justly. I had said "We do not think these facts are all satisfactorily explicable upon the principles of M Ricardo alone["],—it is printed *at all*, which makes a good deal of difference. By the by, have you heard any other critiques on the article. Jeffrey thinks it is not popular enough and probably he is right.'

On 8 April Horner replied: 'Ricardo's reply to your objections is not so well written, in point of clearness, as his usual style. I suspect that upon that dispute the truth lies between you, and that a mode of expressing and stating what takes place might be hit upon, to which you would both assent.'[1]

So far Ricardo and Malthus had never met, and the controversy between them had been carried on only in print. In June 1811, Malthus introduced himself to Ricardo. Malthus's second article on Bullion, in the *Edinburgh Review* for August 1811, contained no criticism of Ricardo,[2] and the further controversy between them was restricted to private discussions and correspondence.[3]

In the present edition the contributions to the *Morning Chronicle* are reprinted from the text of the *Morning Chronicle*, the *High Price of Bullion* from the fourth edition of 1811 (the variants of the previous editions being given in footnotes), and the *Reply to Bosanquet* from the original edition of 1811.

[1] Both MSS, unpublished, are in the possession of Lady Langman.
[2] Cp. below, VI, 47–8.
[3] The Bullion Controversy entered upon its final stage in April and May 1811, with the debates in the House of Commons on the Resolutions of Horner and the counter-Resolutions of Vansittart. Ricardo's Notes on the latter (printed below, p. 411 ff.) are all that he seems to have written on the subject at this stage.

THE PRICE OF GOLD

THREE CONTRIBUTIONS

TO THE

MORNING CHRONICLE

1809

THE PRICE OF GOLD[1]

The present high market price above the mint price of gold, appears to have engrossed a great portion of the attention of the public; but they do not seem to be sufficiently impressed with the importance of the subject, nor of the disastrous consequences which may attend the further depreciation of paper. I am anxious, whilst there is yet time, that we should retrace our steps and restore the currency to that healthful state which so long existed in this country, and the departure from which is pregnant with present evil and future ruin.

The mint price of gold is 3l. 17s. 10½d. and the market price has been gradually increasing, and was within these two or three weeks as high as 4l. 13s. per ounce, not much less than 20 per cent. advance.

It is remarkable that between the years 1777 and 1797 the average price of gold was not higher than 3l. 17s. 7d. During that period, our currency was one of acknowledged purity. It is only since 1797, since the year that the Bank has been restricted from paying its notes in specie, that gold has risen to 4l., 4l. 10s., and latterly to 4l. 13s. per ounce. Whilst the Bank pays its notes in specie, there can never be any great difference between the mint and market-prices of gold. It is well known that, detection being difficult, notwithstanding the most severe, and, perhaps, absurd laws, when it becomes greatly the interest of individuals from a high market price of gold, the coin will be melted and sold as bullion, or exported, as it best suits the views of those who engage in such traffic. If, then, whilst the Bank paid in specie gold rose to 4l. or

[1] *Morning Chronicle*, 29 Aug. 1809.

more per ounce, these dealers would exchange their notes at the Bank, obtaining an ounce of gold for every 3l. 17s. 10½d. in bank notes. This gold would be melted and sold, or exported for 4l. or more in bank-notes per ounce; and as this operation might be repeated daily, or indeed hourly, it would be continued till the Bank had withdrawn the superfluous quantity of their notes from circulation, and had thereby brought the market and mint prices of gold to a level. This is the only check which can exist to an over issue from the Bank, and was so well known that the Bank never ventured on it with impunity.

No efforts of the Bank could keep more than a certain quantity of notes in circulation, and if that quantity was exceeded, its effects on the price of gold always brought the excess back to the Bank for specie. Under such regulations the market price of gold could never rise much above the mint price, for who would give 4l. or more, in bank-notes, for an ounce of gold, when he might obtain the same at the Bank for 3l. 17s. 10½d. It would be the same thing as offering an ounce of gold and 2s. 1½d. for an ounce of gold.—When we talk of a high price of gold, it can have no meaning, if estimated in gold, or in notes which are immediately exchangeable for gold. It may be high, estimated in silver, or in goods of all kinds, and it is only when gold is high compared with goods, or in other words that goods are cheap, that any temptation is offered for its importation. When it is said that we may obtain 1l. 5s. for a guinea by sending it to Hamburg, what is meant but that we may get for it a bill on London for 1l. 5s. in bank-notes? Could this be the case if the bank paid in specie? Would any one be so blind to his interest as to offer me one guinea in specie and four shillings, for a guinea, when he might obtain the same at Hamburgh at par, paying only the expences of freight, &c.? It is only because he cannot get a guinea at the Bank for notes, that he consents to pay it with notes at the best price he can, or in other words he sells 1l. 5s. of his bank-notes for a guinea in specie.

When the Act restricting the Bank from paying in specie took place, all checks to the over issue of notes were removed, excepting that which the Bank voluntarily placed on itself, knowing that if they were not guided by moderation, the effects which would follow would be so notoriously imputable to their monopoly, that the Legislature would be obliged to repeal the Restriction Act.

Whilst the Bank is willing to lend, borrowers will always exist, so that there can be no limit to their over-issues, but that which I have just mentioned, and gold might rise to 8l. or 10l. or any other sum per ounce.—The same effect would be produced in the price of provisions and on all other commodities, and there would be no other remedy for the depreciation of paper, than the Bank withdrawing the superabundant quantity from circulation, by insisting on the merchants paying their bills as they became due, and refusing to renew their loans until the scarcity of circulating medium should so raise its value that it would be at par with gold. It could rise but little above that price, for from that moment importation of gold would commence, and if the Bank were gradually to withdraw all their notes from circulation, the place of those notes would as gradually be supplied by imported gold, which the high price—I mean the high price in goods, would infallibly draw to this country.

If my view of this subject has been correct, we are enabled to ascertain the amount of depreciation at which Bank notes at any time may be, and when gold was at 4l. 13s. per ounce, they appear to have arrived at the enormous discount of 20 per Cent. I may be asked if Bank notes are at so great a discount, how comes it that no shopkeeper will sell more goods for twenty guineas than for 21l. in Bank notes. For this I can only account by supposing that the trade of purchasing guineas at a premium, or in other words selling Bank notes at a discount, is one which would expose the man who openly undertook it to so much obloquy and suspicion, that notwithstanding the profit, no one is hardy enough to encounter the risk, particularly as the law is very severe against melting the coin or exporting it. But that it is practised secretly there can be no doubt, as the profit attending it is enormous, and the number of guineas in circulation, considering that nearly 60 millions have been coined in the present reign, is diminished to a very small amount.

It is sufficient for my argument if I prove that it is a trade which can advantageously be carried on—that if tradesmen could openly and readily sell guineas for twenty-three shillings each, or more in Bank notes, they could afford to sell their goods cheaper for gold than for Bank notes;—and it is sufficiently evident that buying guineas at twenty-three shillings is between 9 and 10 per cent. premium, and selling gold at 4l. 13s. or nearly 20 per cent. premium, is a trade much more advantageous than many carried on in the city of London.

If further proofs of the depreciation of Bank notes were wanting, and that it was caused by an over-issue, it would be found in the present rate of exchange with foreign countries. To make this apparent may require us to consider what is meant by the rate of exchange, and the rules and limits to which it is subject.

If I purchase from a resident in Holland goods of that country, the bargain is made in the money there current. I have consequently contracted to pay him a certain number of ounces of silver of a given purity. As the comparative value of silver and gold is nearly equal all over the world my debt may be either estimated in silver or in the number of ounces of gold for which it would exchange. And if a merchant in Holland has purchased from a resident in London goods which are valued in English money, he has contracted to pay a certain number of ounces of gold of known purity or fineness.

To save the expence of the freight and insurance attending the exporting and importing of a quantity of gold to liquidate these debts, it suits the convenience of both the parties, after agreeing how much money of the one country is equivalent, considering its weight, purity, &c. to that of the other, and which is called the par of exchange, to make a transfer by means of a bill, which is done by my paying to the English merchant the sum which I am indebted to my Correspondent in Holland, the English merchant ordering his Correspondent in Holland to pay to mine the same amount, estimated at the rate of exchange agreed on, in Dutch money. The advantage to both parties is saving freight and insurance. Now if two or more parties had been indebted to merchants in Holland, there would have been a competition between them for the purchase of this bill, and the seller would no longer have been satisfied with saving the freight and insurance on the importation of his gold, but would have exported, and would have obtained a premium for his bill, which it would have been the interest of either of the other parties to have given him, provided such premium did not exceed the expence of the transport of the metals. It is necessarily kept within that limit, for either would say, "the number of ounces of gold which I owe in Holland are ready to pay my debt. I am willing to give them to you to pay it for me, and to add to it the expences which would attend the sending it; but nothing can induce me to give more, as if you do not accept my offer, I shall suffer no further disadvantage by sending the gold!"— This is therefore the natural limit to the fall of the exchange, it can never fall more below par than these expences; nor can it ever rise more above par than the same amount.

But since the restriction on the Bank paying in specie, the fall of the exchange has kept pace with the rise in gold, and is now considerably lower than the limits which I have pointed out, and which may be accounted for in the following manner:—

A merchant can no longer say, that he is possessed of a sufficient number of ounces of gold to send abroad to pay his debt; he may say, indeed, that he has a sufficient number of bank notes, which if he could sell at par, or exchange at the Bank for what they profess to be, viz. an ounce of gold for every 3l. 17s. 10½d. he would have sufficient gold to pay his debt; but as things are, he must either sell his bank notes and be contented to obtain an ounce of gold, or 3l. 17s. 10½d. for every 4l. 13s. of notes, or agree to make an allowance at that rate to the person with whom he negociates his bill. Thus then it appears, that the exchange may not only fall to the limits which I have before mentioned, but also in an inverse proportion to the rise of gold, or rather the discount of bank notes. But these are the limits within which it is even now confined. It cannot on the one hand rise more above par than the expence of freight, &c. on the importation of gold, nor on the other fall more than the expences of freight, &c. on its exportation, added to the discount on bank notes.

If bills of exchange were payable in gold and not in bank notes, the restriction on the Bank from paying in specie, could not in any way affect the exchange beyond the limits which I before specified.

What becomes then of the argument which has so often been urged in Parliament, that whilst the rate of exchange continued against us, it would not be safe for the Bank to pay in specie, when it is evident that their not paying in specie is the cause of the present low exchange.

Let the Bank be enjoined by Parliament gradually to withdraw to the amount of two or three millions of their notes from circulation, without obliging them, in the first instance, to pay in specie, and we should very soon find that the market price of gold would fall to its mint price of 3l. 17s. 10½d. that every commodity would experience a similar reduction; and that the exchange with foreign countries would be confined within the limits above mentioned.

It would then be evident that all the evils in our currency were owing to the over-issues of the Bank, to the dangerous power with which it was entrusted of diminishing at its will, the value of every monied man's property, and by enhancing the price of provisions, and every necessary of life, injuring the public annuitant, and all those persons whose incomes were fixed, and who were consequently not enabled to shift any part of the burden from their own shoulders.

[FIRST REPLY TO 'A FRIEND TO BANK-NOTES']

To the EDITOR of the MORNING CHRONICLE.[1]

Sir,

In the observations which I made on the high price of gold in the *Morning Chronicle* of the 29th ultimo, I expressed my apprehensions of the serious consequences which might attend the increasing depreciation of paper. By lessening the value of the property of so many persons, and that in any degree they pleased, it appeared to me that the Bank might involve many thousands in ruin. I wished, therefore, to call the attention of the public to the very dangerous power with which that body was entrusted; but I did not apprehend, any

[1] *Morning Chronicle*, 20 Sept. 1809.

more than your Correspondent, under the signature of "A Friend to Bank Notes,"[1] that the issues of the Bank would involve us in the dangers of a national bankruptcy.

Allowing to this writer, that the demand for gold has increased, whilst the usual supplies have been withheld, I am not convinced by any arguments which he has advanced, that the market price of gold could have been thereby affected, unless the medium in which the price was estimated was depreciated. That the scarcity of gold should increase its value cannot be doubted; that it would in consequence, when exchanged for other commodities, command an increased quantity of them, is as certain; but no scarcity, however great, can raise the market price much above the mint price, unless it be measured by a depreciated currency.

A pound of gold is coined into forty-four guineas and a half, or 46l. 14s. 6d. This is, therefore, the mint price, and cannot be called, as your Correspondent calls it, an arbitrary value. It is the simple declaration of a fact, that forty-four guineas and a half are of the same weight as a pound of gold, and one-twelfth of that quantity or 3l. 17s. 10½d. of an ounce.

Experience has proved to us, and particularly that of the twenty years preceding 1797, during the vicissitudes of war and peace, of favorable and unfavorable trade, that 46l. 14s. 6d. or a mint pound, would purchase sometimes a little more, and sometimes a little less than a pound of uncoined gold; and whilst an equal amount of bank notes would do the same, they would not be said to be depreciated. This they always did previous to the restriction on the Bank paying in specie, and for some time after it. Will this writer explain to us why any demand, however great, should induce any one to give,

---

[1] The letter, under the title 'Price of Gold', signed 'A Friend to Bank-notes but no Bank Director' and dated 11 September, appeared in the *Morning Chronicle* of 14 September 1809. The writer was Hutches Trower.

as has been lately done, 55l. 16s. in bank notes, for a pound of gold, if they are of equal value with 55l. 16s. in coin? Does he reflect that the gold actually contained in 55l. 16s. weighs one pound and a fifth of a pound? Is it seriously believed that he would give this for a pound? If it is agreed that he would not, then is the fact of the depreciation of bank notes fully established. If for the purchase of gold a greater quantity of corn, hardware, or any other commodity, were given than usual, it might justly be said that the scarcity of gold had increased in value. But what is the fact? If I go to market with corn or hardware, I can purchase 55l. 16s. in bank notes with precisely the same quantity that I am obliged to give to procure a pound of gold, or 46l. 14s. 6d.

I do not dispute with this writer but that it may be advantageous to a foreigner to send his goods to London, and after selling them for 25s. give that sum for the purchase of a guinea. He may possibly be doing it now with profit to himself. But he would not give twenty-five shillings for a guinea, if he did not pay for it in a depreciated medium. Again, I ask, does he think it possible that he would give a guinea and four shillings for a guinea, or bank notes to that amount, if they were exchangeable for that sum?

From the observations of this writer we should be led to suppose, that gold being at a higher price on the Continent than it is here, we might obtain there for it 4l. 15s. or more per ounce; but we should be mistaken in forming such a conclusion. It is paid for there in a medium not depreciated, and is probably somewhere about 4l. per ounce. But a purchaser here at 4l. 10s. can afford to sell it there at that price; because by means of the low exchange, (caused by the depreciation), he can reimburse himself for the depreciation of 15 or 20 per cent. to which our currency has arrived.

It is contended, too, that all the effects on the Exchange,

"which I attribute to the issue of bank notes, would equally be felt if there were not a single bank note in circulation."

If our circulation were wholly carried on by specie, I believe it would be difficult for this writer to convince us, that the exchange might be 20 per cent. against us. What could induce any person owing 100l. in Hamburgh, to buy a bill here for that sum, giving 120l. for it, when the charges attending the exportation of the 100l. to pay his debt could not exceed 4l. or 5l.?

The severity of the law against the exportation of gold coin, prevents *any* one from openly selling bank-notes at a discount, not from any delicacy, as your correspondent supposes me to say, against doing an immoral or an unlawful act, but from the fear that as it is known that no one can purchase guineas but with a view to exportation, he would become an object of suspicion,—he would be watched and unable to effect his purpose. Repeal the law, and what can prevent an ounce of standard gold in guineas from selling at as good a price as an ounce of Portugal coin, when it is known to be rather superior to it in purity? And if an ounce of standard gold, in guineas, would sell in the market (as Portugal coin has lately done) at 4l. 13s. per oz. how long would a shopkeeper sell his goods at the same price either for gold or bank-notes indifferently? The penalties of the law, therefore, have degraded the few guineas in circulation to the value of the bank-notes, but send them abroad and they will purchase exactly what an equal quantity of Portugal coin will.

This is the temptation to their exportation, and operates the same as a demand from abroad. Our currency is already superfluous, and it is worse than useless to retain the guineas here. But diminish the currency by calling in the excess of bank-notes:—Make a partial void, as your correspondent justly observes was done in France and other countries, from the annihilation of their paper-credit, and what can prevent the effectual demand which would thereby be immediately created, from producing an importation of gold, and consequently a favorable exchange?

If our circulating medium has been augmented a fifth, till that fifth be withdrawn the prices of gold and commodities will remain as they are. Increase the quantity of notes, they will rise still higher; but withdraw the fifth, as I earnestly recommend, and gold and every other commodity will find its just level, and whilst the Bank continues to possess the confidence of the public, the representative of an ounce of gold, or 3l. 17s. 10½d. in bank-notes will always purchase an ounce of gold.

The hint thrown out of altering the mint price to the market price of gold, or, in other words, declaring that 3l. 17s. 10½d. in coin, shall pass for 4l. 13s. besides its shocking injustice would only aggravate the evil of which I complain. This violent remedy would raise the market price of gold 20 per cent. above the new mint price, and would further lower the value of bank-notes in the same proportion.[1]

It has been shewn incontrovertibly by that able Writer, Dr. Adam Smith, that the rate of interest for money is regu-

[1] Trower, in the *Morning Chronicle* of 14 September, had written: 'Perhaps, when the period arrives at which it may be deemed proper to take off that restriction which forbids the Bank to pay its notes in specie, it may be necessary to alter the standard price of gold, in order to bring it nearer to the market price; and thereby to prevent that exportation, which otherwise will unquestionably take place.' Ricardo points out here that as long as there is a law prohibiting the exportation of gold coined into guineas, while the exportation of other forms of gold is permitted (cp. p. 24), the latter will continue to exceed the former in price; and if the price of gold in guineas were raised from 3l. 17s. 10½d. to 4l. 13s., the market price of exportable gold would rise from 4l. 13s. to 5l. 11s. 7d. In the *Morning Chronicle* of 30 October, Trower accepted the correction: 'I am ready to admit, that in the suggestion which I hazarded with respect to the alteration in the standard price of coin, I was inadvertently led into an error, which I shortly detected on reflection; but not in time to exclude the remark from my letter.'

lated by the rate of profits on that part of capital only which does not consist of circulating medium, and that those profits are not regulated but are wholly independent of the greater or lesser quantity of money which may be employed for the purposes of circulation; that the increase of circulating medium will increase the prices of all commodities, but will not lower the rate of interest.[1]

We must not, therefore, depend upon the criterion, namely, the rate of interest so strongly recommended by your correspondent, by which to judge of the issues of the Bank; because, if Dr. Smith's reasoning be correct, if our circulating medium were ten times as great as it is, the rate of interest would not be permanently affected.

I think, Sir, I have succeeded in proving that my alarms are not altogether groundless, and that there does exist a great depreciation in our currency, affecting the interests of the public annuitant, and of those whose property consists in money, without any corresponding advantages. The evils attending a variable medium, as it affects all contracts, are too obvious to require to be noticed. The permanency of the value of the precious metals first recommended them as the general medium of exchange. That advantage is now lost to us, and we cannot consider our currency on a solid foundation till it be restored to the value of that of other countries.

By withdrawing a certain quantity of Bank of England notes from circulation it is supposed, by Mr. Cobbett, that their place would be immediately supplied by country bank-notes.[2] No such effect would, in my opinion, take place; on the contrary, I think such a measure would oblige the coun-

---

[1] *Wealth of Nations,* Bk. II, ch. iv.
[2] In an article under the title 'Jacobin Guineas', in *Cobbett's Political Register* of 16 Sept. 1809, referring to 'the philosopher who writes in the Chronicle',

Cobbett had said: 'Besides does this writer imagine, that the country-bankers would not make money to supply the place of any reduction at the Bank of England?'

try-banks to call in at least as many, if not considerably more, of *their* notes.

A Bank of England note and a country bank note are now of equal value, and their quantities are proportioned to the business which they have to perform. By withdrawing Bank of England notes from circulation you increase their value and lower the prices of commodities in those places where they are current. A Bank of England note will then be more valuable than a country bank-note, because it will be wanted to purchase in the cheaper market; and as the country bank is obliged to give Bank of England notes in exchange for their own, they would be called upon for them till the quantity of country paper should be reduced to the same proportion which it before bore to the London paper, producing a corresponding fall of the prices of all commodities for which it was exchangeable.

A writer in *The Pilot* newspaper has been pleased to suppose, that a gentleman who has written in your paper under the signature of "Mercator," has done so "in aid or in imitation of, or in conjunction and conspiracy with me." The fact can of itself be of little importance. If his arguments or mine are weak, let him shew them to be so; but "No Trafficker" is mistaken.—The sentiments of "Mercator" are only known to me as they are to him, through the medium of *The Morning Chronicle.*[1]

I am Sir, &c.

R.

---

[1] A first letter signed 'Mercator' and dated 'London, Sept. 4' appeared in the *Morning Chronicle* of 7 Sept. 1809; the writer unreservedly supported Ricardo's views as expressed in the article of 29 August. A writer who signed himself 'No Trafficker' replied to 'Mercator' in a letter to the *Pilot* newspaper of 8 Sept. 1809, criticising both him and Ricardo. 'Mercator' answered in a second letter, under the title 'The High Price of Gold', in the *Morning Chronicle* of 12 September. A final rejoinder of 'No Trafficker' appeared in the *Pilot* of 13 September; this is the letter to which Ricardo refers.

[SECOND REPLY TO
'A FRIEND TO BANK-NOTES']

To the EDITOR of the MORNING CHRONICLE.[1]

Sir,

Had your Correspondent, "A Friend to Bank-notes," when he first did me the honour to notice my observations on the high price of Gold, contended, as he now does,[2] that Bank-notes were the representatives of Silver, but not of Gold Coin, we should sooner have discovered from whence the difference of our opinions on the subject in dispute between us arose. I should then, Sir, have spared him the trouble of giving so many proofs of that which is indisputable, namely—*that if Silver be the sole measure of value, Gold being at 4l. 13s. per oz. is not, of itself, evidence of Bank notes being at a discount.* Indeed, I thought that in the following observations I had admitted that position—"When we talk of a high price of Gold, it can have no meaning if estimated in Gold, or in Notes which are immediately exchangeable for Gold. It might be high estimated in Silver, or in goods of all kinds."[3] It was evident from the tenor of that and the subsequent paper, that I considered Gold Coin as the standard of commerce, and by it estimated the depreciation of Bank-notes. I had no reason to suppose that it was otherwise considered by your Correspondent. In one place he called Bank-notes a "substitute for Gold"; in another he observes, that "Had not this restriction been imposed, the great and growing demand for Gold upon the Continent would have drawn every Guinea out of the Country, and

---

[1] *Morning Chronicle*, 23 Nov. 1809.
[2] Another letter from 'A Friend to Bank-notes but no Bank Director' (*i.e.* Trower), under the title 'Price of Gold, Letter ii' and dated 23 September had appeared in the *Morning Chronicle* of 30 Oct. 1809.
[3] Above, p. 16.

would have left us without resource in any emergency which might arise, by which its credit would be shaken."[1] The restriction could only have enabled the Directors of the Bank, if they had been so disposed, to prevent the Guineas locked up in the Bank from being exported. Those in circulation have been as liable to be sent out by the Country since, as before that measure. But, if Silver only be the standard of currency, as is now asserted, the Bank might have paid their Notes in our present debased Silver Coin; in Shillings, for example, debased 24 per cent. below their standard weight and value, the Guinea, therefore, would not have needed that protection. The Silver would not have been demanded, because it could not have been either melted or exported, but at a loss of 24 per cent. If Silver be the standard of currency, Bank-notes were, in 1797, at a premium of 24 per cent. and are now at a premium of 14 per cent.

But if, as I shall attempt to prove, Gold be the standard of value, and consequently, Bank Notes the representatives of the Gold-coin, I do expect that this writer will agree with me that Bank Notes are at a discount, and that the excess of the market above the mint price of Gold measures the depreciation.

The price of standard Silver bullion was on Tuesday last 5s. 9½d. per oz. On the same day, the price of standard Gold bullion was 4l. 10s. per oz. An ounce of Gold was therefore equal to about 15½ oz. and not 18 oz. of Silver.

If, then, we estimate the value of Bank Notes by the price of Gold bullion, they will be found to be 15½ per cent. discount. If by the price of Silver bullion 12 per cent. discount. But your Correspondent would no doubt observe, that this conclusion from the price of Silver bullion would be correct,

[1] Both quotations are from Trower's letter in the *Morning Chronicle* of 14 Sept. 1809.

if our Silver currency were not degraded by wearing and clipping, but as it was known to be depreciated by being deficient in standard weight, the high price of Gold bullion might in a great measure, and that of Silver bullion wholly, be caused by that deficiency. Bank Notes are, according to this argument, the representatives, not of our standard Silver currency, but of our debased Silver Coins.

It is observed by Lord Liverpool, in his letter to the King on the state of the coins,[1] that the law now is, and has been since the year 1774, "That no tender in payment of money made in the Silver Coin of this realm, of any sum exceeding the sum of 25l. at any time, shall be reputed in law or allowed to be legal tender, within Great Britain or Ireland, for more than according to its value by weight, after the rate of 5s. 2d. for each ounce of silver."

Bank-notes are not then the representatives of the debased silver coins. A holder of a Bank-note of 1000l. might refuse to take more than 25l. in the present debased Silver currency. If the remaining 975l. were paid him in shillings, he would receive them by weight, at their Mint value of 5s. 2d. per oz. which, with the 25l. of debased Silver, when sold at the present price of 5s. 9½d. per oz. would yield 1110l. in Bank-notes. Here then it is proved, on this writer's own principles, that if Silver be the standard currency, Bank-notes are at a discount of 11 per cent.

For the following reasons given by Lord Liverpool, in the work before mentioned, I consider Gold as the standard measure of value. He observes, "that the Silver Coins are no longer the principal measure of property: all commodities now take their price or value in reference to the Gold Coin,[2]

[1] *A Treatise on the Coins of the Realm; in a Letter to the King*, by Charles Earl of Liverpool, Oxford, 1805, p. 129.

[2] Lord Liverpool says in addition: 'that is, in reference to the quantity of Gold Coins, for which they could be exchanged;'.

in like manner as they took their value in a former period in reference to the Silver Coins. On this account the present deficiency of the Silver Coins, great as it is, is not taken into consideration, in paying the price of any commodity, to the extent in which they are legal tenders. It is clear, therefore, that the Gold Coins are now become, in the practice and opinion of the people, the principal measure of property."[1]

He then states, that in the reign of William the Third, the Guinea was current at even so high a value as 30s.; that the Gold Coins rose or fell as the Silver Coins were more or less perfect. "No such increase or variation in the value of Gold Coin has taken place since the year 1717, when the rate or value of the Guinea was determined by proclamation, and the Mint indenture, to be 21s. and the other Gold Coins in proportion; though the Silver Coins now current have long been, and are still, at least as deficient as they were at the beginning of the reign of King William. The Guinea and other Gold Coins have, notwithstanding, constantly passed since 1717, at the rate or value given them by the Mint indentures."

"The two foregoing reasons clearly prove the opinion of the people of Great Britain on this subject, in their interior commerce and domestic concerns. I will in the next place shew what has been the opinion of foreign nations concerning it." In the reign of King William the exchanges rose or fell according to the perfection or defect of our silver coins. Before the recoinage in 1695, the exchanges with all foreign countries were 4s. in the pound against England, and with some of them considerably more. "The same evil, however, has never existed since the year 1717, though our silver coins have, during all this interval, been very defective. But, on

[1] This and the following quotations occur in Lord Liverpool's *Treatise*, pp. 141–5.

the other hand, our exchanges with foreign countries were very much influenced to our disadvantage, when our gold coins were defective, that is, previous to the reformation of our Gold Coins in the year 1774." Lord Liverpool considers this as a proof that foreigners consider our Gold Coins as the principal measure of property. Another argument is drawn from the prices of gold and silver bullion. When our Gold Coin was defective previous to the re-coinage in 1774, gold bullion advanced considerably above its mint value, but immediately on its being brought to its present state of perfection, gold bullion fell to something under the mint price, and has continued so for twenty years previous to 1797. "It is evident, therefore, from these facts, that the price of gold bullion was affected by the state of our gold coins, though the price of this bullion had not since the year 1717, been so affected by the defective state or condition of our silver coins." The price of silver bullion has, since the year 1717, been affected by the perfection or defect of our Gold Coins, but has not been so by the defective state of our Silver Coins.—"From all which it is evident, that the value of Gold or Silver Bullion has, for 40 years at least, been estimated according to the state of our Gold Coin solely, and not according to that of Silver Coin. The price of both these metals rose when our Gold Coin was defective; it fell when our Gold Coin was brought to its present state of perfection; and it may, therefore, justly be inferred, that, in the opinion of the dealers in the precious metals (who may be considered as the best judges on a subject of this nature), the gold coin has in this respect become the principal measure of property, and consequently the instrument of commerce." In another passage, Lord Liverpool considers a pound sterling to be 20–21 of a guinea.[1] The same opinion is advanced by Sir J.

[1] *ib.* p. 153.

Stewart—"At present (says he) there are no sterling pounds in silver money; there is no silver in England in any proportion to the circulation of trade; and, therefore, the only currency by which a pound can be valued is the guinea."[1]

The Bank-Directors must have been of the same opinion, when they stated in their evidence before Parliament, that it was their usual practice to limit the amount of their notes when the market price of gold exceeded the mint price.[2]

In the Report of the Committee of the House of Lords in 1797, it is observed, that "Gold is the mercantile coin of Great Britain, and silver has for many years been only a commodity, which has no fixed price, and is very rarely carried to the Mint to be coined, but varies according to the demand for it at the market."[3]

I am, Sir, your obedient Servant,

R.

Nov. 4

[APPENDIX TO 'THE PRICE OF GOLD'

The above letter concluded the correspondence in the *Morning Chronicle*. The controversy was continued privately by Ricardo and Trower, and at least two papers were written by each of them, as suggested above, p. 5. Only two of these papers (one by Trower and one by Ricardo) have survived and they are printed

---

[1] *An Inquiry into the Principles of Political Œconomy*, by Sir James Steuart, Bart., London, 1767, vol. II, p. 89.
[2] Cp. below, p. 75.
[3] 'Report of the Lords' Committee of Secrecy. Order of Council 26th February 1797; Relating to the Bank', p. 147 of the reprint in *Parliamentary Papers*, 1810, vol. III.

here. Trower's paper is included since it gives some indication of the contents of a missing paper by Ricardo.]

[A REPLY BY TROWER]

1. It is admitted by Mr. Ricardo[1] that Silver would be the measure of value if there did not exist a law prohibiting the coining of Silver Bullion into money, but that, in consequence of this law, Gold must now be the measure of value.—

By similar reasoning I may contend, that not Gold but Bank Notes are now the measure of value because there exists a law prohibiting the Bank from paying their Notes in Specie.

I allow, that there is this difference between the two cases, that, whereas individuals may, if they choose, take Gold Bullion to the Mint to be coined into money, they cannot do so, with silver bullion; but this difference in the two cases can have no effect upon the question between us, that question being, whether Bank Notes represent Gold or Silver.—Now, in point of fact, they *at present* represent neither, the Bank being prohibited from paying their Notes in either. In speaking of Bank Notes, therefore, as the representatives of specie, reference must be made to the period when the restriction imposed upon the Bank will be removed. If at that period of time the law inhibiting the coinage of silver money shall continue in force, in that case undoubtedly Gold must be considered as the measure of value in this Country. But, at present, that Act according to my notion, has no more influence upon the question between us than the restriction bill itself has.—

We are agreed in opinion with respect to the circumstance[s] which constitute the one metal a measure of value, in preference to the other, to those circumstances therefore, and to those only, must we look in order to determine, which is that measure. That circumstance is the low valuation at which one of the metals is rated at the Mint, compared with its market price. It is admitted, that Silver is the Metal which is, at present, so circumstanced. Silver therefore, must now be the measure of value.—Indeed if we look to the fact we shall find, that there is at present more silver coin in circulation than Gold coin. And how can it be otherwise when the temptation is so great for carrying off the latter.—I confess therefore I do not see the force of the objections urged against Silver being now the measure of value, founded as they are upon the Act prohibiting the coinage of that Metal.—

[1] This and the subsequent references are to a missing paper by Ricardo.

2. It is admitted, that if the debased Silver Coin were legal tender, the excess of the market price, above the mint price of silver bullion would be sufficiently accounted for by that circumstance.

The reply to this observation is, that if the debased Silver Coin were legal tender, *without limitation*, the excess of the market above the mint price of that Bullion would not be merely *8 pC^t* but a great deal more, and nearly in proportion to the extent of the debasement of that coin. The restriction imposed upon the debased Silver Coin as legal tender, is the *cause*, therefore, why the difference between the Mint and Market price of that bullion is not greater than it is.—

3. It is said, 'that it is known, that the debased coin does not pass in circulation according to its intrinsic value, but according to the value of the metal, which it ought to contain.'—This is something like begging the question, for it is asserting the point in dispute, the question between us being whether the debased Silver coin do, or do not, so pass. But in proof of this assertion Mr. R. makes use of an argument, which, I confess, I did not expect to see him advance, as it can, with the strictest propriety, be so completely turned against him. He says, 'Compared with the Gold coin, which is undebased, is it not of equal if not of superior value to it?' My answer is, 'you say that Bank notes are 20 pC^t discount[;] compare them with the Gold coin, which is undebased are they not of equal value to it?' If there be any truth in your argument, there is equal truth in mine; and I may exclaim with you 'What pretence can there be then for saying, that the debased value of Bank Notes is a cause of the increase in the price of commodities?'

The same remarks may be applied to Mr. R's supposed case of a Merchant with his Warehouse full of Goods, desirous of purchasing silver bullion for the purpose of exportation. Mr. R. says 'that if the Merchant could sell his goods, at once, for heavy silver coin, and melt it, he would obtain 8 pC^t more silver than if with the money he purchased Silver bullion.' This I deny, for I contend, that if the heavy silver coin were in circulation, instead of the light, the present difference between the market and mint price of silver bullion would not exist. The cause for that difference being removed, the effect would necessarily cease.

Again, Mr. R. observes, that the fact is 'that £1000 in such debased Silver will purchase precisely as much silver bullion as £1000 in gold coin', to this I may reply, with equal propriety, that the fact is, that £1000 in Bank Notes will purchase precisely as much silver Bullion as £1000 in Gold coin. The argument here employed by Mr. R. will serve my cause equally well with his own, Mr. R. must therefore either *abandon* this *argument* by which he attempts to prove, that the debased silver coin passes in circulation according to the value of the metal which it ought to contain, or he must entirely *abandon* the *question* between us. For it is quite as strong to prove, that Bank Notes are not at a discount, as it is to prove, that our Silver coins are not [at] a discount—or, in other words, if it be sufficient to shew, that the debased Silver coin is not a cause of the increase in the price of commodities, it is equally sufficient to shew, that the amount of Bank Notes in circulation is not a cause of that increase.

I have now observed upon Mr. R's remarks as far as they relate to this point, and wait his reply.—

[A FURTHER REPLY BY RICARDO][1]

'Now, in point of fact,' says Mr. Trower, 'Bank notes, at present, represent neither gold or silver, the Bank being prohibited from paying their notes in either.'[2] The dispute between Mr. Trower and myself, as I understood it, was, whether a bank note was an obligation to pay either. It is true that the bank is by law exempted from fulfilling its obligations, but that fact does not prevent us from ascertaining what their engagement is, and in what manner they would be obliged to perform it if the law were repealed. Here then is the difference in our view of the subject. Mr. Trower contends that if the Bank were suddenly obliged to fulfill their engagements they could and would pay in silver coin it being their interest so to do; I on the contrary maintain that if so called upon they would be obliged to pay in gold coin,—that the silver coin is insufficient for the purpose and that by an express law there can be no silver coined.

[1] In *Letters to Trower* a paper of a later date was prefixed to this Reply; in the present edition it is printed below, p. 407 ff.

[2] This and the subsequent references, up to p. 43, n. 1, are to the preceding paper by Trower.

I admit that if silver could be coined that metal would be preferred because it could be obtained at the least expence,—but that, whilst there is a law against the coinage of silver it is in fact reducing us to the use of gold only. The full extent of what I am contending for is allowed by Mr. Trower when he says, 'If at that period of time' (when the restriction on the bank shall be removed) 'the law inhibiting the coinage of silver money should continue in force, in that case undoubtedly gold must be considered as the measure of value in this country.' Is it fair that Mr. T should not argue on things as they are, but on those which he supposes may take place at some future period? The act prohibiting the coinage of silver may be repealed, and when that happens Mr. Trower may be right, silver may then become the standard measure of value, but whilst the law continues in force gold must necessarily be that measure, and the value of bank notes therefore must be estimated by their comparative value with gold coin or bullion.

The fact of there being more silver coin in circulation than gold can be easily accounted for; in the first place there are no bank notes of less amount than one pound hence a necessity for the use of silver in small payments. Secondly, Bank notes being a substitute for gold coins there is absolutely no use for guineas, this joined to their high value compared with their substitute sufficiently accounts for their disappearing from circulation, and lastly the gold coin having retained its standard weight whilst the silver coin is debased 40 p ct. renders it advantageous to melt guineas and to retain the silver in circulation.

With respect to the second point in dispute, the effect on the prices of commodities, and of gold and silver bullion, which Mr. Trower supposes to have been produced by the debased state of the silver coins. Why, I would ask, if such be the fact was not the same effect produced on the market prices of those metals before the restriction on the Bank in 1797?

It will not be a satisfactory answer to say, because gold coin was then the standard measure, and, *that* coin not being debased no such effects followed. I say this would not be satisfactory because gold was the measure of value, only as it would more advantageously discharge a debt than standard silver coin;—but we are not now speaking of the standard silver coin but of the debased silver coin. The debased silver would then, as well as now have been comparatively cheaper than the gold coin and could then, if it can now, have been more advantageously employed for the discharge of a debt; but no such effects followed then; gold bullion was steadily under its mint price and silver bullion was only above it because of the inaccurate determination of the mint proportions. Perhaps a little further consideration will make this more clear. In 1797 the silver coin was debased 24 p. ct.; at the same time the proportionate value of gold and silver was, in the market, as $14\frac{3}{4}$ to 1 whilst in the coin they were estimated as 15 to 1, gold was therefore the measure of value if the standard metals be compared;—but gold compared with the debased coin was as 19 to 1, there were therefore the same reasons then as there are now for gold bullion being above the mint price, as far as the debasement of silver was concerned; therefore I contend, that if as Mr. Trower supposes the price of commodities be now affected by the debased state of the silver coin, they must for the same reason have been equally so in 1797 and for many years before it. Will Mr. Trower explain why no such effect followed, Gold having been before 1797 for 23 years under its mint price?

I have said 'Compare the debased silver coin with the gold coin which is undebased, is it not of equal value to it?'

Mr. Trower answers 'You say that Bank notes are 20 p.c. disct compare them with the gold coin which is undebased, are they not of equal value to it?' Mr. Trower in another place observes that if the fact be as I state that £1000 in debased silver coin will purchase precisely as much gold or silver bullion as £1000 in gold coin, so is it also a fact that £1000 in Bank notes will do the same. If then it be admitted that at this time £1000 either in gold coin, in debased silver coin, or in Bank notes are precisely of the same value when used in the purchase of commodities, what is the cause that neither of these will purchase as much gold or silver bullion as they did in 1797 previously to the Bank restriction bill? And, tho' they may be of the same value in circulation here at home, is this agreement in their value forced or natural?

It must be evident that it is not by the value of the undebased gold coin, that the values of the bank notes and of debased silver are at present regulated. If they were so, gold would not be above its mint price because Mr. Trower has always agreed that no one would give more than an ounce of gold for an ounce of gold, gold could not therefore be at £4-10/ or £4-13/ per oz, if the value of the circulating medium were generally equal to that of the gold coin. It necessarily follows that the value of the gold coin is brought down to that of the debased silver, or to the Bank notes. But I have already remarked that the debased silver was always previously to 1797 brought up (because it was always moderate in its quantity) to the value of the gold coins, and that altho' it was legal tender to a certain amount, it was neither sufficiently abundant nor sufficiently current to raise the price of gold bullion above its mint price. Not an instance has occurred of a purchaser of gold bullion having paid a penny an ounce more for it in consequence of his wish of paying in debased silver coin.

If then gold and silver coins be of the same value and at the same time are depreciated in their exchangeable value to $\frac{4}{5}$ of their true value; to the value in short of the Bank notes which are in circulation with them, to what can we attribute this phenomenon but to the depreciation of Bank notes? Let us suppose the law against the exportation of guineas repealed, Mr. Trower would not then contend that gold coin, silver coin and bank notes would be of equal value because he has already admitted that more than an ounce of gold would not be given for an ounce of gold; but under those circumstances gold would continue to sell for £4- 10/ or £4- 13/ for bank notes or for debased shillings, but for gold coin it would not be higher than £3-17-10½ per oz.

The present value at which gold coin passes in circulation is a forced value; its natural value is 15 p.c. above its forced value, but repeal the law, withdraw the force by which it is kept down, and it will immediately recover its natural value. If then I were to yield the first point in dispute and allow that Bank notes were obligations to pay silver and not gold coin, it would be evident that no other effect could be produced on the prices of gold or silver bullion, or on any other commodities from the debasement of the silver coin but the trifling one occasioned by a very small proportion of the debased silver coin being considered legal tender.

Before the recoinage of the gold coin in the year 1774, gold bullion, as I have already observed, was at £4 pr oz, being 2/1½ above the mint price. The debasement of the gold coin must have had a similar effect in raising the prices of all other commodities. This is a principle no longer disputed. Immediately on the recoinage gold fell under its mint price.

Whilst the gold coin was thus debased a guinea fresh from the mint and consequently undebased or any other which had been hoarded and had not partaken of the debasement, would have purchased no more goods than a worn and debased guinea, but it would not thence be argued that the debased and the new guinea were of equal value, it being manifest that the prices of all commodities were regulated, not by the quantity of gold in the new guineas, but by the quantity actually contained in the old.

In like manner, now, though a few guineas may be in circulation and may pass in the purchase of commodities for no more than an equal amount in Bank notes, the prices of commodities are regulated not by the quantity of gold which the guineas contain, but by the quantity which the Bank notes will purchase. These two quantities must, if the coin be undebased, and the bank notes not depreciated, be always nearly equal.

The fact of gold coin having been for near a century the principal measure of value is I think placed beyond dispute by the arguments of Lord Liverpool.[1] They are briefly as follows. The debasement of the silver coin has not during that period caused any excess of the market above the mint price of either gold or silver bullion;–neither has it produced any effect on the exchanges with foreign countries, whereas the debasement of the gold coin which occurred during a part of the century never failed to produce a rise in the market price of gold and silver bullion and a corresponding effect on the rate of exchange; that immediately on the gold coin being brought to its present state of perfection the price of bullion fell under its mint price and the foreign exchanges were at par, if not favorable to us.

Lord Liverpool has clearly proved this fact, but has not given any satisfactory reasons why gold should be the standard measure of value in preference to silver.

It appears to me that gold *must* be the principal measure, if not the only measure of value, whilst the relative value of gold and silver is less in the market than the relative value of

---

[1] *A Treatise on The Coins of the Realm*, pp. 132–45.

those metals in the coins, according to the mint regulations.

Gold and silver coins are equally by law legal tender for all sums if of their legal weight.

By the regulations of the mint gold is $15\frac{9}{124}$ times the value of silver. In the market up to the period when Lord Liverpool wrote, gold was only $14\frac{3}{4}$ times, on an average of a very long period, more valuable than silver. It became therefore the interest of every debtor to pay his debt in the gold coin and also the interest of every person, as well as the bank, who carried bullion to the mint to be coined, to carry gold and not silver for that purpose. Thus, if I were a merchant having my warehouses well stocked with goods and was in debt £1000—I could purchase as much gold bullion as is contained in a thousand pounds with less goods than I should be obliged to part with to obtain the quantity of silver bullion contained in a £1000,—this would determine me to purchase the gold and not the silver, and to carry the gold and not the silver to the mint to be coined. Whilst gold was only $14\frac{3}{4}$ the value of silver, the price of silver bullion would be always *above its mint price*, there would be a loss therefore to the bank in purchasing silver bullion to be coined,— whereas there would be no such loss in purchasing gold bullion for that purpose. *It appears therefore evident that it is only whilst gold is less valuable in the market compared with silver, than it is by the mint regulations, that it will be the only measure of value.* Bank notes will whilst this continues be the representatives of the gold coin, because the bank will always pay in the coin which can be coined at the least expence to them.

But, if in the course of time, *as it appears lately to have done, gold should become more valuable,* and be in the market at a greater proportion to silver than it is in the coins,—if it should be $15\frac{1}{2}$ or 16 times the value of silver, gold would be above its mint price and silver would be at or below its mint value. Gold could then be profitably melted and silver could be profitably coined; *silver would therefore become the standard of value; the bank would pay its notes in silver and consequently bank notes would become the representatives of the silver and not the gold coin. Indeed this is Mr. Trower's argument.* The high price of gold bullion, he justly contends, is no proof of the depreciation of bank notes because gold bullion may rise above its mint value from an alteration in its relative value to silver, tho' a bank note were not in existence. It will be seen by what I have already said that *I unequivocally admit the truth of this position.*

But if a high price of gold bullion proceeded from this cause the price of silver bullion would never whilst the coins of full weight only were legal tender, be above the mint price. No one contended when the price of silver bullion was above its mint price and the gold bullion was at or below its mint value (and this was the case generally previous to 1797) that bank notes were depreciated; and, if the price of gold bullion were 20 p.c. above its mint price, and silver bullion were at its mint price, I should allow that bank notes were not at a discount;—but when the prices of both the metals are above the mint prices it is proof conclusive of bank notes being at a discount.

Mr. Trower wishes to account for this from the acknowledged fact of the silver currency being debased.—If this debased currency were legal tender I should not dispute the point with him,—but it is acknowledged by him that it is not;—the debasement of the silver therefore cannot be the cause of the high price of silver bullion.

I shall now answer a few of the observations of Mr. Trower[1] on my last letter in the Chronicle.[2]

[1] These observations of Trower are missing.   [2] Above, p. 28.

I quoted the price of silver at 5/9½ without any view of making my argument better or worse. The price of 5/7 was not I believe mentioned by Mr. Trower at the time he wrote, nor did I reflect that it was on that price that his calculations were made; but as he observes, it is for principles we are contending, therefore 5/7 will suit my purpose just as well as 5/9½.

To Mr. Trower there appear inconsistencies in my saying that, [']if silver be the standard of currency Bank notes were in 1797 at a prem^m of 24 p. c. and are now at a prem^m of 14[']; this is on the supposition of the debased silver currency being the standard, because £100 in bank notes would purchase in 1797 24 p. c. more silver bullion than what was contained in £100 in the debased silver currency and would now at its present price purchase 14 p. c. more. I have said too that 'if we estimate the value of Bank notes by silver bullion they will be found to be 12 p. c. dis^t.' and in another place 'if silver be the standard currency Bank notes are at a disc^t. of 11 p. c.' I am called upon to explain these passages. I meant that if our silver currency was perfectly of its mint weight and consequently as good as an equal quantity of bullion, Bank notes would if estimated by such a medium be 12 p. c. dis^t.,—but, as our currency is not thus pure, as by law in large paym^{ts} a creditor may be forced to accept as much as £25 in debased currency, bank notes were if estimated by our silver currency at a discount of 11 p. c.

In the calculations made by Mr. Trower he attributes all the excess of the market above the mint price of gold to the debasement of the silver coin, except that part of it which is occasioned by an alteration in the relative value of the two metals. He is correct in estimating the alteration in the relative value of gold and silver (at the price he quotes, £4-13/ and 5/7) at 11. 7. 2 pr ct, but he jumps to the con-

clusion in attributing the balance of the rise of gold above
bank notes viz. 8. 1. 3 to the debasement of the silver currency,—he takes for granted that which is the subject of
dispute and does not explain to us his data. By the same rule
if he were to take the present prices of gold and silver bullion
viz. £4. 10/ and 5/9½, he must for the effects of the debasement of the silver coin calculate on no less than 12 p. c. Now
he will not say that the debasement of the silver coin has
increased since this discussion commenced, therefore he
must find out some other cause for the difference between
£8. 1. 3 and £12.—

Mr. Trower says that if one metal only were in circulation
the market would exceed the mint price in exact proportion
to the debasement of the coin, but when it consists of two
metals it does not follow that the bullion should be paid for
in the depreciated currency. From what has already been
said, though we have two metals in circulation one must
necessarily be driven from circulation;—and as the depreciated silver is not legal tender no value can be estimated by it.

I am accused of stating an impossible case and it is asked
'what confidence can be placed upon such an hypothesis?
it is a mode of reasoning as unusual as it is unavailing.' But
is it an impossible case to suppose that my debtor should pay
me in silver coin? I am contending with this gentleman that
Bank notes are at discount, and in proof of my position I
state that if my debtor were to pay me his debt in silver he
would by law be obliged to pay me as much as would be
equal in value to £1120 in Bank notes. Is not this a fair
argument to prove that the silver contained in a £1000 is
more valuable than £1000 in bank notes? That it is impossible that any man should so pay me whilst the law allows
him to pay me in a piece of paper which is called £1000
indeed, but can command as much silver as is contained in

£900 only, is the injury of which I complain, and the fact of its being worth no more which is not denied is a proof of the injury.

I agree with Mr. Trower that silver is a legal tender to any amount as well as gold if it be of its mint weight, but this admission on his part is fatal to his argument. With 62 standard shillings which he admits to be a pound of silver I can always purchase a pound of silver bullion. This he does not deny. It is expressly allowed by him that if silver coin be not debased silver bullion paid for in silver cannot exceed its mint price.

But with 62/ in Bank notes I cannot purchase a pound of silver; I am obliged to give £3. 7 in that medium for a pound of silver or a premium of £8-1-3. With what consistency can it be maintained that 62 standard shillings, such as are legal tender, are of no more value than £3-2 in bank notes?

If the regulations of our mint had been such that every shilling weighed an ounce,—whilst the shillings were of full weight silver could never rise above a shilling an ounce, and tho' the currency were debased and every shilling should come to weigh only half an ounce silver would not rise above one shilling an ounce whilst the law protected the seller of bullion from being paid in the debased coin. 'It is true' he would say 'I have sold you silver at a shilling an ounce but the shilling you tender me is not full weight, you must therefore pay me by weight at the mint price of a shilling.['] The seller would therefore ultimately receive two debased shillings tho' he had sold his silver for one. That such was the state of the silver bullion market we have the experience of near a century. Silver bullion was rarely much above its mint price and the excess which did exist was attributable to the alteration in the relative value of gold and silver. It was paid for in gold, and therefore gold was at its mint value.

THE HIGH PRICE OF BULLION

1810–11

THE HIGH PRICE

OF

BULLION,

A PROOF OF

THE DEPRECIATION

OF

BANK NOTES.

———◆———

BY DAVID RICARDO.

═══════

LONDON:

PRINTED FOR JOHN MURRAY, 32, FLEET-STREET;
AND SOLD BY EVERY OTHER BOOKSELLER
IN TOWN AND COUNTRY.

1810.

THE

HIGH PRICE

OF

B U L L I O N,

A PROOF OF THE

DEPRECIATION OF BANK NOTES.

By DAVID RICARDO.

THE FOURTH EDITION, CORRECTED.

TO WHICH IS ADDED,

AN APPENDIX,

CONTAINING

OBSERVATIONS ON SOME PASSAGES IN AN ARTICLE IN THE
EDINBURGH REVIEW, ON THE DEPRECIATION OF PAPER
CURRENCY; ALSO SUGGESTIONS FOR SECURING TO THE PUB-
LIC A CURRENCY AS INVARIABLE AS GOLD, WITH A VERY
MODERATE SUPPLY OF THAT METAL.

LONDON:

PRINTED FOR JOHN MURRAY, 32, FLEET-STREET;
WILLIAM BLACKWOOD, EDINBURGH; AND
M. N. MAHON, DUBLIN.

1811.

OBSERVATIONS

ON SOME PASSAGES IN AN

ARTICLE IN THE EDINBURGH REVIEW,

ON THE

DEPRECIATION OF PAPER CURRENCY;

ALSO

SUGGESTIONS FOR SECURING TO THE PUBLIC A CUR-
RENCY AS INVARIABLE AS GOLD, WITH A VERY
MODERATE SUPPLY OF THAT METAL.

———

BEING THE

APPENDIX,

TO THE FOURTH EDITION OF "THE HIGH PRICE OF
BULLION," &c.

———

By DAVID RICARDO.

◆

LONDON:

PRINTED FOR JOHN MURRAY, 32, FLEET-STREET;
WILLIAM BLACKWOOD, EDINBURGH; AND
M. N. MAHON, DUBLIN.
———
1811.

INTRODUCTION[1]

THE writer of the following pages has already submitted some reflections to the attention of the public, on the subject of paper-currency, through the medium of the Morning Chronicle. He has thought proper to republish his sentiments on this question in a form more calculated to bring it to fair discussion; and his reasons for so doing, are, that he has seen, with the greatest alarm, the progressive depreciation of the paper-currency. His fears have been augmented by observing, that by a great part of the public this depreciation is altogether denied, and that by others, who admit the fact, it is imputed to any cause but that which to him appears the real one. Before any remedy can be successfully applied to an evil of such magnitude, it is essential that there should be no doubt as to its cause. The writer proposes, from the admitted principles of political economy, to advance reasons, which, in his opinion, prove, that the paper-currency of this country has long been, and now is, at a considerable discount, proceeding from a superabundance in its quantity, and not from any want of confidence in the Bank of England, or from any doubts of their ability to fulfil their engagements. He does this without reluctance, being fully persuaded that the country is yet in possession of the means of restoring the paper-currency to its professed value, viz. the value of the coins, for the payment of which it purports to be a pledge.

He is aware that he can add but little to the arguments which have been so ably urged by Lord King,[2] and which ought

---

[1] The Introduction is contained only in eds. 1–3.
[2] *Thoughts on the Restriction of Payments in Specie at the Banks of England and Ireland,* By Lord King, London, Cadell and Davies, n.d.

[1803]. A 'Second Edition Enlarged, Including Some Remarks on the Coinage' was published, under the title *Thoughts on the Effects of the Bank Restrictions,* in 1804.

long before this to have carried conviction to every mind; but he trusts, that as the evil has become more glaring, the public will not continue to view, without interest, a subject which yields to no other in importance, and in which the general welfare is so materially concerned.

Dec. 1, 1809.

HIGH PRICE OF BULLION,

A PROOF OF

THE DEPRECIATION OF BANK NOTES

THE precious metals employed for circulating the commodities of the world, previously[1] to the establishment of banks, have been supposed by the most approved writers on political economy to have been divided into certain proportions among the different civilized nations of the earth, according to the state of their commerce and wealth, and therefore according to the number and frequency of the payments which they had to perform. While so divided they preserved every where the same value, and as each country had an equal necessity for the quantity actually in use, there could be no temptation offered to either for their importation or exportation.

Gold and silver, like other commodities, have an intrinsic value, which is not arbitrary, but is dependent on their scarcity, the quantity of labour bestowed in procuring them, and the value of the capital employed in the mines which produce them.

"The quality[2] of utility, beauty, and scarcity," says Dr. Smith, "are the original foundation of the high price of those metals,

---

[1] Ed. 1 'previous'.   [2] Adam Smith says 'These qualities'.

or of the great quantity of other goods for which they can every where be exchanged. This value was antecedent to, and independent of their being employed as coin, and was the quality which fitted them for that employment."[1]

If the quantity of gold and silver in the world employed as money were[2] exceedingly small, or abundantly great, it would not in the least affect the proportions in which they would be divided among the different nations—the variation in their quantity would have produced no other effect than to make the commodities for which they were exchanged comparatively dear or cheap. The smaller quantity of money would perform the functions of a circulating medium, as well as the larger. Ten millions would be as effectual for that purpose as one hundred millions. Dr. Smith observes, "that the most abundant mines of the precious metals would add little to the wealth of the world. A produce of which the value is principally derived from its scarcity is necessarily degraded by its abundance."[3]

If in the progress towards wealth, one nation advanced more rapidly than the others, that nation would require and obtain a greater proportion of the money of the world. Its commerce, its commodities, and its payments, would increase, and the general currency of the world would be divided according to the new proportions. All countries therefore would contribute their share to this effectual demand.

In the same manner if any nation wasted part of its wealth, or lost part of its trade, it could not retain the same quantity of circulating medium which it before possessed. A part would be exported, and divided among the other nations till the usual proportions were re-established.

While the relative situation of countries continued unaltered,

---

[1] *Wealth of Nations*, Bk. I, ch. xi, pt. ii; Cannan's ed., vol. I, p. 173.   [2] Ed. 1 'was'.   [3] *ib.* vol. I, p. 174.

they might have abundant commerce with each other, but their exports and imports would on the whole be equal. England might possibly import more goods from, than she would export to, France, but she would in consequence export more to some other country, and France would import more from that country; so that the exports and imports of all countries would balance each other; bills of exchange would make the necessary payments, but no money would pass, because it would have the same value in all countries.

If a mine of gold were discovered in either of these countries, the currency of that country would be lowered in value in consequence of the increased quantity of the precious metals brought into circulation, and would therefore no longer be of the same value as that of other countries. Gold and silver, whether in coin or in bullion, obeying the law which regulates all other commodities, would immediately become articles of exportation; they would leave the country where they were cheap, for those countries where they were dear, and would continue to do so, as long as the mine should prove productive, and till the proportion existing between capital and money in each country before the discovery of the mine, were[1] again established, and gold and silver restored every where to one value. In return for the gold exported, commodities would be imported; and though what is usually termed the balance of trade would be against the country exporting money or bullion, it would be evident that she was carrying on a most advantageous trade, exporting that which was no way useful to her, for commodities which might be employed in the extension of her manufactures, and the increase of her wealth.

If instead of a mine being discovered in any country, a bank were established, such as the Bank of England, with the power of issuing its notes for a circulating medium; after a large

[1] Ed. 1 'was'.

amount had been issued either by way of loan to merchants, or by advances to government, thereby adding considerably to the sum of the currency, the same effect would follow as in the case of the mine. The circulating medium would be lowered in value, and goods would experience a proportionate rise. The equilibrium between that and other nations would only be restored by the exportation of part of the coin.

The establishment of the bank and the consequent issue of its notes therefore, as well as the discovery of the mine, operate as an inducement[1] to the exportation either of bullion or of coin, and are beneficial only in as far as that object may be accomplished. The bank substitutes a currency of no value for one most costly, and enables us to turn the precious metals (which, though a very necessary part of our capital, yield no revenue,) into a capital which will yield one. Dr. A. Smith compares[2] the advantages attending the establishment of a bank to those which would be obtained by converting our highways into pastures and corn-fields, and procuring a road through the air. The highways, like the coin, are highly useful, but neither yield any revenue. Some people might be alarmed at the specie leaving the country, and might consider that as a disadvantageous trade which required us to part with it; indeed the law so considers it by its enactments against the exportation of specie; but a very little reflection will convince us that it is our choice, and not our necessity, that sends it abroad; and that it is highly beneficial to us to exchange that commodity which is superfluous, for others which may be made productive.

The exportation of the specie may at all times be safely left to the discretion of individuals; it will not be exported more than any other commodity, unless its exportation should be advantageous to the country. If it be advantageous to export

[1] Ed. 1 'operates as a stimulus'.   [2] Bk. II, ch. ii; vol. I, p. 304.

it, no laws can effectually prevent its exportation. Happily in this case, as well as in most others in commerce where there is free competition, the interests of the individual and that of the community are never at variance.

Were it possible to carry the law against melting or exporting[1] of coin[2] into strict execution, at the same time that the exportation of gold bullion was freely allowed, no advantage could accrue from it, but great injury must arise to those who might have to pay, possibly, two ounces or more of coined gold for one of uncoined gold. This would be a real depreciation of our currency, raising the prices of all other commodities in the same proportion as it increased that of gold bullion. The owner of money would in this case suffer an injury equal to what a proprietor of corn would suffer, were a law to be passed prohibiting him from selling his corn for more than half its market value. The law against the exportation of the coin has this tendency, but is so easily evaded, that gold in bullion has always been nearly of the same value as gold in coin.

Thus then it appears that the currency of one country can never for any length of time be much more valuable, as far as equal quantities of the precious metals are concerned, than that of another; that excess of currency is but a relative term; that if the circulation of England were ten millions, that of France five millions, that of Holland four millions, &c. &c. whilst they kept their proportions, though the currency of each country were doubled or trebled, neither country would be conscious of an excess of currency. The prices of commodities would every where rise, on account of the increase of currency, but there would be no exportation of money from either. But if these proportions be destroyed by England alone

[1] Eds. 1-2 'the law against the exportation'.
[2] Ed. 4 has 'corn' for 'coin': this misprint is corrected by Ricardo in his own copy, which is preserved at Gatcombe.

doubling her currency, while that of France, Holland, &c. &c. continued as before, we should then be conscious of an excess in our currency, and for the same reason the other countries would feel a deficiency in theirs, and part of our excess would be exported till the proportions of ten, five, four, &c. were again established.

If in France an ounce of gold were more valuable than in England, and would therefore in France purchase more of any commodity common to both countries, gold would immediately quit England for such purpose, and we should send gold in preference to any thing else, because it would be the cheapest exchangeable commodity in the English market; for if gold be dearer in France than in England, goods must be cheaper; we should not therefore send them from the dear to the cheap market, but, on the contrary, they would come from the cheap to the dear market, and would be exchanged for our gold.

The Bank might continue to issue their notes, and the specie be exported with advantage to the country, while their notes were payable in specie on demand, because they could never issue more notes than the value of the coin which would have circulated had there been no bank*.

If they attempted to exceed this amount, the excess would be immediately returned to them for specie; because our currency, being thereby diminished in value, could be advantageously exported, and could not be retained in our circulation.[1] These are the means, as I have already explained, by which our currency endeavours to equalize itself with the currencies of other countries. As soon as this equality was attained,

---

* They might, strictly speaking, rather exceed that quantity, because as the Bank would add to the currency of the world, England would retain its share of the increase.

[1] Eds. 1-2 read 'because our currency being superfluous, there could be no better employment for the superfluity, than the sending it to a better market abroad.'

all advantage arising from exportation would cease; but if the Bank assuming, that because a given quantity of circulating medium had been necessary last year, therefore the same quantity must be necessary this, or for any other reason, continued to re-issue the returned notes, the stimulus which a redundant currency first gave to the exportation of the coin would be again renewed with similar effects; gold would be again demanded, the exchange would become unfavourable, and gold bullion would rise, in a small degree,[1] above its mint price, because it is legal to export bullion, but illegal to export the coin, and the difference would be about equal to the fair compensation for the risk.

In this manner if the Bank persisted in returning their notes into circulation, every guinea might be drawn out of their coffers.

If to supply the deficiency of their stock of gold they were to purchase gold bullion at the advanced price, and have it coined into guineas, this would not remedy the evil, guineas would be still demanded, but instead of being exported would be melted and sold to the Bank as bullion at the advanced price. "The operations of the Bank," observed Dr. Smith, alluding to an analogous case,[2] "were upon this account somewhat like the web of Penelope, the work that was done in the day was undone in the night." The same sentiment is expressed by Mr. Thornton[3]:—"Finding the guineas in their coffers to lessen every day, they must naturally be supposed to be desirous of replacing them by all effectual and not extravagantly expensive means. They will be disposed, to a certain degree, to buy gold, though at a losing price, and to coin it into new

[1] Eds. 1-2 do not contain ', in a small degree,'.
[2] Bk. IV, ch. vi; vol. II, p. 52. Adam Smith actually says 'The operations of the mint'.
[3] *An Enquiry into the Nature and Effects of the Paper Credit of Great Britain*, by Henry Thornton, London, Hatchard, 1802, pp. 124-5.

guineas; but they will have to do this at the very moment when many are privately melting what is coined. The one party will be melting and selling while the other is buying and coining. And each of these two contending businesses will now be carried on, not on account of an actual exportation of each melted guinea to Hamburgh, but the operation or at least a great part of it will be confined to London; the coiners and the melters living on the same spot, and giving constant employment to each other.

"The Bank," continues Mr. Thornton, "if we suppose it, as we now do, to carry on this sort of contest with the melters, is obviously waging a very unequal war; and even though it should not be tired early, it will be likely to be tired sooner than its adversaries."

The Bank would be obliged therefore ultimately to adopt the only remedy in their power to put a stop to the demand for guineas. They would withdraw part of their notes from circulation, till they should have increased the value of the remainder to that of gold bullion, and consequently to the value of the currencies of other countries. All advantage from the exportation of gold bullion would then cease, and there would be no temptation to exchange bank-notes for guineas.

In this view of the subject, then, it appears, that the temptation to export money in exchange for goods, or what is termed an unfavourable balance of trade, never arises but from a redundant currency. But[1] Mr. Thornton, who has considered this subject very much at large, supposes[2] that a very unfavourable balance of trade may be occasioned to this country by a bad harvest, and the consequent importation of corn; and that there may be at the same time an unwillingness in

---

[1] Eds. 1-2 do not contain the preceding sentence and open the paragraph with 'Mr. Thornton, who has considered'.

[2] *ib.* pp. 131-4.

the country, to which we are indebted, to receive our goods in payment; the balance due to the foreign country must therefore be paid out of that part of our currency, consisting of coin, and that hence arises the demand for gold bullion and its increased price. He considers the Bank as affording considerable accommodation to the merchants, by supplying with their notes the void occasioned by the exportation of the specie.[1]

As it is acknowledged by Mr. Thornton, in many parts of his work, that the price of gold bullion is rated in gold coin; and as it is also acknowledged by him,[2] that the law against melting gold coin into bullion and exporting it is easily evaded, it follows, that no demand for gold bullion, arising from this or any other cause, can raise the money price of that commodity. The error of this reasoning proceeds from not distinguishing between an increase in the value of gold, and an increase in its money price.

If there were a great demand for corn its money price would advance; because, in comparing corn with money, we in fact compare it with another commodity; and for the same reason, when there is a great demand for gold its corn price will increase; but in neither case will a bushel of corn be worth more than a bushel of corn, or an ounce of gold more than an ounce of gold. An ounce of gold bullion could not, whatever the demand might be, whilst its price was rated in gold coin, be of more value than an ounce of coined gold, or 3*l*. 17*s*. 10½*d*.

If this argument should not be considered as conclusive, I should urge, that a *void* in the currency, as here supposed, can only be occasioned by the annihilation or limitation of

---

[1] Eds. 1-2 do not contain the three paragraphs that follow. Cp. for their substance Ricardo's letter to Horner of 5 Feb. 1810, below, VI, 5–7.

[2] *Enquiry into Paper Credit*, pp. 123–4.

paper currency, and then it would speedily be filled by importations of bullion, which its increased value, in consequence of the diminution of circulating medium, would infallibly attract to the advantageous market. However great the scarcity of corn might be, the exportation of money would be limited by its increasing scarcity. Money is in such general demand, and in the present state of civilization is so essential to commercial transactions, that it can never be exported to excess; even in a war such as the present, when our enemy endeavours to interdict all commerce with us, the value which the currency would bear, from its increasing scarcity, would prevent the exportation of it from being carried so far as to occasion a void in the circulation.

Mr. Thornton has not explained to us, why any unwillingness should exist in the foreign country to receive our goods in exchange for their corn; and it would be necessary for him to show, that if such an unwillingness were to exist, we should agree to indulge it so far as to consent to part with our coin.

If we consent to give coin in exchange for goods, it must be from choice, not necessity. We should not import more goods than we export, unless we had a redundancy of currency, which it therefore suits us to make a part of our exports. The exportation of the coin is caused by its cheapness, and is not the effect, but the cause of an unfavourable balance: we should not export it, if we did not send it to a better market, or if we had any commodity which we could export more profitably. It is a salutary remedy for a redundant currency; and as I have already endeavoured to prove, that redundancy or excess is only a relative term, it follows, that the demand for it abroad arises only from the comparative deficiency of the currency of the importing country, which there causes its superior value.

It resolves itself entirely into a question of interest. If the sellers of the corn to England, to the amount I will suppose of a million, could import goods which cost a million in England, but would produce, when sold abroad, more than if the million had been sent in money, goods would be preferred; if otherwise, money would be demanded.

It is only after a comparison of the value in their markets and in our own, of gold and other commodities, and because gold is cheaper in the London market than in theirs, that foreigners prefer gold in exchange for their corn. If we diminish the quantity of currency, we give an additional value to it: this will induce them to alter their election, and prefer the commodities. If I owed a debt in Hamburgh of 100*l.* I should endeavour to find out the cheapest mode of paying it. If I send money, the expence attending its transportation being I will suppose 5*l.* to discharge my debt will cost me 105*l.* If I purchase cloth here, which, with the expences attending its exportation, will cost me 106*l.* and which will, in Hamburgh, sell for 100*l.* it is evidently more to my advantage to send the money. If the purchase and expences of sending hardware to pay my debt, will take 107*l.* I should prefer sending cloth to hardware, but I would send neither in preference to money, because money would be the cheapest exportable commodity in the London market. The same reasons would operate with the exporter of the corn, if the transaction were on his own account. But if the Bank, "fearful for the safety of their establishment,"[1] and knowing that the requisite number of guineas would be withdrawn from their coffers at the mint price, should think it necessary to diminish the amount of their notes in circulation, the proportion between the value of the money, of the cloth, and of the hardware, would no longer be as 105, 106, and 107; but the money would become the

[1] Cp. the quotations from Thornton, below, p. 75–6.

most valuable of the three, and therefore would be less advantageously employed in discharging the foreign debts.[1]

If, which is a much stronger case, we agreed to pay a subsidy to a foreign power, money would not be exported whilst there were any goods which could more cheaply discharge the payment. The interest of individuals would render the exportation of the money unnecessary*.[2]

Thus then specie will be sent abroad to discharge a debt only when it is superabundant; only when it is the cheapest exportable commodity. If the Bank were at such a time paying their notes in specie, gold would be demanded for that purpose. It would be obtained there at its mint price, whereas its price as bullion would be something above its value as coin, because bullion could, and coin could not, be legally exported.

It is evident, then, that a depreciation of the circulating medium is the necessary consequence of its redundance; and that in the common state of the national currency this depre-

---

* This is strongly corroborated, by the statement of Mr. Rose in the House of Commons, that our exports exceeded our imports by (I believe) sixteen millions.[3] In return for those exports no bullion could have been imported, because it is well known, that the price of bullion having been during the whole year higher abroad than in this country, a large quantity of our gold coin has been exported. To the value of the balance of exports, therefore, must be added the value of the bullion exported. A part of the amount may be due to us from foreign nations, but the remainder must be precisely equal to our foreign expenditure, consisting of subsidies to our allies, and the maintenance of our fleets and armies on foreign stations.[4]

---

[1] Eds. 1-3 'debt.'
[2] In eds. 1-2 the two paragraphs that follow are placed below; see p. 74, footnote.
[3] Probably in a speech on 26 Jan. 1810. *Hansard* (XV, 156) reports him as saying simply that 'for a very long time past our export trade had been carried on in in manufactures, with a perpetual balance of millions in favour of this country.' George Rose was then Vice-President of the Board of Trade.
[4] Eds. 1-2 do not contain this footnote.

ciation is counteracted by the exportation of the precious metals*.

* It has been observed, in a work of great and deserved repute, the Edinburgh Review †, that an increase in the paper currency will only occasion a rise in the *paper* or *currency* price of commodities, but will not cause an increase in their bullion price.

This would be true at a time when the currency consisted wholly of paper not convertible into specie, but not while specie formed any part of the circulation. In the latter case the effect of an increased issue of paper would be to throw out of circulation an equal amount of specie; but this could not be done without adding to the quantity of bullion in the market, and thereby lowering its value, or in other words, *increasing the bullion price of commodities*. It is only in consequence of this fall in the value of the metallic currency, and of bullion, that the temptation to export them arises; and the penalties on melting the coin is the sole cause of a small difference between the value of the coin and of bullion, or a small excess of the market above the mint price. But exporting of bullion is synonymous with an unfavourable balance of trade. From whatever cause an exportation of bullion, in exchange for commodities, may proceed, it is called (I think very incorrectly) an unfavourable balance of trade.[1]

When the circulation consists wholly of paper, any increase in its quantity will raise the *money* price of bullion without lowering its *value*, in the same manner, and in the same proportion, as it will raise the prices of other commodities, and for the same reason will lower the foreign exchanges; but this will only be a *nominal*, not a *real* fall, and will not occasion the exportation of bullion, because the real value of bullion will not be diminished, as there will be no increase to the quantity in the market.[2]

† Vol. I, p. 183.[3]

[1] Ed. 3 has here an additional paragraph: 'It is highly essential to a due understanding of this subject, that we should accurately distinguish between cause and effect. In the work to which I have already alluded, it is said, (Page 184) "When the local rise of the price of goods consists in the actual increase of their bullion price, a real fall in the foreign exchange will generally take place, and will *occasion*, by the demand for bullion to be exported, a fluctuating excess of the market price above the mint price of gold." Here, and in many other parts of the same article, the fall in the exchange, or the unfavourable balance of trade, is stated to be the *cause* of the excess of the market above the mint price of gold, but to me it appears to be the *effect* of such excess. An increase of paper currency we have just seen, lowers the value of gold bullion but raises its money price. It is the fall in its value which causes its exportation, and therefore the fall of the exchange.'

[2] Eds. 1-2 do not contain this footnote.

[3] October 1802, Art. xxv (by Francis Horner), on Thornton's *Paper Credit*.

Such, then, appear to me to be the laws that regulate the distribution of the precious metals throughout the world, and which cause and limit their circulation from one country to another, by regulating their value in each. But before I proceed to examine on these principles the main object of my enquiry, it is necessary that I should shew what is the standard measure of value in this country, and of which, therefore, our paper currency ought to be the representative, because it can only be by a comparison to this standard that its regularity, or its depreciation, may be estimated.

No permanent* measure of value can be said to exist in any nation while the circulating medium consists of two metals, because they are constantly subject to vary in value with respect to each other. However exact the conductors of the mint may be, in proportioning the relative value of gold to silver in the coins, at the time when they fix the ratio, they cannot prevent one of these metals from rising, while the other remains stationary, or falls in value. Whenever this happens, one of the coins will be melted to be sold for the other. Mr. Locke[1], Lord Liverpool, and many other writers, have ably considered this subject, and have all agreed, that the only remedy for the evils in the currency proceeding from this source, is the making one of the metals only the standard measure of value. Mr. Locke considered[2] silver as the most

---

* Strictly speaking, there can be no permanent measure of value. A measure of value should itself be invariable; but this is not the case with either gold or silver, they being subject to fluctuations as well as other commodities. Experience has indeed taught us, that though the variations in the *value* of gold or silver may be considerable, on a comparison of distant periods, yet for short spaces of time their value is tolerably fixed. It is this property, among their other excellencies, which fits them better than any other commodity for the uses of money. Either gold or silver may therefore, in the point of view in which we are considering them, be called a measure of value.

[1] Eds. 1-3 'The great Mr. Locke'.
[2] *Some Considerations of the Consequences of the Lowering of Interest,* and *Raising the Value of Money,* London, 1692, pp. 166–8.

proper metal for this purpose, and proposed that gold coins should be left to find their own value, and pass for a greater or lesser number of shillings, as the market price of gold might vary with respect to silver.

Lord Liverpool, on the contrary, maintained[1] that gold was not only the most proper metal for a general measure of value in this country, but that, by the common consent of the people, it had become so, was so considered by foreigners, and that it was best suited to the increased commerce and wealth of England.

He, therefore, proposed, that gold coin only should be a legal tender for sums exceeding one guinea, and silver coins for sums not exceeding that amount. As the law now stands, gold coin is a legal tender for all sums; but it was enacted in the year 1774, "That no tender in payment of money made in the silver coin of this realm, of any sum exceeding the sum of twenty-five pounds at any one time, shall be reputed in law, or allowed to be legal tender within Great-Britain or Ireland, for more than according to its value by weight, after the rate of 5s. 2d. for each ounce of silver."[2] The same regulation was revived in 1798, and is now in force.[3]

For many reasons given by Lord Liverpool,[4] it appears proved beyond dispute, that gold coin has been for near a century the principal measure of value, but this is, I think, to be attributed to the inaccurate determination of the mint proportions. Gold has been valued too high; no silver, therefore, can remain in circulation which is of its standard weight.

If a new regulation were to take place, and silver to be valued too high, or (which is the same thing) if the market proportions between the prices of gold and silver were to

[1] *A Treatise on the Coins of the Realm*, Oxford, 1805, pp. 152–5.
[2] 14 Geo. III, c. 42.
[3] 38 Geo. III, c. 59. The quotation from the Statute, and this sentence, are from Lord Liverpool's *Treatise*, p. 129.
[4] *ib*. pp. 132–45.

become greater than those of the mint, gold would then disappear, and silver become the standard currency.[1]

This may require further explanation. The relative value of gold and silver in the coins is as $15\frac{9}{124}$ to 1. An ounce of gold which is coined into $3l.$ $17s.$ $10\frac{1}{2}d.$ of gold coin, is worth, according to the mint regulation, $15\frac{9}{124}$ ounces of silver, because that weight of silver is also coined into $3l.$ $17s.$ $10\frac{1}{2}d.$[2] of silver coin. Whilst the relative value of gold to silver is in the market under 15 to 1, which it has been for a great number of years till lately, gold coin would necessarily be the standard measure of value, because neither the Bank, nor[3] any individual, would send $15\frac{9}{124}$ ozs. of silver to the mint to be coined into $3l.$ $17s.$ $10\frac{1}{2}d.$ when they could sell that quantity of silver in the

[1] In place of the six paragraphs that follow in the text, ending on p. 69 (which Ricardo takes, with slight alterations, from his letter to Horner of 5 Feb. 1810, below, VI, 3–5), ed. 1 and, unless stated otherwise, ed. 2, read 'Gold has lately experienced a considerable rise compared with silver; an ounce of standard gold, which, on an average of many years, was of equal value to $14\frac{3}{4}$ oz. of standard silver, being now in the market of the same value as $15\frac{1}{2}$ oz. The proportion in our coin, as regulated by the mint, is as 1 to $15\frac{9}{124}$. It is therefore probable, that if the present market relative value of gold and silver should be permanent, and that we should be so fortunate as to restore our currency to the state in which it was previous [ed. 2 'previously'] to 1797, by the repeal of the Bank Restriction-bill, silver would in effect become the standard measure of value. Silver bullion only would then be carried to the mint to be coined; and as gold coin might be advantageously melted, it would disappear from circulation. This would continue till the mint should adopt more just proportions, or till government should follow the recommendations [ed. 2 'recommendation'] of Lord Liverpool, and make silver a legal tender for sums not exceeding a guinea.' (See *A Treatise on the Coins of the Realm*, Oxford, 1805, p. 168.)

At the end of this passage, eds. 1–2 attach a footnote which begins 'Since writing the above, I have seen an act of parliament, passed in the 39th of Geo. III. wherein is the following clause:—'. The clause quoted is that given in the text of eds. 3–4, below, p. 68; the footnote is concluded by the two paragraphs which in the text of eds. 3–4 follow immediately the quotation from the Act (and which begin 'This law is now' and end 'standard of currency.').

[2] Ed. 3 misprints '$3l.$ $17s.$ $10\frac{3}{4}d.$'.

[3] Ed. 3 'or'.

market for more than 3*l.* 17*s.* 10½*d.* in gold coin, and this they could do by the supposition, that less than 15 ounces of silver would purchase an ounce of gold.

But if the relative value of gold to silver be more than the mint proportion of $15\frac{9}{124}$ to 1, no gold would then be sent to the mint to be coined, because as either of the metals are a legal tender to any amount, the possessor of an ounce of gold would not send it to the mint to be coined into 3*l.* 17*s.* 10½*d.* of gold coin, whilst he could sell it, which he could do in such case, for more than 3*l.* 17*s.* 10½*d.* of silver coin. Not only would not gold be carried to the mint to be coined, but the illicit trader would melt the gold coin, and sell it as bullion for more than its nominal value in the silver coin. Thus then gold would disappear from circulation, and silver coin become the standard measure of value. As gold has lately experienced a considerable rise compared with silver, (an ounce of standard gold, which, on an average of many years, was of equal value to $14\frac{3}{4}$ ozs. of standard silver, being now in the market of the same value as $15\frac{1}{2}$ oz.) this would be the case now were the Bank Restriction-bill repealed, and the coinage of silver freely allowed at the mint, in the same manner as that of gold; but in an act of parliament of 39 Geo. III. is the following clause:—

"Whereas inconvenience may arise from any coinage of silver until such regulations may be formed as shall appear necessary; and whereas from the present low price of silver bullion, owing to temporary circumstances, a small quantity of silver bullion has been brought to the mint to be coined, and there is reason to suppose that a still further quantity may be brought; and it is therefore necessary to suspend the coining of silver for the present; be it therefore enacted, That from and after the passing of this act, no silver bullion shall be coined at the mint, nor shall any silver coin that may have been coined there be delivered, any law to the contrary notwithstanding."

This law is now in force.

It would appear, therefore, to have been the intention of the legislature to establish gold as the standard of currency in this country. Whilst this law is in force, silver coin must be confined to small payments only, the quantity in circulation being barely sufficient for that purpose. It might be for the interest of a debtor to pay his large debts in silver coin if he could get silver bullion coined into money; but being prevented by the above law from doing so, he is necessarily obliged to discharge his debt with gold coin, which he could obtain at the mint with gold bullion to any amount. Whilst this law is in force, gold must always continue to be the standard of currency.

Were the market value of an ounce of gold to become equal to thirty ounces of silver, gold would nevertheless be the measure of value, whilst this prohibition continued in force. It would be of no avail, that the possessor of 30 ounces of silver should know that he once could have discharged a debt of 3*l.* 17*s.* 10½*d.* by procuring $15\frac{9}{124}$ ounces of silver to be coined at the mint, as he would in this case have no other means of discharging his debt but by selling his 30 oz. of silver at the market value, that is to say, for one ounce of gold, or 3*l.* 17*s.* 10½*d.* of gold coin.[1]

The public has sustained, at different times, very serious loss from the depreciation of the circulating medium, arising from the unlawful practice of clipping the coins.

In proportion as they become debased, so the prices of every commodity for which they are exchangeable rise in nominal value, not excepting gold and silver bullion: accordingly we find, that before the re-coinage in the reign of King William the Third, the silver currency had become so degraded, that an ounce of silver, which ought to be contained in sixty-two pence, sold for seventy-seven pence; and a guinea, which was valued at the mint at twenty shillings, passed in all contracts

[1] Here end the six paragraphs referred to on p. 67, footnote 1.

In eds. 1-2 the three paragraphs that follow in the text (together with the footnote attached to the third paragraph) are placed below; see p. 74, footnote 1.

for thirty shillings. This evil was then remedied by the re-coinage. Similar effects followed from the debasement of the gold currency, which were again corrected in 1774 by the same means.

Our gold coins have, since 1774, continued nearly at their standard purity; but our silver currency has again become debased. By an assay at the mint in 1798, it appears that our shillings were found to be twenty-four per cent., and our sixpences thirty-eight per cent. under their mint value; and I am informed, that by a late experiment they were found considerably more deficient. They do not, therefore, contain as much pure silver as they did in the reign of King William. This debasement, however, did not operate previously[1] to 1798, as on the former occasion. At that time both gold and silver bullion rose in proportion to the debasement of the silver coin. All foreign exchanges were against us full twenty per cent., and many of them still more. But although the debasement of the silver coin had continued for many years, it had neither, previously[2] to 1798, raised the price of gold nor[3] silver, nor had it produced any effect on the exchanges. This is a convincing proof, that gold coin was, during that period, considered as the standard measure of value. Any debasement of the gold coin would then have produced the same effects on the prices[4] of gold and silver bullion, and on the foreign exchanges, which were formerly caused by the debasement of the silver coins*.

While the currency of different countries consists of the

* When the gold coin was debased, previously[5] to the re-coinage in 1774, gold and silver bullion rose above their mint prices, and fell immediately on the gold coin attaining its present perfection. The exchanges were, owing to the same causes, from being unfavourable rendered favourable.

[1] Ed. 1 'previous'.
[2] Ed. 1 'previous'.
[3] Eds. 1-3 'or'.
[4] Eds. 1-3 'price'.
[5] Ed. 1 'previous'.

precious metals, or of a paper money which is at all times exchangeable for them; and while the metallic currency is not debased by wearing, or clipping, a comparison of the weight, and degree of fineness of their coins, will enable us to ascertain their par of exchange. Thus the par of exchange between Holland and England is stated to be about eleven florins, because the pure silver contained in eleven florins is equal to the pure silver contained in twenty standard shillings.

This par is not, nor can it be, absolutely fixed; because, gold coin being the standard of commerce in England, and silver coin in Holland, a pound sterling, or $\frac{20}{21}$ of a guinea, may at different times be more or less valuable than twenty standard shillings, and therefore more or less valuable than its equivalent of eleven florins. Estimating the par either by silver or by gold will be sufficiently exact for our purpose.

If I owe a debt in Holland; by knowing the par of exchange, I also know the quantity of our money which will be necessary to discharge it.

If my debt amount[1] to 1100 florins, and gold have not varied in value, 100l. in our pure gold coin will purchase as much Dutch currency as is necessary to pay my debt. By exporting the 100l. therefore in coin, or (which is the same thing) paying a bullion merchant the 100l. in coin, and allowing him the expences attending its transportation, such as freight, insurance, and his profit, he will sell me a bill which will discharge my debt; at the same time he will export the bullion, to enable his correspondent to pay the bill when it shall become due.

These expences then are the utmost limits of an unfavourable exchange. However great my debt may be, though it equalled the largest subsidy ever given by this country to an ally; while I could pay the bullion-merchant in coin of standard value, he

[1] Ed. 1 reads 'amounts' here; and 'has', in place of 'have', six words later.

would be glad to export it, and to sell me bills. But if I pay him for his bill in a debased coin, or in a depreciated paper-money, he will not be willing to sell me his bill at this rate; because if the coin be debased, it does not contain the quantity of pure gold or silver which ought to be contained in 100*l*., and he must therefore export an additional number of such debased pieces of money, to enable him to pay my debt of 100*l*., or its equivalent, 1100 florins. If I pay him in paper-money; as he cannot send it abroad, he will consider whether it will purchase as much gold or silver bullion as is contained in the coin for which it is a substitute; if it will do this, paper will be as acceptable to him as coin; but if it will not, he will expect a further premium for his bill, equal to the depreciation of the paper.

While the circulating medium consists, therefore, of coin undebased, or of paper-money immediately exchangeable for undebased coin, the exchange can never be more above, or more below, par, than the expences attending the transportation of the precious metals. But when it consists of a depreciated paper-money, it necessarily will fall according to the degree of the depreciation.

The exchange will, therefore, be a tolerably accurate criterion by which we may judge of the debasement of the currency, proceeding either from a clipped coinage, or a depreciated paper-money.

It is observed by Sir James Stuart,[1] "That if the foot measure was altered at once over all England, by adding to it, or taking from it, any proportional part of its standard length, the alteration would be best discovered, by comparing the new foot with that of Paris, or of any other country, which had suffered no alteration.

[1] *An Inquiry into the Principles of Political Œconomy*, London, 1767, vol. 1, p. 534.

"Just so, if the pound sterling, which is the English unit, shall be found any how changed; and if the variation it has met with be difficult to ascertain, because of a complication of circumstances; the best way to discover it will be to compare the former and the present value of it, with the money of other nations which has suffered no variation. This the exchange will perform with the greatest exactness."

The Edinburgh reviewers, in speaking of Lord King's pamphlet, observe,[1] that "it does not follow because our imports always consist partly of bullion, that the balance of trade is therefore permanently in our favour. Bullion," they say, "is a commodity, for which, as for every other, there is a varying demand; and which, exactly like any other, may enter the catalogue either of imports or exports; and this exportation or importation of bullion will not affect the course of exchange in a different way from the exportation or importation of any other commodities."

No person ever exports or imports bullion without first considering the rate of exchange. It is by the rate of exchange that he discovers the relative value of bullion in the two countries between which it is estimated. It is therefore consulted by the bullion-merchant in the same manner as the price-current is by other merchants, before they determine on the exportation or importation of other commodities. If eleven florins in Holland contain an equal quantity of pure silver as twenty standard shillings, silver bullion, equal in weight to twenty standard shillings, can never be exported from London to Amsterdam whilst the exchange is at par, or unfavourable[2] to Holland. Some expence and risk must attend its exportation, and the very term *par* expresses that a quantity of silver bullion, equal to that weight and purity, is to be

[1] *Edinburgh Review*, July 1803, Art. XI (by Francis Horner), p. 419. [2] Ed. 1, by an error, 'favourable'.

obtained in Holland by the purchase of a bill of exchange, free of all expence. Who would send bullion to Holland at an expence of three or four per cent. when, by the purchase of a bill at par, he in fact obtains an order for the delivery to his correspondent in Holland of the same weight of bullion which he was about to export?

It would be as reasonable to contend, that when the price of corn is higher in England than on the Continent, corn would be sent, notwithstanding all the charges on its exportation, to be sold in the cheaper market.

Having already noticed the disorders to which a metallic currency is exposed, I will proceed to consider those which, though not caused by the debased state of either the gold or silver coins, are nevertheless more serious in their ultimate consequences.[1]

Our circulating medium is almost wholly composed of paper, and it behoves us to guard against the depreciation of

---

[1] Eds. 1-2, in place of this paragraph, contain a passage, which in eds. 3-4 (the text printed above) is broken up and inserted in two different places earlier in the pamphlet. The passage in eds. 1-2 is made up as follows:

First, the paragraph 'Thus then specie', printed above, p. 63;

Second, a paragraph which reads 'It is evident, then, that a depreciation of the circulating medium is the necessary consequence of its redundance; and that in the common state of the national currency this depreciation is counteracted by the exportation of the precious metals: but another very serious injury has been at different times sustained by the public from the depreciating of the circulating medium, by the unlawful practice of clipping the coins'. This paragraph in eds. 3-4 is split in two: the first half, 'It is evident', appears above, p. 63, and the second half, 'The public has', above, p. 69.

Third, the two paragraphs beginning 'In proportion as' and 'Our gold coins' (together with the footnote attached to the latter) which are given above, pp. 69–70.

Finally, a paragraph which begins 'But the disorders now affecting our currency, although not proceeding either from the debased state of the gold or silver coin, are nevertheless more serious in their ultimate consequences. Our circulating medium' etc., from this point agreeing with the text of eds. 3-4.

the paper currency with at least as much vigilance as against that of the coins.

This we have neglected to do.

Parliament, by restricting the Bank from paying in specie, have enabled the conductors of that concern to increase or decrease at pleasure the quantity and amount of their notes; and the previously existing checks against an over-issue having been thereby removed, those conductors have acquired the power of increasing or decreasing the value of the paper currency.

In tracing the present evils to their source, and proving their existence by an appeal to the two unerring tests I have before mentioned, namely, the rate of exchange and the price of bullion, I shall avail myself of the account given by Mr. Thornton of the conduct of the Bank before the restriction, to shew how clearly they acted on the principle which he has expressly acknowledged, viz. that the value of their notes is dependent on their amount, and that they ascertained the variation in their value by the tests I have just referred to.

Mr. Thornton tells us, "That if at any time the exchanges of the country became so unfavourable as to produce a material excess of the market above the mint price of gold,[1] the directors of the Bank, as appears by the evidence of some of their body, given to parliament, were disposed to resort to a reduction of their paper, as a means of diminishing or removing the excess, and of *thus providing for the security of their establishment*. They moreover have at all times," he says, "been accustomed to observe some limit as to the quantity of their notes for the same prudential reasons."[2] And in another place: "When the price which our coin will fetch in foreign countries is such as to

---

[1] In eds. 1-3 Ricardo inserts in square brackets '[here the cause is mistaken for the effect]'. Cp. above, p. 64, n. 1.

[2] *Enquiry into Paper Credit*, pp. 231–2. Ricardo's italics.

tempt it out of the kingdom, the directors of the Bank naturally diminish, in some degree, the quantity of their paper *through an anxiety for the safety of their establishment*. By diminishing their paper, they raise its value; and in raising its value, they raise also the value in England of the current coin which is exchanged for it. Thus the value of our gold coin conforms itself to the value of the current paper, and the current paper is rendered by the Bank-directors, of that value which it is necessary that it should bear in order to prevent large exportations;—a value sometimes rising a little above, and sometimes falling a little below, the price which our coin bears abroad."[1]

The necessity which the Bank felt itself under to guard the safety of its establishment, therefore, always prevented, before the restriction from paying in specie, a too lavish issue of paper money.

Thus we find that, for a period of twenty-three years previously[2] to the suspension of cash payments in 1797, the average price of gold bullion was 3*l*. 17*s*. 7$\frac{3}{4}$*d*. per oz. about 2$\frac{3}{4}$*d*. under the mint price; and for sixteen years previously[3] to 1774, it never was much above 4*l*. per oz. It should be remembered that during these sixteen years our gold coin was debased by wearing, and it is therefore probable that 4*l*. of such debased money did not weigh as much as the ounce of gold for which it was exchanged.

Dr. A. Smith considers[4] every permanent excess of the market above the mint price of gold, as referrible to the state of the coins. While the coin was of its standard weight and purity, the market price of gold bullion, he thought, could not greatly exceed the mint price.

Mr. Thornton contends that this cannot be the only cause.

[1] *ib.* p. 208, note. Ricardo's italics.
[2] Ed. 1 'previous'.
[3] Ed. 1 'previous'.
[4] *Wealth of Nations*, Bk. 1, ch. v; vol. 1, p. 47.

"We have," he says,[1] "lately experienced fluctuations in our exchanges, and correspondent variations in the market, compared with the mint price of gold, amounting to no less than eight or ten per cent.; the state of our coinage continuing in all respects the same." Mr. Thornton should have reflected that at the time he wrote, specie could not be demanded at the Bank in exchange for notes; that this was a cause for the depreciation of the currency which Dr. Smith could never have anticipated. If Mr. Thornton had proved that there had been a fluctuation of ten per cent. in the price of gold, while the Bank paid their notes in specie, and the coin was undebased, he would then have convicted Dr. Smith of "having treated this important subject in a defective and unsatisfactory manner."[2]*

* An excess in the market above the mint price of gold or silver bullion, may, whilst the coins of both metals are legal tender, and there is no prohibition against the coinage of either metal,[3] be caused by a variation in the relative value of those metals; but an excess of the market above the mint price proceeding from this cause will be at once perceived by its affecting only the price of one of the metals. Thus gold would be at or below, while silver was above, its mint price, or silver at or below its mint price, whilst gold was above.

In the latter end of 1795, when the Bank had considerably more notes in circulation than either the preceding or the subsequent year, when their embarrassments had already commenced, when they appear to have resigned all prudence in the management of their concerns, and to have constituted Mr. Pitt sole director, the price of gold bullion did for a short time rise to 4l. 3s. or 4l. 4s. per oz.; but the directors were not without their fears for the consequences. In a remonstrance sent by them to Mr. Pitt, dated October 1795, after stating, "that the demand for gold not appearing likely soon to cease," and "that it had excited great apprehension in the court of directors," they observe, "The present price of gold being 4l. 3s. to 4l. 4s.† per ounce, and our guineas being

† It is difficult to determine on what authority the directors made this assertion, as by a return lately made to parliament it appears that during the year 1795 they did not purchase gold bullion at a price higher than 3l. 17s. 6d.[4]

[1] *Enquiry into Paper Credit*, pp. 206–7.
[2] Thornton, *ib.* p. 203.
[3] Eds. 1–2 do not contain 'and there is no prohibition against the coinage of either metal,'.
[4] Eds. 1–3 do not contain this footnote. For the return referred to, which is dated 22 Feb. 1811, see below, V, 462, n. 3.

But as all checks against the over-issues of the Bank are now removed by the act of parliament, which restricts them from paying their notes in specie, they are no longer bound by "*fears for the safety of their establishment,*" to limit the quantity of their notes to that sum which shall keep them of the same value as the coin which they represent. Accordingly we find that gold bullion has risen from 3*l.* 17*s.* 7¾*d.* the average price previously[1] to 1797, to 4*l.* 10*s.* and has been lately as high as 4*l.* 13*s.* per oz.

We may therefore fairly conclude that this difference in the relative value, or, in other words, that this depreciation in the actual value of bank-notes has been caused by the too abundant quantity which the Bank has sent into circulation. The same cause which has produced a difference of from fifteen to twenty per cent. in bank-notes when compared with gold bullion, may increase it to fifty per cent. There can be no limit to the depreciation which may arise from a constantly increasing quantity of paper. The stimulus which a redundant currency gives to the exportation of the coin has acquired new force, but cannot, as formerly, relieve itself. We have paper money only in circulation, which is necessarily confined to ourselves. Every increase in its quantity degrades it below the value of gold and silver bullion, below the value of the currencies of other countries.

The effect is the same as that which would have been produced from clipping our coins.

If one-fifth[2] were taken off from every guinea, the market

to be purchased at 3*l.* 17*s.* 10½*d.*, clearly demonstrates the grounds of our fears; *it being only necessary to state those facts to the Chancellor of the Exchequer.*"[3] It is remarkable that no price of gold above the mint price is quoted during the whole year in Wetenhall's list. In December it is there marked 3*l.* 17*s.* 6*d.*

[1] Ed. 1 'previous'.
[2] Should be 'one-sixth', to agree with the calculations that follow.
[3] 'Report of the Lords' Committee of Secrecy...Relating to the Bank', 1797 (reprint 1810), p. 84.

price of gold bullion would rise one-fifth above the mint price. Forty-four guineas and a half (the number of guineas weighing a pound, and therefore called the mint price), would no longer weigh a pound, therefore a fifth more than that quantity, or about 56*l.* would be the price of a pound of gold, and the difference between the market and the mint price, between 56*l.* and 46*l.* 14*s.* 6*d.* would measure the depreciation.

If such debased coin were to continue to be called by the name of guineas, and if the value of gold bullion and all other commodities were rated in the debased coin, a guinea fresh from the mint would be said to be worth 1*l.* 5*s.* and that sum would be given for it by the illicit trader; but it would not be the value of the new guinea which had increased, but that of the debased guineas which had fallen. This would immediately be evident, if a proclamation were issued, prohibiting the debased guineas from being current but by weight at the mint price of 3*l.* 17*s.* 10½*d.*; this would be constituting the new and heavy guineas, the standard measure of value, in lieu of the clipped and debased guineas. The latter would then pass at their true value, and be called 17 or 18 shilling-pieces. So if a proclamation to the same effect were now enforced, bank-notes would not be less current, but would pass only for the value of the gold bullion which they would purchase. A guinea would then no longer be said to be worth 1*l.* 5*s.* but a pound note would be current only for 16 or 17 shillings. At present gold coin is only a commodity, and bank-notes are the standard measure of value, but in that case gold coin would be that measure, and bank-notes would be the marketable commodity.[1]

"It is," says Mr. Thornton,[2] "the maintenance of our general exchanges, or, in other words, it is the agreement of

---

[1] Eds. 1-2 do not contain this paragraph. [2] *Enquiry into Paper Credit*, p. 191.

the mint price with the bullion price of gold, which seems to be the true proof that the circulating paper is not depreciated."

When the motive for exporting gold occurs, while the Bank do not pay in specie, and gold cannot therefore be obtained at its mint price, the small quantity that can be procured will be collected for exportation, and bank-notes will be sold at a discount for gold in proportion to their excess. In saying however that gold is at a high price, we are mistaken; it is not gold, it is paper which has changed its value. Compare an ounce of gold, or 3*l.* 17*s.* 10½*d.* to commodities, it bears the same proportion to them which it has before done; and if it do not, it is referrible to increased taxation, or to some of those causes which are so constantly operating on its value. But if we compare the substitute of an ounce of gold, 3*l.* 17*s.* 10½*d.* in bank-notes, with commodities, we shall then discover the depreciation of the bank-notes. In every market of the world I am obliged to part with 4*l.* 10*s.* in bank-notes to purchase the same quantity of commodities which I can obtain for the gold that is in 3*l.* 17*s.* 10½*d.* of coin.

It is often asserted, that a guinea is worth at Hamburgh 26 or 28 shillings;[1] but we should be very much deceived if we should therefore conclude that a guinea could be sold at Hamburgh for as much silver as is contained in 26 or 28 shillings. Before the alteration in the relative value of gold and silver, a guinea would not sell at Hamburgh for as much silver coin as is contained in 21 standard shillings; it will at the present market price sell for a sum of silver currency, which, if imported and carried to our mint to be coined, will produce in our standard silver coin 21*s.* 5*d.**

* The relative value of gold and silver is on the Continent nearly the same as in London.

[1] Ricardo in his letter to Horner of 5 Feb. 1810 had quoted this assertion as J. Marryat's; see below, VI, 7.

It is nevertheless true, that the same quantity of silver will, at Hamburgh, purchase a bill payable in London, in bank-notes, for 26 or 28 shillings. Can there be a more satisfactory proof of the depreciation of our circulating medium?[1]

It is said,[2] that, if the Restriction-bill were not in force, every guinea would leave the country.*

This is, no doubt, true; but if the Bank were to diminish the quantity of their notes until they had increased their value fifteen per cent., the restriction might be safely removed, as there would then be no temptation to export specie. However long it may be deferred, however great may be the discount on their notes, the Bank can never resume their payments in specie, until they first reduce the amount of their notes in circulation to these limits.

The law is allowed by all writers on political economy to be a useless barrier against the exportation of guineas: it is so easily evaded, that it is doubted whether it has had the effect of keeping a single guinea more in England than there would have been without such law. Mr. Locke, Sir J. Stuart, Dr. A. Smith, Lord Liverpool, and Mr. Thornton, all agree on this subject. The latter gentleman observes,[3] "That the state of the British law unquestionably serves to discourage and limit, though not effectually to hinder, that exportation of guineas which is encouraged by an unfavourable balance of trade, and perhaps scarcely lessens it when the profit on exportation becomes very great." Yet after every guinea that can in the

---

* It must be meant that every guinea in the Bank would leave the country; the temptation of fifteen per cent. is amply sufficient to send those out which can be collected from the circulation.

[1] Eds. 1–2 do not contain the last two paragraphs or the footnote attached. Cp. letter to Horner, 5 Feb. 1810, below, VI, 7.

[2] By 'A Friend to Bank-notes' (Trower) in the *Morning Chronicle*, 14 Sept. 1809; cp. above, p. 28.

[3] *Enquiry into Paper Credit*, p. 124.

present state of things be procured by the illicit trader has been melted and exported, he will hesitate before he openly buys guineas with bank-notes at a premium, because, though considerable profit may attend such speculation, he will thereby render himself an object of suspicion. He may be watched, and prevented from effecting his object. As the penalties of the law are severe, and the temptation to informers great, secrecy is essential to his operations. When guineas can be procured by merely sending a bank-note for them to the Bank, the law will be easily evaded; but when it is necessary to collect them openly and from a widely diffused circulation, consisting almost wholly of paper, the advantage attending it must be very considerable before any one will encounter the risk of being detected.

When we reflect that above sixty millions sterling have been coined into guineas during his present Majesty's reign, we may form some idea of the extent to which the exportation of gold must have been carried.—But repeal the law against the exportation of guineas, permit them to be openly sent out of the country, and what can prevent an ounce of standard gold in guineas from selling at as good a price for bank-notes, as an ounce of Portugueze gold coin, or standard gold in bars, when it is known to be equal to them in fineness? And if an ounce of standard gold in guineas would sell in the market, as standard bars do now, at 4*l.* 10*s.* per oz., or as they have lately done at 4*l.* 13*s.* per oz., what shopkeeper would sell his goods at the same price either for gold or bank-notes indifferently?[1] If the price of a coat were 3*l.* 17*s.* 10½*d.* or an ounce of gold, and if at the same time an ounce of gold would sell for 4*l.* 13*s.*, is it conceivable that it would be a matter of

[1] The last two sentences are reproduced almost verbatim from Ricardo's letter to the *Morning Chronicle*, 20 Sept. 1809, above, p. 24.

indifference to the tailor whether he were paid in gold or in bank-notes?

It is only because a guinea will not purchase more than a pound-note and a shilling, that many hesitate to allow that bank-notes are at a discount. The Edinburgh Review[1] supports the same opinion; but if my reasoning be correct, I have shewn such objections to be groundless.

Mr. Thornton has told us that an unfavourable trade will account for an unfavourable exchange; but we have already seen that an unfavourable trade, if such be an accurate term, is limited in its effects on the exchange. That limit is probably four or five per cent. This will not account for a depreciation of fifteen or twenty per cent. Moreover Mr. Thornton has told us,[2] and I entirely agree with him, "That it may be laid down as a general truth, that the commercial exports and imports of a state naturally proportion themselves in some degree to each other, and that the balance of trade therefore cannot continue for a very long time to be either highly favourable or highly unfavourable to a country." Now the low exchange, so far from being temporary, existed before Mr. Thornton wrote in 1802, and has since been progressively increasing, and is now from fifteen to twenty per cent. against us. Mr. Thornton must therefore, according to his own principles, attribute it to some more permanent cause than an unfavourable balance of trade, and will, I doubt not, whatever his opinion may formerly have been, now agree that it is to be accounted for only by the depreciation of the circulating medium.[3]

[1] July 1803, Art. XI (by Francis Horner), pp. 417–18.
[2] Enquiry into Paper Credit, p. 116.
[3] In a speech in the House of Commons, on 14 May 1811, Thornton acknowledged the change of his opinion. Referring to 'that dangerous doctrine' according to which the high price of gold 'was no indication of an excess of paper or of a depreciation of it, but was simply an evidence of an unfavourable balance of trade' he said: 'It was an error to which he himself had once inclined, but he had stood corrected after a fuller considera-

It can, I think, no longer be disputed that bank-notes are at a discount. While the price of gold bullion is 4*l.* 10*s.* per oz., or in other words, while any man will consent to give that which professes to be an obligation to pay nearly an ounce, and a sixth of an ounce of gold, for an ounce, it cannot be contended that 4*l.* 10*s.* in notes and 4*l.* 10*s.* in gold coin are of the same value.

An ounce of gold is coined into 3*l.* 17*s.* 10½*d.*; by possessing that sum therefore I have an ounce of gold, and would not give 4*l.* 10*s.* in gold coin, or notes which I could immediately exchange for 4*l.* 10*s.*, for an ounce of gold.

It is contrary to common sense to suppose that such could be the market value, unless the price were estimated in a depreciated medium.

If the price of gold were estimated in *silver* indeed, the price might rise to 4*l.*, 5*l.*, or 10*l.* an ounce, and it would, of itself, be no proof of the depreciation of paper currency, but of an alteration in the relative value of gold and silver. I have, however, I think proved, that silver is not the standard measure of value, and therefore not the medium in which the value of gold is estimated. But if it were; as an ounce of gold is only worth in the market 15½ oz. of silver, and as 15½ ounces of silver is precisely equal in weight, and is therefore coined into 80 shillings, an ounce of gold ought not to sell for more than 4*l.*

Those then who maintain that silver is the measure of value cannot prove that any demand for gold which may have taken place, from whatever cause it may have proceeded, can have raised its price above 4*l.* per oz. All above that price must, on their own principles, be called a depreciation in the value of

tion of the subject.' See *Substance of Two Speeches of Henry Thornton, Esq. in the Debate in the House of Commons, on the Report of the Bullion Committee,* London, Hatchard, 1811, pp. 60–61.

bank-notes. It therefore follows, that if bank-notes be the representative of silver coin, then an ounce of gold, selling as it now does for 4*l.* 10*s.* sells for an amount of notes which represent 17½ ounces of silver, whereas in the bullion market it can only be exchanged for 15½ ounces. Fifteen ounces and a half of silver bullion are therefore of equal value with an engagement of the Bank to pay to *bearer* seventeen ounces and a half.[1]

The market price of silver is at the present time 5*s.* 9½*d.* per oz. estimated in bank-notes, the mint price being only 5*s.* 2*d.*, consequently the standard silver in 100*l.* is worth more than 112*l.* in bank-notes.

But bank-notes, it may be said, are the representatives of our debased silver coin, and not of our standard silver. This is not true, because the law which I have already quoted[2] declares silver to be a legal tender for sums only not exceeding 25*l.* except by weight. If the Bank insisted on paying the holder of a bank-note of 1000*l.* in silver coin, they would be bound either to give him standard silver of full weight, or debased silver of an equal value, with the exception of 25*l.* which they might pay him in debased coin. But the 1000*l.* so consisting of 975*l.* pure money, and 25*l.* debased, is worth more than 112*l.* at the present market value of silver bullion.

---

[1] In place of the last two paragraphs (which Ricardo reproduces from his letter to Horner of 5 Feb. 1810, below, VI, 6), eds. 1-2 read: 'But it has been contended, that bank-notes are the representatives of silver and not of gold coin.

'Bank-notes must necessarily be the representative of that coin which is the standard of currency, and there can be no doubt that for near a century gold has been the standard metal. But if a change have taken place, and silver be now the standard of value, and consequently bank-notes the representative of the silver coins, this will not remove the difficulty.' (These two paragraphs of eds. 1-2, and the two which follow them in the text, are based on Ricardo's letter to the *Morning Chronicle*, 23 Nov. 1809, above, pp. 28-31.)

[2] Above, p. 68.

It is said that the amount of bank-notes has not increased in a greater proportion than the augmentation of our trade required, and therefore cannot be excessive. This assertion would be difficult to prove, and if true, no argument but what is delusive could be founded on it. In the first place, the daily improvements which we are making in the art of economizing the use of circulating medium, by improved methods of banking, would render the same amount of notes excessive now, which were necessary for the same state of commerce at a former period. Secondly, there is a constant competition between the Bank of England and the country-banks to establish their notes, to the exclusion of those of their rivals, in every district where the country banks are established.

As the latter have more than doubled in number within very few years, is it not probable that their activity may have been crowned with success, in displacing with their own notes many of those of the Bank of England?

If this have happened, the same amount of Bank of England notes would now be excessive; which, with a less extended commerce, was before barely sufficient to keep our currency on a level with that of other countries. No just conclusion can therefore be drawn from the actual amount of bank-notes in circulation, though the fact, if examined, would, I have no doubt, be found to be, that the increase in the amount of bank-notes, and the high price of gold, have usually accompanied each other.

It is doubted, whether two or three millions of Bank-notes (the sum which the Bank is supposed to have added to the circulation, over and above the amount which it will easily bear,) could have had such effects as are ascribed to them; but it should be recollected, that the Bank regulate the amount of the circulation of all the country banks, and it is probable, that if the Bank increase their issues three millions, they enable the country banks to add more than three[1] millions to the general circulation of England.

The money of a particular country is divided amongst its different provinces by the same rules as the money of the world is divided amongst the different nations of which it is composed. Each district will retain in its circulation such a proportionate share of the currency of the country, as its trade, and consequently its payments, may require, compared to the trade of the whole; and no increase can take place in the circulating medium of one district, without being generally diffused, or calling forth a proportionable quantity in every other district. It is this which keeps a country bank note always of the same value as a Bank of England note. If in London, where Bank of England notes only are current, one million be added to the amount in circulation, the currency will become cheaper there than elsewhere, or goods will become dearer. Goods will, therefore, be sent from the country to the London market, to be sold at the high prices, or which is much more probable, the country banks will take advantage of the relative deficiency in the country currency, and increase the amount of their notes in the same proportion as the Bank of England had done; prices would then be generally, and not partially affected.

In the same manner, if Bank of England notes be diminished one million, the comparative value of the currency of London will be increased, and the prices of goods diminished. A Bank of England note will then be more valuable than a country-bank note, because it will be wanted to purchase goods in the cheap market; and as the country banks are obliged to give Bank of England notes for their own when demanded, they would be called upon for them till the quantity of country paper should be reduced to the same proportion which it before

[1] Eds. 1-3 'twelve' in place of 'three'.

bore to the London paper, producing a corresponding fall in the prices of all goods for which it was exchangeable.[1]

The country banks could never increase the amount of their notes, unless to fill up a relative deficiency in the country currency, caused by the increased issues of the Bank of England*. If they attempted it, the same check which compelled[2] the Bank of England to withdraw part of their notes from circulation when they used[3] to pay them on demand in specie, would oblige the country banks to adopt the same course. Their notes would, on account of the increased quantity, be rendered of less value than the Bank of England notes, in the same manner as Bank of England notes were rendered of less value than the guineas which they represented. They would therefore be exchanged for Bank of England notes until they were of the same value.

The Bank of England is the great regulator of the country paper. When they increase or decrease the amount of their notes, the country banks do the same; and in no case can country banks add to the general circulation, unless the Bank of England shall have previously increased the amount of their notes.

It is contended,[4] that the rate of interest, and not the price of gold or silver bullion, is the criterion by which we may always judge of the abundance of paper-money; that if it were too abundant, interest would fall, and if not sufficiently so, interest would rise. It can, I think, be made manifest, that the

---

* They might, on some occasions, displace Bank of England notes, but that consideration does not affect the question which we are now discussing.

[1] This sentence is reproduced almost verbatim from Ricardo's letter to the *Morning Chronicle*, 20 Sept. 1809, above, p. 27.

[2] Eds. 1-2 'obliged' in place of 'compelled'.

[3] Eds. 1-2 'were obliged' in place of 'used'.

[4] By 'A Friend to Bank-notes' in the *Morning Chronicle*, 14 Sept. 1809; cp. above, p. 26.

rate of interest is not regulated by the abundance or scarcity of money, but by the abundance or scarcity of that part of capital, not consisting of money.

"Money," observes Dr. A. Smith, "the great wheel of circulation, the great instrument of commerce, like all other instruments of trade, though it makes a part, and a very valuable part of the capital, makes no part of the revenue of the society to which it belongs; and though the metal pieces of which it is composed, in the course of their annual circulation, distribute to every man the revenue which properly belongs to him, they make themselves no part of that revenue.[1]

"When we compute the quantity of industry which the circulating capital of any society can employ, we must always have regard to those parts of it only which consist in provisions, materials, and finished work: the other, which consists in money, and which serves only to circulate those three, must always be deducted. In order to put industry into motion, three things are requisite:—materials to work upon, tools to work with, and the wages or recompense for the sake of which the work is done. Money is neither a material to work upon, nor a tool to work with; and though the wages of the workman are commonly paid to him in money, his real revenue, like that of all other men, consists not in money, but in money's worth;[2] not in the metal pieces, but what can be got for them."[3]

And in other parts of his work,[4] it is maintained, that the discovery of the mines in America, which so greatly increased the quantity of money, did not lessen the interest for the use of it: the rate of interest being regulated by the profits on the employment of capital, and not by the number or quality of the pieces of metal, which are used to circulate its produce.

[1] Bk. II, ch. ii; vol. I, p. 275.
[2] Adam Smith says 'not in the money, but in the money's worth'.
[3] ib. vol. I, pp. 278–9.
[4] Bk. II, ch. iv; vol. I, pp. 335–6.

Mr. Hume has supported the same opinion.[1] The value of the circulating medium of every country bears some proportion to the value of the commodities which it circulates. In some countries this proportion is much greater than in others, and varies, on some occasions, in the same country. It depends upon the rapidity of circulation, upon the degree of confidence and credit existing between traders, and above all, on the judicious operations of banking. In England so many means of economizing the use of circulating medium have been adopted, that its value, compared with the value of the commodities which it circulates, is probably (during a period of confidence*) reduced to as small a proportion as is practicable. What that proportion may be has been variously estimated.

No increase or decrease of its quantity, whether consisting of gold, silver, or paper-money, can increase or decrease its value above or below this proportion. If the mines cease to supply the annual consumption of the precious metals, money will become more valuable, and a smaller quantity will be employed as a circulating medium. The diminution in the quantity will be proportioned to the increase of its value. In like manner, if new mines be discovered, the value of the precious metals will be reduced, and an increased quantity used in the circulation; so that in either case the relative value of money, to the commodities which it circulates, will continue as before.

If, whilst the Bank paid their notes on demand in specie, they were to increase their quantity, they would produce little permanent effect on the value of the currency, because nearly an equal quantity of the coin would be withdrawn from circulation and exported.

* In the following observations, I wish it to be understood, as supposing always the same degree of confidence and credit to exist.

[1] Essay 'Of Interest', in *Political Discourses*, 1752

If the Bank were restricted from paying their notes in specie, and all the coin had been exported, any excess of their notes would depreciate the value of the circulating medium in proportion to the excess. If twenty millions had been the circulation of England before the restriction, and four millions were added to it, the twenty-four millions would be of no more value than the twenty were before, provided commodities had remained the same, and there had been no corresponding exportation of coins; and if the Bank were successively to increase it to fifty, or a hundred millions, the increased quantity would be all absorbed in the circulation of England, but would be, in all cases, depreciated to the value of the twenty millions.

I do not dispute, that if the Bank were to bring a large additional sum of notes into the market, and offer them on loan, but that they would for a time affect the rate of interest. The same effects would follow from the discovery of a hidden treasure of gold or silver coin. If the amount were large, the Bank, or the owner of the treasure, might not be able to lend the notes or the money at four, nor perhaps, above three per cent.; but having done so, neither the notes, nor the money, would be retained unemployed by the borrowers; they would be sent into every market, and would every where raise the prices of commodities, till they were absorbed in the general circulation. It is only during the interval of the issues of the Bank, and their effect on prices, that we should be sensible of an abundance of money; interest would, during that interval, be under its natural level; but as soon as the additional sum of notes or of money became absorbed in the general circulation, the rate of interest would be as high, and new loans would be demanded with as much eagerness as before the additional issues.

The circulation can never be over-full. If it be one of gold and silver, any increase in its quantity will be spread over the world. If it be one of paper, it will diffuse itself only in the country where it is issued. Its effects on prices will then be only local and nominal, as a compensation by means of the exchange will be made to foreign purchasers.

To suppose that any increased issues of the Bank can have the effect of permanently[1] lowering the rate of interest, and satisfying the demands of all borrowers, so that there will be none to apply for new loans, or that a productive gold or silver mine can have such an effect, is to attribute a power to the circulating medium which it can never possess. Banks would, if this were possible, become powerful engines indeed. By creating paper money, and lending it at three or two per cent. under the present market rate of interest, the Bank would reduce the profits on trade in the same proportion; and if they were sufficiently patriotic to lend their notes at an interest no higher than necessary to pay the expences of their establishment, profits would be still further reduced; no nation, but by similar means, could enter into competition with us, we should engross the trade of the world. To what absurdities would not such a theory lead us! Profits can only be lowered by a competition of capitals not consisting of circulating medium. As the increase of Bank-notes does not add to this species of capital, as it neither increases our exportable commodities, our machinery, or our raw materials, it cannot add to our profits nor lower interest*.

---

* I have already allowed[2] that the Bank, as far as they enable us to turn our coin into "materials, provisions, &c."[3] have produced a national benefit, as they have thereby increased the quantity of productive capital; but I am here speaking of an excess of their notes, of that quantity which adds to our circulation without effecting any corresponding exportation of coin, and which, therefore, degrades the notes below the value of the bullion contained in the coin which they represent.

[1] Eds. 1-2 do not contain 'permanently'.

[2] Above, p. 55.

[3] See quotation above, p. 89.

When any one borrows money for the purpose of entering into trade, he borrows it as a medium by which he can possess himself of "materials, provisions, &c." to carry on that trade; and it can be of little consequence to him, provided he obtain the quantity of materials, &c. necessary, whether he be obliged to borrow a thousand, or ten thousand pieces of money. If he borrow ten thousand, the produce of his manufacture will be ten times the nominal value of what it would have been, had one thousand been sufficient for the same purpose. The capital actually employed in the country is necessarily limited to the amount of the "materials, provisions, &c." and might be made equally productive, though not with equal facility, if trade were carried on wholly by barter. The successive possessors of the circulating medium have the command over this capital: but however abundant may be the quantity of money or of bank-notes; though it may increase the nominal prices of commodities; though it may distribute the productive capital in different proportions; though the Bank, by increasing the quantity of their[1] notes, may enable A to carry on part of the business formerly engrossed by B and C, nothing will be added to the real revenue and wealth of the country. B and C may be injured, and A and the Bank may be gainers, but they will gain exactly what B and C lose. There will be a violent and an unjust transfer of property, but no benefit whatever will be gained by the community.

For these reasons I am of opinion that the funds are not indebted for their high price to the depreciation of our currency. Their price must be regulated by the general rate of interest given for money. If before the depreciation I gave thirty years' purchase for land, and twenty-five for an annuity in the stocks, I can after the depreciation give a larger sum for the purchase of land, without giving more years' purchase,

[1] Ed. 1 'its'.

because the produce of the land will sell for a greater nominal value in consequence of the depreciation; but as the annuity in the funds is paid in the depreciated medium, there can be no reason why I should give a greater nominal value for it after than before the depreciation.

If guineas were degraded by clipping to half their present value, every commodity as well as land would rise to double its present nominal value; but as the interest of the stocks would be paid in the degraded guineas, they would, on that account, experience no rise.

The remedy which I propose for all the evils in our currency, is that the Bank should gradually decrease the amount of their notes in circulation until they shall have rendered the remainder of equal value with the coins which they represent, or, in other words, till the prices of gold and silver bullion shall be brought down to their mint price. I am well aware that the total failure of paper credit would be attended with the most disastrous consequences to the trade and commerce of the country, and even its sudden limitation would occasion so much ruin and distress, that it would be highly inexpedient to have recourse to it as the means of restoring our currency to its just and equitable value.

If the Bank were possessed of more guineas than they had notes in circulation, they could not, without great injury to the country, pay their notes in specie, while the price of gold bullion continued greatly above the mint price, and the foreign exchanges unfavourable to us. The excess of our currency would be exchanged for guineas at the Bank and exported, and would be suddenly withdrawn from circulation. Before therefore they can safely pay in specie, the excess of notes must be gradually withdrawn from circulation. If gradually done, little inconvenience would be felt; so that the principle were fairly admitted, it would be for future consideration whether the object should be accomplished in one year or in five. I am fully persuaded that we shall never restore our currency to its equitable state, but by this preliminary step, or by the total overthrow of our paper credit.

If the Bank directors had kept the amount of their notes within reasonable bounds; *if they had acted up to the principle which they have avowed to have been that which regulated their issues when they were obliged to pay their notes in specie, namely, to limit their notes to that amount which should prevent the excess of the market above the mint price of gold, we should not have been now exposed to all the evils of a depreciated, and perpetually varying currency.*

Though the Bank derive considerable advantage from the present system, though the price of their capital stock has nearly doubled[1] since 1797, and their dividends have proportionally increased, I am ready to admit with Mr. Thornton,[2] that the directors, as monied men, sustain losses in common with others by a depreciation of the currency, much more serious to them than any advantages which they may reap from it as proprietors of Bank stock[3]. I do therefore acquit them of being influenced by interested motives, but their mistakes, if they are such, are in their effects quite as pernicious to the community.

The extraordinary powers with which they are entrusted enable them to regulate at their pleasure the price at which those who are possessed of a particular kind of property, called money, shall dispose of it. The Bank directors have imposed upon these holders of money all the evils of a maximum. To-day it is their pleasure that 4*l.* 10*s.* shall pass for 3*l.* 17*s.* 10½*d.*, to-morrow they may degrade 4*l.* 15*s.* to the same value, and in another year 10*l.* may not be worth more. By what an

[1] Eds. 1-2 repeat here 'in price'.
[2] *Enquiry into Paper Credit,* pp. 68–9.
[3] Eds. 1-2 do not contain 'as proprietors of Bank stock'.

insecure tenure is property consisting of money or annuities paid in money held! What security has the public creditor that the interest on the public debt, which is now paid in a medium depreciated fifteen per cent., may not hereafter be paid in one degraded fifty per cent.? The injury to private creditors is not less serious. A debt contracted in 1797 may now be paid with eighty-five per cent. of its amount, and who shall say that the depreciation will go no further?

The following observations of Dr. Smith on this subject are so important, that I cannot but recommend them to the serious attention of all thinking men.

"The raising the denomination of the coin has been the most usual expedient by which a real public bankruptcy has been disguised under the appearance of a pretended payment. If a sixpence, for example, should either by act of parliament or royal proclamation be raised to the denomination of a shilling, and twenty sixpences to that of a pound sterling, the person who under the old denomination had borrowed twenty shillings, or near four ounces of silver, would, under the new, pay with twenty sixpences, or with something less than two ounces. A national debt of about a hundred and twenty[1] millions, nearly the capital of the funded[2] debt of Great Britain, might in this manner be paid with about sixty-four millions of our present money. It would indeed be a pretended payment only, and the creditors of the public would[3] be defrauded of ten shillings in the pound of what was due to them. The calamity too would extend much further than to the creditors of the public, and those of every private person would suffer a proportionable loss; and this without any advantage, but in most cases with a great additional loss, to the creditors of the

---

[1] Adam Smith says 'about a hundred and twenty-eight'.

[2] Adam Smith says 'funded and unfunded'.

[3] Adam Smith says 'would really'.

public. If the creditors of the public indeed were generally much in debt to other people, they might in some measure compensate their loss by paying their creditors in the same coin in which the public had paid them. But in most countries the creditors of the public are the greater part of them wealthy people, who stand more in the relation of creditors than in that of debtors towards the rest of their fellow-citizens. A pretended payment of this kind, therefore, instead of alleviating, aggravates in most cases the loss of the creditors of the public; and without any advantage to the public, extends the calamity to a great number of other innocent people. It occasions a general and most pernicious subversion of the fortunes of private people; enriching in most cases the idle and profuse debtor at the expence of the industrious and frugal creditor, and transporting a great part of the national capital from the hands which are likely to increase and improve it, to those which are likely to dissipate and destroy it. When it becomes necessary for a state to declare itself bankrupt, in the same manner as when it becomes necessary for an individual to do so, a fair, open, and avowed bankruptcy is always the measure which is both least dishonourable to the debtor, and least hurtful to the creditor. The honour of a state is surely very poorly provided for, when in order to cover the disgrace of a real bankruptcy, it has recourse to a juggling trick of this kind, so easily seen through, and at the same time so extremely pernicious."[1]

These observations of Dr. Smith on a debased money are equally applicable to a depreciated paper currency. He has enumerated but a few of the disastrous consequences which attend the debasement of the circulating medium, but he has sufficiently warned us against trying such dangerous experiments. It will be a circumstance ever to be lamented, if this

[1] Bk. v, ch. iii; vol. ii, pp. 415–16.

great country, having before its eyes the consequences of a forced paper circulation in America and France, should persevere in a system pregnant with so much disaster. Let us hope that she will be more wise. It is said indeed that the cases are dissimilar: that the Bank of England is independent of government. If this were true, the evils of a superabundant circulation would not be less felt; but it may be questioned whether a Bank lending many millions more to government than its capital and savings can be called independent of that government.

When the order of council for suspending the cash payments became necessary in 1797, the run upon the Bank was, in my opinion, caused by political alarm alone, and not by a superabundant, or a deficient quantity (as some have supposed) of their notes in circulation*.

This is a danger to which the Bank, from the nature of its institution, is at all times liable. No prudence on the part of the directors could perhaps have averted it: but if their loans to government had been more limited; if the same amount of notes had been issued to the public through the medium of discounts; they would have been able, in all probability, to have continued their payments till the alarm had subsided. At any rate, as the debtors to the Bank would have been obliged to discharge their debts in the space of sixty days, that being the longest period for which any bill discounted by the Bank has to run, the directors would in that time, if necessary, have been enabled to redeem every note in circulation. It was then owing to the too intimate connection between the Bank and government that the restriction became necessary; it is to that cause too that we owe its continuance.

To prevent the evil consequences which may attend the

* At that period the price of gold kept steadily under its mint price.

perseverance in this system, we must keep our eyes steadily fixed on the repeal of the Restriction-bill.

The only legitimate security which the public can possess against the indiscretion of the Bank is to oblige them to pay their notes on demand in specie; and this can only be effected by diminishing the amount of bank-notes in circulation till the nominal price of gold be lowered to the mint price.

Here I will conclude; happy if my feeble efforts should awaken the public attention to a due consideration of the state of our circulating medium. I am well aware that I have not added to the stock of information with which the public has been enlightened by many able writers on the same important subject. I have had no such ambition. My aim has been to introduce a calm and dispassionate enquiry into a question of great importance to the state, and the neglect of which may be attended with consequences which every friend of his country would deplore.

APPENDIX[1]

THE public having called for a new edition of this pamphlet, I avail myself of the occasion to consider the observations which the Edinburgh Reviewers, in the last number of their publication, have done me the honour to make on some of the passages contained in it.[2] I am induced to do this from the

[1] Eds. 1–3 do not contain this Appendix. It was also published as a separate pamphlet under the title *Observations on Some Passages in an Article in the Edinburgh Review, on the Depreciation of Paper Currency; also Suggestions for Securing to the Public a Currency as Invariable as Gold, with a Very Moderate Supply of That Metal. Being the Appendix, to the Fourth Edition of "The High Price of Bullion," &c.*, London, Murray, etc., 1811.

[2] *Edinburgh Review*, February 1811, Art. v. The article, which is by Malthus, reviews Ricardo's *High Price of Bullion* and *Reply to Bosanquet*, together with pamphlets on the depreciation of the currency by Mushet, Blake, Huskisson and Bosanquet.

conviction that discussion on every point connected with this important subject will hasten the remedy against the existing abuse, and will tend to secure us against the risk of its recurrence in future.

In the article on the depreciation of money, the Reviewers observe, "The great fault of Mr. Ricardo's performance is the partial view which he takes of the causes which operate upon the course of exchange. He attributes," they say, "a favourable or an unfavourable exchange *exclusively* to a redundant or deficient currency, and overlooks the varying desires and wants of different societies, as an original cause of a temporary excess of imports above exports, or exports above imports."[1] They then comment on the passage in which I have maintained, that a bad harvest will not occasion the export of money, unless money is relatively cheap in the exporting country,[2] and conclude their observations by giving it as their decided opinion, that the exportation of money in the supposed case of a bad harvest, "is not occasioned by its cheapness. It is not, as Mr. Ricardo endeavours to persuade us, the cause of the unfavourable balance, instead of the effect. It is not merely a salutary remedy for a redundant currency: but it is owing precisely to the cause mentioned by Mr. Thornton—the unwillingness of the creditor nation to receive a great additional quantity of goods not wanted for immediate consumption, without being bribed to it by excessive cheapness; and its willingness to receive bullion—the currency of the commercial world—without any such bribe. *It is unquestionably true, as stated by Mr. Ricardo, that no nation will pay a debt in the precious metals, if it can do it cheaper by commodities;* but the prices of commodities are liable to great depressions from a

[1] pp. 342 and 343. The two sentences quoted are not consecutive in the original. [2] Above, p. 61.

glut in the market; whereas the precious metals, on account of their having been constituted by the universal consent of society, the general medium of exchange, and instrument of commerce, will pay a debt of the largest amount at its nominal estimation, according to the quantity of bullion contained in the respective currencies of the countries in question, and, whatever variations between the quantity of currency and commodities may be stated to take place subsequent to the commencement of these transactions, it cannot be for a moment doubted that the cause of them is to be found in the wants and desires of one of the two nations, and not in any original redundancy or deficiency of currency in either of them."[1]

They agree with me, "that no nation will pay a debt in the precious metals, if it can do it cheaper by commodities, *but the prices of commodities*," they say, "*are liable to great depressions from a glut in the market;*" of course they must mean in the foreign market, and then the words express the opinion which they are endeavouring to controvert, viz. that when goods cannot be sent out so advantageously as money, money will be exported,—which is another way of saying that money will never be exported, unless it is relatively redundant with commodities, as compared with other countries. Yet immediately after[2] they contend, that the exportation of the "precious metals is the *effect of a balance of trade**, originating in causes which may exist without any relation whatever to redundancy or deficiency of currency." These opinions appear to me directly contradictory. If however the precious metals can be exported from a country in exchange for commodities,

---

* We are here speaking of a *balance of trade* abstracted from a *balance of payments*. A balance of trade may be favourable whilst a balance of payments is unfavourable. It is the balance of payments only which operates on the exchange.

[1] p. 345. The italics are Ricardo's.   [2] Actually before, p. 342.

although they should be as dear in the exporting as in the importing country, what are the effects which will follow from such improvident exportation?

"A comparative deficiency in one country, and redundancy in the other," say the Reviewers, p. 343.[1] "and this state of things could not fail to have a speedy effect in changing the direction of the balance of payments, and in restoring that equilibrium of the precious metals, which had been for a time disturbed by the naturally unequal wants and necessities of the countries which trade with each other." Now it would have been well if the Reviewers had told us at what point this re-action would commence,—as at the first view it appears that the same law which will permit money to be exported from a country, when it is no cheaper than in the importing country, may also allow it to be exported when it is actually dearer. It is self-interest which regulates all the speculations of trade, and where that can be clearly and satisfactorily ascertained, we should not know where to stop if we admitted any other rule of action. They should have explained to us therefore, why, if the demand for the commodity imported should continue, the country importing might not be entirely exhausted of its coin and bullion. What is under such circumstances to check the exportation of the currency? The Reviewers say, because "a country with a diminished quantity of bullion would evidently soon be limited in its powers of paying with the precious metals."[2] Why soon? Is it not admitted "that excess and deficiency of currency are only relative terms; that the circulation of a country can never be superabundant," (and therefore can never be deficient,) "except in relation to other countries."[3] Does it not follow from these admissions, that if the balance of trade may become unfavourable to a

[1] The two parts of the quotation are not consecutive.
[2] p. 343.
[3] p. 341.

country, though its currency be not relatively superabundant, that there is no check against the exportation of its coin, whilst any amount of money remains in circulation; as the diminished sum, (by acquiring a new value,) will as readily and as effectually make the required payments as the larger sum did before? A succession of bad harvests might, on this principle, drain a country of its money, whatever might be its amount, although it consisted exclusively of the precious metals. The observation that its diminished value in the importing country, and its increasing value in the exporting country, would make it revert again to the old channel, does not answer the objection. When will this happen? and in exchange for what will it be returned? The answer is obvious—for commodities. The ultimate result then of all this exportation and importation of money, is that one country will have imported one commodity in exchange for another, and the coin and bullion will in both countries have regained their natural level. Is it to be contended that these results would not be foreseen, and the expence and trouble attending these needless operations effectually prevented, in a country where capital is abundant, where every possible economy in trade is practised, and where competition is pushed to its utmost limits? Is it conceivable that money should be sent abroad for the purpose merely of rendering it dear in this country and cheap in another, and by such means to ensure its return to us?

It is particularly worthy of observation that so deep-rooted is the prejudice which considers coin and bullion as things essentially differing in all their operations from other commodities, that writers greatly enlightened upon the general truth of political economy seldom fail, after having requested their readers to consider money and bullion merely as commodities subject to "the same general principle of supply and demand which are unquestionably the foundation on which the whole superstructure of political economy is built;"[1] to forget this recommendation themselves, and to argue upon the subject of money, and the laws which regulate its export and import, as quite distinct and different from those which regulate the export and import of other commodities. Thus the Reviewers, if they had been speaking of coffee or of sugar, would have denied the possibility of those articles being exported from England to the continent, unless they were dearer there than here. It would have been in vain to have urged to them, that our harvest had been bad, and that we were in want of corn; they would confidently and undeniably have proved that to whatever degree the scarcity of corn might have existed, it would not have been possible for England to send, or for France (for example) to be willing to receive, coffee or sugar in return for corn, whilst coffee or sugar cost more money in England than in France. What! they would have said, do you believe it possible for us to send a parcel of coffee to France to sell there for 100*l.* when that coffee cost here 105*l.*—when by sending 100*l.* of the 105*l.* we should equally discharge the debt contracted for the imported corn? And, I say, do you believe it possible that we shall agree to send, or France agree to receive (if the transaction is on her account) 100*l.* in money, when 95*l.* invested in coffee and exported will be equally valuable as the 100*l.* when it arrives in France? But coffee is not wanted in France, there is a glut of it;—allowed, but money is wanted still less, and the proof is, that a hundred pounds worth of coffee will sell for more than a hundred pounds worth of money. The only proof which we can possess of the relative cheapness of money in two places, is by comparing it with commodities. Commodities measure the value of money in the same manner as money measures the value of commodities. If then commodities will purchase

[1] p. 341.

more money in England than in France, we may justly say
that money is cheaper in England, and that it is exported to
find its level, not to *destroy* it. After comparing the relative
value of coffee, sugar, ivory, indigo, and all other exportable
commodities in the two markets, if I persist in sending money,
what further proof can be required of money being actually
the cheapest of all these commodities in the English market,
in relation to the foreign markets, and therefore the most
profitable to be exported? What further evidence is necessary
of the relative redundance and cheapness of money between
France and England, than that in France it will purchase more
corn, more indigo, more coffee, more sugar, more of every
exportable commodity than in England?

I may, indeed, be told that the Reviewer's supposition is
not that coffee, sugar, indigo, ivory, &c. &c. are cheaper than
money, but that these commodities and money are equally
cheap in both countries, that is to say, that one hundred pounds
sent in money, or invested in coffee, sugar, indigo, ivory,
&c. &c. will be of equal value in France. If the value of all
these commodities were so nicely poised, what would determine
an exporter to send the one in preference to the other, in
exchange for corn; in relation to which they are all cheaper
in England? If he sends money, and thereby destroys the
natural level, we are told by the Reviewers that money would
on account of its increasing quantity in France, and its decreasing quantity in England, become cheaper in France than
in England, and would be re-imported in exchange for goods
till the level were restored. But would not the same effects
take place if coffee or any of the other commodities were
exported, whilst they were equally valuable in relation to
money in both countries? Would not the equilibrium between
supply and demand be destroyed, and would not the diminished
value of coffee, &c. in consequence of their increased quantity

in France, and their increased value in England, from their diminished quantity, produce their re-importation into England? Any of *these* commodities might be exported without producing much inconvenience from their enhanced price; whereas money, which circulates all other commodities, and the increase or diminution of which, even in a moderate proportion, raises or falls prices in an extravagant degree, could not be exported without the most serious consequences. Here then we see the defective principle of the Reviewers. On my system, however, there would be no difficulty in determining the mode in which, in a case so extremely improbable, as that of an equal value in both countries, for *all* commodities, money included, and corn alone excepted, the returns would be made so as to preserve the relative amount and the relative value of their respective currencies.

If the circulating medium of England consisted wholly of the precious metals, and were a fiftieth part of the value of the commodities which it circulated, the whole amount of money which would under the circumstances supposed be exported in exchange for corn, would be a fiftieth part of the value of such corn: for the rest we should export commodities, and thus would the proportion between money and commodities be equally preserved in both countries. England, in consequence of a bad harvest, would come under the case mentioned at page [53] of this work, of a country having been deprived of a part of its commodities, and therefore requiring a diminished amount of circulating medium. The currency which was before equal to her payments would now become superabundant and relatively cheap, in the proportion of one fiftieth part of her diminished production; the exportation of this sum, therefore, would restore the value of her currency to the value of the currencies of other countries. Thus it appears to be satisfactorily proved that a bad harvest operates on the exchange in no other way than by causing the currency which was before at its just level to become redundant, and thus is the principle that an unfavourable exchange may always be traced to a relatively redundant currency most fully exemplified.

If we can suppose that after an unfavourable harvest, when England has occasion for an unusual importation of corn, another nation is possessed of a superabundance of that article, *"but has no wants for any commodity whatever,"* it would unquestionably follow that such nation would not export its corn in exchange for commodities: but neither would it export corn for money, as that is a commodity which no nation ever wants absolutely, but relatively, as is expressly admitted by the Reviewers. The case is, however, impossible, because a nation possessed of every commodity necessary for the consumption and enjoyment of all its inhabitants who have wherewithal to purchase them, will not let the corn which it has over and above what it can consume rot in its granaries. Whilst the desire of accumulation is not extinguished in the breast of man, he will be desirous to realise the excess of his productions, above his own consumption, into the form of capital. This he can only do by employing, himself, or by loans to others, enabling them to employ, an additional number of labourers, as it is by labour only that revenue is realized into capital. If his revenue be corn, he will be disposed to exchange it for fuel, meat, butter, cheese, and other commodities in which the wages of labour are usually expended, or, which is the same thing, he will sell his corn for money, pay the wages of his labourers in money, and thereby create a demand for those commodities which may be obtained from other countries in exchange for the superfluous corn. Thus will be reproduced to him articles more valuable, which he may again employ in the same manner, adding to his own riches, and augmenting the wealth and resources of his country.

No mistake can be greater than to suppose *that a nation can ever be without wants for commodities of some sort.* It may possess too much of one or more commodities for which it may not find a market at home. It may have more sugar, coffee, tallow, than it can either consume or dispose of, but no country ever possessed a general glut of all commodities. It is evidently impossible. If a country possesses every thing necessary for the maintenance and comfort of man, and these articles be divided in the proportions in which they are usually consumed, they are sure, however abundant, to find a market to take them off. It follows therefore, that whilst a country is in possession of a commodity for which there is no demand at home, it will be desirous of exchanging it for other commodities in the proportion in which they are consumed.

No nation grows corn, or any other commodity, with a view to realise its value in money, (the case supposed, or involved in the case supposed, by the Reviewers), as this would be the most unprofitable object to which the labour of man could be devoted. Money is precisely that article which till it is re-exchanged never adds to the wealth of a country: accordingly we find, that to increase its amount is never the voluntary act of any country any more than it is that of any individual. Money is forced upon them only in consequence of the relatively less value which it possesses in those countries with which they have intercourse.

Whilst a country employs the precious metals for money, and has no mines of its own, it is a conceivable case that it may greatly augment the amount of the productions of its land and labour without adding to its wealth, because at the same time those countries which are in possession of the mines may possibly have obtained so enormous a supply of the precious metals as to have forced an increase of currency on the industrious country, equal in value to the whole of its increased productions. But by so doing the augmented currency, added to that which was before employed, will be of no more real value than the original amount of currency. Thus then will this industrious nation become tributary to those nations which are in possession of the mines, and will carry on a trade in which it gains nothing and loses every thing.

That the exchange is in a constant state of fluctuation with all countries I am not disposed to deny, but it does not generally vary to those limits at which remittances can be more advantageously made by means of bullion than by the purchase of bills. Whilst this is the case, it cannot be disputed that imports are balanced by exports. The varying demands of all countries may be supplied, and the exchanges of all deviate in some degree from par, if the currency of any one of them is either redundant or deficient, as compared with the rest. Suppose England to send goods to Holland, and not to find there any commodities which suit the English market; or, which is the same thing, suppose that we can purchase those commodities cheaper in France. In this case we confine our operation to the sale of goods in Holland, and the purchase of other goods in France. The currency of England is not disturbed by either transaction, as we shall pay France by a bill on Holland, and there will neither be an excess of imports nor of exports. The exchange may, however, be favourable to us with Holland, and unfavourable with France; and will be so, if the account be not balanced by the importation into France of goods from Holland, or from some country indebted to Holland. If there be no such importation, it can arise only from a relative redundancy of the circulation of Holland, as compared with that of France, and in payment of the bill it will suit both those countries that bullion should be transmitted. If the balance be settled by the transmission of goods, the exchange between all the three countries will be at par. If by bullion, the exchange between Holland and England will be as much above par, as that between France and England will be below the par, and the difference will be equal to the expenses attending the passage of bullion from Holland to France. It will make no difference in the result, if every nation of the world were concerned in the transaction. England having bought goods from France and sold goods to Holland, France might have purchased to the same amount from Italy; Italy may have done the same from Russia, Russia from Germany, and Germany within 100,000*l.* of the same amount from Holland; Germany might require this amount of bullion either to supply a deficient currency, or for the fabrication of plate. All these various transactions would be settled by bills of exchange, with the exception of the 100,000*l.* which would be either transmitted from an existing redundancy of coin or bullion in Holland, or it would be collected by Holland from the different currencies of Europe. It is not contended, as the Reviewers infer, "that a bad harvest, or the necessity of paying a subsidy in one country, should be immediately and invariably accompanied by an unusual demand for muslins, hardware, and colonial produce," as the same effects would be produced if the country paying the subsidy, or suffering from a bad harvest, were to import less of other commodities than it had before been accustomed to do.

The Reviewers observe, page 345, "The same kind of error which we have here noticed pervades other parts of Mr. Ricardo's pamphlet, particularly the opening of his subject. He seems to think that when once the precious metals have been divided among the different countries of the earth, according to their relative wealth and commerce, that each having an equal necessity for the quantity actually in use, no temptation would be offered for their importation or exportation, till either a new mine or a new bank was opened;

or till some marked change had taken place in their relative prosperity." And afterwards at page 361, "We have already adverted to the error (confined, however, principally to Mr. Ricardo, and from which the Report is entirely free) of denying the existence of a balance of trade or of payments not connected with some original redundancy or deficiency of currency." "But there is *another point* in which almost all the writers on this side of the question concur, where, notwithstanding, we cannot agree with them, and feel more inclined to the mercantile view of the subject. Though they acknowledge that bullion occasionally passes from one country to another from causes connected with the exchange, yet they represent these transactions as quite inconsiderable in degree. Mr. Huskisson observes[1] 'that the operations in the trade of bullion originate almost entirely in the fresh supplies which are yearly poured in from the mines of the New World, and are chiefly confined to the distribution of those supplies through the different parts of Europe. If this supply were to cease altogether, the dealings in gold and silver, as objects of foreign trade, would be very few, and those of short duration.'"

"Mr. Ricardo, in his reply to Mr. Bosanquet, refers[2] to this passage with particular approbation." Now I am at a loss to discover in what this opinion of Mr. Huskisson differs from that which I had before given, and on which the Reviewers had been commenting.

The passages are in substance precisely the same, and must stand or fall together. If "we acknowledge that bullion occasionally passes from one country to another, from causes connected with the exchange," we do not acknowledge that it would so pass till the exchange had fallen to such limits as

---

[1] *The Question concerning the Depreciation of our Currency...*, 1810, pp. 49–50.

[2] Below, p. 171, note.

would make the exportation of bullion profitable, and I am of opinion that if it should so fall, it is in consequence of the cheapness and redundance of currency, which "would originate almost entirely in the fresh supplies which are yearly poured in from the mines of the New World." This, then, is not *another point* in which the Reviewers differ with me, but the same.

If "it is well known that most states, in their usual relations of commercial intercourse, have an almost constantly favourable exchange with some countries, and an almost constantly unfavourable one with the others,"[1] to what cause can it be ascribed but to that mentioned by Mr. Huskisson? "The fresh supplies of bullion which are yearly poured in, (and in nearly the same direction) from the mines of the New World." Dr. A. Smith does not seem to have been sufficiently aware of the powerful and uniform effects which this stream of bullion had on the foreign exchanges, and he was inclined much to overrate the uses of bullion in carrying on the various round-about foreign trades which a country finds it necessary to engage in.[2] In the early and rude transactions of commerce between nations, as in the early and rude transactions between individuals, there is little economy in the use of money and bullion; it is only in consequence of civilization and refinement that paper is made to perform the same office between the commonwealth of nations, as it so advantageously performs between individuals of the same country. The Reviewers do not appear to me to be sufficiently aware of the extent to which the principle of economy in the use of the precious metals is extended between nations, indeed they do not seem to acknowledge its force even when confined to a single nation, as from a passage in page 346, their readers would be induced to sup-

---

[1] p. 362.

[2] *Wealth of Nations*, Bk. IV, ch. i; vol. I, pp. 409–10.

pose their opinion to be, that there are frequent transfers of currency between the distant provinces of the same country, for they tell us that "there have been and ever will be a quantity of the precious metals in use destined to perform the same part with regard to the different nations connected with each other by commerce, which the currency of a particular country performs with regard to its distant provinces." Now what part does the currency of a country perform with regard to the distant provinces?

I am well persuaded that in all the multiplicity of commercial transactions which take place between the distant provinces of this kingdom, the currency performs a very inferior part, imports being almost always balanced by exports*, and the proof is, that the local currency of the provinces (and they have no other) is seldom circulated at any considerable distance from the place where it is issued.

It appears to me that the Reviewers were induced to admit the erroneous doctrine of the merchants, *that money might be exported in exchange for commodities, although money were no cheaper in the exporting country,* because they could in no other way account for the rise of the exchange having, on some occasions, accompanied the increased amount of Bank notes, as stated by Mr. Pearse, the late deputy-governor and now governor of the Bank, in a paper delivered by him to the Bullion Committee.[1] They say, "according to this view[2] of the subject, it certainly is not easy to explain an improving exchange under an obviously increasing issue of notes: an event

---

* Part of the produce of the provinces is exported without any return, as it constitutes the revenue of absentees, but this consideration can have no effect on the question of currency.

[1] *Bullion Report*, 'Appendix of Accounts', No. 49, and cp. 'Minutes of Evidence', p. 121.
[2] *i.e.* the view of Ricardo who, according to the Reviewers, considered 'redundancy or deficiency of currency as the mainspring of all commercial movements'.

that not unfrequently happens, and was much insisted upon by the deputy-governor of the Bank, as a proof that our foreign exchanges had no connexion with the state of our currency."[1]

These are circumstances, however, which are not absolutely irreconcileable. Mr. Pearse, as well as the Edinburgh Reviewer, appears to have wholly mistaken the principle advanced by those who are desirous of the repeal of the restriction bill. They do not contend, as they are understood to do, that the increase of *bank notes* will permanently lower the exchange, but that such an effect will proceed from a redundant currency. It remains, therefore, to be considered whether an increase of bank notes is necessarily, at all times, accompanied with a permanently increased currency, as if I can make it appear that it is not, there will be no difficulty in accounting for a rise in the exchange, with an increased amount of bank-notes.

It will be readily admitted, that whilst there is any great portion of coin in circulation, every increase of bank-notes, though it will for a short time lower the value of the whole currency, paper as well as gold, yet that such depression will not be permanent, because the redundant and cheap currency will lower the exchange and will occasion the exportation of a portion of the coin, which will cease as soon as the remainder of the currency shall have regained its value, and restored the exchange to par. The increase of small notes, then, will ultimately be a substitution of one currency for another, of a paper for a metallic currency, and will not operate in the same way as an actual and permanent increase of circulation*. We are not, however, without a criterion by which we may deter-

* That an increase of bank-notes under 5*l.* should be considered as a substitute for the coins exported, rather than an actual increase of circulation, is often and justly maintained by those who oppose the reasoning of the Bullion Report; but when these same gentlemen want to establish their favourite theory, that there is no connection between the amount

[1] p. 359.

mine the relative amount of currency at different periods, as distinguished from bank-notes, on which though we cannot infallibly rely, it will probably be a sufficiently accurate test to determine the question which we are now discussing. This criterion is the amount of notes of 5*l.* and upwards in circulation, which we may reasonably calculate always bear some tolerably regular proportion to the whole circulation. Thus, if since 1797 the bank-notes of this description have increased from twelve to sixteen millions, we may infer that the whole circulation has increased one-third, if the districts in which bank-notes circulate have neither been enlarged nor contracted. The notes under 5*l.* will be issued in proportion as the metallic currency is withdrawn from circulation, and will be further augmented, if there be also an augmentation of notes of a higher denomination.

If I am correct in this view of the subject, that the increase in the amount of our currency is to be inferred from the increased amount of bank-notes of 5*l.* and upwards, and can by no means be proved by an increase of 1*l.* and 2*l.* notes which have been substituted in the place of the exported or hoarded guineas, I must wholly reject the calculations of Mr. Pearse, because they are made on the supposition that every increase of this description of notes is an increase of currency to that amount. When it is considered that in 1797 there were no notes of 1*l.* and 2*l.* in circulation, but that their place was wholly filled with guineas; and that since that period there have been no less than seven millions issued, partly to supply the place of our exported and hoarded guineas, and partly to keep up the proportion between the circulation for

of the circulation and the rate of exchange, they do not forget to bring to their aid these small notes which they had before discarded.[1]

[1] The allusion is to Trotter's *Principles of Currency and Exchanges*, 1810, pp. 24 and 50; cp. below, pp. 384 and 395.

the larger and for the smaller payments, we shall observe to what errors such reasoning may lead. I can consider the paper in question of no authority whatever as opposed to the opinion which I have ventured to give, namely, that an unfavourable balance of trade, and a consequently low exchange, may in all cases be traced to a relatively redundant and cheap currency*. But if the reasoning of Mr. Pearse were not incorrect as his *facts* are, he is no way warranted in the conclusions which he has drawn from them.

Mr. Pearse states the increase of bank-notes from January, 1808, to Christmas, 1809, to have been from $17\frac{1}{2}$ to 18 millions, or 500,000*l.*, the exchange with Hamburgh during the same period having fallen from 34s. 9g. to 28s. 6g. an increase in the amount of notes of less than three per cent, and a fall in the exchange of more than eighteen per cent.

But from whence did Mr. Pearse obtain this information, of 18 millions of bank-notes *only* being in circulation at Christmas in 1809? After looking at every return, with which I have been able to meet, of the amount of bank-notes in circulation at the end of 1809, I cannot but conclude that Mr. Pearse's statement is incorrect. Mr. Mushet in his tables gives four returns of bank-notes in the year. In the last, for the year 1809, he has stated the amount of bank-notes in circulation at 19,742,998

In the Appendix to the Bullion Report, and in
    returns lately made to the House of Commons,
    the amount of bank-notes in circulation ap-
    pears to have been on December 12, 1809, . 19,727,520

On the 1st January, 1810 20,669,320

On the 7th January, 1810, ... 19,528,030

* It is not meant to be denied, that the sudden invasion of an enemy, or a convulsion in a country of any kind which renders the possession of property insecure, may form an exception to this rule, but the exchange will in general be unfavourable to a country thus circumstanced.

For many months previously to December it was not lower. When I first discovered this inaccuracy I thought Mr. Pearse might have omitted the bank post bills in both estimates, although they did not in December, 1809, exceed 880,880*l.*; but on looking at the return of bank-notes in circulation, including bank post bills, in January, 1808, I find Mr. Pearse has stated it larger than I can any where find it: indeed his estimate exceeds the return made by the Bank for the 1st of January, 1808, by nearly 900,000*l.*, so that from the 1st of January, 1808, to the 12th of December, 1809, the increase was from 16,619,240 to 19,727,520, a difference of more than three millions, instead of 500,000, as stated by Mr. Pearse, and of two millions if Mr. Pearse's statement for any time in January, 1808, be correct.

Mr. Pearse's statement too, that from January 1803, to the end of 1807, the amount of bank-notes had increased from 16 and a half to eighteen millions, an increase of a million and a half appears to me to exceed the fact by half a million. The increase of notes of 5*l.* and upwards, including bank post bills, did not, during that period, exceed 150,000*l.* It is material that these errors should be pointed out, that those who may, in spite of what I have urged, agree in principle with Mr. Pearse, may see that the facts of the case do not warrant the conclusions which that gentleman has drawn from them, and, indeed, that all calculations founded on the particular amount of bank-notes for a day, or for a week, when the general average has been for some time before, or some time after, greater or less, will be of little avail in overturning a theory which has every other proof of its truth. Such I consider the theory which asserts that the unlimited multiplication of a currency which is referrible to no fixed standard may and must produce a permanent depression of the exchange, estimated with a country whose currency is founded on such standard.

Having considered the weight which ought to be attached to Mr. Pearse's paper, I beg the reader's attention to the table which I have drawn out from the statements in the Bullion Report, and from the papers which have since been presented to the House of Commons. I request him to compare the amount of the circulation of the larger notes with the variations in the exchange, and I trust he will find no difficulty in reconciling the principle maintained by me with the actual facts of the case, particularly if he considers that the operations of an increased currency are not instantaneous, but require some interval of time to produce their full effect,—that a rise or fall in the price of silver, as compared with gold, alters the relative value of the currencies of England and Hamburgh, and therefore makes the currency of one or other relatively redundant and cheap;—that the same effect is produced, as I have already stated, by an abundant or deficient harvest, either in this country or in those countries with which we trade, or by any other addition or diminution to their real wealth, which by altering the relative proportion between commodities and money alters the value of the circulating medium. With these corrections, I have no fear but that it will be found that Mr. Pearse's objections may be refuted without having recourse to the abandonment of a principle, which, if yielded, will establish the mercantile theory of exchange, and may be made to account for a drain of circulating medium, so great, that it can only be counteracted by locking up our money in the bank, and absolving the directors from the obligation of paying their notes in specie.

The average amount of bank notes from the year 1797 to 1809 inclusive, in the following table,[1] is copied from the Report of the Bullion Committee.[2] The rates of exchange are extracted from a list presented by the mint to parliament. There

---

[1] See below, p. 121.   [2] *Report*, p. 60.

* Mr. Pearse's statement, as presented to the Bullion Committee:

	Total of Bank notes. *Millions.*	Rate of Hambro' Exchange. *s. g.*
27th February, 1797 . . .	8½	35 6
Rose gradually in 1797 and 1798 to .	13	38 0
March, 1799	13½	37 7
After this period, great commercial distress, large importation of corn, heavy subsidies, and the Hambro' Exchange continued falling, and on the 2d January, 1801, was as low as		29 8
Between the end of the year 1799 to the end of 1802, an increased quantity of 1l. and 2l. notes were issued, swelling the sum total of *all* notes to .	Fluctuation {13½ to 16¼}	{from 33 3 to 29 8}
From January, 1803, to the end of 1807 .	Fluctuation {16¼ to 18}	{from 32 10 to 35 10}
From January, 1808, to Christmas 1809 .	Fall {17½ to 18}	{from 34 9 to 28 6}

The rate of the Hambro' Exchange is taken from Lloyd's list.

* I have omitted as much of Mr Pearse's paper as regarded the amount of bank notes in circulation before the restriction on bank payments, because whilst the public possessed the power of obtaining specie for their notes, the exchange could not but be momentarily lowered by the amount of the bank issues.

have been three returns made to parliament by the Bank, of the
amount of their notes in circulation in the year 1810; the first
for the 7th and 12th of each month; the second a weekly return
from the 19th January, 1810, to 28th December; and the third
also a weekly account from the 3d March to 29th December,
1810. The average amount of notes above 5l. including bank
post bills, according to the first account is

	£15,706,226	of notes under 5l.	£6,560,674
Second . . .	16,192,110		6,758,895
Third . . .	16,358,230		6,614,721
	3)48,256,566		19,934,290
General average	16,085,522		6,644,763

In the years marked thus * the value of silver as compared
with gold exceeded the mint valuation,—this was the case
particularly in the year 1801, when less than 14oz. of silver
could purchase an ounce of gold,—the mint valuation is as
1 to 15·07; the present market value is as 1 to 16 nearly.

"If," say the Reviewers,[1] "considerable portions of the
currency were taken from the idle, *and those who live upon
fixed incomes,*[2] and transferred to farmers, manufacturers, and
merchants,—the proportion between capital and revenue would
be greatly altered to the advantage of capital; and in a short
time the produce of the country would be greatly augmented."
It is no doubt true "that it is not the *quantity*" of circulating
medium which adds to the national wealth, "but the *different
distribution* of it." If, therefore, we could be fully assured that
the effects of the abundance, and the consequent depreciation
of the currency, would diminish the powers of consumption
in the idle and unproductive class, whilst it increased the number
of the industrious and productive class, the effect would undoubtedly be to augment the national wealth, as it would

[1] p. 364.   [2] The italics are Ricardo's.

Average amount of Bank of England Notes in circulation in each of the following years:

Year	Notes of 5l. and upwards, including Bank Post Bills.	Notes under 5l.	Total.	Highest rate of Exchange with Hamburgh.		Lowest rate of Exchange with Hamburgh.	
1798	£11,527,250	£1,807,502	£13,334,752	38.2	Jan.	37.4	Dec.
*1799	12,408,522	1,653,805	14,062,327	37.7	Jan.	31.6	Oct.
*1800	13,598,666	2,243,266	15,841,932	32.5	May.	31.—	Feb.
*1801	13,454,367	2,715,182	16,169,594	31.8	Oct.	29.8	Jan.
*1802	13,917,977	3,136,477	17,054,454	34.—	Dec.	32.—	Feb.
1803	12,983,477	3,864,045	16,847,522	35.—	Dec.	34.—	Jan.
1804	12,621,348	4,723,672	17,345,020	36.—	June.	34.8	Feb.
*1805	12,697,352	4,544,580	17,241,932	35.8	March.	32.9	Nov.
*1806	12,844,170	4,291,230	17,135,400	34.8	Dec.	33.3	Jan.
*1807	13,221,988	4,183,013	17,405,001	34.10	March.	34.2	Sept.
*1808	13,402,160	4,132,420	17,534,580	35.3	July.	32.4	Dec.
1809	14,133,615	4,868,275	19,001,890	31.3	Jan.	28.6	Nov.
1810	16,085,522	6,644,763	22,730,285	31.2	June.	28.6	Dec.
1811				26.6	Jan.	24.—	March.

The Bank have made a return of the amount of their notes for eighteen days in this present year 1811. The average amount of notes of 5l. and upwards in circulation for those eighteen days, including bank post bills, is £16,286,950

And of those under 5l. 7,260,575

Total . 23,547,525

realize into capital that which was before expended as revenue. But the question is, will it so operate? Will not a thousand pounds saved by the stockholder from his income and lent to the farmer, be equally productive as if it had been saved by the farmer himself? The Reviewers observe,[1] "On every fresh issue of notes, not only is the quantity of the circulating medium increased, but the distribution of the whole mass is altered. A large proportion falls into the hands of those who consume and produce, and a smaller proportion into the hands of those who only consume." But is this necessarily so? They appear to take it for granted, that those who live on fixed incomes *must* consume the whole of their income, and that no part of it can be saved and annually added to capital. But this is very far from being the true state of the case, and I would ask, Do not the stockholders give as great a stimulus to the growth of the national wealth by saving half their incomes and investing it in the stocks, thereby liberating a capital which will ultimately be employed by those who consume and produce, as would be done if their incomes were depreciated 50 per cent. by the issues of bank-notes, and the power of saving were in consequence entirely taken from them, although the Bank should lend to an industrious man an amount of notes equal in value to the diminished income of the stockholder? The difference, and the only difference appears to me to be this, that in the one case the interest on the money lent would be paid to the real owner of the property, in the other it would ultimately be paid in the shape of increased dividends or bonuses to the bank proprietors, who had been enabled unjustly to possess themselves of it. If the creditor of the Bank employed his loan in less profitable speculations than the employer of the savings of the stockholders would have done, there would result a real loss to the country; so that a depreciation of cur-

[1] p. 364.

rency may, as far as it is considered as a stimulus to production, be beneficial or otherwise.

I see no reason why it should diminish the idle, and add to the productive class of society. At any rate the evil is certain. It must be accompanied with a degree of injustice to individuals which requires only to be understood to excite the censure and indignation of all those who are not wholly insensible to every honourable feeling.

With the sentiments of the remainder of the article I most cordially agree, and trust the efforts of the Reviewers will powerfully contribute to overturn the mass of error and prejudice which pervades the public mind on this most important subject.

It is often objected to the recommendation of the Bullion Committee, namely that the Bank should be required to pay their notes in specie in two years, that, if adopted, the Bank would be exposed to considerable difficulty in providing themselves with the requisite amount of bullion for such purpose; and it cannot be denied, that before the Restriction Bill can be repealed, the Bank would be in prudence bound to make ample provision for every demand which might by possibility be made on them. It is observed by the Bullion Committee, that the average amount of Bank notes in circulation, including Bank Post Bills, in the year 1809, was 19 millions. During the same period the average price of gold was 4l. 10s.—exceeding its mint price by nearly 17 per cent, and proving a depreciation of the currency of nearly 15 per cent. A diminution therefore of 15 per cent. in the amount of the Bank circulation in 1809, should, on the principles of the Committee, raise it to par, and reduce the market price of gold to 3l. 17s. 10½d.; and till such reduction take place, there would be imminent danger to the Bank as well as to the public, that the Restriction Bill should cease to operate. Now, admitting (which we are far from doing) the truth of your principles, say the advocates for the Bank, admitting that after such a reduction in the amount of Bank notes, the value of the remainder would be so raised, that it would not be the interest of any person to demand specie at the Bank in exchange for notes, because no profit could be made by the exportation of bullion; what security would the Bank have that caprice or ill-will might not render the practice general of discontinuing the use of small notes altogether, and demanding guineas of the Bank in lieu of them? Not only then must the Bank reduce their circulation 15 per cent. on their issues of 19 millions,—not only must they provide bullion for 4 millions of 1l. and 2l. notes which would remain in circulation, but they must also furnish themselves with the means of meeting the demands which may be made on them to pay the small notes of all the country banks in the kingdom,—and all this within the short period of two years. It must be confessed, that whether these apprehensions are likely or not likely to be realized, the Bank could not but make some provision for the worst that might happen; and though it is a situation in which their own indiscretion has involved them, it would be desirable, if possible, to protect them against the consequences of it.

If the same benefits to the public,—the same security against the depreciation of the currency, can be obtained by more gentle means, it is to be hoped that all parties, who agree in principle, will concur in the expediency of adopting them. Let the Bank of England be required by Parliament to pay (if demanded) all notes above 20l.—and no other, at their option, either in specie, in gold standard bars, or in foreign coin (allowance being made for the difference in its purity) at the English mint value of gold bullion, viz. 3l. 17s. 10½d. per oz., such payments to commence at the period recommended by the Committee.

This privilege of paying their notes as above described might be extended to the Bank for three or four years after such payments commenced, and if found advantageous, might be continued as a permanent measure. Under such a system the currency could never be depreciated below its standard price, as an ounce of gold and 3*l.* 17*s.* 10½*d.* would be uniformly of the same value. By such regulations we should effectually prevent the amount of small notes necessary for the smaller payments from being withdrawn from circulation, as no one who did not possess to the amount of 20*l.* at least of such small notes could exchange them at the Bank, and even then bullion, and not specie, could be obtained for them. Guineas might indeed be procured at the Mint for such bullion, but not till after the delay of some weeks or months, the loss of interest for which time would be considered as an actual expence; an expence which no one would incur, whilst the small notes could purchase as much of every commodity as the guineas which they represented. Another advantage attending the establishment of this plan would be to prevent the useless labour, which, under our system previously to 1797, was so unprofitably expended on the coinage of guineas, which on every occasion of an unfavourable exchange (we will not enquire by what caused) were consigned to the melting pot, and in spite of all prohibitions exported as bullion. It is agreed by all parties that such prohibitions were ineffectual, and that whatever obstacles were opposed to the exportation of the coin they were with facility evaded.

An unfavourable exchange can ultimately be corrected only by an exportation of goods,—by the transmission of bullion,—or *by a reduction in the amount of the paper circulation.* The facility therefore with which bullion would be obtained at the Bank cannot be urged as an objection to this plan, because an equal degree of facility actually existed before 1797, and must exist under any system of Bank payments. Neither ought it to be urged, because it is now no longer questioned by all those who have given the subject of currency much of their consideration, that not only is the law against the exportation of bullion, whether in coin or in any other form, ineffectual, but that it is also impolitic and unjust; injurious to ourselves only, and advantageous to the rest of the world.

The plan here proposed appears to me to unite all the advantages of every system of banking which has been hitherto adopted in Europe. It is in some of its features similar to the banks of deposit of Amsterdam and Hamburgh. In those establishments bullion is always to be purchased from the Bank at a fixed invariable price. The same thing is proposed for the Bank of England; but in the foreign banks of deposit, they have actually in their coffers, as much bullion, as there are credits for bank money in their books; accordingly there is an inactive capital as great as the whole amount of the commercial circulation. In our Bank, however, there would be an amount of bank money, under the name of bank-notes, as great as the demands of commerce could require, at the same time there would not be more inactive capital in the bank coffers than that fund which the Bank should think it necessary to keep in bullion, to answer those demands which might occasionally be made on them. It should always be remembered too, that the Bank would be enabled by contracting their issues of paper to diminish such demands at pleasure. In imitation of the Bank of Hamburgh, who purchase silver at a fixed price, it would be necessary for the Bank to fix a price *very little below* the mint price, at which they would at all times purchase, with their notes, such gold bullion as might be offered to them.

The perfection of banking is to enable a country by means of a paper currency (always retaining its standard value) to carry on its circulation with the least possible quantity of coin or bullion. This is what this plan would effect. And with a silver coinage, on just principles, we should possess the most economical and the most invariable currency in the world. The variations in the price of bullion, whatever demand there might be for it on the continent, or whatever supply might be poured in from the mines in America, would be confined within the prices at which the Bank bought bullion, and the mint price at which they sold it. The amount of the circulation would be adjusted to the wants of commerce with the greatest precision; and if the Bank were for a moment so indiscreet as to overcharge the circulation, the check which the public would possess would speedily admonish them of their error. As for the country Banks, they must, as now, pay their notes when demanded in Bank of England notes. This would be a sufficient security against the possibility of their being able too much to augment the paper circulation. There would be no temptation to melt the coin, and consequently the labour which has been so uselessly bestowed by one party in recoining what another party found it their interest to melt into bullion, would be effectually saved. The currency could neither be clipped nor deteriorated, and would possess a value as invariable as gold itself, the great object which the Dutch had in view, and which they most successfully accomplished by a system very like that which is here recommended.

THREE LETTERS

TO THE

MORNING CHRONICLE

ON THE

BULLION REPORT

1810

[THREE LETTERS ON THE BULLION REPORT]

REPORT OF THE BULLION COMMITTEE[1]

To the EDITOR of the MORNING CHRONICLE.

SIR,

The able Report of the Bullion Committee can leave no doubt, in the minds of all unprejudiced persons, that there exists at this moment a great depreciation in the paper currency of this country; and though the Committee have treated the Bank Directors with a great degree of lenity, they justly attribute to their ignorance of the principles which should regulate them in their issues of paper, all those consequences which we at present deplore, and the remedy for which is now sought with so much anxiety. The fatal effects attending the interference of Government in commercial concerns, and which has been so frequently and so ably insisted on, are in this instance fully exemplified. Had the Bank, at the period of their difficulties in the year 1797, been suffered to have extricated themselves as well as they were able, they might possibly, under the peculiar pressure of the times, have been obliged for a short time to have ceased paying in specie, and their notes might in consequence have suffered a trifling discount; but as they could easily have convinced the public that their assets were fully equal to the discharge of all demands on them, it would in all probability have been of short duration, for who would have consented to accept much less than twenty shillings in the pound, when, by the delay of a few weeks, the Bank would have been enabled to pay him that amount. The creditors of the Bank

[1] *Morning Chronicle*, 6 Sept. 1810.

would have seen how little foundation there was for alarm. That opulent Company would in a short time have resumed their payments in specie, and would have continued to be what Sir F. Baring in his evidence before the Committee represented them to have been for above a century previously to 1797, highly conducive to the prosperity of England.[1]

The law which gave the Bank the power of refusing to pay their notes in specie, has entailed upon us the evil of a depreciation in our currency of nearly 20 per cent., and has rendered it extremely difficult to restore it to the true standard by which it should be regulated—the value of the gold which is actually contained in the coin for which it is a substitute.

We have advanced so far in this ruinous path, that we are beset with dangers on every side;—to proceed will inevitably plunge us into increasing and accumulated difficulties, from which we shall be unable hereafter to extricate ourselves; and to return, though by far the safest course, will be attended with trials which will require a great degree of ability, integrity, and firmness to surmount.

The Legislature has, by the restriction law, sanctioned for many years a most unjust interference in all contracts, benefiting one of the contracting parties at the expence of the other. No complaint has been so common as the increased prices of every commodity, but very few know, or can be made to understand, how large a portion of the inconvenience[2] which they suffer, is to be ascribed, wholly, to the improper use which the Bank Directors have made of the extraordinary powers with which the Legislature has entrusted them. The evil is not less real because its source is concealed from ordinary optics.

[1] *Bullion Report*, 'Minutes of Evidence', 8vo edition, p. 198.

[2] Misprinted 'convenience' in the *Morning Chronicle*.

The Bullion Committee has most ably illustrated the principles upon which a paper currency should be regulated; and I trust the day is not far distant when we shall look back with astonishment at the delusion to which we have so long been subject, in allowing a company of merchants, notoriously ignorant of the most obvious principles of political œconomy, to regulate at their will, the value of the property of a great portion of the community; in a country, too, justly famed for the protection which it affords to the produce of the industry of the meanest of its inhabitants.

In treading back our steps we must necessarily again interfere, not only in contracts already made, but in those now making; this is an evil inseparable from the situation in which we are involved, it must ever attend the reformation of a debased or of a depreciated currency, and, I fear, admits of no equitable remedy.

It is by many supposed that the mode recommended by the Bullion Committee for the adoption of Parliament, namely, to oblige the Bank to pay their notes on demand in specie, at the expiration of two years, will materially lessen the amount of our exports and imports. If it is meant that the nominal amount will be less, it cannot be denied, because they will be estimated in undepreciated money, but the real amount, the number of pieces of cloth, for example, exported —or the number of hogsheads of sugar imported—they must for ever be independent of the quantity or value of the circulating medium. If a merchant has a monied capital of 1000l. with which he can purchase and export 50 pieces of cloth— and if the Bank by increasing the amount of circulating medium by advances to B. and C. so affect its value as to enable A. to purchase and export with his 1000l. only 40 pieces of cloth, they, in fact, enable B. and C. to purchase and export the remaining 10 pieces; and if they withdraw their advances to B. and C. and thereby lessen the amount of the circulating medium, the 100l. of A. will regain its original value, and he will again become the exporter of fifty pieces of cloth.

The effect of the late great advances of the Bank has been precisely this, and is the same as if A. had contented himself with the employment of 80l. only, in the purchase and exportation of cloth, and had lent the 20l. to B. and C. and thereby enabled them to export the remaining ten pieces. There is this difference, indeed, that in the latter case A. would have received the interest on the 20l.—whereas in the former the Bank would have received it, and it would have been divided amongst the Proprietors of their Capital Stock.

If the Bank had doubled the circulation, A.'s 100l. would have purchased only 25 pieces, but the new holders of the Bank paper, would have been enabled to purchase and export the remaining 25. As in all these cases the 50 pieces of cloth would be exported, the proposed remedy for restoring the standard currency cannot have the effect of lessening the real amount of exports.

In the same manner it might be shewn that the amount of imports will not be diminished. This principle is perhaps only strictly applicable to the regular export trade of the country, as it is founded on the supposition that the speculators, who are called into existence by the abundance of paper, will be governed by the same prudence and circumspection which had before guided the transactions of real Capitalists; but, unfortunately, this is not the case. They wish to acquire fortune by a *coup-de-main*, and are enabled to force exportation, unnaturally, to every part of the world; not waiting for the regular demands of trade, but forestalling it, and thereby inverting its regular course. They forcibly divert a part of the National Capital to a trade which it would

not otherwise seek. The markets abroad become glutted—
no returns are made, and these speculative exporters, if they
are unable to renew their bills when they become due, are
not only ruined themselves, but involve in their fall the
whole chain with which they are connected. This I conceive
to be the true history of the present failures. Exportations so
injurious can well be dispensed with.

Experience has, indeed, proved, that every alteration in
the regular routine of commercial concerns, is attended with
some shock to general credit. If a war break out, though no
loss of capital should be sustained, the employment for that
part of it which is diverted from the old channels of trade,
must be sought in new directions; and the consequence
generally is attended with convulsions in the commercial
world, in which those who are trading on borrowed capitals,
and who depend on the continuance of commercial credit,
cannot answer the demands suddenly made on them. As the
paper system, pushed to the extravagant length which it now
is, affords great facilities to this description of persons, there
can be no doubt that every measure which tends to correct
that system, every material reduction in the quantity of paper,
will greatly embarrass and cause much distress amongst those
who depend upon its continuance; and though the mis-
fortunes of every part of the community must be deplored,
it is to the pernicious system which has lately prevailed, that
it will be alone to be ascribed. The remedy may be postponed, but can never be effectual without risking the safety
of those individuals.

But whatever may be lost in consequence of the difficulties to which the persons of whom we have been speaking may be exposed, cannot be regarded as a national loss,
as the capital which they could command by the credit which
the abundance of circulating medium afforded them will

revert to those hands which have been heretofore dispossessed of it, and where it will at least be as profitably employed as in those where this ruinous system has placed it.

A merchant trading with a monied capital has been injured by the depreciation of money, as his capital has not been equal to the same extent of business as before the depreciation; but there are few merchants in this situation:—their capitals, as well as that of tradesmen, are invested in goods, ships, &c. they are rather debtors than creditors to the rest of the community. A varying circulating medium, though injurious to every class of the community, is least so to mercantile men; as the prices of their commodities will undergo the same variations as the prices of all others, their comparative value will, under all circumstances, be the same, and their nominal, not their real value, will be affected.

The depreciation of the circulating medium has been most injurious to monied men.—By monied men I mean, that class whose property consists wholly of money, the amounts of which must, in this country, far exceed the total amount of the circulating medium.

It may be laid down as a principle of universal application, that every man is injured or benefited by the variation of the value of the circulating medium in proportion as his property consists of money, or as the fixed demands on him in money exceed those fixed demands which he may have on others. Thus the farmer is injured by any increase in the value of money, from whatever cause it may arise, whilst he has a fixed money rent, and fixed money taxes to pay. His produce will in consequence of the increased value of money sell for less, whilst his taxes and his rent continue the same. He must sell a greater number of quarters of corn, or whatever may be the produce of his land, to pay the same rent and the same taxes. He, more than any other class of the community, is benefited by the depreciation of money, and injured by the increase of its value. He has contracted to pay certain fixed sums,—the merchant and tradesman have done the same, but they have perhaps equal demands on others. The farmer trusts wholly to the sale of his produce; whatever, therefore, lowers the price of produce is injurious to him, without any corresponding benefit. The landlord will gain a great part of what the farmer loses, he will receive a greater real rent than he contracted for.

The landholder will be no loser, as the price of his produce will conform itself to the price of other commodities. Inasmuch as his taxes will be really increased in the same proportion as those of the farmer he will be a sufferer. But he cannot complain of injury—because, if the Bank had continued since 1797, to pay in specie as it had done before, he would not only now have to pay this amount of taxes but would have been obliged to do so for some years past. He has had an exemption which it would be unjust to continue to him.

Applying the principle which I have already noticed to the monied man, he must of course be greatly benefited by the restoration of the currency, as he stands in relation of creditor to all those with whom he has dealings. The rate of interest, it is true, is not affected by the increased value of the circulating medium, but the value of that interest is. He may receive in both cases 500l. for the use of 10,000l. but he will be sensible of the real increase of his revenue, by the fall in the prices of all the commodities which he consumes. He will, as well as the landholder and farmer, have increased taxes to pay, though the same nominal amount, but he will be amply compensated by the real increase of his income. He will regain by the restoration of the currency to its original standard, that portion of his revenue of which he has long been unjustly deprived, and which has been enjoyed by the issuers of paper money. The stock-holder and annuitant will, for the same reasons and in the same degree, be benefited.

The revenue will no doubt suffer some diminution, as an increase of 20 per cent. on all the existing taxes, can scarcely be paid without a considerable defalcation; in addition to which we must calculate on a deficiency in those taxes which are levied on the value of goods, such as many of the export and import duties,—the duty on houses by the rent,—the Income tax, and several others. It is certain that there will be a great deficiency in the amount of those taxes. But those who should, on account of these difficulties, contend for a continuance of the present system, should consider that a much less annual amount of loan and war taxes would be adequate to carry on the present expensive contest than what is now necessary. The loans and taxes being paid in a depreciated medium, and prices being affected in exact proportion to the depreciation, larger loans and larger taxes are requisite than what there would be, if the circulating medium were restored to its standard value. This is capable of an easy illustration. They should also consider that the longer the remedy is delayed, the more will the nation have ultimately to pay for it. We shall have to pay on every loan which may be raised, and on which the dividend shall hereafter be paid in standard currency, not only the interest really contracted for, but also the difference between the value of the dividends estimated in the present depreciated medium and their future value to which it is intended that they shall attain. This is a consideration of no trifling importance. Will it be contended that it would be wise and prudent to render the present system permanent?—Should such a plan be adopted, it is easy to foresee that we shall fare the fate of all those countries who have run the same ruinous course before us. It is impossible that a paper-money issuable by Government, or by a chartered company, at pleasure, and which is not exchangeable for specie, at the will of the holder, can retain a permanent value. Its value must be constantly vacillating, and it is not difficult to foretell what the consequences must be of uncontrouled power remaining in the hands of the issuers of paper, whilst their interest and that of the public must necessarily be at variance.

R.

[ON SIR JOHN SINCLAIR'S 'OBSERVATIONS']

BULLION REPORT[1]

To the EDITOR *of the* MORNING CHRONICLE.

SIR,

I have read with attention the observations of Sir John Sinclair on the Report of the Bullion Committee,[2] and am surprised that his ingenuity could not furnish him with any arguments against their conclusions, but such as have been again and again refuted.

It is not possible in the limits, to which, notwithstanding your indulgence, I must be confined, to point out all the false principles and uncandid statements with which the observations abound; neither would it be necessary, as the Bullion Report, though attacked, is itself an able, a satisfactory, and a conclusive answer.

Sir John takes much pains to inform us, that the increase of our commerce and of our public revenue require an additional amount of circulating medium. Who has denied it?—

[1] *Morning Chronicle*, 18 Sept. 1810.
[2] *Observations on the Report of the Bullion Committee*, by the Rt. Hon. Sir John Sinclair, Bart., M.P., London, Cadell and Davies, 1810.

Did he suppose that the Bullion Committee would refuse its assent to this principle? But might they not have successfully contended, that if no increase of Bank Notes beyond such necessity had taken place, no depreciation could have occurred? That it is the excess above this amount, only, whilst the Bank possesses the confidence of the public, which causes depreciation.

Before 1797, when the Bank paid in specie, increased commerce, and increased taxation might have required, precisely as they do now, an addition to the circulating medium, which the Bank might have supplied with their notes without causing any depreciation in their value as compared with gold; but if they had refused or neglected to do so, the increased demand for money would have raised the foreign exchange above par, and the mint price of gold above the market price; or in more popular language, the market price of gold would have fallen below the mint price, and would have so continued till the Bullion Merchants had availed themselves of the advantage attending the importation of gold at the favourable exchange, and the subsequent coining of it into money, and thereby supplied the demand for currency. The exchange would then have been at or about par, and the market and mint prices of gold at the usual level. The paper given in to the Committee by Mr. Pearse, and on which Sir John rests his assertion, that it is proved ["]as a matter of fact, that there is no connection whatever between the amount of paper currency issued by the Bank of England, and the rate of exchange["]¹, appears to confirm this reasoning. This paper attempted to prove, that "from January 1803, to the end of the year 1807, a period of not less than about four years, the amount of Bank Notes fluctuated from 16½ to 18 millions, and the exchange on Hamburgh varied from 32.10

¹ *Observations*, pp. 22–3.

to 35.6, becoming more favourable as the amount of Bank Notes increased."[1]

To which I answer, that no such additions could have been made in those years to the circulating medium, without lowering the foreign exchanges, and raising the price of Gold Bullion, if our increased commerce, and increased taxation, had not rendered an addition to the circulating medium necessary.

That this country has since 1797 greatly increased in wealth and prosperity, is not denied; but it cannot be justly estimated by a comparison of the nominal amount of our exports and imports, at that period and at this, because they are now estimated in a depreciated circulating medium. If the currency were now doubled, the nominal value of the exports and imports would double also, but some more solid proof would be required of the country having increased its wealth in the same proportion.

The difference of the rate of interest at which the loans have been raised, is an argument of much more weight.[2]

Sir John informs us, on the authority of the Bullion Committee, that the exchange was greatly unfavourable to this country during the reign of King William, and that in consequence guineas were then as high as thirty shillings each. Here his information ends, but it would have been candid if he had added from the same authority, that at that period the silver coin (which was then the standard measure of value) was greatly debased, and Bank Notes were in excess. "At length," says the Report, "the true remedies were resorted to: first by a new coinage of silver, which restored that part

---

[1] *ib.* p. 23, n. The paper referred to by Sinclair is published as No. xlix in the 'Appendix of Accounts' of the *Bullion Report*.

[2] According to Sinclair (*Observations*, p. 12) the interest on the loan of 1796 had been £4. 4s. 2¾d. per cent. and on the loan of 1809, £4. 13s. 3d.

of the currency to its standard value, though the scarcity of money, occasioned by calling in the old coin, brought the Bank into streights, and even for a time affected its credit; secondly, by taking out of the circulation the excess of Bank notes."[1]

Sir John dwells with much complacency, in his own opinion, that coin or bullion ought to be considered merely as merchandize, being sanctioned by the authority of many respectable witnesses examined before the Committee. I cannot find this principle questioned in the Report, though when Sir John informs us, that under the influence of respect for the Report of the Committee, he provided himself with some gold on his journey from Edinburgh to London, but found that the depreciated currency was equally useful with the coin, he seems to have forgotten its value as merchandize, as in that state it would certainly have procured him a few additional luxuries on his journey.

Sir John accuses the Committee of recommending the exportation of at least 20 millions of goods, and the importation in return of bullion, the absurdity of which, he observes, is self-evident. I have in vain looked over the Report for any foundation for this charge. Such a measure might be necessary in the contemplation of Sir John, if the Bank paid in specie, but on the principles of the Bullion Committee, that the circulation is in excess, and the excess could well be spared, there could be no necessity for any material importation of gold. Their recommendation is to lessen the amount of the circulating medium, and not to exchange one currency for another. Neither do the Committee express any expectation that the exchange will be brought to par, when the Bank is open, by the exportation of bullion, but by a reduction in the amount of the circulating

[1] *Bullion Report*, 8vo ed., p. 42.

medium, which will increase its value, not only at home but in its relation to the value of the currencies of other countries. The assertion, therefore, "that there is a great fallacy in the argument that opening the Bank would improve the exchange by the exportation of bullion,"[1] will not apply to the Report.

One of the advantages attending the increase of paper circulation is, according to Sir John Sinclair, that the interest for the use of money is thereby reduced. "Let us suppose," he says, "the total circulation of Great Britain to be 40 millions sterling in coin and in paper, bearing an interest of 5 per cent.; if it were reduced to 30 millions, bearing an interest of 6 per cent. how much would not the industry of the nation be cramped? whereas, were it raised to 50 millions, bearing an interest of 4 per cent. and the whole of it actively employed in various industrious pursuits, it cannot be doubted, that the prosperity of the country would increase with a celerity, and be carried to a height, which would not otherwise have been attainable."[2] If this reasoning be just, how incalculable would the prosperity of the country become, if the Bank would increase their notes to 100 millions and lend them at 3 per cent.

If Sir John will take the trouble to consult the 4th chap. 2d book, of Dr. A. Smith's celebrated work, he will there see it undeniably demonstrated, that the rate of interest for money is totally independent of the nominal amount of the circulating medium. It is regulated solely by the competition of capital, not consisting of money. The real amount of the circulating medium, with the same amount of commerce and confidence, must always be the same; it may, indeed, be called 100 millions, or 20 millions, but the real value of the one or the other sum must be the same. He will also see in

[1] *Observations*, p. 45.   [2] *ib.* pp. 56–7.

the same work, that the power of "effecting lasting improvements, such as roads, canals, bridges, harbours, mines, buildings, &c. &c."[1] depends upon the real wealth and capital of the country, and can neither be accelerated or retarded by the amount of the circulating medium.

"Let us suppose," says Sir John, "that the goods annually produced in the united kingdom are worth 100 millions sterling, per annum; if the quantity were increased one-fifth, and if the price were lowered in proportion, we should not, *in a pecuniary point of view*, be one farthing richer; and in regard to finance, the people at large would, in fact, be less able than before to furnish supplies to the Exchequer. Those who purchased goods cheaper, and consumed them, might, to a certain extent, be benefitted, and be enabled of course to pay more to the public; but all the various classes of the community, by whose industry the goods were made and brought to market, would not be able to pay near so much as they did before, and would necessarily be impoverished."[2]

2. "Let us next suppose," says Sir John, "that the quantity of goods remains the same, but that the price increases one-fifth. The amount of the annual income of the nation would then rise from 100 to 120 millions in value, and there would be a much larger fund for paying the demands of the public."[3]

That is to say, that a country which by its industry adds one-fifth to the annual produce of her land and labour becomes less capable of contributing to the exigencies of the state.

It would, to me, appear that if the prices of commodities be increased a fifth, a greater nominal revenue might possibly be levied on the people, but as the money raised would be

[1] *Observations*, p. 56.   [3] *ib*. p. 59.
[2] *ib*. pp. 58–9.

expended by Government in the purchase of commodities which had also increased a fifth in price, no considerable advantage would attend this ingenious experiment.

Nothing is wealth, according to these principles, but money, a doctrine which has been before maintained, but ably refuted by Dr. Adam Smith. It was reserved for this writer to contend not only that money is exclusively wealth, but paper money depreciated to any possible extent. How inexhaustible are our resources! Is it by such arguments that the reasoning of the Bullion Committee is to be overturned?

I am, Sir, &c.

R.

[ON MR RANDLE JACKSON'S SPEECH]

BULLION REPORT[1]

To the EDITOR of the MORNING CHRONICLE.

Permit me, Sir, through the medium of your Paper, to make a few remarks on the speech of Mr. Randle Jackson, delivered at the Bank Court on Thursday last, on the subject of the Report of the Bullion Committee.[2]

I cannot help lamenting, that those who differ from the Report, should endeavour, by every means in their power,

---

[1] *Morning Chronicle*, 24 Sept. 1810.

[2] Jackson's speech was delivered at the General Court of the Bank of England held on 20 Sept. 1810, and was reported in the *Morning Chronicle* of the following day. An enlarged version was published as a pamphlet under the title *The Speech of Randle Jackson, Esq. delivered at the General Court of the Bank of England, held on the* 20th of September, 1810, respecting the Report of the Bullion Committee of the House of Commons; with Notes on the Subject of that Report, London, Butterworth, n.d. [1810]. Ricardo's quotations are from the report in the *Morning Chronicle*; the page references here given in footnotes are to the pamphlet.

to impress on the public mind, that the question in dispute is a party question, and that in this attempt they should have received the sanction of Mr. Jackson. If ever there was a question, which, from its importance, peculiarly required to be considered on its own merits only, it is the present state of our currency, connected as it necessarily is with the best interests of the community.

When the Hon. Proprietor commenced his speech, I hoped he would have discussed it as a subject of science, admitting of clear and obvious deductions from the known principles of political œconomy. I anxiously waited for his proofs of the fallacious propositions with which he stated the Report abounded—I expected that he would have grappled with some of its leading principles—have traced them to their source—detected their errors and exposed their sophistry. I expected that he would have favoured us with his own theory on the subject of money, adorned by all the graces of his eloquence, and supported by such authorities as must have commanded respect and attention. I expected, in short, to have quitted the Court enlightened and informed on a subject which possesses peculiar interest to me; but, Sir, these expectations were not to be realized; I was doomed to listen to an unmeaning attack on what was called the party spirit which dictated the Report, and to a repetition of the worst of the erroneous opinions which were delivered in evidence to the Committee, and which the Report itself has so ably confuted.

One of the first observations made by Mr. Jackson was, that the Committee had reported contrary to the evidence. He of course did not mean to charge them with any misstatement of facts, but of drawing conclusions directly contrary to the *opinion* given by the gentlemen whom they examined. As the evidence were not unanimous in their opinion, as the respectable authority of the late Sir F. Baring was with the Committee, they would have been equally liable to this charge on whichever side they had reported. This censure the Committee had no means of avoiding. The charge in fact means, that they erred in not agreeing with the opinions of the Bank Directors. Now, Sir, this is the feature in the Report which, I think, is its peculiar recommendation; —it has demonstratively proved that those opinions were founded on false principles, and has, I hope, for ever, rescued us from their further and fatal influence. It is to be regretted, that truth is but slow in its progress; but it will not fail ultimately to triumph. We may be deprived for a time of the beneficial efforts of the labours of the Bullion Committee, but the true principles of currency, developed in their Report, can happily never be stifled. Did Mr. Jackson mean to contend, that the Committee were not to exercise their judgment on the facts laid before them, but that they were bound to report the opinions of others? To what consequences would not such an opinion lead? Merchants may understand the details of business—they may give much useful information; but it does not therefore follow that they are qualified to give sound opinions on points of theory and science. Glass-makers and dyers are not necessarily chemists, because the principles of chemistry are intimately connected with their trades.

If it be true "that it is impossible that any greater aspersion could be thrown on the Bank, than that it was they who had increased the price of the necessaries of life,"[1] I fear they must continue to suffer under it, notwithstanding the defence made for them by Mr. Jackson. "But what is meant," he asks, "by an excessive issue, to which these high prices are[2]

---

[1] *Speech of Randle Jackson*, p. 17.
[2] Misprinted 'is'; corrected by

Ricardo on the cutting from the *Morning Chronicle* which is in *R.P.*

imputed?"[1]—Though this question has been often answered, I will again endeavour to satisfy it, and for that purpose will avail myself of the assistance of Dr. Adam Smith.

"Let us suppose," says that writer, "that the whole circulating money of some particular country, amounted, at a particular time, to one million sterling, that sum being then sufficient for circulating the whole annual produce of their land and labour. Let us suppose too that some time thereafter different banks and bankers issued promissory notes, payable to the bearer, to the extent of one million, reserving in their different coffers two hundred thousand pounds for answering occasional demands. There would remain, therefore, in circulation eight hundred thousand pounds in gold and silver, and a million of bank notes, or eighteen hundred thousand pounds of paper and money together. But the annual produce of the land and labour of the country had before required only one million to circulate and distribute it to its proper consumers, and that annual produce cannot be immediately augmented by those operations of banking. One million will therefore be sufficient to circulate it after them. The goods to be bought and sold being precisely the same as before, the same quantity of money will be sufficient for buying and selling them. The channel of circulation, if I may be allowed such an expression, will remain precisely the same as before. One million we have supposed sufficient to fill that channel. Whatever, therefore, is poured into it beyond this sum cannot run into it, but must overflow. One million eight hundred thousand pounds are poured into it, 800,000l. therefore, must overflow that sum, being over and above what can be employed in the circulation of the country.[2]

[1] *Speech of Randle Jackson*, p. 18.
[2] Adam Smith says in addition: 'But though this sum cannot be employed at home, it is too valuable to be allowed to lie idle.'

It will, therefore, be sent abroad, in order to seek that profitable employment which it cannot find at home. But the paper cannot go abroad, because at a distance from the Banks which issue it, and from the country in which payment of it can be exacted by law, it will not be received in common payments. Gold and silver, therefore to the amount of eight hundred thousand pounds, will be sent abroad, and the channel of home circulation will remain filled with a million of paper, instead of a million of those metals which filled it before."[1]

So far there is no excess, but if, as is the case in this country, the Bank should be protected from paying its notes in specie, and should increase their issues to 1,200,000l, I should call the 200,000l. excessive. It could not, as formerly, overflow and be exported, because every part of the currency consisted of paper, it must therefore either enlarge the channel of circulation, raising in the same proportion the prices of all commodities, not excepting gold and silver bullion, or it must, as is contended by the Bank Directors in their evidence before the Committee, return to them in the payment of bills discounted, as no one would consent, they say, to pay interest for 200,000l. which was superfluous and excessive. Here then the whole dispute rests, and Mr. Jackson should have exercised his talents in defence of this main prop of the Bank Directors.

If this falls, and it be proved that the 200,000l. will remain in circulation, and admits of being increased to two millions, or any other amount, all the ingenious reasoning of Mr. Jackson on the hardship to which the Bank will be subjected, by a repeal of the Restriction Bill, in being obliged to purchase gold bullion, not only at the present high price, but at any advance which the avarice of the dealers in bullion will

[1] *Wealth of Nations*, Bk. ii, ch. ii; Cannan's ed., vol. i, pp. 276–7.

add to it, must fall with it—as it will then appear evident that
the Bank have the power of raising or falling, at their pleasure, not only the prices of bullion, but of every other commodity for which their notes are exchangeable.

In defence of my opinion, that the channel of circulation
admits of indefinite enlargement, I have the authority of historical facts, the discovery of the mines of America must at
least have trebled the amount of money. This increased
amount of circulating medium, according to Dr. Smith,
could have had no effect on the rate of interest for money.
In the 4th chapter of the 2d book of the Wealth of Nations,
to which I, in my last letter referred,[1] it is demonstrated that
the rate of interest depends on the rate of profits, which again
is totally independent of the nominal amount of the circulating medium. Admitting this fact; if profits be high, and
the Bank is willing to lend at a low interest, can there be any
conceivable number of Bank Notes which may not be applied
for? Let us suppose that the Bank had a mine of gold on its
own premises and that England were insulated from all other
countries—might they not have their gold coined into guineas
and discount bills with them to an indefinite amount?[2] Where
is the difference in the present case? our currency is insulated
from all others, and may, by the same rule, be indefinitely
increased. But the Bank never discount bills, but such as are
for bona fide transactions.—Suppose A. to sell a hogshead of
sugar to B. and draw a bill for its value at two months;—
suppose further, that B. sells the sugar to a grocer either in
London or the country, and to draw another bill at two
months, are not these both *bona fide* transactions? And will
not the Bank discount both bills? Can it be seriously con-

[1] Above, p. 143.
[2] Three minor corrections in this sentence, written by Ricardo on the cutting in *R.P.*, have been adopted here: 'premises and that' for 'premises.—'; 'guineas and' for 'guineas—'; 'with them' for 'with it'.

tended that these are checks which will keep the currency within proper limits.

It is observed by Dr. Adam Smith, "that the whole paper money of every kind which can easily circulate in any country, never can exceed the value of the gold and silver, of which it supplies the place, or which (the commerce being supposed the same) would circulate there if there were no paper money."[1]

Let us try our circulation by this test. Let it be supposed possible that the Bank of England, and the Country Banks, could pay every note in circulation with specie, could the whole be kept in circulation? No; the excess would at the present exchange go abroad as bullion, and there seek a better market.

This is admitted by the Directors and their defenders. The circulation of England, therefore, according to Dr. Smith's rule, is excessive, because it exceeds the quantity of gold and silver of which it supplies the place, and which would circulate there if there were no paper. "But the Bank has been surprisingly parsimonious in their issues," says Mr. Jackson; "they have not, since 1797, exceeded their average issues more than 7 millions, whilst the Country Banks have increased theirs 20 millions."[2] So then it is allowed, that the town and country issues have been increased 27 millions; and yet we are gravely asked, what is meant by excessive issues? and it is deemed an aspersion of the character of the Bank, who have the power of regulating the amount of the country currency, because they are accused of being the cause of the high price of provisions, and of the other necessaries of life.

The Bank might make a simple experiment, by which the

[1] *Wealth of Nations*, Bk. II, ch. ii;   [2] *Speech of Randle Jackson*, p. 20.
Cannan's ed., vol. I, p. 283.

soundness of the principles on which the Bullion Report is founded might be fairly tried. Let them withdraw one million of notes from circulation, and if in three months no effect should thereby be produced on the price of bullion and the rates of exchange, they may then fairly exult in the justness of their views.

Mr. Jackson thinks the Directors blameless because they have to receive eighteen millions of the public, whilst the amount of their notes does not exceed twenty millions; he informs us that the Bank could raise the remaining two millions in half an hour, if it were wanted. This would be a good argument to prove the solvency of the Bank, of which no man doubts, but is of no avail against the accusation of an excessive currency. The same might be urged if 100 millions of Bank notes were in circulation and 98 had been issued in discounts. What again can the fact of the public participating in the profits of the Bank have to do with the question at issue?

Most willingly do I agree with Mr. Jackson in the just tribute which he paid to the disinterestedness and integrity of the Bank Directors; but I can go no further with him, and must deny them the character for ability and discretion, which he also bestows on them. But if men less scrupulous had been in the Direction, they might, with the power which they possessed, have alternately raised and depressed the price of Bullion, by the increase or diminution of their notes, and might either in their corporate or individual capacities have taken advantage of the successive variations.

I do not recollect that any of the Merchants in their evidence stated, as Mr. Jackson asserts, that the price of Bullion has no influence on foreign exchanges;[1] neither was he correct in his statement, that in the year 1797, when the price of

[1] Cp. below, pp. 358–9.

Bullion was very low, the exchange upon Hamburgh was, *as now*, 38 and a fraction.

This, which he considers as a strong instance against the opinion of the Committee, was unfortunately chosen, the fact being directly otherwise. The price of bullion is now high, and[1] the exchange is proportionally low, being at 31. 6. and not at 38. I believe Mr. Jackson can bring no proof of a high price of bullion being unaccompanied by a low exchange—and a low price of bullion by a high exchange. But, Sir, the Report is the best antidote to these attacks—if that be but read I shall not fear the result, as it cannot fail to carry conviction to every unprejudiced mind.

I am, Sir, &c.

R.

[1] 'and' is inserted by Ricardo on the cutting in *R.P.*

REPLY

TO

MR. BOSANQUET'S

PRACTICAL OBSERVATIONS

ON THE

REPORT

OF

THE BULLION COMMITTEE.

BY

DAVID RICARDO.

LONDON:

PRINTED FOR JOHN MURRAY, 32, FLEET-STREET;
WILLIAM BLACKWOOD, EDINBURGH; AND
M. N. MAHON, DUBLIN.

1811.

CONTENTS

CHAPTER I.

CHAPTER II.

Mr. Bosanquet's alleged Facts, drawn from the History of the State of Exchange, considered.

SECTION I.

SECTION II.

SECTION III.

SECTION IV.

CHAPTER III.

Mr. Bosanquet's alleged Facts, in supposed Refutation of the Conclusion that a Rise in the Market Price of Bullion above the Mint Price proves a Depreciation of the Currency, considered.

SECTION I.

SECTION II.

SECTION III.

SECTION IV.

CHAPTER IV.

CHAPTER V.

CHAPTER VI.

CHAPTER VII.

CHAPTER VIII.

CHAPTER IX.

REPLY, &c.

CHAPTER I

Preliminary Observations.—Mr. Bosanquet's Objections to the Conclusions of the Bullion Committee briefly stated.

THE question concerning the depreciation of our currency has lately assumed peculiar interest, and has excited a degree of attention in the public mind which promises the most happy results. To the Bullion Committee we are already most particularly indebted, for a more just exposition of the true principles which should regulate the currency of nations, than has before appeared in any authoritative shape, in this or any other country. It could not, however, be expected that a reform, so important as that which the Committee recommend, could be effected without calling forth the warmest opposition, dictated by the erroneous principles of some, and by the interested views of others. Hitherto this opposition has been attended with the best effects; it has tended to prove more fully the correctness of the principles laid down by the Committee; it has called forth new champions in the field of argument; and discussion has daily produced new converts to the cause of truth. Of all the attacks on the report of the Committee, however, that of Mr. Bosanquet[1] has appeared to me the most formidable. He has not, as his predecessors have done, confined himself to declamation alone; and though he disclaims all reasoning and argument, he has brought forward, what he thought were irrefragable proofs of the discordance of the theory with former practice. It is these proofs which

[1] *Practical Observations on the Report of the Bullion-Committee,* by Charles Bosanquet, London, Richardson, 1810.

I propose to examine, and am confident that it will be from a deficiency of ability in me, and not from any fault in the principles themselves, if I do not shew that they are wholly unfounded. Mr. Bosanquet commences, by availing himself of the vulgar charge, which has lately been so often countenanced, and in places too high, against theorists. He cautions the public against listening to their speculations before they have submitted them to the test of fact; and he kindly undertakes to be their guide in the examination. If this country had hitherto carried on trade by barter, and it were, for the first time, going to establish a system by which the intervention of money should facilitate the operations of trade, there might be some foundation for calling the principles which might be offered to public attention wholly theoretical; because, however clearly dictated by the experience of the past, their practical effects would not have been witnessed. But, when the principles of a currency, long established, are well understood; when the laws which regulate the variations of the rate of exchange between countries have been known and observed for centuries, can that system be called wholly theoretical which appeals to those principles, and is willing to submit to the test of those laws?

To such an examination the report of the Committee is now submitted, and the public is called upon to believe that a theory which its adversary allows to be unassailable by reasoning and argument, is to be battered down by an appeal to facts. We are told, "that boldly as the principle is asserted, *and strongly as reason appears to sanction it*, that it is not generally true, and is at variance with fact."[1] This is the test to which I have long wished to see this important question brought. I have long wished that those who refused their assent to principles which experience has appeared to sanction, would either state their

[1] *Practical Observations*, p. 16. The italics are Ricardo's.

own theory as to the cause of the present appearances in the state of our currency, or that they would point out those facts which they considered at variance with that which, from the firmest conviction, I have espoused.

To Mr. Bosanquet, then, I feel considerably obliged. If, as I trust, I shall be able to obviate his objections; to prove them wholly untenable; to convince him that *his* statements are at variance with fact; that for his supposed proofs he is indebted to the wrong application of a principle, and not to any deficiency in the principle itself:—I shall confidently expect that he will abjure his errors, and become the foremost of our defenders.

Mr. Bosanquet has thus stated[1] the principal positions of the Committee, to which he is induced to object:

1st, "That the variations of the exchange with foreign countries can never, for any considerable time, exceed the expense of transporting and insuring the precious metals from one country to the other.

2d, "That the price of Gold Bullion can never exceed the mint price, unless the currency in which it is paid, is depreciated below the value of gold.

3d, "That, so far as any inference is to be drawn from Custom-house returns of exports and imports, the state of the exchanges ought to be peculiarly favourable.

4th, "That the Bank, during the restriction, possesses exclusively the power of limiting the circulation of Bank notes.

5th, "That the circulation of country bank-notes depends upon, and is proportionate to, the issues from the Bank.

Lastly, "That the paper currency is now excessive, and depreciated in comparison with gold, and that the high price of Bullion and low rates of exchange are the consequences as well as the sign of such depreciation."

These principles being in all essential points the same as

[1] p. 8.

those which I have avowed, and on which Mr. Bosanquet has attacked me, to avoid the necessity of speaking at one time of the opinion of the Bullion Committee, and at another of my own, I shall, in the future pages of this work, consider them as the principles of the Bullion Committee only, and shall take occasion to mention any shade of difference that may occur between theirs and mine.

CHAPTER II

Mr. Bosanquet's alleged Facts, drawn from the History of the State of Exchange, considered.

SECTION I

Exchange with Hamburg.

THE first position controverted is, "That the variations of the exchange with foreign countries can never, for any length of time, exceed the expense of transmitting and insuring the precious metals from one country to the other."[1]

Can this be called a theoretical opinion, now brought forward for the first time? Has it not been sanctioned by the writings of Hume and Smith? and has it not been undisputed even by practical men?

Mr. ——, in his evidence before the Bullion Committee, observes, "that the extent to which the exchange can fall is the charge of transporting Bullion, together with an adequate profit to the risk the transporting such specie is liable to."[2]

Mr. A. Goldsmid "never recollected the exchange to have differed more from par than 5 per cent. before the suspension of cash payments."[3]

Mr. Grefulhe stated, "that since he had been in business he recollected no period prior to the suspension of the cash payments by the Bank, when the exchange was considerably below par."[4]

The same opinions were given by many practical men before the Lords Committee in 1797.

[1] This is quoted more accurately on p. 161 above.
[2] *Bullion Report*, 'Minutes of Evidence', p. 83; a loose quotation. On 'Mr. —' see below, p. 427 ff.
[3] A. Goldsmid's actual statement is 'I have known it differ as much as 5 per cent. either way.' And in reply to a further question 'I have known it 5 per cent. but very seldom, and not for a long time together.' *ib.* p. 117.
[4] *ib.* p. 130.

But in opposition to all these opinions, Mr. Bosanquet has facts which he boldly thinks will prove the unsoundness of the doctrine. "In the years 1764 to 1768," he observes, "prior to the recoinage, when the imperfect state of the coins occasioned gold to be 2 to 3 per cent. above the mint price, the exchange with Paris was 8 to 9 per cent. against London,—at the same time the exchange with Hamburgh was, during the whole period, 2 to 6 per cent. in favour of London; here appears, then, a profit of 12 to 14 per cent. for the expense, in time of peace, of paying the debt to Paris with gold from Hamburgh, which must have exceeded the fact by at least 8 or 10 per cent.; and it is worthy of remark, that the average exchange with Hamburgh, for the years 1766 and 1767, of 5 per cent. in favour of London, added to the[1] 2 per cent. the price of gold above the mint price constituted a premium of 7 per cent. on the importation of gold into England, or, deducting $1\frac{1}{2}$ per cent. for expenses in time of peace, a net profit of 5 per cent, yet the exchange was not rectified thereby. Again, in 1775, 6, and 7, after the recoinage, we find the exchange on Paris 5, 6, 7, and 8 per cent. against London in time of peace, when half the amount would have conveyed gold to Paris, and one-fourth have paid the debts of Paris at Amsterdam.

"In the years 1781, 2, and 3, being years of war, the exchange was constantly from 7 to 9 per cent. in favour of Paris; and, during this period, gold was the common circulation of this country; and the Bank was compelled to provide it for the public at the mint price. It has been already shewn how little effect the precious metals produced towards equalising the exchange with Hamburgh during the years 1797 and 1798; and another instance may be adduced in the years 1804 and 1805, when the Paris exchange varied from 7 to 9 per cent. in favour of London.

[1] 'the' is not in Bosanquet's text.

"In every case here cited, the fluctuations of the exchanges greatly exceeded the expense of conveying gold from one country to the other, and to a much greater degree in most of them than in the present instance; the circumstances of the times were, it will readily be admitted, more favourable to intercourse on those occasions than they now are, and the state of metallic circulation afforded facilities not now experienced here. Yet, under all these disadvantages, the principle assumed by the Committee was not operative, and cannot therefore be admitted as a solid foundation for the superstructure of excess and depreciation attempted to be raised upon it."[1]

If the facts had been as here stated by Mr. Bosanquet, I should have found it difficult to reconcile them with my theory. That theory takes for granted, that whenever enormous profits can be made in any particular trade, a sufficient number of capitalists will be induced to engage in it, who will, by their competition, reduce the profits to the general rate of mercantile gains. It assumes that in the trade of exchange does this principle more especially operate; it not being confined to English merchants alone; but being perfectly understood, and profitably followed, by the exchange and bullion merchants of Holland, France, and Hamburgh; and competition in this trade being well known to be carried to its greatest height. Does Mr. Bosanquet suppose that a theory which rests on so firm a basis of experience as this can be shaken by one or two solitary facts not perfectly known to us? Even should no explanation of them be attempted, they might safely be left to produce their natural effects on the public mind.

But before the reasoning of the Committee can be proved defective by Mr. Bosanquet's facts, we must examine the source from whence those supposed facts are derived.

---

[1] *Practical Observations*, pp. 17–19.

Mr. Bosanquet tells us that[1] "there is annexed to Mr. Mushet's pamphlet a table, shewing, 1st, the rate of exchange with Hamburgh and Paris for 50 years past, and how much it has been, in each instance, above or below par.

2d, "The price of gold in London, and a comparison of this price with the English standard or mint price.

3d, "The amount of Bank notes in circulation, and the rate of their assumed depreciation, by a comparison with the price of gold."[2]

Now the accuracy of these tables must be admitted or proved before the conclusions, which result from the inspection of them, can command assent;—but so far from this being the case, their accuracy is disowned by Mr. Mushet himself, who, in the second edition of his pamphlet, acknowledged the false principle upon which his first tables were calculated, and has given us a new and amended set.

The following notice accompanied the second edition of Mr. Mushet's pamphlet:[3] "In the first edition of this work I stated the par of exchange with Hamburgh at 33 schillings and 8 grotes, and at that considered it as a fixed par; from the best information which I have been able to obtain upon 'Change since, $34.11\frac{1}{4}$ are considered as the par, and in the present edition I have stated it as such. *I have also corrected the mistake of considering the par to be fixed;* because gold being the standard of the money of England, and silver in Hamburgh, there can

---

[1] By a misprint the inverted commas open at the beginning of the paragraph.

[2] p. 9.

[3] *An Enquiry into the Effects Produced on the National Currency and Rates of Exchange, by the Bank Restriction Bill; Explaining the Cause of the High Price of Bullion; with Plans for Maintaining the National Coins in a State of Uniformity and perfection. The second Edition, With some Observations on Country Banks, and on Mr. Grenfell's Examination of the Tables of Exchange annexed to the first Edition.* By Robert Mushet, of His Majesty's Mint, London, Baldwin, 1810, pp. 94–5.

be no fixed par between those two countries; it will be subject to all the variations which take place in the relative value of gold and silver. For example, if 34 schillings 11 grotes and $\frac{1}{4}$ of Hamburgh currency be equal in value to a pound sterling, or $\frac{20}{21}$ of a guinea, when silver is 5s. 2d. per oz., they can no longer be so when silver falls to 5s. 1d. or 5s. per oz., because a pound sterling in gold being then worth more silver, is also worth more Hamburgh currency.

"To find the real par, therefore, we must ascertain what was the relative value of gold and silver when the par was fixed at 34.11$\frac{1}{4}$, and what is the relative value at the time we wish to calculate it.

"For example, if the price of standard gold was 3l. 17s. 10$\frac{1}{2}$d. per oz. and silver 5s. 2d. an ounce of gold would then be worth 15.07 ounces of silver, being the mint proportions; 20 of our standard shillings would then contain as much pure silver as 34 schillings 11 grotes and $\frac{1}{4}$; but if the ounce of gold was 3l. 17s. 10$\frac{1}{2}$d., and silver 5s. (which it was on the 2d January, 1798) the ounce of gold would then be worth 15.57 ounces of silver. If 1l. sterling at par, therefore, be worth 15.07 ounces of silver, then at 15.57 it would be at 3 per cent. premium; and 3 per cent. premium on 34.11$\frac{1}{4}$ is 1 schilling 1 grote and $\frac{9}{10}$, so that the par, when gold is to silver as 15.57 to 1, will be 36 schillings 1 grote and $\frac{1}{10}$.

"The above calculation will be more easily made by stating as follows:

$$\text{As } 15.07 : 34.11\tfrac{1}{4} :: 15.57 : 36\tfrac{1}{10}.\text{"}[1]$$

As it is universally admitted, that gold is the standard measure of value in this country, and that silver performs the same office at Hamburgh, it is evident that no tables can be correct which assume a fixed invariable par. The true par must

---

[1] The last figure should be '36.1$\frac{1}{10}$', as given by Mushet.

vary with every variation in the relative value of the two metals.

There are some objections, however, which I have yet to offer against the perfect accuracy of Mr. Mushet's present tables.

In the first place, he has taken the par of silver against silver too low; he has calculated on the information which he had received, that 20 standard shillings in silver contained as much of that pure metal as thirty-four schillings and $11\frac{1}{4}$ grotes; but it appears by Dr. Kelly's table (Bullion Rep. page 207),[1] that by actual assay, as well as by computation, 20 shillings are of equal value with 35 schillings and 1 grote. This difference amounts to little more than $\frac{3}{8}$ per cent.; and I have only noticed it because I think it highly desirable that we should be able, at all times, to ascertain the true par.

Secondly, Mr. Mushet has calculated the degree in which the exchange was above or below par by a reference to the prices which he has quoted from Lloyd's list. Now, invariably have those prices been for bills at $2\frac{1}{2}$ usances, and as the par of exchange is computed from a comparison of the actual value of the coins of the two countries, payable at the same time in both, and not in one of them at the end of $2\frac{1}{2}$ months, an allowance for interest must be made for this period, which will amount to about 1 per cent.*

A deduction of $1\frac{3}{8}$ per cent. must therefore be made from

---

* By Mr. —— evidence to the Bullion Committee (Appendix, page 74),[2] it appears that the course of exchange from Hamburgh to London in ordinary times differs 1 Flemish schilling from the course of London to Hamburgh, to compensate the $2\frac{1}{2}$ usances and commission allowed on bills both ways; when the difficulties of communication existed to the greatest extent the difference of exchange was full 2s. Flemish.

[1] The reference is to the folio ed.;   [2] Octavo ed., pp. 79–80.
in the octavo ed., 'Appendix of Ac-
counts', p. 73.

the column for the favourable exchange to England in Mr. Mushet's tables.[1]

There are also, in all calculations on the true par of exchange, other sources of error, some of which will be presently noticed; so that it is not possible to ascertain with perfect accuracy, unless all those facts were before us, the actual difference which at any time existed between a remittance by bullion, and by the purchase of a bill.

To Mr. Mushet's amended tables, thus corrected, I am willing to submit the truth of the principle now disputed. It will then appear, that at no period since 1760 has the exchange with Hamburgh been more in favour of England than 7 per cent., with one exception only; and the reader will not be surprised that there should have been such an exception, when he learns that it was in the memorable year of 1797, just after the suspension of cash payments at the Bank. At this period the currency of this country was reduced particularly low; the amount of bank notes in circulation being less than it had been for ten years preceding. That, under such circumstances, the exchange should have become favourable to England, and, consequently, that there should have been large importations of bullion, is entirely conformable with the principle of the Bullion Committee, and confirms the efficacy of the remedy which they have proposed. A great circulation of paper, and a too abundant currency, are stated by them to be the causes of the present nominally low exchange, and they confidently predict, that a reduction of its quantity will, as in the year 1797, raise the exchange, and by that means render the importation of bullion profitable. That this favourable exchange did, in the year 1797, produce an immense importation of gold

---

[1] Neither of these corrections was made in Mushet's 3rd ed., 1811, although he there (p. 103) refers the reader to Ricardo's 'very ingenious and masterly' *Reply to Bosanquet*.

can, by indirect evidence, be amply proved. The amount of foreign gold coined in his Majesty's mint was,

In the year 1795 in value £255,721 11   8
                   1796 .   .   72,179 14 11
                   1797 .   . 2,486,410   6   0
                   1798 .   . 2,718,425   9   0
                   1799 .   .   271,846 12   8

But, it will be asked, how do those who contend that the exchanges of a country cannot, for any length of time, be either highly favourable, or highly unfavourable, account for the exchange with Hamburgh being permanently in favour of England for two or three years?

This was the case, Mr. Bosanquet observes,[1] during the years 1797 and 1798, and he affirms that the precious metals produced little effect in equalising the exchange. It appears by Mr. Mushet's amended tables (always corrected by the $1\frac{3}{8}$ per cent.) that, during those years, the exchange was favourable to England, and fluctuated from 5.6 to 4.3 per cent. But the principle I understand to be this, that no country can, for any length of time, have the exchange highly favourable or highly unfavourable, because it supposes either such an increase on the one hand in her stock of money and bullion, or on the other such a diminution in that stock, as would destroy that equilibrium in the value of the currencies of countries which they naturally have a tendency to find.

The assertion is true when applied to the exchanges in general of any country, but is false if the rate of her exchange with one country only be considered. It is possible that her exchange with one particular country may be permanently unfavourable, in consequence of a continued demand for

----

[1] p. 18.

bullion, but this by no means proves that her stock of coin
and bullion is decreasing, unless her exchange should be also
unfavourable with other countries. She may be importing
from the north the bullion which she is exporting to the south
—she may be collecting it from countries where it is relatively
abundant, for countries where it is relatively scarce, or where,
from some particular causes, it is in particular demand; but
it by no means follows, as an undeniable consequence, that
her own stock of money shall be reduced below its natural
level. Spain, for example, who is the great importer of bullion
from America, can never have an unfavourable exchange with
her colonies; and as she must distribute the bullion she receives
amongst the different nations of the world, she can seldom have
a favourable exchange with the countries with which she
trades.*

Applying then these principles to the state of our exchange
with Hamburgh, in 1797 and 1798, we shall observe, that it
was not in consequence of what is usually termed a balance of
trade that the exchange was permanently favourable to England;
it was not because Hamburgh had contracted a debt to us for
the balance of commodities which she had imported, that she
was necessitated to pay us in gold and silver bullion, but
because she could advantageously export bullion in the same
way as any other commodity, in consequence of an unusual
demand for that article in England. This demand proceeded
from two causes: First, from the unusually low amount of our

---

* Mr. Huskisson has commented with great ability upon the few
transactions, few comparatively, which take place in bullion, and has
observed, that those transactions are principally confined to the distribution of the produces of the mines to the different countries where gold
and silver are in use.[1]

[1] *The Question concerning the De-   and Examined*, London, Murray,
preciation of our Currency Stated   1810, pp. 49-50.

currency; secondly, from the exportation of silver to Asia by the East India Company.

In consequence of the first of these causes, and of the immense amount of guineas which at that period had been withdrawn from circulation, for the purpose of hoarding, by timid people, we have already seen that the foreign gold coined into guineas, during those years, amounted to no less a sum than 5,200,000*l.* Here then was a demand for gold unprecedented in the history of the Mint, and of itself abundantly sufficient to account both for the high exchange, and the length of time which it continued. It is a practical illustration of the truth of a most satisfactory theory.

To this however must be added, the demand for silver bullion in consequence of the exportation of the East India Company. It appears, by the account delivered to the Bullion Committee, (No. 9.) that the whole amount of foreign silver coin, exported by the Company on their own account, as well as on account of private persons, amounted

$$
\begin{array}{lcl}
\text{In the year } 1795 & . \text{ to } . & 151,795 \text{ ounces} \\
1796 & . \quad . \quad . & 290,777 \\
1797 & . \quad . \quad . & 962,880 \\
1798 & . \quad . \quad . & 3,565,691 \\
1799 & . \quad . \quad . & 7,287,327.
\end{array}
$$

From this time the exportation of silver to the East Indies was considerably reduced, and has now almost wholly ceased. Thus then it appears, that a high exchange was followed by an unusually great importation of bullion, and that when that demand ceased the exchange regained its natural level. On a further inspection of the table, it will appear, that in proportion as the amount of Bank notes increased, the exchange became depressed, and was in 1801 more than 11 per cent. against

England; and at the same time the price of gold bullion rose to 4*l.* 6*s.*—more than 10 per cent above the mint price*.

It must be confessed, that from September 1766 to September 1767, the exchange continued permanently in favour of England from 7.4 to 6.8 per cent.; and from that period to September 1768 it continued generally favourable above 3 per cent.; but what circumstances in the situation of Europe might then have made it profitable for England to become the agent in collecting bullion from Hamburgh for some other country, it is not now material to enquire. Of this I am fully assured, that, if all the circumstances were fairly before us, it might be satisfactorily explained.

But whether explained or not explained, it proves nothing in favour of Mr. Bosanquet's theory (for theory Mr. B. has just as much as the Committee);—it only proves that the

---

* Lord King satisfactorily accounted[1] for the long duration of an exchange favourable to this country with Hamburgh, from the circumstance of the demands of the India Company for silver bullion for their settlements in the East. Mr. Blake comments in his late publication[2] upon what he calls "the erroneous opinions" entertained by Lord King on this subject; and observes, "that the exportation of bullion is affected like that of any other commodity, when there is such a difference in its real prices, at any two places, as will afford a profit on its transit; an occurrence that will frequently take place with an exchange at par." An occurrence, I should say, which can never take place, with an exchange at par. Who would send bullion from Hamburgh to London at an expence of 4 or 5 per cent, whilst the exchange was at par, when by means of a bill he could obtain the same amount of bullion in London free from all charges?

I am happy that an opinion similar to that which I have expressed is also entertained by Mr. Bosanquet, page 12. "In the event of an unfavourable balance of payments, the depression of the exchange must necessarily attain this limit (the expences of conveying and insuring the precious metals from one country to the other) before the balance can be adjusted by the exportation of gold."

[1] *Thoughts on the Effects of the Bank Restrictions*, 2nd ed., 1804, pp. 55–9 and 153–62.
[2] *Observations on the Principles which Regulate the Course of Exchange; and on the Present Depreciated State of the Currency*, London, Lloyd, 1810, pp. 35–6.

precious metals might continue to be imported from one quarter while they were exported to another; which the theory of the Committee not only allows but requires. To prove any thing in favour of Mr. B.'s theory, it must be proved that the precious metals came in permanently in greater proportion than they went out; not from one place only, but from all places taken together.

The following considerations go a certain way in accounting for the phenomena which have misled Mr. Bosanquet: the tables of Mr. Mushet are calculated on a comparison of the relative value of silver with bar gold. Now bar gold is generally 2 or 3s. per ounce worse in price than gold in coin; and, therefore, if the gold imported be intended for re-exportation, the true par will differ from 2 to 3 per cent, according as the calculation is made by reference to coined or to bar gold.*

When money is wanted for our own circulation I do not object to the calculation of the true par of exchange being made, on a comparison of the relative value of the silver of the foreign country with the value of standard gold bars in this; but in that case there must be added to the amount of expences attending the transportation of the silver, the interest which the purchaser of gold will lose, during the detention of the gold in the Mint whilst coining into money. The natural destination of a great part of all the bar gold is to some of the

---

* Mr. Mushet's calculations take for granted, that the relative value of gold and silver was the same in both countries, and that the gold and silver were of the same description, viz. in bars. But it is chiefly by the value of gold in coin that a foreigner determines whether he shall export gold to this country, or make a remittance by bill, and the price of gold in coin in England must necessarily enter into his calculation. On a reference to the Appendix of the Bullion Report, No. 6, it will appear that the transactions in gold with the continent are mostly confined to gold in coin. For 15 months, ending in March 1810, the whole amount of sales of bar gold, by private dealers, transacted through the Bullion Office at the Bank, did not exceed in value 60,867l., whilst the sales of gold in coin during the same period amounted to 683,067l.

Mints of Europe, as it is in the state of coin only that gold can be made productive of interest to the owner. In comparing, therefore, the value of the currency of one country with the value of bullion in another, we must not leave out of our consideration the trifling superior value which coin bears above bullion in the importing country. Thus, if a merchant in Hamburgh were indebted 1*l*. sterling to a merchant in England, and should export to England as much silver as would purchase the quantity of gold contained in 1*l*., he would not be able to discharge his debt till the gold were manufactured into coin. In addition, then, to his other expences, the interest which he would have to pay to his creditor till the coin was returned to him would enter into his calculation at the time that he was making a comparison of the advantages which would attend either the purchase of a bill, or the remittance of bullion.

This loss of interest the Bullion Committee have estimated at one per cent.[1]

If these principles are correct, there must be deducted from the favourable Hamburgh exchanges of Mr. Mushet's tables 1 per cent. more than we have already stated when the bullion is wanted for our own coin, and from 2 to 3 per cent. when it is required for re-exportation. It is also necessary to observe, that the relative value of gold to silver is constantly varying in all countries, though always tending in all to an equality of value; and that the test of our currency being depreciated is more certainly proved by the high market price of bullion than by the low exchanges*.

* I have read in a small French tract, "Sur L'Institution des Principales Banques de L'Europe,"[2] that on one occasion the Bank of Hamburgh was obliged to suspend its payments in consequence of having made too great advances on gold bullion. I have in vain endeavoured to find out

[1] *Report*, p. 12.
[2] *Considérations sur l'institution des principales banques de l'Europe, particulièrement sur celle de France;*   *ses statuts, son administration, sa solidité et son crédit,* par M. Monbrion, Paris, an XIV, 1805, p. 23.

SECTION II

Exchange with Paris.

Having thus examined the objections made by Mr. Bosanquet to the conclusions of the Committee, as far as the exchanges with Hamburgh are concerned, I shall now proceed to consider the circumstances which appear to him to be at variance with the principle I am defending, in the account of the exchanges between this country and Paris.

In the consideration of the par of exchange with Hamburgh, the principle on which it is calculated is easy and simple, not so that with Paris. The difficulty proceeds from this—that France as well as England has two metals, gold and silver, in circulation, both of which are legal tender in all payments.

In my former publication[1] I endeavoured to explain the principles which appeared to me to fix the standard measure of value in a country where silver and gold are both in circulation, and both a legal tender.

Lord Liverpool supposed,[2] that when gold became the standard measure of value in this country, it arose from some capricious preference of the people to gold; but it can, I think, be clearly proved that it was caused entirely from the circumstance of the market value of silver relatively to gold having become greater than the Mint proportions. This principle is not only most fully admitted, but also most ably illustrated by his lordship.

in what year this occurred. It is evident that a circumstance of this sort must have had some influence on the exchange,—and it is not impossible that it might have happened in the years 1766-7.[3]

[1] *High Price of Bullion,* above, p. 65 ff.

[2] Cp. above, p. 66.

[3] The Bank of Hamburg did in fact suspend specie payments in 1766 and resumed them by a decision of the Hamburg Senate of 9 December 1767. See A. Soetbeer, 'Die Hamburger Bank', in *Vierteljahrsschrift für Volkswirthschaft,* 1866, vol. III, pp. 42-3.

The Mint will coin an ounce of gold into 3*l.* 17*s.* 10½*d.* of gold money, and they will also coin 15.07 ounces of silver into the same amount of silver money. What is it, then, that determines the Bank or any individual to carry an ounce of gold in preference to 15.07 ounces of silver to the Mint to be coined, as they are both by law equally useful to discharge a debt to the amount of 3*l.* 17*s.* 10½*d.*? No other consideration but their interest. If 15.07 ounces of silver can be purchased for less than an ounce of gold, silver will be coined; and if an ounce of gold can be procured for less than 15.07 ounces of silver, gold will be taken to the Mint for that purpose.

In the first case silver will become the measure of value, in the second, gold.

Now as the relative market value of these metals is subject to constant variation, gold or silver may alternately become the standard measure of value. Since the recoinage of silver, in the reign of King William, an ounce of[1] gold has almost uniformly been of less value than 15.07 ounces of silver, and consequently gold has, since that period, been the standard of value in this country. In the year 1798 the coinage of silver was altogether prohibited by law. Whilst that law remains in force gold must necessarily be the standard measure, whatever may be the variations in the relative value of the two metals*.

Whichever metal is the standard measure of value, it will

---

* The Bullion Committee,[2] as well as Mr. Huskisson,[3] consider gold as the standard measure of value, in consequence of the 39th of the king, which declares that silver shall not be a legal tender for sums exceeding 25*l.* except by weight at the rate of 5*s.* 2*d.* per ounce. But this law would not have prevented the coinage of silver when under its mint price, and, therefore, under its mint relative value to gold. In 1798, for example, when the price of silver was 5*s.* per ounce, and the relative market value of silver to gold as 1 to 15.57, and when therefore silver could be profitably coined, the new silver fresh from the Mint would have been a legal tender to any amount.

[1] 'an ounce of' had been omitted in the text, and was added in *Errata.*
[2] *Report,* p. 10.
[3] *The Question,* etc., p. 6.

also regulate the par of exchange with foreign countries, because it will be in that metal, or in paper currency representing
that metal, that bills will be paid.

In France there are also two metals in circulation, and both
legal tender to any amount. The relative value of gold to silver
in the coins of France, previously to the Revolution, was as
15 to 1 (Bullion Report, No. 59.), and is now 15½ to 1;—but
we are informed by a letter of Mr. Grefulhe to the Bullion
Committee (No. 56.), that in 1785 an alteration had been made
in the number of louis which were coined from a marc of gold,
that number having been increased from 30 to 32. Previously
to 1785, therefore, gold must have been valued in the French
Mint somewhere about 14 to 1. For the same reasons that the
standard of value was subject to change from gold to silver,
and from silver to gold in England, it would also be subject
to do so in France. When the relative value of gold to silver
was under 14 to 1, gold would have become the standard
measure of value in France, and consequently the rate of
exchange with England would have been estimated by a comparison of the gold coins of the two countries. When above
14 and under 15.07 to 1, gold would have been the standard
in England, and silver in France, and the exchange rated
accordingly. The par would then have been fixed by a comparison of the gold of England with the silver of France. And
when the relative value was above 15.07 to 1, silver would have
been the standard in both countries. The exchange would then
have been rated in silver. But after 1785, when the Mint
valuation of the metals was altered in France, and became
nearly the same as that of England, the par of exchange would
have been reckoned either in gold or in silver in both countries.

I have already observed[1] that, to compare the amount of
deviation of the exchange from par with the expences of trans-

[1] Above, pp. 174–5.

mitting the precious metals from one country to the other is not sufficient to prove that such trade would be profitable, we must also consider what the price of bullion is in the country to which it is transmitted, or the amount of expence which would be incurred in procuring the bullion to be coined into money. In this country no seignorage is charged. If an ounce of gold or silver is carried to the Mint, an ounce of coined money is returned. The only inconvenience therefore that an importer of bullion can experience in receiving bullion from abroad, instead of the money of England, is the delay during its detention at the Mint, and which the Bullion Committee have valued at 1 per cent.[1] One per cent. appears, therefore, to be the natural value of English coin above bullion, provided the coin be not debased, and the currency be not excessive. But in France the seignorage, according to Dr. Smith, amounted to no less than 8 per cent., besides the loss of interest during its detention at the Mint. And we have his authority too, that no sensible inconvenience resulted from it*.[2] An ounce of gold or silver coin was in France, therefore, of more value by 8 per cent. than an ounce of gold or silver bullion. It results from these facts that no bullion could have been imported into France, unless there was not only a profit equal to the expences

* Since writing the above I have seen an extract from a Moniteur of the year 1803,[3] by which it appears that the seignorage in France was

	In 1726 on gold	$7\frac{9}{16}$ per c.	on silver	$7\frac{4}{11}$
1729	,,	$5\frac{3}{16}$	,, ,,	$5\frac{7}{16}$
1755	,,	$4\frac{1}{16}$	,, ,,	$3\frac{10}{11}$
1771	,,	$1\frac{4}{7}$	,, ,,	$2\frac{7}{9}$
1785	,,	$2\frac{9}{17}$	,, ,,	—

And was fixed in 1803 at $\frac{1}{3}$ per c. for gold, and $1\frac{1}{2}$ for silver.

[1] *Report*, p. 12.
[2] *Wealth of Nations*, Bk. IV, ch. vi, art. iii; Cannan's ed., vol. II, p. 53.
[3] *Gazette Nationale ou le Moniteur Universel*, 8 Germinal, An XI (29 March 1803), vol. 28, pp. 842–4, reports a speech by Darn in the Tribunat which contains the table reproduced here. There is among Ricardo's papers a summary of this speech in Ricardo's handwriting.

attending its importation, but a further profit of 8 per cent., the par of exchange being calculated not on the value which the coin actually passed for in currency, but on its intrinsic value as bullion*.

To make this appear more evident, let us suppose that the exchange with London was, as Mr. Bosanquet informs us,[1] 8 per cent. in favour of France, in the year 1767, and that at the same time it was 6 per cent. in favour of London with Hamburgh, and that the expences of sending gold from Hamburgh to Paris were no more than 1½ per cent. Will it not be cheaper, he asks, by 12½ per cent. to pay the debt at Paris, by sending the gold from Hamburgh †, than by remitting a bill? I answer, No; because, when the gold arrives at Paris, it must either be coined into money, or sold as bullion. If it be coined into money, 8 per cent. must be paid to the Mint; if it be sold as bullion, it will sell at 8 per cent. under the Mint price‡. The profit then, if all the other calculations be correct,

* It is only whilst the currency of France was kept at its proper level that the price of gold could continue 8 per cent. under the Mint price, in the same manner as the price of gold would and did continue under the Mint price of England. The currency of England was rather above its level when gold was 3*l.* 17*s.* 6*d.*, as 4*d.* an ounce is not sufficient compensation for the delay of the Mint. It follows therefore that the principle here contended for can only have its full force whilst the currency is not excessive.

† As silver is the currency of Hamburgh, it would be silver, and not gold, which an English creditor would be entitled to send from Hamburgh to Paris.

‡ "In France, a duty of 8 per cent. is deducted for the coinage, which not only defrays the expence of it, but affords a small revenue to the government. In England, as the coinage costs nothing, the current coin can never be much more valuable than the quantity of bullion which it actually contains. In France, the workmanship, as you pay for it, adds to the value, in the same manner as to that of wrought plate. A sum of French money, therefore, containing a certain weight of pure silver is more valuable than a sum of English money containing an equal weight of pure silver, and must require more bullion, or other commodities, to purchase it. Though the current coin of the two countries, therefore,

[1] p. 17.

will be reduced from $12\frac{1}{2}$ to $4\frac{1}{2}$ per cent. But they are not correct, being subject to further deductions from the causes already stated.

Keeping these principles in view, it will, I believe, appear, that the exchange with Paris was in favour of England during a great portion of the four years, from 1764 to 1768, and at all the other periods mentioned by Mr. Bosanquet.

I cannot help here observing, that it must excite astonishment, that a British merchant should seriously believe it possible, that, in time of peace, a net profit, after paying all expences, of from $10\frac{1}{2}$ to $12\frac{1}{2}$ per cent. should have been made by the exportation of gold from Hamburgh to Paris during four years; —a profit, which, from the quick returns, would have enabled any person engaging in such undertakings to have cleared more than 100 per cent. per ann. on the capital employed; and that too in a trade, the slightest fluctuations of which are watched by a class of men proverbial for their shrewdness, and in which competition is carried to the greatest extent. For any man to compare the account of the Hamburgh exchange, and of the Parisian, and not to see that the accounts were incorrect, that the facts could not be as so stated, is very like a man who is all for fact and nothing for theory. Such men can hardly ever sift their facts. They are credulous, and necessarily so, because they have no standard of reference. Those two sets of sup-

were equally near the standards of their respective Mints, a sum of English money could not well purchase a sum of French money, containing an equal number of ounces of pure silver, nor, consequently, a bill upon France for such a sum. If for such a bill no more additional money was paid than what was sufficient to compensate the expence of French coinage, the real exchange might be at par between the two countries, their debts and credits might mutually compensate one another, while the computed exchange was considerably in favour of France. If less than this was paid, the real exchange might be in favour of England, while the computed was in favour of France."—*Wealth of Nations*, Chap. iii. Book iv.[1]

[1] Cannan's ed., vol. I, p. 442.

posed facts, those in the Hamburgh exchange on the one hand, and those in the Parisian on the other, are absolutely inconsistent, and disprove one another. That facts such as these should be brought forward to invalidate a theory, the reasonableness of which is allowed, is a melancholy proof of the power of prejudice over very enlightened minds.

SECTION III

Supposed Fact of a Premium on English Currency in America—favourable Exchange with Sweden.

The next point on which I wish to make a few observations, is that first mentioned by Mr. Grefulhe,[1] and now brought forward by Mr. Bosanquet. I allude to the premium which it is asserted was given in America, in hard dollars, for the depreciated currency of England. I have examined this fact with the greatest attention, and to me it appears evident; first, that the price which was called a premium of 9 per cent. given for a bill upon England *was really a discount* of $3\frac{1}{4}$ per cent.; and secondly, that at that price it was a cheaper remittance than if the dollars with which the bill was bought had been exported.

The par of exchange with America is reckoned in dollars; the par is called 4*s.* 6*d.* sterling for a dollar, consequently, 444.4 dollars ought to contain as much pure silver as 100*l.* sterling. But this is not the fact. An American dollar, according to the mint regulation of America, ought to weigh 17 dwt. 8 grains, and is $8\frac{1}{2}$ dwts.[2] worse than English standard silver; consequently, the value of an American dollar in our standard silver is 4*s.* $3\frac{3}{4}d.$ According to this value, 463.7 dollars is the true par for 100*l.* of our English silver currency; but we are comparing the dollars of America with the pound sterling of

---

[1] In his evidence to the Bullion Committee, 'Minutes', p. 71, quoted by Bosanquet, p. 20.

[2] Misprinted '$8\frac{1}{4}$ grains': corrected in *Errata.*

England, which is gold, therefore, the true par for 100*l.* sterling at the relative value of dollars and gold in May 1809, the period alluded to, was 500 dollars. Now for a bill of 100*l.* on London, bought with dollars in America at the highest exchange that year, viz. 109, no more was paid than 484 dollars; it was therefore purchased at 3¼ per cent. under the real par*.

It should be recollected that the embargo laws were at that time most strictly enforced; that captains of packets were obliged, before they were permitted to proceed on their voyage, to swear that they had no specie on board; and on one occasion one of these captains was obliged to re-land the specie which he had smuggled on board his vessel. At the same time the rate of insurance was immoderately high, and a premium of 8 per cent. was paid on a few ships which broke the embargo, the underwriters being guaranteed too from the loss which would have attended their seizure by the American government. Now 8 per cent. insurance, besides commission, freight, and other expences, together with 3¼ per cent., the actual discount of the bill bought, would, perhaps, not be much under the discount which then existed on our paper currency; so that our depreciated paper was not bought at a premium for hard dollars, but was bought at a discount, and at its actual value.

But we are told[1] the exchange with Sweden is favourable to England, and that the currency of Sweden is regulated in a manner precisely similar to ours, the Bank not issuing specie whenever the exchange becomes unfavourable. There is no

---

* The weight of the American dollar in circulation is not more, according to Mr. Williams's evidence,[2] than 17 dwt. 6 gr., which would make the true par somewhat lower than 4*s.* 3¼*d.*; and, according to Ede's book of Coins,[3] the American dollar is 11 dwts.[4] worse than standard, and contains no more pure silver than 4*s.* 2¼*d.* of English standard silver coin.

[1] Bosanquet, pp. 20–21.
[2] 'Minutes of Evidence', p. 141.
[3] *A View of the Gold and Silver Coins of all Nations...*, by Js. Ede,
London, J. M. Richardson, n.d. [1808], p. 8.
[4] Misprinted '11 grains': corrected in *Errata.*

doubt a perfect agreement in the two cases, and for that reason they are followed by similar effects, and the depreciation of both currencies requires the same remedy. This remedy is a diminution in the amount of the circulating medium, either by the exportation of the coins, or by a reduction of Bank paper. If the exchange with Sweden is, as stated, 24 per cent. in favour of London, it proves only that the excess of paper currency not convertible into specie is, in Sweden, proportionably greater than in England*.

SECTION IV

A Statement, concerning the Par of Exchange, by the Bullion Committee, examined.

Having now considered every fact, or supposed fact, advanced by Mr. Bosanquet on the subject of the exchange, with a view to prove that the principle which the Committee have avowed, namely, that the variations in the exchange with foreign countries can never exceed for any length of time the expence of transporting and insuring the precious metals; having proved the conclusion to which the writer would lead us to be unsupported by his facts, of which not one is, as I think, at variance with the principle of the Committee; I must beg leave to point out an error in the report itself, an error on which Mr. Bosanquet founds his opinion, that all remedy may safely be delayed.

"Thus, then," says Mr. Bosanquet,[1] "it appears that, on a full admission of all the principles adopted by the Committee, and of their application to the present case, the foreign exchanges were at the time when the report was presented, and

* Before however it can be admitted that the exchange with Sweden is 24 per cent. in favour of London, we must be informed whether both gold and silver be legal tender in Sweden, and, if so, at what relative value those metals are rated in the Swedish Mint. I suspect that a part of this favourable exchange may be accounted for by the rise in the relative value of gold to silver.

[1] pp. 14–15.

for three months prior thereto, about 2 per cent. below the natural limit of depression."

"It will probably be thought that the question, as a practical question of national importance, is altogether at rest.—That there is no necessity, at least, for the adoption of hasty remedies, even though the correctness of the general reasoning of the Committee should, on full enquiry, be conceded."

When the exchange is admitted to be exceedingly depressed, we are told that to oblige the Bank to pay in specie would be attended with the most dangerous consequences; that we must wait till the exchange becomes more favourable; and when it is supposed to have risen within 2 per cent. of its natural limit, then we are again desired to pause, because it is no longer a question of national importance. By this mode of reasoning, a motive may be found for refusing *ad infinitum* to renew the payments of the Bank. I confidently hope that no such fallacious reasoning will be listened to; that we shall at last open our eyes to the dangers that beset us,—that we shall examine coolly and decide manfully.

The principle upon which Mr. Mushet's amended tables are constructed has been most fully admitted, and most correctly and concisely stated in the Report (page 10).[1]

"If one country uses gold for its principal measure of value, and another uses silver, the par between those countries cannot be estimated for any particular period, without taking into account the relative value of gold and silver at that particular period."

The Committee have, moreover, in their endeavours to find out the real par between this country and Hamburgh, kept this principle constantly in view, as will appear from the questions put to Mr. ——, (Report, page 73).[2] Mr. —— also fully

---

[1] Octavo ed., p. 23.

[2] Octavo ed., 'Minutes of Evidence', p. 78.

admitted the principle, and yet, when he was requested to "state in what manner he applied those general ideas to the statement of the par of exchange as between England and Hamburgh," he answered, "taking gold at the coinage price of 3*l*. 17*s*. 10½*d*., and taking it at Hamburgh at what we call its par, which is 96 stivers banco for a ducat, and further reducing 55 ounces of standard gold as being equal to 459 ducats, it produces a par of exchange of 34*s*. 3½*g*. Flemish for a pound sterling: a ducat contains at the rate of 23½ carats fine."

Now here is not one word said about the relative value of gold to silver in the market, and the only information which is obtained from this answer is, that 34*s*. 3½*g*. Flemish, in gold coin, is equal to a pound sterling of gold;—and this calculation agrees within ½ grote with that of Dr. Kelly (Rep. No. 59). If the purchaser of a bill in London for 34*s*. 3*g*. could obtain at Hamburgh 34*s*. 3*g*. in gold currency, that might truly be called the par, but he can only obtain 34*s*. 3*g*. in silver, which is not worth by 8 per cent. as much as 34*s*. 3*g*. in gold coin. The question proposed by the Committee was, in effect, What amount of Hamburgh currency contains the same quantity of pure silver as can be purchased by a pound sterling in gold?

At the period when the report was made, the answer would have been 37*s*. 3*g*. Flemish; 37*s*. 3*g*. therefore was then the true par of exchange. If the Committee had calculated according to this par, instead of 34*s*. 3*g*., they would not have reported that the exchange with Hamburgh was not more unfavourable to England than 9 per cent., but nearly 17 per cent.; and Mr. Bosanquet would not have had an opportunity for observing, that, admitting the reasoning of the Committee, the evil was not of sufficient magnitude to make any immediate interference necessary.

CHAPTER III

SECTION I

That the Negation of the above Conclusion implies the Impossibility of melting or exporting English Coin—an Impossibility contended for by Nobody.

THE next proposition of the Committee, the justness of which Mr. Bosanquet disputes, he has thus stated: "That the price of gold bullion can never exceed the Mint price, unless the currency in which it is paid is depreciated below the value of gold." But this is not exactly the principle of the Committee. Their principle, when fairly stated, is, not that gold as a commodity may not rise above its value as coin, but that it cannot continue so, because the convertibility of coin into bullion would soon equalize their value. The words of the Committee are these; "Your Committee are of opinion that, in the sound and natural state of the British currency, the foundation of which is gold, no increased demand for gold from other parts of the world, however great, or from whatever causes arising, can have the effect of producing here, *for a considerable period of time*, a material rise in the market price of gold."[1] Nothing appears to me to be wanting to make this a self-evident proposition but the admission, that the law, which forbids the conversion of gold coin into gold bullion, cannot be successfully executed.

I should have expected, therefore, that any one who denied its truth would have contended that the law was fully efficient

[1] *Report*, pp. 4–5; Ricardo's italics.

for the purposes for which it was enacted; and that he would have brought forward authorities to justify this view which he had taken of it. But authorities for such an opinion would have been difficult to have been found. From the days of Locke till the present time I have nowhere seen the fact disputed. It is by all writers indiscriminately allowed, that no penalties can prevent the coin from being melted when its value as bullion becomes superior to its value as coin.

Locke calls the law which forbids the melting and exporting coin, "a law to hedge in the cuckoo."[1] Smith observes, "that no precautions of government can prevent it."[2] On this subject too we have the authority of practical men:

The Bank Directors, in the year 1795, when the price of gold rose to $4l.$ $3s.$ or $4l.$ $4s.$ per ounce, after acquainting Mr. Pitt with that fact, observe, "our guineas being to be purchased at $3l.$ $17s.$ $10\frac{1}{2}d.$ per ounce, clearly demonstrates the grounds of our fears; it being only necessary to state those facts to the Chancellor of the Exchequer."[3] Now, what were those fears, but that there would be a run upon them for gold coin, for the purpose of melting it into bullion? Mr. Newland, too, when asked (by the Committee of the Lords, 1797),[4] "If there were now to be a new coinage, do you think a great deal would be melted down and privately exported?" Answered, "That depends entirely upon the price of bullion." In the same Committee Mr. Newland was also asked, "Is it more difficult to prevent false coining, or to prevent the melting down or exporting, when it is for their advantage to export it?"—Answer. "I am at a loss to guess how you can prevent either."

[1] *Some Considerations on the Consequences of the Lowering of Interest and Raising the Value of Money*, 2nd ed., London, 1696, p. 24.
[2] Bk. IV, ch. vi, art. iii; vol. II, p. 52.
[3] 'Report of the Lords' Committee of Secrecy relating to the Bank', 1797 (reprint 1810), p. 84.
[4] *ib.* p. 40.

These are but a few of the opinions which might be brought forward in support of the fact of the coin being melted into bullion whenever the price of bullion rises above the price of coin. I shall conclude, however, with the opinion of Mr. Bosanquet himself. Speaking of the Committee, he observes, "They say nothing about the price of bullion, which is expected, doubtless, to return when the Bank shall have sufficiently controuled the exchange; although Mr. Locke and many other writers have clearly demonstrated that the coins of any country can only be retained within it when the general balance of trade and payments is not unfavourable."[1] Now, under the circumstances supposed of a low exchange, what should take our coins from us but their superior value as bullion? Who would export coins if bullion could be bought at its Mint price? It is their superior value as bullion, therefore, that is the cause of their being melted and exported.

But the Committee have not been satisfied with simply stating a position which is almost self-evident; they have appealed to facts, and distinctly assert,[2] that for a period of 24 years, since the recoinage, gold bullion in standard bars had not been at a higher price than 3*l*. 17*s*. 10½*d*. per ounce, with the exception of one year, beginning in May 1783 and ending in May 1784, when the price was 3*l*. 18*s*. per ounce. We are indeed informed by a letter from the Bank Directors to Mr. Pitt in October 1795, and it is on that authority reported by the Committee, that gold bullion was then as high as 4*l*. 3*s*. or 4*l*. 4*s*. per ounce; and it was stated by Mr. Newland to the Lords' Committee in 1797, that the Bank had been frequently obliged to buy gold higher than the Mint price; and

---

[1] pp. 104–5. The words following 'although' are quoted by Bosanquet from Lord Liverpool's *Treatise on the Coins of the Realm*, p. 109.
[2] *Bullion Report*, pp. 7–8.

upon one occasion gave as much for a small quantity, which their agent procured in Portugal, as 4*l.* 8*s.**

These are the only facts on which Mr. Bosanquet relies for overturning the principle in question. Prices not known to the public; not recorded in any list; given too by a corporation not remarkable for the good management of their concerns, are to be deemed the fair market price; and such exceptions as these are to overturn opinions grounded on a just theory, sanctioned by practical men, and confirmed by experience.

Is there any evidence that these prices continued even for a week? If we consult the price list, we shall find, that in July

* It appears that it was in 1795, and most probably in October, that the Bank gave 4*l.* 8*s.* for gold, as stated by Mr. Newland. On being asked concerning the time by the Lords' Committee, he answered, "I believe it was about two years since the Bank gave about 4*l.* 8*s.* per ounce for gold; it was but a small quantity, it was soon stopt on account of its price. The Bank at that time thought it expedient to obtain gold from Portugal, which their agent could not do at a less price than 4*l.* 8*s.*"[1]

Mr. Newland was speaking on the 28th March, 1797.

It is a case by no means improbable that the Bank may frequently have bought foreign gold above the Mint price, at the same time that they could have obtained gold in bars, not exportable, at a comparatively cheaper price. They might flatter themselves that, by not purchasing English gold, they would lessen the temptation to melt the guineas: at the same time their diminished stock required them to replenish their coffers. This opinion is very much confirmed by an examination of the account in the Appendix of the Bullion Report, No. 19, where it appears, that from 1797 to 1810 the amount in value of gold coined at his Majesty's Mint was 8,960,113,11*l.*, of which only 2,296,056 was coined from English gold, the remainder, 7,044,282 was coined from foreign gold.[2] It appears too that since 1804, 1,402,542*l.* has been coined from foreign gold, and not one guinea from British gold. During the whole of this period the price of foreign gold in the market exceeded the price of English gold. Is it not probable, therefore, that the Bank, who are the only importers of gold into the Mint, have been guided by some such policy as I have supposed?

[1] 'Report of the Lords' Committee', 1797 (reprint 1810), p. 40.
[2] According to the Appendix referred to, the two latter figures represent not the amounts of gold coined but the amounts received by the Mint, which accounts for the discrepancy in the sum.

of that year 1795, the price of gold is quoted 3*l*. 17*s*. 6*d*.; in
December it is again quoted 3*l*. 17*s*. 6*d*., and in the intervening
four months no price is marked. Does Mr. Bosanquet think
it possible that such a price as 4*l*. 4*s*. for gold could have continued, whilst it was to be obtained, by melting the coin, at
3*l*. 17*s*. 10½*d*.? Has he so good an opinion of the self-denial
and virtues of all classes of the community? If he has, why
are they not now to be trusted? What is the plea urged for
not paying in specie? That at the present exchange, and present
price of gold, it would be advantageous to export and melt the
coin, so that there would be danger that every guinea would
leave the country. But when you tell us, that bullion has no
connection with coin, "that there is no point of contact between
English and foreign gold,"[1] there can be no danger of any
one's being particularly desirous to possess coin, as, for the
mere purposes of circulation, Bank notes are equally, if not
more, convenient.

"*If*," says Mr. Bosanquet,[2] "the demand for foreign gold
was at any time very great, and the melting and exportation
of guineas, however abundant, by any means effectually
prevented, foreign gold might rise to[3] double its price in
English gold, and yet the intrinsic value of guineas remain
undiminished."

I might apply to this *if* of Mr. Bosanquet the observation
which he has made on the same word, when used by the Committee, *your, if, is, a great peace-maker*.[4] But the above is not
our case; the law cannot be effectually enforced. The remark,
therefore, is of no use in the question before us.

If the law, however, could be effectually enforced, it would
be attended with the most cruel injustice. Why should not the
holder of an ounce of gold in coin have the same advantages

[1] In substance, Bosanquet, p. 31.
[2] pp. 31–2. Ricardo's italics.
[3] 'rise to' is not in Bosanquet.
[4] Bosanquet, p. 99.

from the increase in the value of his property, as the holder of an ounce of uncoined gold? From the mere circumstance of its having had a stamp put on it, is he to be made to suffer all the inconveniences from the *fall* in the value of his gold, in consequence of the opening of new mines, or from any other circumstances? and derive none of the benefits which may result from a *rise* in its value? This injustice to individuals would not be compensated by the slightest advantages to the community; as the exportation of the coin, were it freely permitted, would always cease when the value of our currency had risen to its true bullion value, and that is precisely the value at which the currencies of all countries are permanently fixed.

Such, in spite of the law, was the value of our currency till the Bank restriction bill, and for some time after. There it would inevitably fix itself again, if that most impolitic act were repealed. Increase the value of your currency to its proper level, and you are sure to retain it. No policy can be worse than forcibly detaining a million, for example, to perform those offices, to which 800,000*l.* are fully adequate.

SECTION II

Consequences which would follow on the Supposition that the Currencies of other Countries (exclusive of England) were diminished or increased one half.

Let us suppose that the circulation of all countries were carried on by the precious metals only, and that the proportion which England possessed were one million; let us further suppose, that, at once, half of the currencies of all countries, excepting that of England, were suddenly annihilated, would it be possible for England to continue to retain the million which she before possessed? Would not her currency become relatively excessive compared with that of other countries? If a quarter of wheat, for example, had been both in France and England of the same value as an ounce of coined gold, would not half an ounce now purchase it in France, whilst in England it continued of the same value as one ounce*? Could we by any laws, under such circumstances, prevent wheat or some other commodity (for all would be equally affected) from being imported into England, and gold coin from being exported? If we could, and the exportation of bullion were free, gold might rise 100 per cent.; and for the same reason, if 35 Flemish schillings in Hamburgh had before been of equal value with a pound sterling, $17\frac{1}{2}$ schillings would now attain that value. If the currency of England only had been doubled, the effects would have been precisely the same.

Suppose again the case reversed, and that all other currencies remained as before, while half of that of England was retrenched. If the coinage of money at the Mint was on the present footing, would not the prices of commodities be so reduced here that their cheapness would invite foreign purchasers, and would not this continue till the relative proportions in the different currencies were restored?

If such would be the effects of a diminution of money below its natural level, and that such would be the consequences the most celebrated writers on political economy are agreed, how

---

* That commodities would rise or fall in price, in proportion to the increase or diminution of money, I assume as a fact which is incontrovertible.—Mr. Bosanquet in his admission[1] of the effects on prices from the discovery of a mine shews, that he has no such doubts on this subject as the governor of the Bank, who, when asked by the Committee, "Do you conceive that a very considerable reduction of the amount of the circulating medium would not tend in any degree to increase its relative value compared with commodities, and that a considerable increase of it would have no tendency whatever to augment the price of commodities in exchange for such circulating medium?"—Answered, "It is a subject on which such a variety of opinions are entertained, I do not feel myself competent to give a decided answer."[2]

[1] See quotation below, pp. 215–16.   [2] *Bullion Report*, 'Minutes of Evidence', p. 187.

can it be justly contended that the increase or diminution of money has nothing to do either with the foreign exchanges, or with the price of bullion?

Now a paper circulation, not convertible into specie, differs in its effects in no respect from a metallic currency, with the law against exportation strictly executed.

Supposing then the first case to occur whilst our circulation consisted wholly of paper, would not the exchanges fall, and the price of bullion rise in the manner which I have been representing; and would not our currency be depreciated, because it was no longer of the same value in the markets of the world as the bullion which it professed to represent? The fact of depreciation could not be denied, however the Bank Directors might assure the public that they never discounted but good bills for bonâ fide transactions; however they might assert that they never forced a note into circulation; that the quantity of money was no more than it had always been, and was only adequate to the wants of commerce, which had increased and not diminished*; that the price of gold, which was here at twice its mint value, was equally high, or higher, abroad, as might be proved by sending an ounce of bullion to Hamburgh, and having the produce remitted by bill payable in London in bank-notes; and that the increase or diminution of their

* The Bank could not on their own principles then urge that most erroneous opinion, that the rate of interest would be affected in the money market if their issues were excessive, and would therefore cause their notes to return to them, because in the case here supposed the actual amount of the money of the world being greatly diminished, they must contend that the rate of interest would generally rise, and they might therefore increase their issues. If after the able exposition of Dr. Smith[1] any further argument were necessary to prove that the rate of interest is governed wholly by the relation of the amount of capital with the means of employing it, and is entirely independent of the abundance or scarcity of the circulating medium, this illustration would, I think, afford it.

[1] Bk. II, ch. iv; vol. I, p. 335.

notes could not possibly either affect the exchange or the price of bullion. All this, except the last, might be true, and yet would any man refuse his assent to the fact of the currency being depreciated? Could the symptoms which I have been enumerating proceed from any other cause but a relative excess in our currency? Could our currency be restored to its bullion value by any other means than by a reduction in its quantity, which should raise it to the value of the currencies of other countries; or by the increase of the precious metals, which should lower the value of theirs to the level of ours?

Why will not the Bank try the experiment by a reduction in the amount of their notes of two or three millions for the short period of three months? If no effects were produced on the price of bullion and the foreign exchange, then might their friends boast that the principles of the Bullion Committee were the wild dreams of speculative theorists.

SECTION III

The trifling Rise in the Price of Gold on the Continent, owing solely to a Variation in the Relation of Silver to Gold.

But the price of gold, we are told,[1] has risen on the continent even more than it has here, because when it was 4*l*. 12*s*. in this country, 4*l*. 17*s*. might be procured for it at Hamburgh, a difference of 5½ per cent. This is so often repeated, and is so wholly fallacious, that it may be proper to give it particular consideration.

When an ounce of gold was to be bought in this country at 3*l*. 17*s*. 10½*d*, and the relative value of gold was to silver as 15.07 to 1, it would have sold on the continent for nearly the same as here, or 3*l*. 17*s*. 10½ in silver coin. In Hamburgh, for example, we should have received in payment of an ounce of gold 136 Flemish schillings and 7 grotes, that quantity of

---

[1] Bosanquet, p. 24.

silver containing an equal quantity of pure metal, as $3l.$ $17s.$ $10\frac{1}{2}d.$ in our standard silver coin.

Gold has since that period risen in this country 18 per cent, and is now at $4l.$ $12s.$ per ounce, and it is said that the $4l.$ $12s.$ with which it is paid for is not depreciated. Now as gold has risen $5\frac{1}{2}$ more abroad than it has here, it must be there $23\frac{1}{2}$ per cent higher than when it was sold for $136s.$ $7g.$, and we therefore should be led to expect that we should now obtain for it at Hamburgh 167 Flemish schillings: but what is the fact? this ounce of gold, which we are told we sell at Hamburgh for $4l.$ $17s.$, actually produces no more than 140 schillings 8 grotes, an advance only of 3 per cent.; and for this the seller is indebted to the rise in the relative value of gold to silver, which from 15.07 to 1 is now about 16 to 1. It is true, that when the ounce of gold was sold at Hamburgh at $3l.$ $17s.$ $10\frac{1}{2}d.$ or for its equivalent, 136 schillings 7 grotes, the currency of England was not depreciated; that sum, therefore, could only purchase a bill payable in London in Bank notes for $3l.$ $17s.$ $10\frac{1}{2}d.$; but the currency of England being now depreciated, and being estimated on the Hamburgh exchange at 28 or 29 Flemish schillings, instead of 37, the true value of a pound sterling, 140 schillings 8 grotes, or 3 per cent. more than $136s.$ $7g.$ will now purchase a bill payable in London in Bank notes for $4l.$ $17s.$; so that gold has not risen more than 3 per cent. in Hamburgh, but the currency of England, on a comparison with the currency of Hamburgh, has fallen $23\frac{1}{2}$ per cent.

In further proof of the truth of my assertion, that it is not gold which has risen 16 or 18 per cent. in the general market of the world, but that it is the paper currency in which the price of gold is estimated in England, which alone has fallen; I will subjoin an account of the lowest prices of gold in Hamburgh, Holland, and England, in the year 1804, and the highest prices in each of those countries in the year 1810, by which we shall be enabled to ascertain the actual rise in the price of gold measured in the currencies of each. This account was furnished to the Bullion Committee by Mr. Grefulhe, and is numbered 56.

	lowest price.	highest price.	
Hamburgh	1804—97$\frac{3}{8}$	1810—101 being a rise of 3$\frac{3}{4}$ per cent.	
Holland	1804—392$\frac{1}{4}$	1810—406$\frac{7}{16}$	3$\frac{5}{8}$
England	1804—4l.	1810—4l. 13s.	16

Now in Hamburgh and in Holland, where the currency is silver, gold may not rise 3 per cent. only, but 30 per cent., without its being any proof of the depreciation of the currency; it proves only an improvement in the relative value of gold to silver. But in England, where the price of gold is estimated in gold coin, or in Bank notes representing that coin, a rise of 1 per cent. cannot take place without its proving a corresponding *depression** of the coin or paper. This observation is equally applicable to the fact mentioned by Mr. Bosanquet,[1] and of which he himself seems aware, of gold having varied in Hamburgh no less than 8 per cent. within a period of two years.

As there is an acknowledged difference between the price of standard gold bars and the price of gold coin reduced to the English standard, arising out of the latter being a more marketable commodity on the continent †; I cannot admit the inferences which Mr. Bosanquet draws from the comparison of Mr. Grefulhe's paper (No. 58), with the paper No. 60, in the Report. It would be first necessary to ascertain whether the prices of gold, as quoted in these papers (and they do not quite agree), were for gold in coin, or for gold of any other

---

* This expression has been noticed by Mr. Bosanquet[2] as extremely theoretical, but I consider it so exceedingly correct that I have taken the liberty of using it after the Committee.

† See note to page [174].

[1] p. 26.　　　　　　　　[2] p. 31, n.

description; and whether the prices of gold in this country at different periods were always for gold of the same quality.

Mr. Bosanquet observes, that "From the calculation furnished by Mr. Grefulhe to the Committee, it appears that in the spring of 1810 an ounce of gold of English standard weight was worth at Hamburgh 4*l.* 17*s.* sterling; the price being 101, and the exchange 29*s.* At this time the extreme price of bullion in London was 4*l.* 12*s.*—or 5½ per cent. below the price of Hamburgh."[1] The reader must recollect, that it is 4*l.* 17*s.* in Bank notes that is here meant, as I have already explained. But I cannot admit the perfect accuracy of this statement. The exporter of an ounce of gold purchased here at 4*l.* 12*s.* would at least have had to wait three months before he could have received the 4*l.* 17*s.* because after the gold is sold at Hamburgh the remittance is made by a bill at $2\frac{1}{2}$[2] usances; so that allowing for interest for this period he would actually have obtained a profit of $4\frac{1}{4}$ per cent. only; but as the expence of sending gold to Hamburgh is stated in evidence to be 7 per cent.,[3] a bill would at this time have been a cheaper remittance by $2\frac{3}{4}$ per cent.

Now allowing that Mr. Bosanquet is perfectly accurate in his statement, that the price of gold was in this country at 4*l.* 12*s.* during the months of June, July, August, and September, 1809, as well as in the spring of 1810, and that in all these instances such price was given for gold of the same quality; his conclusion that in those months in the year 1809 a profit of 5½ per cent. could be made by the exportation of gold, over

[1] pp. 23–4. The last sentence of the quotation, which had been omitted, was inserted in *Errata.*

[2] Misprinted '$2\frac{1}{4}$', corrected in *Errata.*

[3] 'From 4 to 7 per cent. for all charges covering the risk, as well as the cost of transportation', according to Abraham Goldsmid, 'Minutes', p. 115; 'from $1\frac{1}{2}$ to 2 per cent.', plus 'about 4 per cent.' for the premium of insurance, according to 'Mr. ——', *ib.* p. 84.

and above the expences, is not warranted by the fact. "If at 101 and 29, observes Mr. Bosanquet,[1] there was a profit on the export of gold from hence to Hamburgh of $5\frac{1}{2}$[2] per cent.; it follows that at $104\frac{1}{2}$ (the prices in Hamburgh June, July, August and September, 1809), and 28s. there was a profit of $12\frac{1}{2}$ per cent.; or, deducting the expences of conveyance, that gold, if bought here at 4l. 12s. per ounce, was a cheaper remittance by $5\frac{1}{2}$ per cent. than a bill at the current exchange." As I have already shewn that when the exchange was 29, and the price of gold in Hamburgh 101, gold was a dearer remittance than by bill by $2\frac{3}{4}$ per cent.; it follows that at 28s. and $104\frac{1}{2}$, it was only cheaper by $4\frac{1}{4}$ per cent.

These facts prove that in June, July, August, and September, 1809, whilst the exchange was at Hamburgh 28s. and gold $104\frac{1}{2}$, the real exchange was in favour of Hamburgh; whilst in the spring of 1810 it was so much less favourable, that it would not cover the expences attending the importation of gold.

As for the rise of gold in Hamburgh with an invariable exchange, it is what would have been naturally expected if there had been a corresponding rise in the price of gold here. In proportion as the English currency becomes depreciated, as compared with gold, will it become worth fewer of the schillings of Hamburgh, unless a rise in the value of gold at Hamburgh should counteract the depreciation, by making a gold pound sterling more valuable.

The exchanges again would partake in all the variations in the value of a depreciated pound sterling, whilst the price of gold continued invariable at Hamburgh.

"It appears," says Mr. Bosanquet,[3] "by the return from the Bullion-office at the Bank, Nos. 7 and 8 in the Appendix to the

[1] p. 24.
[2] Misprinted $5\frac{1}{4}$', corrected in *Errata*.
[3] pp. 32–3.

Report, that the total amount of gold bullion imported and deposited in the Bullion-office in 1809 amounted in value to only . . . . £. 520,225
That during the same period, the quantity of
gold delivered out of the Bullion-office amounted
in value to . . . . £. 805,568
of which only 592*l.* was not exportable.

"The amount of the importation is therefore such as, when compared with the amount of exports and imports, and that of the circulating medium, to justify the assumption of comparative scarcity; and the excess of delivery beyond the importation is sufficient evidence of unusual demand."

The fact itself here insisted on would be of little importance in the question which we are now discussing; but it appears to me that Mr. Bosanquet is not warranted in his conclusions by the statements in the accounts to which he refers.

The excess of delivery beyond the importation is not any evidence of unusual demand, as it is accounted for by the following note to No. 7, from which the larger sum is extracted.

"*Note.*—The above is the amount of gold which has passed the Bullion-office in the time above named, as sales and purchases by private dealers, but *which may have passed more than once*[1] the Bullion-office, having no information generally from whence the seller procures his gold."

The importations stated in No. 8 are actually deposited by importers from abroad, and can only be received once. Besides this objection, these accounts were not fair subjects of comparison, No. 7 being made up to the 18th April, 1810; No. 8 to 30th March, 1810.

"The point of view in which these facts are important," continues Mr. Bosanquet, "is that which places the amount

[1] Ricardo's italics.

of gold imported or delivered in line of comparison with the amount of paper currency supposed to be depreciated on the evidence of the increased price of bullion. The advance of 12s. per oz. on the total quantity of gold delivered in one year, about 200,000 ounces, amounts to 120 or 130,000l.; and this is assumed as an unequivocal symptom of a depreciation of 12 or 13 per cent. on 30 or 40 millions of paper, the probable amount of our paper currency." "We may soon expect to be told that the value of Bank notes has increased, because the paper on which they are made is somewhat dearer than heretofore."[1]

The value of a Bank note is ascertained, not by the number of transactions which may take place in the purchase or sale of gold, but by the actual comparative value of the note with the value of the coin for which it professes to be a substitute.

As it is allowed[2] that a Government Bank might force a circulation of paper, *although our Bank cannot*, how would Mr. Bosanquet calculate the depreciation of such forced notes, but by a comparison of their value with the value of bullion? Would he think it necessary to enquire whether 100 ounces only had been the amount transacted in the year, or whether it had been a million? If gold be not a test by which to estimate depreciation, what is? Whilst it is a criminal offence to buy guineas at a premium, it does not seem probable that we can possess the only test which would satisfy these gentlemen, namely, two prices for commodities, a price in guineas, and another in Bank notes. They might, even in that case, contend, that it was the scarcity of gold abroad which had raised the value of the guinea.

[1] Bosanquet omits this sentence in his 2nd ed.   [2] See quotation below, pp. 215–16.

SECTION IV

Failure ascribed to Mr. Locke's Theory relative to the Recoinage in 1696.

It is correctly stated by Mr. Bosanquet[1] that Mr. Locke's theory was similar to that now held. He did most certainly maintain that an ounce of silver in coin could not be less valuable than an ounce of silver bullion of the same standard. And the Committee now maintain[2] that in the sound state of the British currency an ounce of gold bullion cannot, for any length of time, be of more value than 3*l.* 17*s.* 10½*d.*, or an ounce of gold coin: but neither of these opinions have been yet found incorrect. The effects expected from the recoinage in King William's reign failed of being realised, not because Mr. Locke's theory was followed, but because it was not followed. It did not fail, because he could not be convinced that "the value of silver bullion was become greater than the standard or mint price" (that being impossible if estimated in silver coin), but because his suggestions were not adopted.

It was proposed by Mr. Locke that silver coin should be the only fixed legal standard of currency, and that guineas should pass current in all payments at their bullion value. Under such a system, a guinea would have partaken of all the variations in the relative value of gold and silver; it might at one time have been worth 20 shillings, and at another 25; but contrary to Mr. Locke's principle, the value of the guinea was first fixed at 22 shillings, and afterwards at 21 shillings and sixpence, whilst its value as bullion was considerably below it*.

---

* It may be said, that although guineas were by law prohibited from passing at more than 21*s.* 6*d.*, they were not declared a legal tender till 1717; and, therefore, that no creditor was obliged to accept of them in discharge of a debt at that rate. But if Government received them in the payment of taxes at such value, the effects would be nearly the same as if they had by act of Parliament been made a legal tender.

[1] pp. 35–7.   [2] *Report*, pp. 4–5.

At the same time the silver coin, for the very reason that gold was rated too high, passed in currency at a value less than its bullion value. It was to be expected, therefore, that the gold coin would be retained, and that the silver coin would disappear from circulation. If the value of the guinea in currency had been lowered to its true market value in silver, the exportation of the silver coin would immediately have ceased, and, in fact, this was the remedy which was at last adopted. The matter being referred to Sir I. Newton in 1717, then master of the Mint, he reported "the principal cause of the exportation of the silver coin was, that a guinea, which then passed for 21s. 6d., was generally worth no more than 20s. 8d., according to the relative value of gold to silver at the market, though its value occasionally varied." "He then suggested, that 6d. should be taken off from the value of the guinea, in order to diminish the temptation to export and melt down the silver coin, acknowledging, however, that 10d. or 12d. ought to be taken from the guinea, in order that gold might bear the same proportion with silver money in England, which it ought to do by the course of trade and exchange in Europe*." The same effects would have followed without the intervention of Government, if the relative value of gold and silver in the market had so varied as to have made them agree with the Mint proportions.

Lord Liverpool, in speaking of the recoinage in 1696, is of a very different opinion from Mr. Bosanquet;—so far from considering that measure as having "subjected the nation to disappointment and inconvenience, under which we still labour, and to an unprofitable expence of nearly three millions sterling," [1] he observes, "that great as this charge was, the losses which the Government as well as the people of this kingdom con-

* Lord Liverpool's letter to the King.[2]

[1] Bosanquet, p. 36.   [2] p. 82.

tinued daily to suffer till the recoinage was completed, justified almost any expence which might be incurred for their relief."[1]

Mr. Bosanquet is not quite correct in saying, page 34, that the price of silver has never been under the Mint price since the recoinage in the reign of King William. On a reference to Mr. Mushet's tables, it appears that it was as low as 5s. 1d. in 1793 and 1794, and in 1798 it fell to 5s., which was the occasion of the law for prohibiting the coinage of silver which I have already noticed[2]*.

* Since this was sent to the press I have seen the second edition of Mr. Bosanquet's work, in which this inaccuracy is corrected.

[1] Lord Liverpool, p. 76.   [2] Above, p. 177.

CHAPTER IV

Mr. Bosanquet's Objections to the Statement, that the Balance of Payments has been in Favour of Great Britain, examined.

HAVING considered all those points deemed so important by Mr. Bosanquet in contradiction of the opinion of the Committee, "that it is by a comparison of the market and Mint value of bullion, that the fact of the depreciation of the currency can be estimated;" and having, I trust, made it evident that there is no other test singly, by which we are enabled to judge of the sound or unsound state of our paper currency, I shall proceed to the consideration of the next disputed position of the Bullion Committee; namely, "That so far as any inference is to be drawn from Custom House returns of exports and imports, the state of the exchanges ought to be peculiarly favourable."

Mr. Bosanquet has been at the trouble of consulting numerous documents to prove that the Committee have not only committed an error to the amount of 7,500,000*l.* in their estimate of the balance of exports, but other errors to a still greater amount; and that, in fact, so far from their opinion being well founded, that the state of the exchange ought to have been favourable to this country during the past year, the actual amount of the balance of payments to the continent had been unusually great.

As I am desirous only of defending the principles of the Committee, and as these facts are by no means essential to those principles, I shall not enter into any examination of the correctness either of the statements of the Committee, or of those of Mr. Bosanquet, but will at once concede to him the facts, difficult as he would find it to prove all of them, for which he contends.

That the balance of payments has been against this country cannot, I conceive, admit of dispute. The state of the real exchange sufficiently proves it, as that infallibly indicates from which country bullion is passing. It would, however, have been of some satisfaction to those who are desirous of clearly understanding this difficult subject, if Mr. Bosanquet had acquainted us with the means which we possessed of paying the very large unfavourable balance for which he contends. Does he imagine that it has actually been discharged with our own hoard of gold? Do we usually keep unemployed such a large amount of bullion that we can afford to pay such balances year after year?

As we have no mines of our own, if we do not actually possess it, we must purchase it from foreign countries; but Bank notes will be useless for such purpose. If the price of gold in Bank notes be 4*l.* per ounce, or 10*l.* per ounce, we shall not obtain the slightest addition to our quantity of bullion, as it can only be procured by the exportation of goods. If we obtain it from America, for example, it is with goods we must purchase it. In that case, on a view of the whole trade of the country, we have discharged a debt in Europe by the exportation of goods to some other part of the world, and the balance of payments, however large it may be, must ultimately be paid by the produce of the labour of the people of this country. Bills of exchange never discharge a debt from one country to another; they enable a creditor of England to receive, at the place where he is resident, a sum of money from a debtor to England; they effect a transfer of a debt, but do not discharge it. That a demand for gold (if it could be allowed that our creditor would accept nothing but gold) might occasion a rise in its value no one denies. If, therefore, goods had become

exceedingly cheap, it would have been the natural effect of
such a cause. But how is any rise in its price in Bank notes
to procure it, even if we suppose it hoarded in England?

The seller is not to be deluded with an increase of nominal
value; it will be to him of little importance whether he sells
his gold at 3*l.* 17*s.* 10½*d*, or at 4*l.* 12*s.* per ounce, provided either
of those sums will procure him the commodities for which he
intends ultimately to exchange his gold. If then Bank notes
to the amount of 3*l.* 17*s.* 10½*d.* be rendered of equal value in
procuring the commodities which he seeks to purchase, with
4*l.* 12*s.*, as much gold will be procured at one price as at the
other. Now can it be denied, that by reducing the amount of
Bank notes their value will be increased? If so, how can the
reduction of Bank notes prevent us from obtaining the same
amount of gold both at home and abroad to discharge our
foreign debt, as we now obtain by a nominal and fictitious price?

"At a moment," says Mr. Bosanquet,[1] "when we were
compelled to receive corn, even from our enemy, without the
slightest stipulation in favour of our own manufacturer, and
to pay neutrals for bringing it, Mr. Ricardo tells us,[2] that the
export of bullion and merchandize, in payment of the corn
we may import, resolves itself entirely into a question of
interest, and that, if we give corn[3] in exchange for goods, it
must be from choice, not necessity. Whilst providing against
famine, he tells us, that we should not import more goods than
we export, unless we had a redundancy of currency."

Mr. Bosanquet speaks as if the nation collectively, as one
body, imported corn and exported gold, and that it was compelled by hunger so to do, not reflecting that the importation
of corn, even under the case supposed, is the act of individuals,

---

[1] p. 47. The italics are Ricardo's.
[2] *High Price of Bullion*, above,
p. 61.

[3] Bosanquet's misquotation, for
'coin'.

and governed by the same motives as all other branches of trade. What is the degree of *compulsion* which is employed to make us receive corn from our enemy? I suppose no other than the want of that commodity which makes it an advantageous article of import; but if it be a voluntary, as it most certainly is, and not a compulsory bargain between the two nations, I do still maintain that gold would not, even if famine raged amongst us, be given to France in exchange for corn, unless the exportation of gold was attended with advantage to the exporter, unless he could sell corn in England for more gold than he was obliged to give for the purchase of it.

Would Mr. Bosanquet, would any merchant he knows, import corn for gold on any other terms? If no importer would, how could the corn be introduced into the country, unless gold or some other commodity were cheaper here? As far as those two commodities are concerned, do not these transactions as certainly indicate that gold is dearer in France, as that corn is dearer in England?

Seeing nothing in Mr. Bosanquet's statement to induce me to change my opinion, I must continue to think that it is interest, and interest alone, which determines the exportation of gold, in the same manner as it regulates the exportation of all other commodities. Mr. Bosanquet would have done well, before he had deemed this opinion so extravagant, to have used something like argument to prove it so; and he would not have hurt his cause, if, even in the year 1810, he had explained his reason for supporting a principle advanced by Mr. Thornton in 1802, the correctness of which was questioned in 1809.

Bullion will not be exported unless we have previously imported it for such purpose, or unless from some circumstances in our internal circulation it has been rendered cheap and less useful to us. If Milan decrees, embargoes, non-intercourse acts, &c. affect the exportation of commodities, they also affect their importation, as no country can long continue to buy unless it can also sell; and least of all England, who by the abundance of her paper has driven from her circulation every vestige of the precious metals.

"If the currency be depreciated below the value of gold," Mr. Bosanquet tells us, "it is so positively, not relatively, and all exchanges must equally feel the influence of the depreciation." (Page 20.) Most true; and therefore if Mr. Bosanquet could have shewn that with *any one country in the world*, whose currency is not debased nor depreciated, the exchange had been favourable to England, more than the expences of transporting bullion,[1] he would have successfully controverted the opinion of the Committee.

Some able writers on this subject have lately taken, I think, a mistaken view of the exportation of money, and of the effects produced on the price of bullion by an increase of currency through paper circulation.

Mr. Blake observes,[2] "All writers upon the subject of political economy that I have met with, seem to be persuaded that when the rate of exchange has deviated from par beyond the expences of the transit of bullion, bullion will immediately pass; and the error has arisen from not sufficiently distinguishing the effects of a *real* and a *nominal* exchange;" and many pages are employed in proving, that on every addition to the paper circulation, even when a great part of the currency consists of the precious metals, the price of bullion will be raised in the same proportion as other commodities; and as the foreign exchange will be nominally depressed in the same degree, no advantage will arise from the exportation of bullion. The same opinion is maintained by Mr. Huskisson,[3] page 27.

[1] 'more than the expences of transporting bullion,' was inserted in *Errata*.

[2] *Observations on…the Course of Exchange*, p. 52.

[3] *The Question concerning the Depreciation of our Currency*.

"If the circulation of a country were supplied partly by gold and partly by paper, and the amount of that circulation were doubled by an augmentation of that paper, the effect upon prices at home would be the same as in the former case," (a rise in the price of commodities). "But gold not becoming by this augmentation of currency more abundant in such a country than in other parts of the world, as a *commodity*, its relative value to other commodities would remain unaltered; as a commodity also, its price would rise in the same proportion as that of other commodities, although, in the state of coin, of which the *denomination* is fixed by law, it could only pass current according to that *denomination*.

"When paper is thus augmented in any country, the exportation of the gold coin, therefore, will take place; not because gold, as a *commodity*, is become more abundant and less valuable with reference to other commodities in such a country; but, from the circumstance of its value as currency remaining the same, while its price in that currency is increased in common with the prices of all other commodities."

I should perfectly agree with these writers, that the effects on the value of gold as an exportable commodity would be as they describe, provided the circulation consisted wholly of paper, but no rise would take place in the price of bullion, in consequence of an addition of paper currency, whilst the currency was either wholly metallic, or consisted partly of gold and partly of paper.

If an addition be made to a currency consisting partly of gold and partly of paper, by an increase of paper currency the value of the whole currency would be diminished, or, in other words, the prices of commodities would rise, estimated either in gold coin or in paper currency. The same commodity would purchase, after the increase of paper, a greater number of ounces of gold coin, because it would exchange for a greater quantity of money. But these gentlemen do not dispute the fact of the convertibility of coin into bullion, in spite of the law to prevent it. Does it not follow, therefore, that the value of gold in coin, and the value of gold in bullion, would speedily approach a perfect equality? If then a commodity would sell in consequence of the issue of paper for more gold coin, it would also sell for more gold bullion. It cannot therefore be correct to say that the relative value of gold bullion and commodities would be the same after as before the increase of paper.

The diminution in the value of gold, as compared with commodities, in consequence of the issues of paper in a country where gold forms part of the circulation, is, in the first instance, confined to that country only. If such country were insulated, and had no commerce whatever with any other country, this diminution in the value of gold would continue till the demand for gold for its manufactures had withdrawn the whole of its coin from circulation, and not till then would there be any visible depreciation in the value of paper as compared with gold, whatever the amount of paper might be which was in circulation.

As soon as the gold had been wholly withdrawn, the demand for manufactures still continuing, gold would rise above the value of paper, and would soon obtain that relative value to other commodities which subsisted before any addition had been made to the circulation by the issues of paper. The mines would then supply the quantity of gold required, and the paper currency would continue to be permanently depreciated. During this interval the gold mines of such country, if it possessed any, could not be worked, because of the low value of gold, which would have reduced the profits on capital employed in the mines below the level of the profits of other mercantile concerns. As soon as this equality of profit were established, the supply of gold would be as regular as before.

These would be the consequences of a great issue of paper in a country having no intercourse with any other.

But if the country supposed, as is the case with England, had intercourse with all other countries, any excess of her currency would be counteracted by an exportation of specie, and if that excess did not exceed the amount of coin in circulation which could be easily collected by those who evade the law, no depreciation of the currency would take place.

Suppose England to have 1000 ounces of gold in the state of bullion, and 1000 ounces in the state of coin, whilst her exchange with foreign countries was at par; that is to say, whilst the value of gold abroad was precisely the same as here, and therefore could be neither advantageously exported nor imported.

Suppose, too, that the Bank were at such time to issue notes to an amount which should represent 1000 ounces more of gold, and that they were not exchangeable for specie. If her bullion retained the same value after as before the issue of paper (which is the point contended for), how could a single guinea be exported? Who would be at the trouble and risk of sending guineas to the continent to be sold there for their value as bullion, while the value of bullion continued here as high as before, and consequently as high as the price abroad? Would not the coin be melted and sold as bullion at home, till the value of bullion had so much diminished in its relative value to the bullion of other countries, and therefore to the relative value of commodities here, as to pay the expences of transportation; or, in other words, till the exchange had fallen to the price at which it would repay such expences? At that price the whole 1000 ounces would go at once, or if any part were retained in circulation, it would not be of less value than an equal weight of gold bullion. I am all along considering the law as having no effect in preventing exportation, and if it be contended that the law could be strictly executed, that argument would be equally applicable if the addition to the currency had been made in gold coin, and not in paper currency.

It appears, therefore, evident, first, that by the addition of paper to a currency consisting partly of gold and partly of paper, gold bullion will not necessarily rise in the same degree as other commodities; and, secondly, that such addition will cause depression not in the nominal but in the real exchange, and therefore that gold will be exported.

But to return to Mr. Bosanquet. He observes,[1] "that the three propositions," viz. those on which I have been commenting, "appear to have been brought forward by the Committee as well as by the authors on whose theories the report is founded, to induce the admission of the depreciation of the paper currency of this country as the necessary consequence of the impossibility of accounting for the depression of the exchanges and the increased price of bullion in any other way. They may be termed negative arguments."

Now, as far as I, who am one of the authors arraigned, am concerned, Mr. Bosanquet is incorrect: the third of these propositions was not on any occasion brought forward by me. The fact of the balance of payments being for or against this country could be of little consequence, in my estimation, to the proof of the theory which I maintain. Whether a part of our exports or a part of our imports consisted of gold cannot in the least affect this question, it is abundantly certain that our currency is neither by ourselves nor by foreigners estimated at its bullion value. And why should our currency be degraded below such value more than those of America, France, Hamburgh, Holland, &c.? The answer is, because neither of those countries have a paper currency not convertible into specie at the will of the holder.

[1] p. 48.

CHAPTER V

Mr. Bosanquet's Argument to prove that the Bank of England has NOT *the Power of forcing the Circulation of Bank Notes—considered.*

THE fourth proposition is what now presents itself for discussion:

"That the Bank, during the restriction, possesses exclusively the power of limiting the circulation of Bank notes."

It is difficult to determine whether Mr. Bosanquet thinks that even a forced paper circulation could have the effect of lowering the exchange; so confidently is it asserted by him that there is no connexion between the exchanges and the amount of Bank notes. If the Bank were to become truly a government Bank, in the sense in which Mr. Bosanquet somewhere uses that term; if they were to advance all the money requisite for the service of the year; if from twenty millions they were to raise the amount of their notes to fifty millions, would not such a Bank be justly said to force a circulation of paper? and would not the effect of such a forced circulation of paper be, that their notes would be depreciated, that the price of bullion would rise and the foreign exchanges fall? Would not these effects take place although Government were to guarantee the notes of the Bank, and the final payment of them should by no one be doubted? Would not the abundance of the circulation alone produce depreciation? Or is it to be maintained that no abundance of paper money, provided its final redemption be certain, can cause depreciation? A proposition so extravagant will hardly, I think, be supported, and it must therefore be admitted that depreciation may arise from the abundance of notes alone, however great might be the funds of those who were the issuers of them. As these symptoms, then, which accompany a forced paper currency are, at this moment, too glaring to be denied, as they cannot be accounted for in any other way either by theory or by an appeal to experience, are we not justified in our suspicions that the Bank of England, as at present constituted, is not so devoid of the power of forcing a circulation as their friends would have us believe? It is not intended by the words forced circulation to accuse the Bank of having departed from those cautions which have usually accompanied the issue of their paper; it is meant only that the restriction bill enables them to keep in circulation an amount of notes (allowance made for the coin that would then be in circulation) greater than they could maintain but for that measure. It is this surplus sum which I consider as producing precisely the same effects as if it were forced on the public by a Government Bank. The plea that no more is issued than the wants of commerce require is of no weight; because the sum required for such purpose cannot be defined. Commerce is insatiable in its demands, and the same portion of it may employ 10 millions or 100 millions of circulating medium; the quantity depends wholly on its value. If the mines had been ten times more productive, ten times more money would the same commerce employ. This Mr. Bosanquet admits, but denies the analogy between the issues of the Bank and the produce of a new gold mine.

On this subject Mr. Bosanquet makes the following observations.[1]

"Mr. Ricardo[2] has assimilated the Bank of England during the restriction, so far as relates to the effects of its issues, to a gold mine, the produce of which being thrown into circulation, in addition to the circulating medium already sufficient, is an excess; and has the acknowledged effect of depreciating the value of the existing medium, or, in other words, of raising

---

[1] pp. 51–3.   [2] Above, p. 54.

the prices of commodities for which it is usually exchanged. But Mr. Ricardo has not stated what is essential to the comparison, *why* it is that the discovery of a gold mine would produce this effect. It would produce it, because the proprietors would issue it, for whatever services, without any engagement, to give an equal value for it again to the holders, or any wish, or any means, of calling back and annihilating that which they have issued. By degrees, as the issues increase they exceed the wants of circulation; gold produces no benefit to the holder as gold; he cannot eat it, nor clothe himself with it; to render it useful, he must exchange it either for such things as are immediately useful, or for such as produce revenue. The demand and consequently the prices of commodities and real properties measured in gold, increases; and will continue to increase as long as the mine continues to produce. And this effect will equally follow whether, under the circumstances I have supposed, the issue be gold from a mine or paper from a government-bank. All this I distinctly admit; but in all this statement, there is not one point of analogy to the issues of the Bank of England.

"But the principle on which the Bank issues its notes is that of loan. Every note is issued at the requisition of some party, who becomes indebted to the Bank for its amount, and gives security to return this note, or another of equal value at a fixed and not remote period; paying an interest proportioned to the time allowed."

Now supposing the gold mine to be actually the property of the Bank, even to be situated on their own premises, and that they procured the gold which it produced to be coined into guineas, and in lieu of issuing their notes when they discounted bills or lent money to Government that they issued nothing but guineas; could there be any other limit to their issues but the want of the further productiveness in their mine?

In what would the circumstances differ if the mine were the property of the king, of a company of merchants, or of a single individual? In that case Mr. Bosanquet admits that the value of money would fall, and I suppose he would also admit that it would fall in exact proportion to its increase.

What would be done with the gold by the owner of the mine? It must be either employed at interest by himself, or it would finally find its way into the hands of those who would so employ it. This is its natural destination; it may pass through the hands of 100, or 1000 persons, but it could be employed in no other manner at last. Now if the mine should double the quantity of money, it would depress its value in the same proportion, and there would be double the demand for it. A merchant who before required the loan of 10,000*l.* would now want 20,000*l.*; and it could be of little importance to him whether he continued to borrow 10,000*l.* of the Bank, and 10,000*l.* of those with whom the money finally rested, or whether he borrowed the whole 20,000*l.* of the Bank. The analogy seems to me to be complete, and not to admit of dispute. The issues of paper not convertible are guided by the same principle, and will be attended with the same effects as if the Bank were the proprietor of the mine, and issued nothing but gold. However much gold may be increased, borrowers will increase to the same amount, in consequence of its depreciation; and the same rule is equally true with respect to paper. If money be but depreciated sufficiently, there is no amount which may not be absorbed, and it would not make the slightest difference whether the Bank with their notes actually purchased the commodities themselves, or whether they discounted the bills of those who would so employ them.

If it were granted to Mr. Bosanquet that a given sum, and no more, could be absorbed in the circulation, the effects he states would follow: but I deny that there would be a surplus seeking in vain for advantageous employment, and which, not being able to find it, would necessarily either return to the Bank in payment of a bill already discounted, or would prevent an application to them for an advance of money to that amount.

If money, however abundantly issued, could retain its value, such might be the effects; but as, when once it is brought into circulation, depreciation commences, the employment for the additional sum would retain it in the currency.

Let us recur to the effect which would result from the establishment of a Bank of undoubted credit in a country where the circulation was wholly metallic.

Such a Bank would discount bills or make advances to government as our Bank does; and if the principle now contended for by Mr. Bosanquet be correct, their notes would necessarily return on them as soon as issued; because the metallic currency being before sufficient for the commerce of the country, no additional quantity could be employed.—But this is contrary both to theory and experience. The issues of the Bank would, as they now do, not only depreciate the currency, but the value of bullion at the same time, as I have endeavoured to explain at page 211; this, again, would be the temptation to exportation, and the diminution of the currency would make it regain its value. The Bank would issue more notes, and the same effects would follow; but in no case would there be such an excess as would induce any holder of notes to return them to the Bank in payment of loans, if the law against the exportation of money could be effectually executed. Money would be demanded because it could be profitably exported, and not because it could not be absorbed in the circulation. But let us suppose a case in which money could not be profitably exported—Let us suppose all the countries of Europe to carry on their circulation by means of the precious metals, and that each were at the same moment to establish a Bank on the same principles as the Bank of England—Could they, or could they not, each add to the metallic circulation a certain portion of paper? and could or could they not permanently maintain that paper in circulation? If they could, the question is at an end, an addition might then be made to a circulation already sufficient, without occasioning the notes to return to the Bank in payment of bills due. If it is said they could not, then I appeal to experience, and ask for some explanation of the manner in which Bank notes were originally called into existence, and how they are permanently kept in circulation.

I should find it laborious to follow up in all its bearings the analogy between the first establishment of a Bank, the discovery of a mine, and the present situation of our Bank; but of this I am fully certain, that if the principle advanced by the Bank Directors be correct, not a Bank note could ever have been permanently kept in circulation, nor would the discovery of the mines of America have added one guinea to the circulation of England. The additional gold would, according to this system, have found a circulation already adequate, and in which no more could be admitted.

The refusal to discount any bills but those for *bonâ fide* transactions would be as little effectual in limiting the circulation; because, though the directors should have the means of distinguishing such bills, which can by no means be allowed, a greater portion of paper currency might be called into circulation, not than the wants of commerce could employ, but greater than what could remain in the channel of currency without depreciation. It is well known that the same thousand pounds may settle 20 *bonâ fide* transactions in one day. It may pay for a ship; the seller of a ship may pay with it his rope-maker;— he again may pay the Russian merchants for hemp, &c. &c. Now as each of these was a *bonâ fide* transaction, a bill might have been drawn by each, and the Bank, by their rule, might discount them all; so that 20,000*l.* might be called into circulation to perform those payments for which 1000*l.* was equal. I am aware that the opinion of Dr. Smith, as quoted by Mr. Bosanquet, appears to favour his opinion[1]; but that able writer has in various passages of his work, and within a few pages of that from whence Mr. Bosanquet has quoted, declared that, "The whole paper money of every kind which can easily circulate in any country can never exceed the value of the gold and silver of which it supplies the place, or which (the commerce being supposed the same) would circulate there if there were no paper money."[2]

To this test we must not submit our currency. If at its present amount it consisted of gold and silver, no laws, however severe, could retain it in circulation; a part would be melted and exported till it was reduced to its just level. At that level it would be as impossible to force the exportation of it. In such case we should no longer hear of the balance of payments being against us, nor of the necessity of exporting gold in return for corn. That such would be the consequences cannot be doubted by those who are familiar with the writings of Dr. Smith. But if it should be otherwise, if the continent should adopt the almost impossible, absurd policy of wishing to buy more of that of which they already had too much, what evil consequences would ensue to us, even if our currency were reduced to the same level at which it stood before the discovery of America? Would not this be a national gain? inasmuch as the circulation of the same commerce being carried on with a smaller amount of gold, the balance might be profitably employed in procuring a return of more useful and more productive commodities. And if the circulation of paper were reduced in the same pro-

[1] Bosanquet, pp. 63–4, quotes Smith, Bk. II, ch. ii; vol. I, p. 287. [2] *ib.* vol. I, p. 283.

portion, would not the profits now gained by the Bank be enjoyed by those who can shew a much better title to them?

It is fortunate for the public that there should exist the disinclination to discount at the Bank which Mr. Bosanquet mentions,[1]—as without some such check, it is impossible to say to what amount Bank notes might by this time have been multiplied. Indeed, to all those who have given the subject any consideration it is matter of suprise that our circulation has been confined within such moderate bounds, after knowing the principles which the Bank Directors have avowed as their guide in regulating their issues.

[1] p. 57.

CHAPTER VI

Observations on the Principles of Seignorage.

DR. Smith, though favourable to a small seignorage on the coin, was fully aware of the evils which might attend a large one.

The limits, beyond which a seignorage cannot be advantageously extended, are the actual expences incurred by the manufacturing of bullion into coin. If a seignorage exceeds these expences, an advantage will accrue to false coiners by imitating the coins, although they should actually make them of their legal weight and standard; but even in this case, as the addition of money to the circulation beyond the regular demands of commerce will diminish the value of that money, the trade of false coiners must cease when the value of the coin does not exceed the value of bullion more than the actual expences of fabrication. If the public could be secured from such illegal additions to the circulating medium, there could be no seignorage so high which a government might not advantageously exact; as the coined money would, in the same degree, exceed the value of bullion. If the seignorage amounted to 10 per cent. bullion would necessarily be 10 per cent. under the Mint price; and if it were 50 per cent., that also would the value of coin exceed the value of bullion. It appears then, that although a given weight of bullion can never exceed in value a given weight of coin, a given weight of coin may exceed in value a given weight of bullion by the whole expence of seignorage, however great that seignorage may be, provided that there was effectual security against the increase of money through the imitation of the coins by illegal means. And it appears also, that if no such security could be given, the trade of the false coiner would cease as soon as he had added so much to the amount of the coin as to diminish its value, on a comparison with bullion, to the actual expences incurred. That these principles are correct may be proved from the consideration of the circumstances which give value to a Bank note. A Bank note is of no more intrinsic value than the piece of paper on which it is made. It may be considered as a piece of money on which the seignorage is enormous, amounting to all its value; yet if the public is sufficiently protected against the too great increase of such notes, either by the indiscretion of the issuers, or by the practices of false coiners or forgers, they must, in the ordinary operations of trade, retain their value.

Whilst such money is kept within certain limits any value may be given to it as currency; 3*l*. 17*s*. 10½*d*. may be worth an ounce of gold bullion, the value at which it was originally issued, or it may be reduced to the value of half an ounce; and if the Bank which issued had the exclusive privilege of procuring money to be coined at the Mint, 3*l*. 17*s*. 10½*d*. of their notes might be rendered of equal value to 1, 2, 3, or any number of ounces of gold bullion.

The value of such money must depend wholly upon its quantity, and in the case supposed the Bank would not only have the power of limiting the amount of paper money, but of metallic money also.

I have before endeavoured to show, that previously to the establishment of banks the precious metals, employed as money, were necessarily distributed amongst the different countries of the world in the proportion that their trade and payments required; that whatever the value of the bullion so employed for the purposes of currency might be, the equal demands and necessities of all countries would prevent the quantity allotted to each from being either increased or diminished, unless the proportions in the trade of countries should undergo some alteration which should make a different division necessary;

that England or any other country might substitute paper instead of bullion for the uses of money, but that the value of such paper must be regulated by the amount of coin of its bullion value, which would have circulated had there been no paper.

Under this point of view the paper currency of any particular country represents a certain weight of bullion which, her commerce and payments continuing the same, could neither be increased nor diminished; 3*l.* 17*s.* 10½*d.* of coin or paper currency might represent an ounce of gold bullion, or 4*l.* 13*s.* might, in consequence of some internal regulation, do the same; but the actual amount of bullion so represented would, under the same circumstances of commerce and payments, be eternally the same.

Suppose that England's share amounted to a million of ounces, if by a law which could be effectually executed a million and a half of ounces in coin could be forced or retained in circulation, by preventing its being melted or exported, or if by means of a restriction bill the Bank should be enabled to maintain an amount of paper which should represent a million and a half of ounces of coined gold in circulation, such million and a half would be of no more value in currency than a million of ounces; and consequently an ounce and a half of coined gold, or bank-notes which represented that amount, would purchase no more of any commodity than an ounce of gold bullion. If, on the other hand, Government were to charge a seignorage of 50 per cent. or if the issues of the Bank were to be exceedingly limited, whilst they had also the exclusive right of coining, so that the whole amount of their notes did not exceed what should represent at the mint price half a million of ounces of gold, that half million would in currency pass for the same value as the million of ounces in one case, and the million and a half in the other did before.

From these principles it results, that there can exist no

depreciation of money but from excess; however debased a coinage may become it will preserve its mint value, that is to say, it will pass in circulation for the intrinsic value of the bullion which it ought to contain, provided it be not in too great abundance. It is a mistaken theory, therefore, to suppose that guineas of 5 dwts. and 8 grains cannot circulate with guineas of 5 dwts. or less. As they might be in such limited quantity that both the one and the other might actually pass in currency for a value equal to 5 dwts. 10 grains, there would be no temptation to withdraw either from circulation; there would be a real profit in retaining them. In practice, indeed, it would seldom occur that the heavier pieces would escape the melting pot, but it would arise wholly from the augmentation of such currency, either by the liberal issues of the Bank, or by the supply of false money which the arts of the false coiner would throw into circulation.

Our silver currency now passes at a value in currency above its bullion value, because, notwithstanding the profit obtained by the counterfeiter, it has not yet been supplied in sufficient abundance to affect its value.

It is on this principle too that the fact must be accounted for, that the price of bullion previously to the recoinage in 1696, did not rise so high as might have been expected from the then debased state of the currency; the quantity had not been increased in the same proportion as the quality had been debased.

It also follows from these principles, that in a country where gold is the measure of value, the price of gold bullion (where the law offers no restraint against exportation) can never exceed its mint price; and that it can never fall more below it than the expences of coinage; and that these variations depend wholly on the supply of coin or paper currency being proportioned to the trade of the country, or, in other words, that nothing can raise the value of bullion even so high as the mint price but an excess of circulation. If, indeed, any power in the state have the privilege of increasing the paper currency at pleasure, and be at the same time protected from the payment of its notes, there is no other limit to the rise of the price of gold than the will of the issuers.

CHAPTER VII

*Mr. Bosanquet's Objections to the Proposition, that the Circulation of
the Bank of England regulates that of the Country Banks, considered.*

THE next proposition which Mr. Bosanquet attempts to disprove is that in which the Committee give it as their opinion,
"That the circulation of country bank-notes depends upon,
and is proportionate to, the issues from the Bank."

There are many practical authorities for the truth of this
principle also. It appears to be singularly unfortunate,
that few of the principles of the Bullion Committee which
Mr. Bosanquet has selected have not the authority of practical
men, to whose opinions on these subjects so much deference
is paid. That the exchange can never vary for any length
of time beyond the limits defined by the Committee has
been, and is, the opinion of the ablest practical men.

That the price of bullion cannot long continue, with a sound
system of currency, above the mint price has received full
confirmation from the same quarter, and the proposition
now under discussion is not without the same sanction.
Mr. Huskisson[1] has already availed himself of the authority
of the Governor of the Bank for its truth, who declared in his
evidence to the Committee, page 127,[2] "The country banks
by not regulating their issues on the principle of the Bank
of England might send forth a superabundance of their notes;
but this excess, in my opinion, would no sooner exist in any
material degree, than it would be corrected by its own operation, for the holders of such paper would immediately return
it to the issuers, when they found that in consequence of the

[1] *The Question concerning the De-*   [2] Octavo ed., 'Minutes of Evi-
preciation of our Currency, pp. 35–6.   dence', pp. 187–8.

over issue its value was reduced, or likely to be reduced, below par; thus, though the balance might be slightly and transiently disturbed, no considerable or permanent over issue could possibly take place, as from the nature of things the amount of bank-notes in circulation must always find its level in the public wants." Mr. Gilchrist of the Bank of Scotland stated to the Committee, that "If the Bank of England were to restrict their issues, of course the Scotch banks would find it necessary to diminish theirs." "The issues of the Bank of England," he observed, "operate upon the issues of the banks of Scotland in this manner. If the banks of Scotland issue more than they ought to do in proportion to the issues of the Bank of England, they would be called upon to draw bills upon London at a lower rate of exchange." (Page 114, App.)[1] Mr. Thompson, a country banker, and a member of the Committee, was asked, "By what criterion do the country banks now regulate their issues of paper?"—Ans. "By the plenty or scarcity of bank-notes."[2] "Then their issues bear a proportion to the issues of the Bank?"—Ans. "In my opinion they do."

"The Committee," Mr. Bosanquet observes,[3] "has not defined the sense in which they use the term excess of currency; I, therefore," he continues, "suppose it to be used in the Report in the sense in which it is used by Dr. Smith, as denoting a quantity greater than the circulation of the country can easily absorb or employ." And in another place,[4] "As the fact is not *apparent* at least (I mean that there is more paper than the country can easily absorb and employ), the *onus probandi* seems to lie on the Committee."

This is not the sense in which I consider the Committee to use the word *excess*. In that sense there can be no excess whilst

[1] Octavo ed., 'Minutes of Evidence', p. 162.
[2] *ib.*, p. 163. The Minutes actually read 'of Bank of England notes'.
[3] p. 75.
[4] p. 83.

the Bank does not pay in specie, because the commerce of the
country can easily employ and absorb any sum which the
Bank may send into circulation. It is from so understanding
the word excess that Mr. Bosanquet thinks the circulation cannot be excessive, because the commerce of the country could
not easily employ it. In proportion as the pound sterling
becomes depreciated will the want of the nominal amount
of pounds increase, and no part of the larger sum will be
excessive, more than the smaller sum was before. By excess,
then, the Committee must mean the difference in amount of
circulation between the sum actually employed, and that sum
which would be employed if the pound sterling were to regain
its bullion value. This is a distinction of more consequence
than at first sight appears, and Mr. Bosanquet was well aware
that it was in this sense that it was used by me. He has been
so obliging as to express my meaning in a passage where it
appeared obscure; he has done it most ably, and completely
understood the sense in which I used the words *an excessive
circulation.*[1] He observes upon the passage, page 86, "If this
interpretation be adopted, it will be nearly useless to search
for, and enquire after, excess of paper as a fact; we must be
content to admit proof of its existence from its effects, and
our attention must be directed to ascertain depreciation, or an
increased price of commodities, solely arising out of, and
occasioned by, the increased amount of the circulating medium."
I do most unequivocally admit, that whilst the high price of
bullion and the low exchanges continue, and whilst our gold

---

[1] 'Mr. Ricardo states, "that the
circulation can never be overful",
meaning thereby, as I apprehend,
(for in this instance Mr. Ricardo's
language is not quite so clear and
perspicuous as it usually is) that, as
the nominal price of commodities
rises in proportion to any increase
of currency, the currency, though
of greater numerical amount, will
not bear a higher proportion to the
value of the commodities; and
although there is an obvious depreciation there is no excess.'
(Bosanquet, pp. 85–6.)

is undebased, it would to me be no proof of our currency not being depreciated if there were only five millions of bank-notes in circulation. When we speak, therefore, of an excess of bank-notes, we mean that portion of the amount of the issues of the Bank, which can now circulate, but could not, if the currency were of its bullion value. When we speak of an excess of country currency, we mean a portion of the amount of the country bank-notes, which cannot be absorbed in the circulation, because they are exchangeable for, and are depreciated below, the value of bank-notes.

This distinction appears to me to be an answer to Mr. Bosanquet's objection, where he says, "But does it follow that the country bank paper, if issued to excess, will not be checked, because there is already more bank paper in circulation than the country can absorb and employ["]?[1] If it be admitted, and how can it be denied? that the price of commodities must every where rise or fall in proportion to the increase or diminution of the money which circulates them; must not an increase of London money increase the prices of commodities in London only, unless a part of that money can be employed in the country circulation? and, on the contrary, must not the same rise take place in the country prices only if the country currency be increased, and if it be not convertible into London currency; or cannot circulate in London? If the case put by Mr. Bosanquet be supposed possible, that the London currency only should be increased, and that London bank-notes were not current in the country, then we should have an exchange with the country in the same manner as we have with Hamburgh or France, and that exchange would shew that London paper was on a comparison with country paper depreciated.

If each of the country banks were protected by a restriction act from paying their notes in any other medium than their

[1] p. 76.

own paper, and if these notes were each confined to the circulation of their particular districts, they would each be depreciated on a comparison with bullion, in proportion as their amount exceeded the amount of money of bullion value, which would have circulated in those districts if they had not been protected by such an act. The notes of one bank might be depreciated 5 per cent. of another 10, another 20, and so on. The restriction bill being confined to the Bank of England alone, and all other notes being convertible into their notes, country notes can never be issued in a greater proportion than those of the London bank. Mr. Bosanquet thinks, "I was bound to shew that some physical impossibility obstructs the increase of bank-notes at the expence of country notes, and *vice versa*, before I assume that an increase of bank-notes must produce an increase of country notes." [1]

From what I have already said, I think it will appear that unless London notes are employed in the circulation of places where they were not before admitted, there is, if not a physical, at least an *absolute*, impossibility, that an increase of Bank of England notes should not either be followed by an increase of country bank-notes, or by a depreciation in the value of the London notes, as compared with the country notes.

But how is this effected? How do the issues of the Bank produce an increase in the country circulation? Mr. Gilchrist has informed us.[2] Reverse the case which he has supposed, and it would stand thus: If the Bank of England increase their issues, the country banks might increase theirs: the prices of commodities being raised in London, whilst those of the country continued as before, money would be wanted in the country to purchase in the cheaper market; bills would be demanded for

---

[1] p. 83, n. Bosanquet says 'Mr. Ricardo was bound' and 'before he assumes'.   [2] See above, p. 228.

that purpose upon the country, which would therefore sell at a premium, or, in other words, bank-notes would be depreciated below the value of the country currency. Such demand would cease as soon as the country currency were either brought up to the level of the London currency, or the London currency reduced to the level of the country currency.

I should not have thought that a principle so clear could have been questioned: the value of our gold currency formerly regulated the value of a pound sterling all over England. If gold became abundant from the discovery of new mines, and more money were therefore employed in the circulation of London, a proportionate increase must necessarily have taken place in the country to preserve the equality of prices. Bank-notes perform now the same office, and if they be increased the country currency must either partake in the use of the additional quantity, or the country banks must make a proportional increase to their issues. It is not difficult, under such circumstances, to determine what will be the choice of the country banks.

The Committee having stated,[1] that "If an excess of paper be issued in a country district, while the London circulation does not exceed its due proportion, there will be a local rise in prices in that country district, but prices in London will remain as before; that those who have the country paper will prefer buying in London, where things are cheaper, and will therefore return that country paper upon the banker who issued it, and will demand of him Bank of England notes, or bills upon London; and that thus the excess of country paper being returned[2] upon the issuers for Bank of England paper, the quantity of the latter necessarily and effectually limits the quantity of the former."

[1] *Report*, p. 67.   [2] The *Report* actually reads 'being continually returned'.

Mr. Bosanquet asks,[1] "Does this follow as a consequence? Admitting the accuracy of the reasoning, under the supposition that the country notes were actually paid in bank-notes, does it apply under the admission that they are paid by bills on London, since, as we have already shewn, the payment of these has very little reference to bank notes?" Most certainly it does. Suppose the excess of country paper to be 1000*l.* and in consequence a thousand pounds in Bank of England notes is demanded of the issuer, and sent up to London for the purchase of goods, will not 1000*l.* be added to the London circulation, whilst that of the country is diminished 1000*l.* Now suppose that, instead of a Bank of England note of 1000*l.* a bill on London is given to the holder of the country note: this will as sufficiently answer his purpose of making a purchase in London, but as a bill is only an order to A in London to pay to B in London, the London currency will remain as before; but the country currency will be reduced 1000*l.*

Now the only difference in the two cases is this, that in the former 1000*l.* was added to the London circulation, in the latter it continued at the same amount. But will not the country banker, having by the payment of the thousand pound Bank of England note diminished that deposit, which he thinks it necessary for the safety of his establishment to have by him, give directions to his correspondent, either by the sale of an exchequer bill, or in any other way that might be agreed upon, to send him Bank of England notes to the amount of 1000*l.*?

"If things are cheaper in Liverpool than in London, I shall prefer buying there, and if I have too many bank-notes, I shall send them to Liverpool in payment,"[2]—provided they can circulate there. If they can, Liverpool will partake with London in the increase of circulation, but it is not improbable that a Liverpool banker will find an opportunity of persuading the

---

[1] p. 76.   [2] Bosanquet, p. 77.

people of Liverpool, that his note will answer their purposes as well as the Bank of England note*; he will, therefore, possess himself of it for one of his own, and will send it to London, thus will the circulation of Liverpool be increased by the issues of the Bank of England; and thus Mr. Bosanquet is mistaken, when he observes[1] that "they may restrict, but can never augment, one shilling the circulation of the Liverpool banks." The Committee having "assumed as an axiom, that country bank paper is a superstructure raised on the foundation of the paper of the Bank of England," Mr. Bosanquet asks,[2] where they have learnt this? "They learned from Mr. Stuckey," he continues, "a considerable and experienced banker in Somersetshire, that his houses regulate their issues by the assets they have in London to pay them, consisting of stock, exchequer bills, and other convertible securities, without much reference to the quantity of Bank of England notes or specie which they have, although they always keep a quantity of both to pay occasional demands.[3] What is there in this evidence to sanction the opinion, that bank-notes either generate or limit country notes?"

It may, I think, be shewn, that the increased issues of the Bank would induce Mr. Stuckey, or any other country banker, to increase the amount of his issues, although he kept precisely the securities which he has enumerated. There would be such a demand for country notes, in consequence of the alteration of prices in London, that a country banker would be enabled to obtain bills upon London in return for his notes. With the produce of the bills he might possess himself of a larger sum

* The Committee asked Mr. Stuckey, "Is it not your interest as a banker to check the circulation of Bank of England notes, and with that view do you not remit to London such Bank of England notes as you may receive beyond the amount which you may think it prudent to keep as a deposit in your coffers?" Ans. Unquestionably.[4]

[1] p. 77.
[2] p. 78.
[3] Ricardo here omits two sentences.
[4] 'Minutes of Evidence', p. 212.

of stock, exchequer bills, &c. the foundation being thus increased, the superstructure might be further raised.

The Committee could not have supposed that the Scotch Bank in the year 1763, when they reduced their circulation by giving bills at 40 days upon London, actually deposited banknotes, in the first instance, in the hands of their London correspondents. They might, if such were the case, have redeemed their notes at once with bank-notes in Scotland. No; the Scotch Bank were situated as Mr. Stuckey describes; they had securities of some sort in London, which they authorised their correspondents to turn into money in time to pay their bills. There was a transfer of money from A to B in London, and the Scotch note was withdrawn.

CHAPTER VIII

Mr. Bosanquet's Opinion—that Years of Scarcity and Taxes have been the sole Cause of the Rise of Prices, excessive Circulation no Cause—considered.

M R. Bosanquet, after having shewn, as he imagines, the insufficiency of the arguments of the Committee, to prove that the Bank circulation is excessive, brings forward positive arguments to prove that it is not. The ground of these arguments is, the cause of an advance of prices which arises from years of scarcity, and increased taxation. He has quoted[1] a passage from Dr. Smith in support of this opinion, which I regard as in favour of the opinion which I hold on that subject.

"A prince," says Dr. Smith,[2] "who should enact that a certain proportion of his taxes should be paid in a paper money of any kind, might thereby give a certain value to this paper money, even though the time of its final discharge and redemption should depend altogether on the will of the prince. If the bank which issued this paper were careful to keep the quantity of it always somewhat below what could easily be employed in this manner, the demand for it might be such as even to make it bear a premium, or sell for somewhat more in the market than the quantity of gold and silver for which it was issued."

Now, asks Mr. Bosanquet, as the annual amount of taxes far exceeds the amount of bank-notes, how can paper according to this principle be depreciated? But where does Dr. Smith talk of the annual amount of taxes? It might as fairly be contended, that the comparison of the amount of paper should be

---

[1] pp. 86–7.
[2] Bk. II, ch. ii; vol. I, p. 311. The slight inaccuracies in quotation are Bosanquet's, whom Ricardo follows.

made with the amount of two or three years taxes. I understand Dr. Smith to mean, that if the quantity of paper does not
exceed that amount, which can be wholly and solely employed
in the payment of taxes, it will not be depreciated; he never
could have maintained so extravagant a proposition as that
which Mr. Bosanquet ascribes to him. To try our paper circulation by this rule of Dr. Smith, it should be proved that the
daily payment of taxes is equal in amount to the whole of the
bank-notes in circulation. According to Mr. Bosanquet's interpretation of this passage, as the amount of the total payments
into the exchequer is 76,805,440*l.*, bank-notes cannot become
excessive or depreciated till they exceed that amount. Who, on
reading the passage, can believe that such was the fair meaning
of Dr. Smith's words?

When Mr. Bosanquet talked[1] of a premium having been
given for bank-notes, I conceived he meant a premium in gold
or in silver; I can have no other idea of a premium: but it
seems Mr. Bosanquet meant that a premium was given for
them in paper more depreciated than themselves; in exchequer
bills or banker's checks. Now both of these securities being
payable in bank-notes at some future period, may, on some
occasions, be less valuable than the notes which are wanted
for immediate use, and which will sufficiently account for the
preference. An assignat at a discount of 50 per cent might
have borne such a premium as Mr. B. supposes.

One of the proofs with which Mr. Bosanquet has favoured
his readers[2] of the very small increase that has taken place in
the actual amount of bank-notes, compared with the business
which it has to perform, is, that the increase in the amount
of currency since the year 1793 is three millions, and the
increased amount of payments to Government alone above
sixty millions.

[1] p. 87.   [2] p. 90.

In this calculation the addition to the country currency is wholly omitted. I shall endeavour presently to shew, that it does not by any means necessarily follow that this enormous increase in the amount of taxes should have made any increase of circulation necessary, unless during the same time there had been an increase of commerce and trade.

At present it will be sufficient for me to remark, that had Mr. Bosanquet made a comparative statement from the year 1793 to 1797, he would have possibly seen reason to doubt the accuracy of his *theory* on this subject. During those four years there must have been a considerable addition to the taxes; and, therefore, on Mr. Bosanquet's principles, there should also have been an addition to the circulating medium, which does not appear to be the fact. It is not probable that any very great addition was made to the amount of the coin in circulation; on the contrary, from the very great coinage in 1797 and 1798, the metallic currency must, in 1797, have been at an unusually low level. And it appears from the account delivered in to the Lords' Committee,[1] that the amount of Bank notes in circulation

In the year 1793 amounted to £11,451,180
1796 it varied from . . . 10,713,460
to
9,204,500

and in 1797 the general average, even after the restriction, did not exceed the amount of 1793.

The amount of Bank notes in circulation in 1803 was nearly 18 millions. In 1808 it was not more; and yet no one will deny that in those five years our taxes and expences must have been greatly augmented.—Thus, then, it appears, that considerable additions may be made to the taxes of a country without a corresponding increase in its circulating medium.

[1] 'Report of the Lords' Committee', 1797 (reprint 1810), p. 96.

The Committee is charged by Mr. Bosanquet with not having sufficiently considered the effect of taxation on the prices of commodities; and it is implied in that accusation, that they have exclusively attributed the rise in the prices of commodities to the depreciation of the currency. The Committee would indeed have been highly deserving of censure, if they had held out hopes to the people of this country, that the reformation of the currency could possibly reduce the prices of commodities to that level at which they were previously to the restriction bill. The effect produced on prices by the depreciation has been most accurately defined, and amounts to the difference between the market and the mint price of gold. An ounce of gold coin cannot be of less value, the Committee say,[1] than an ounce of gold bullion of the same standard; a purchaser of corn therefore is entitled to as much of that commodity for an ounce of gold coin, or 3*l*. 17*s*. 10½*d*., as can be obtained for an ounce of gold bullion. Now, as 4*l*. 12*s*. of paper currency is of no more value than an ounce of gold bullion, prices are actually raised to the purchaser 18 per cent., in consequence of his purchase being made with paper instead of coin of its bullion value. Eighteen per cent. is, therefore, equal to the rise in the price of commodities, occasioned by the depreciation of paper. All above such rise may be either traced to the effects of taxation, to the increased scarcity of the commodity, or to any other cause which may appear satisfactory to those who take pleasure in such enquiries.

The theory which Mr. Bosanquet has advanced with respect to taxation, and the effects which it produces on the amount of circulating medium, is exceedingly curious, and is a proof that even practical men are sometimes tempted to wander from the sober paths of practice and experience, to indulge in speculations the most wild, and dreams the most chimerical.

[1] *Bullion Report*, pp. 4–5.

Mr. Bosanquet observes,[1] there are two causes of the augmentation of prices in Great Britain since the date of the restriction bill. 1st, "The altered state of the corn trade, and the scarcity arising out of it, in 1800 and 1801." 2dly, "The increase of taxes since the commencement of the war in 1793."

That the scarcity of corn, and the expences which have attended its importation, must have produced some rise in the prices of commodities I do most readily admit. But is it a self-evident proposition—is it, as Mr. Bosanquet lays it down,[2] an axiom in political economy, that the effect of taxation is to raise the prices of commodities in the full amount of the taxes levied? Does it by any means follow, because taxes since the year 1793 have increased to the enormous amount of forty-eight millions, that all that sum must have gone to the increase of the prices of commodities, and that, therefore, this fact alone will account for a rise of 50 per cent. on the prices of 1793? Does it follow that every person, excepting the stockholder, has the power of indemnifying himself for the taxes which he pays?

Does it make no difference, for example, whether the tax be laid on consumable commodities, or whether it be such a tax as an income tax, assessed taxes, and twenty others that may be named? Do they all tend to raise the prices of commodities? And is every contributor but the stockholder enabled to rid himself of the burthen? If this argument were correct, it would appear that the whole weight of taxation falls exclusively on the stockholders; that the whole annual augmentation since 1793, amounting now to fifty-three millions, must have come from their pockets. Their taxes must at this rate have exceeded their income, because they exceeded the interest of the national debt. This I do not consider very correct doctrine; and, if true, it would not make stockholders

[1] p. 92.   [2] pp. 94-5.

very much enamoured with that species of property. Wars would, on such a principle, never impoverish, and the sources of taxation could never be exhausted.

To me, however, it appears convincingly certain, that neither the income tax, the assessed taxes, nor many others, do in the least affect the prices of commodities.

Unfortunate indeed would be the situation of the consumer, if he had to pay additional prices for those commodities which were necessary to his comfort, after his means of purchasing them had been by the tax considerably abridged.

The income tax, were it fairly imposed, would leave every member of the community in the same relative situation in which it found him. Each man's expences must be diminished to the amount of his tax; and if the seller would wish to relieve himself from the burthen of the tax by raising the price of his commodity, the buyer for the same reason would wish to buy cheaper. These contending interests would so exactly counter-act each other, that prices would undergo no alteration. The same observations are applicable to the assessed taxes, and to all other taxes which are not levied on commodities. But if the tax should in its operation be unequal, if it should fall par-ticularly heavy on one class of trade, the profits of that trade would be diminished below the general level of mercantile profits, and those engaged in it would either desert it for one more profitable, or they would raise the price of the com-modities in which they dealt, so as to bring it to produce the same rate of profits as other trades.

Taxes on commodities would certainly raise the price of the commodity taxed to the full amount of the tax. The price for such commodities may be considered as divided into two portions; one portion, its original and natural price, and the other a tax for the liberty of consuming it. If this tax again were laid on a commodity, the consumption of which, by each individual, was in exact proportion to his income, no other commodity would rise but the one taxed; but if it were not in such proportion, those who paid more than their just portion would demand an increased price for the commodity in which they dealt, and, by obtaining it, the society would be put in the same relative situation in which they were before placed.

If, instead of the tax being laid on the commodity, each individual were to pay no more for the commodity than the original price, and were to pay the amount of the tax at once to government for a licence to consume it, it would act precisely as the assessed taxes do, there would be only a partial rise in the prices of some commodities to compensate the inequality which, in spite of the best wishes of the legislature, must accompany every tax.

If this view of the effect of taxation be correct, it will follow that Mr. Bosanquet's estimate, that 48 millions has been actually added to the prices of commodities in consequence of taxation since the year 1793, and that such addition will sufficiently account for the rise in the prices of commodities, without having recourse to the depreciation of the circulating medium as the cause, is a false theory, neither supported by reason nor probability.

From these statements Mr. Bosanquet has deduced another consequence, viz. that

As the value of commodities has been raised 48 millions since 1793, and the circulation only increased 3 millions, such increase cannot be called excessive*.

Although in the preceding statement I have conceded to Mr. Bosanquet, that in consequence of some of our taxes the

---

* If we add to these 3 millions the increase in the country circulation, and bear in mind the economy in the use of circulating medium, so ably and so clearly explained by Mr. Bosanquet, it would appear to me that, granting all the facts for which Mr. Bosanquet contends, the circulating medium has increased in an undue proportion.

prices of commodities will be increased, it does not appear necessarily to follow that more money will be requisite to circulate them.

That amount of money which is received by government in the shape of taxes, is taken from a fund which would otherwise have been expended on consumable commodities.

In proportion as the taxes are great, must the expences of the people diminish. If my income amounts to 1000*l.*, and government requires 100*l.* in taxes from me, I shall have but 900*l.* to expend on such necessaries and comforts as are requisite for the use of my family. If government take 200 I shall have but 800 for such purposes. Now, as the amount of money actually expended by government and by me cannot exceed 1000*l.*, no additional circulating medium would, I think, be required, although the taxes were 50 per cent. of each man's income. If the tax were laid upon bread, and, in consequence, the wages of labour were raised, the tax would eventually fall on all those who consumed the produce of the labour of man. It would make no real difference to these consumers if they had at once paid the amount of such tax into the exchequer, or if it had gone through the circuitous channel which it would then take.

Nor would any additional sum be required. Government would be in the daily receipt of a portion of the taxes, whether it was paid to the exciseman or to the tax-gatherer, and their expences in the one case would be precisely the same as in the other. Whatever the government expended would cause a diminished expenditure in the people to the same amount: the same amount of commodities would be circulated, and the same money would be adequate to their circulation.

This is on the supposition that the people were sufficiently prudent or sufficiently rich to pay all the taxes from their annual income, and were not tempted or compelled to diminish their capital to satisfy the calls of government. If capital were however diminished, the aggregate amount of productions would also diminish; and if the money which was before necessary for their circulation were to continue of the same amount, it would bear a larger proportion to the goods, and it might therefore be expected that commodities would rise; but we must not forget that the amount of money in a country is regulated by its value, and as its value would in this case be diminished, it would become relatively excessive to the money of other countries, and the excess would therefore be exported.

When we talk of a scarcity of corn, and a consequent increase of price, it is naturally concluded, because its value is doubled, that double the value of money will be necessary to circulate it, but this is by no means obvious or necessary. If double the money be necessary, there should be an equal quantity of corn at double the usual price,—but it is because there is a diminished quantity of corn that its price is doubled.

If the commerce of a country increases, that is to say, if by its savings it is enabled to add to its capital, such country will require an additional amount of circulating medium; but, under all circumstances, the currency ought to retain its bullion value; that is the only sure test by which we may know that it is not excessive.

CHAPTER IX

Mr. Bosanquet's Opinion, that Evil would result from the Resumption of Cash Payments—considered.

To conclude, Mr. Bosanquet is persuaded[1] that much evil will ensue from the resumption of cash payments, and he cannot anticipate any improvement in the course of exchange, or any fall in the price of bullion from a reduction of the circulation, unless our imports are diminished and our exports increased.

To me, however, it appears perfectly clear, that a reduction of Bank notes would lower the price of bullion and improve the exchange, without in the least disturbing the regularity of our present exports and imports. It would neither enable us to export or import gold in any way different to what is now actually taking place. Our transactions with foreigners would be precisely the same, we should possess only a more valuable money of the same name; and instead of being credited by Hamburgh for a depreciated pound sterling, which will only purchase 104 grains of gold, at the rate of 28 Flemish schillings, we should, by restoring our pound sterling to its true bullion value, viz. 123 grains, have a credit at the rate of 34 schillings. The difference, however, of six schillings, which would thus appear in our favour, would be an advantage in name and appearance solely. No mistake would be greater than to suppose there was in it any real advantage.

If, by a reduction of Bank notes, they were so raised in value as to be above the value of gold bullion, we should then interfere with the real course of exchange; we should disturb the present equilibrium of imports and exports; and we should cause an importation of bullion, or, in the language of merchants, a favourable balance of trade.

If Mr. Bosanquet's view of our affairs were indeed correct,

[1] pp. 102–3.

gloomy would be our prospects. Obliged to support a great foreign expenditure, "to import articles with which we cannot dispense," and in return for which nothing but gold will be accepted, we might almost calculate the period at which the contest must terminate, from a want of this most essential commodity. For a balance of payments so enormous as he calculates, gold could not be found in this country for one twelvemonth; and if our goods can no where purchase it, how hopeless must be our condition!

For my part, however, I have no such apprehensions. I am persuaded that our foreign expenditure is neither paid with gold nor with bills of exchange,—that it must eventually be discharged with the produce of the labour and industry of our people.

It is only to a blind perseverance in our present system of circulation that I look with alarm,—a system which is gradually undermining our resources, and the inconveniences and evils of which, in the language of the Committee,[1] "if not checked, must at no great distance of time work a practical conviction upon the minds of all those who may still doubt their existence; but even if their progressive increase were less probable, the integrity and honour of Parliament are concerned not to authorize longer than is required by imperious necessity, the continuance in this great commercial country of a system of circulation in which that natural check or controul is absent, which maintains the value of money, and, by the permanency of that common standard of value secures the substantial justice and faith of monied contracts and obligations between man and man."

May we be permitted to hope, that what an enlightened Committee has so happily begun, is a pledge of what will be accomplished by the wisdom of Parliament?

[1] *Report*, p. 74.

APPENDIX

AFTER the preceding sheets were sent to the press, I read the supplementary observations of Mr. Bosanquet, annexed to the second edition of his pamphlet.[1] I shall have but few remarks to make on them.

1st, From what I have already said[2] it may be seen that I deny the accuracy of all Mr. Bosanquet's calculations concerning the exchange with Hamburgh. Those calculations are made on the assumption of a fixed invariable par, whilst the true par, on which they should have been made, is subject to all the variations to which the relative value of gold and silver is exposed. These two metals having varied no less since the year 1801, than from $6\frac{1}{2}$ per cent. under the mint proportions, to 9 per cent. above those proportions; calculations made on such a principle may involve errors to no less an amount than $15\frac{1}{2}$ per cent. 2dly, The argument attempted to be founded on the fact of the increase or diminution in the amount of Bank notes, not having invariably been accompanied by a fall or rise in the exchange, or by a rise or fall in the price of bullion, is of no avail against a theory which admits that the demand for circulating medium is subject to continual fluctuations, proceeding from an increase or decrease in the amount of capital and commerce; from a greater or less facility which at one period may be afforded to payments by a varying degree of confidence and credit; and, in short, which supposes that the same commerce and payments may require very different amounts of circulating medium. An amount of Bank notes which at one time may be

[1] *Practical Observations*, 'Second Edition, Corrected, with A Supplement', 1810. The latter was also published as a separate pamphlet under the title *Supplement to Practical Observations on the Report* of the *Bullion-Committee*, London, Richardson, 1810 (24 pp., numbered 111 to 134, as in the 2nd ed. of the complete work).
[2] Above, p. 166.

excessive, in the sense in which I use that term,[1] and which may therefore be depreciated,—may, at another, be barely sufficient for the payments which it may have to perform, barring the effect of a temporary increase in its value above that of the bullion which it represents. It will therefore be useless to admit or to deny the correctness of the grounds on which Mr. Bosanquet's calculation of the amount of country paper in circulation is founded. Those facts do not, in my opinion, bear upon the subject in dispute. Whether the paper currency be 25 or 100 millions, I consider it equally certain that it is excessive, because I am not aware of any causes but excess or a want of confidence in the issuers[2] of the paper (which I am sure does not now exist), which could produce such effects as we have for a *considerable time** witnessed.

Mr. Bosanquet has thrown the inferences which he wishes to be drawn from the facts he has newly brought forward into the shape of four problems;[3] the solution of which, upon the principles of the Committee, he presumes to be impossible. I hope I have already shewn that his facts fall abundantly short of proving the points which he makes to rest upon them, and I think the difficulty will not be great in giving him even a

* Mr. Bosanquet has remarked as incorrect, my having used the words "length of time"[4] in reference to a discount on Bank notes, because Mr. Mushet's tables did not indicate a very unfavourable exchange for more than a year before I wrote, in Dec. 1809. We should once have thought a year a *considerable time*, when speaking of a discount on Bank notes, but as I have constantly maintained that the high price of bullion was the test on which I most relied for the proof of depreciation, and as the price of gold has not been under the Mint price for about ten years, the correctness of my conclusion cannot, I think, on my principles, be questioned.

[1] Cp. above, p. 229, n. 1.
[2] Misprinted 'issues', corrected in *Errata*.
[3] *Supplement*, pp. 129–30.
[4] 'I conclude, that Mr. Ricardo's opinion, that the paper-currency *had long been excessive*, when he wrote in 1809, was incorrect'. (*Practical Observations*, pp. 10–11.) Cp. *High Price of Bullion*, above, p. 51.

solution of his problems in perfect conformity with the principles of the Committee.

The first problem is, "The fall of the exchange, from an average of 6 per cent. in favour, from 1790 to 1795, to 3 per cent. below par, in 1795 and 6, with an equal circulation of eleven millions of Bank paper, convertible into specie on demand, and the advance of the exchange to 11 per cent. above par, on average in 1797 and 1798, the circulation being increased to thirteen millions and not so convertible."

The reader will perceive that this problem has already received its solution in the body of the work. The exchanges are not correctly stated, and no one denies that the exchanges may rise and fall from many causes.

It has been proved[1] that the demand for gold for the Mint, and for silver for the East Indies, in the years 1797 and 1798, had their natural effect on the exchange, and was not counteracted by an extravagant issue of paper currency. The gold was required to fill up the exhausted coffers of the Bank; it was therefore not sent into circulation; and the addition of two millions in Bank notes served only to supply the vacuum which the hoarding of money had occasioned; so that there was no real increase to the circulation of those years.

The second problem is, "The fall of the exchange to 6 per cent. below par, and gold 9 per cent. above the mint price in 1800 and 1801, the Bank circulation rather above 15 millions, and the advance to 3 per cent. above par, on average of six years, from 1803 to 1808, and gold nearly at the mint price, with an augmented circulation of 17 to 18 millions."

Besides the effects from a varying degree of commerce and credit, it should be recollected that whilst our circulation consisted partly of gold and partly of paper, the effect of an increased issue of paper, both on the exchanges and the price of

[1] Above, pp. 171-2.

bullion, was corrected, after a sufficient interval, by the exportation of the coin. That resource has been for some time lost to us.

The third problem, viz. "The fall of the exchange, from 5 per cent. above par, in July 1808, to 10 per cent. below par, in June 1809, the Bank circulation being the same in both instances;" is of easy solution. I cannot find the document from which Mr. Bosanquet has stated that the amount of Bank notes was the same in July 1808 as in June 1809; but, admitting its correctness, are they fair subjects of comparison? One period is immediately after the payment of the dividends, the other immediately before. In January and July 1809 there was no less an increase in the amount of Bank notes, after the payment of the dividends, than 2,450,000*l.* and in the January following, 1,878,000*l.*

I am not disposed to contend that the issues of one day, or of one month, can produce any effect on the foreign exchanges; it may possibly require a period of more permanent duration; an interval is absolutely necessary before such effects would follow. This is never considered by those who oppose the principles of the Committee. They conclude that those principles are defective, because their operation is not immediately perceived. But what are the facts respecting the circulation of Bank notes in the years 1808 and 1809? There are only three returns of their amount in the year 1808 made to the Bullion Committee. Let us compare them with the returns for the same periods in 1809, and I think my readers will agree with me, that these facts will rather confirm than appear to be at variance with the principles of the Committee.

Amount of Bank notes In 1808.		Amount of Bank notes In 1809.	
1 May . .	17,491,900	1 May . .	18,646,880
1 August .	17,644,670	1 August .	19,811,330
1 November .	17,467,170	1 November .	19,949,290

As for the fourth problem, viz. "The gradually increasing price of commodities, during the American war, when the circulation was gold, and during the six years from 1803 to 1808, when the exchange was in favour," where has it been disputed that there are not other causes besides the depreciation of money which may account for a rise in the prices of commodities? The point for which I contend is, that when such rise is accompanied by a permanent rise in the price of that bullion which is the standard of currency, then to the amount of that rise is the currency depreciated. During the American war the rise in the prices of commodities was not attended with any rise in the price of bullion, and was therefore not occasioned by a depreciation of the currency.

We are now, for the first time, left to doubt, whether the principles of the Committee against which Mr. Bosanquet in the body of his work had so strongly contended, are really at variance with his own. We are now told not that the theory is erroneous, but "that the facts must be established before they can be reasoned upon,"[1] "and that the importance of those facts[2] would, in no degree, be lessened even by an unreserved admission of the accuracy of the principles assumed." Does this declaration accord with Mr. Bosanquet's conclusions? Certain principles are brought forward by the Bullion Committee, and which, if true, prove the fact of the depreciation of the currency. Your principles are plausible, and reason appears to sanction them, says Mr. Bosanquet, but here are facts to prove that they are inconsistent with past experience; and he further observes[3] from Paley, "that when a theorem is proposed to a mathematician, the first thing he does with it is to try it on a simple case; if it produce a false result, he is sure there must

---

[1] *Supplement*, p. 115.
[2] Bosanquet actually says 'the importance of what, in the preceding pages, I have offered to the public' (*Supplement*, p. 113).
[3] *Practical Observations*, p. 4.

be some error in the demonstration." "The public must proceed in this way with the report, and submit its theories to the test of fact." Can, then, Mr. Bosanquet be consistent in contending[1] "that the importance of what, in his preceding pages, he had offered to the public, would be in no degree lessened even by an unreserved admission of the accuracy of the principles assumed?"

If the theory of the Committee is allowed to be accurate on the one hand, and Mr. Bosanquet's facts are accurate on the other, what follows? Either that Mr. Bosanquet agrees with the Committee, or that his facts are totally inapplicable to the question. One other conclusion there is, but one which I have no intention to ascribe to Mr. Bosanquet;—That there may be a theory on the one side, and facts on the other; both true, and yet inconsistent.

As for Dr. Paley's test, of trying the Committee's theory by a simple case; Mr. Bosanquet might have tried it by a thousand, and would have found it accurately to correspond. Had he employed his leisure and ingenuity in tracing its application to the thousands of cases with which it accords, instead of hunting for two or three cases *seemingly* contradictory, and adopting them with fond credulity, he would have probably arrived at more just conclusions.

Mr. Bosanquet[2] calls in question the accuracy of the following proposition of Mr. Huskisson,[3] "that if one part of the currency of a country (provided such currency be made either directly or virtually legal tender according to its denomination) be depreciated, the whole of that currency, whether paper or coin, *must* be equally depreciated."

The fact brought forward by Mr. Bosanquet,[4] that the "extraordinary depreciation of the silver coin, in the reign of King

---

[1] *Supplement*, p. 113.
[2] p. 117.
[3] *The Question...*, p. vii.
[4] *Supplement*, p. 118.

William, did not depreciate the gold; that, on the contrary, the
guinea, worth 21 perfect shillings, passed currently for 30
shillings," does not prove the principle advanced by Mr. Huskisson to be at variance with experience, because gold was not
then the current coin; it was not either *directly* or *virtually* legal
tender; nor was it estimated at a fixed value by public authority:
it passed in all payments as a piece of bullion of known weight
and fineness. If by law it could not have passed for more than
21*s.* of the debased silver currency, it would, whilst in the state
of coin, have been equally debased with the 21*s.* for which it
would have exchanged. If guineas were now to be considered
as a commodity, and were not by law prohibited from being
exported or melted, they might pass in all payments at 24 or
25 shillings, whilst the Bank note continued of its present value.

Neither is the following principle of Mr. Huskisson,[1] from
which Mr. Bosanquet dissents,[2] *contrary to authority;* "That
if the quantity of gold, in a country whose currency consists of
gold, should be increased in any given proportion, the quantity
of other articles and the demand for them remaining the same,
the value of any given commodity measured in the coin of that
country would be increased in the same proportion." Mr. Huskisson does not question, as Mr. Bosanquet supposes, the truth
of the principle advanced by Dr. Adam Smith,[3] "that the increase in the quantity of the precious metals, which arises in
any country from an increase of wealth, has no tendency to
diminish their value;" but says, that if the quantity of the
precious metals increases in any country, whilst its wealth does
not increase, or whilst its commodities remain the same in
quantity, then will the value of the gold coin of such country
diminish, or, in other words, goods will rise in price. Mr. Bosanquet himself, in the argument relating to the mine, has

---

[1] *The Question...*, p. 5.
[2] *Supplement*, p. 118.

[3] In substance, *Wealth of Nations*,
Bk. I, ch. xi, pt. iii; vol. I, p. 191.

admitted that such would be the effect.[1] To this passage from
Mr. Huskisson's book, however, I have an objection to offer,
because he adds, that an increase in the prices of commodities
would take place (page 5) under the circumstances supposed,
"although no addition should actually be made to the coin of
the country." I hold it as a conclusion which will not admit of
dispute, that if neither commodities, nor the demand for them,
nor the money which circulates them, suffer either increase or
diminution, prices must continue unaltered, whatever quantity
of gold or silver may exist in the state of bullion in such
country*. It is hardly necessary to remark, that the case is
wholly hypothetical, and is indeed impossible. There can be
no great addition to the bullion of a country the currency of
which is of its standard value, without causing an increase in
the quantity of money.

I confess I was not a little surprised by the next point brought
forward by Mr. Bosanquet, and I have no doubt it must have
excited equal astonishment in many of his readers. Having
contended throughout his work that Bank notes were not depreciated as compared with gold coin, that the same rise in the
price of gold might have taken place, and actually had, on some
occasions, taken place, whilst our currency consisted partly of
gold, and partly of paper convertible into gold, at the will of
the holder; after denying that there was any point of contact
between gold for exportation and gold in coin, and that it was
for want of such contact that its price had risen, we are now
seriously told by Mr. Bosanquet that, "applying to this subject
the most approved theories, he inclines to the belief that gold,
since the new system of the Bank of England payments has been
fully established, has *not*, in truth, continued to be the measure

* It is to be understood that I am supposing no increased or diminished
confidence operating, so as to give a diminished or increased value to
the coin.

[1] See above, pp. 216–17.

of value. Bank notes," he maintains, "have since 1797 unquestionably become the measure of commerce, and the money
of account, and it is on these grounds that he considers the
proposition respecting the price of gold, on which so much
reliance is placed, as one of those which, though he admits the
principle, he hesitates at the application."[1] Whether the Bank
Directors, or others who have so confidently asserted that, admitting gold to be the standard, its high price did not prove
the depreciation of the currency, will be pleased with a defence
on such principles, which yields all for which the Committee
contend, it is not for me to enquire. That gold is no longer in
practice the standard by which our currency is regulated is a truth.
It is the ground of the complaint of the Committee (and of all
who have written on the same side) against the present system.

The holder of money has been injured, inasmuch as there is
no standard reference by which his property can be protected.
He has suffered a loss of 16 per cent. since 1797, and there is no
security for him that it may not shortly be 25, 30, or even 50
per cent. more. Who will consent to hold money or securities,
the interest on which is payable in money, on such terms? There
is no sacrifice which a man holding such property should not
make, to secure to himself some provision for the future whilst
such a system is avowed. Mr. Bosanquet has, in these few
words, said as much in favour of the repeal of the restriction
bill as all the writers, all the theorists, have advanced since the
discussion of this subject commenced. What, then, does Mr.
Bosanquet admit that we have no standard because it is no
longer gold? Let us hear what he says[2]: "If a pound note be
the *denomination*, it will, of course, be asked what is the
standard?

"The question is not easy of solution. But, considering the

---

[1] The quotation is made up of non-consecutive passages from the *Supplement*, pp. 119, 121 and 122.
[2] *ib.* pp. 122–3.

high proportion which the dealings between government and
the public bear to the general circulation, it is probable the
standard may be found in those transactions; and it seems not
more difficult to imagine that the standard value of a one pound
note may be the interest of 33*l*. 6*s*. 8*d*.—3 per cent. stock, than
that such standard has reference to a metal, of which none
remains in circulation, and of which the annual supply, even
as a commodity, does not amount to one twentieth part of the
foreign expences of government in one year."

So then we *have* a standard for a pound Bank note, it is
the interest of 33*l*. 6*s*. 8*d*.—3 per cent. stock. Now, in what
medium is this interest paid? because *that* must be the standard.
The holder of 33*l*. 6*s*. 8*d*. stock receives at the Bank a one pound
note. Bank notes are, therefore, according to the theory of a
practical man, the standard by which alone the depreciation of
Bank notes can be estimated !

A puncheon of rum has 16 per cent. of its contents taken out,
and water poured in for it. What is the standard by which
Mr. Bosanquet attempts to detect the adulteration? A sample
of the adulterated liquor taken out of the same cask.

We are next told, that "if the Bank really possess a large
stock of gold, or only to the extent of six or seven millions, the
best use they can make of it is to call in all the notes under 5*l*.,
and not re-issue any of this description." [1]

How could bankers and manufacturers be enabled to effect
their small payments if the gold, thus partially issued, were at
the present exchange and price of bullion to be either exported
or melted? If the Bank did not issue small notes, and they could
not procure guineas for large ones, they would be obliged to
cease such payments altogether. The more I have reflected on
this subject, the more convinced I am that the evil admits of no
other safe remedy but a reduction in the amount of Bank notes.

[1] *Supplement*, pp. 133–4.

NOTES FROM RICARDO'S
MANUSCRIPTS
1810–1811

NOTES ON BENTHAM'S
'SUR LES PRIX'
1810–1811

NOTE ON 'NOTES ON BENTHAM'

RICARDO wrote his comments on Dumont's French translation of Bentham's papers on currency between 25 December 1810 and 11 January 1811. They are here published for the first time.

Mill, who had been consulted by Dumont as to 'the propriety of publishing', sent Dumont's MS to Ricardo, asking him to read it and to write down his remarks, 'and to make them pretty minute.' Mill's own opinion, after having read the first part of Dumont's MS, was not favourable: 'they are loose papers of the author, not put in order, on a subject which he ceased to study before he had probed it to the bottom.'[1] Ricardo and Mill seem to have agreed in advising against publication; but as Dumont was anxious to proceed with it, a meeting between the three of them was arranged for 11 January at Ricardo's house at Mile End;[2] the outcome of their discussion is not recorded, but in the end publication did not take place.[3]

Bentham had written his papers on currency many years before. On 25 February 1801, writing to arrange for the publication of a reply which he intended to make to Boyd's recent pamphlet,[4] he said that the subject of currency had 'occupied a considerable share of [his] attention for some time', and added that 'one day, perhaps' he might devote to the subject 'a regular

---

[1] Letter of Mill, 25 Dec. 1810; below, VI, 14.

[2] See below, VI, 18–21.

[3] The discussion was renewed in 1822 when Ricardo visited Geneva. Of this the Duc de Broglie later said to Senior: 'I remember a conversation at Coppet, which lasted for one or two days, between Ricardo and Dumont, as to Bentham's Political Economy. Dumont produced many manuscripts of Bentham's on that subject. There were few of his doctrines to which Ricardo did not object, and, as it seemed to me, victoriously.' (Entry of 8 March 1858 in *Conversations with M. Thiers, M. Guizot, and Other Distinguished Persons, during the Second Empire*, by N. W. Senior, 1878, vol. II, p. 176.)

[4] *A Letter to the Rt Hon. W. Pitt, on the Influence of the Stoppage of Issues in Specie at the Bank of England on the Prices of Provisions, and Other Commodities*, by Walter Boyd, London, Wright, 1801.

work, not dependent on times or persons'.[1] Two months later he appears to have amalgamated the two projects, intending to publish a single work to deal with Boyd and at the same time to expound his own views on the subject. In a letter of 20 April 1801 to Nicholas Vansittart, he wrote that 'for about these two years' the chief part of his time had been occupied with the subject of money: 'I am preparing a pamphlet, to which I think of giving for a title, *The True Alarm*, (in contradistinction and reference to Mr Boyd's, which appears to me to be in great measure, though perhaps not wholly, false) or Thoughts on Pecuniary Credit,— its advantages, inconveniencies, dangers, and their remedies. By the *inconveniences*, I mean *rise of prices*, (allowance made for the still greater, but temporary effects of bad seasons.) By the danger, I mean that of general bankruptcy. By the remedy, I do *not* mean the *suppression* of paper money,—a remedy which would at once convert the *danger* into the hight of the disease.'[2]

Of these early projects of Bentham, Dumont later wrote in the Introduction to his own translation: 'L'auteur avoit entrepris son ouvrage à une epoque où il regnoit une grande alarme en Angleterre rélativement à la disette, à la hausse des prix et à la multiplication du papier-monnoie: *Alarme* etoit le titre general de tous les manuscrits. L'intention de l'auteur etoit de justifier les craintes publiques relativement à la hausse des prix et à la ruine probable du credit pecuniaire par l'augmentation indefinie du papier-monnoie—mais il ne vouloit se joindre aux alarmistes et augmenter l'effroi que pour se faire ecouter en proposant les remedes. Alarme etoit le principe—securité etoit le résultat.'[3]

The project of publication came to nothing and Bentham entirely abandoned the papers which he had written on the subject. Some time between 1802 and 1810[4] he handed over all the

---

[1] Letter to H. J. Pye, in Bentham's *Works*, ed. Bowring, vol. x, p. 361.
[2] *Works*, vol. x, p. 364.
[3] Fols. 31–2 of the MS.
[4] There is no direct evidence to determine more closely the date of Dumont's translation. That it

was in the earlier part of the period in question is suggested by his having preserved Bentham's reference to 1801 as the 'present' (below, p. 269), and by the early watermark of the paper used (1794). That Dumont was working on Bentham's economic

MSS to Dumont, at the request of the latter, who intended to translate and arrange for publication this disorganised mass of material, as he had done for other works of Bentham.

A note written by Dumont at some later date on the MS of the translation, runs: 'Ces manuscrits avoient été entierement abandonnés par l'auteur—il me les remit à ma demande en m'avertissant que d'essai en essai il avoit souvent changé d'avis, qu'il étoit sans cesse revenu sur ses pas et qu'il n'y avoit point d'ordre dans les Mss. quoiqu'il y en eut un dans le résultat &c. J'ai cherché à le trouver en divisant l'ouvrage en 3 parties qui me paroissent distinctes—mais il y a un grand nombre d'essais qui ne contiennent que des repetitions, entre lesquelles il faudroit choisir.'[1]

It is the MS of this translation, still somewhat chaotic, which Dumont, when the interest in currency questions had been stimulated by the Bullion Controversy, sent to James Mill, who passed it on to Ricardo.

Ricardo's comments amounted to a detailed criticism of the work. They add little to what was already known of his views on currency at this time, and their chief interest lies in that they provide some indication of his early views on other questions of political economy.[2]

Dumont's MS, with Ricardo's commentary, remained among Dumont's papers and was presented by his heir, Dr Duval, to the Bibliothèque Publique et Universitaire de Genève in 1870, where it is preserved. It is there catalogued under the title

writings in 1804 appears from their correspondence in that year, but whether he was engaged on this or some other work is uncertain. (See Bentham's *Works*, vol. x, pp. 413 and 416.)

[1] Fol. 35 of the MS. A still later note on the same folio reads: 'en 1808,—j'ai remis ces Mss. dont je n'ai pu me tirer à ma satisfaction à Mr Ricardo,—les notes en anglais sont de lui,—mais malheureusement les renvois sont perdus.' The reference to 1808 is undoubtedly a mistake for 1810, and shows that this note was written many years later. The allusion to the 'renvois' is obscure; Ricardo's MS at present at any rate seems complete.

[2] See, *e.g.* on wages and prices, p. 270; on accumulation, pp. 274 and 276; on utility and value, p. 284; on diminishing returns, p. 287, etc.

'Matériaux d'un traité sur la hausse des prix et les effets du papier-monnaie', and classmarked Ms. D. 50 (Inventaire 1495).

Dumont's papers bear no general title, but in one place (fol. 338) the work is referred to as *Sur les prix*. The work is composed of a number of separate Chapters or Propositions, each written on a separate quire, of a variable number of sheets. These Chapters were grouped by Dumont in three Books, as follows:

> Livre I. Préliminaires. De la Richesse considérée dans ses modifications, sa valeur et ses sources.
> Livre II. De la hausse des prix et des effets du papier-monnoye.
> Livre III. Remedes.[1]

On Livres I and II of Dumont's MS Ricardo marked the passages on which he commented with marginal numbers (1–39 for Livre I, and 1–71 for Livre II) which correspond to those of his Notes. The Notes themselves were written on other sheets.

Within each Book Dumont numbered neither the pages, nor the quires, nor the Chapters.[2] In the present edition the Chapters are arranged in the order of Ricardo's Notes, which must have been that of the MS as he received it. For Book I, however, Dumont wrote, apparently at a later period, on paper water-marked 1807, a Table of Contents in which the Chapters were numbered.[3] These numbers have been here prefixed to the Chapter headings.

The Geneva Ms. D. 50 consists of 488 folios (including 43 blanks), made up as follows:

[1] Livre III was not commented on by Ricardo and therefore none of it is printed here.

[2] The leaves must have got mixed up in more recent times, and the confusion has been crystallised by the pagination given to them a few years ago.

[3] The order given in Dumont's Table of Contents agrees in general with that followed by Ricardo in the numbering of his Notes. The Section, however, headed 'Diminution de valeur par augmentation d'argent' (below, p. 276), which appears from the sequence of Ricardo's Notes to have occurred between Chapters 2 and 4 in the MS as he saw it, is entered in Dumont's Table as a separate Chapter at the end of Book I.

Fols. 1–19. Ricardo's Notes, covering 14 folios of quarto note-paper and 5 of large foolscap.

Fols. 20–29. A series of notes in English on a French book of political economy, not identified, in John Stuart Mill's youthful handwriting, with corrections in James Mill's handwriting, on paper watermarked 1824. (These have no connection with the Dumont-Ricardo MS and must have been included under a misapprehension.)

Fols. 30–137. Livre I (including the Introduction and one quire of Livre II).

Fols. 138–337. Livre II.

Fols. 338–433. Livre III.

(Fols. 30–433 are written in Dumont's handwriting, on one side only, on quarto paper watermarked 1794, of English make; except fol. 30, containing the Table of Contents mentioned above, p. 264, which is watermarked 1807.)

Fols. 434–439. 'Essai d'un resumé general' (of Bentham's work) in Dumont's handwriting, on foolscap paper watermarked 1802, of English make.

The remainder of the MS, ending with fol. 488, consists of miscellaneous papers in Dumont's handwriting on various economic subjects (including an essay on Thornton's *Paper Credit*).

Of the original papers of Bentham which Dumont used for his work, none are among the MSS at Geneva. There are, however, some fragments among the Bentham MSS at University College, London: they are described in the Catalogue as 'Political economy—paper mischief; 1800' and 'Alarm remedies; 1801' (Box III (a), fols. 84–147 and 148–171).[1]

The same method of printing has been adopted in this case as for the *Notes on Malthus* in Vol. II. So much of Dumont's MS as is necessary for the understanding of Ricardo's *Notes* has been

[1] One sheet headed 'Alarm remedies. Contents' is dated '2 March, 1801' and 'Oct. 1, 1801', and inscribed, probably later, 'for Dumont'. Dr Stark has added the information that Box I contains some further fragments of the Alarm papers (fols. 617–626).

printed in smaller type on the upper part of the page (omissions being indicated by points); and the corresponding Notes of Ricardo are printed in larger type on the lower part of the page. (An opening, *i.e.* two pages facing one another, is for this purpose regarded as a single page.) The reference numbers have been placed as Ricardo placed them on Dumont's MS. All but the purely verbal corrections in Ricardo's MS have been noticed in footnotes. Dumont's own remarks written on the margins of his MS and referring to difficulties in Bentham's original papers have been inserted in the text in square brackets.

———

Since the above Note and the text below have been in page-proof Mr E. Silberner has published Ricardo's notes (together with Ricardo's letter to Dumont of 6 Jan. 1811[1]) in the *Revue d'Histoire économique et sociale*, vol. xxv (1940), p. 195 ff. On the basis of Dumont's statement that he sent the MS to Ricardo in 1808, Mr Silberner has argued at some length in his Introduction that Bentham had a decisive intellectual influence in directing Ricardo's interest towards the study of monetary questions, some time before Ricardo had published anything. Since, however, as we have seen above (p. 263, n. 1), Dumont's statement about the date is a mistake for 1810, and the MS was in fact sent to Ricardo almost exactly a year *after* the publication of his *High Price of Bullion*, this argument loses its basis.

A letter of Ricardo to Mill of 1 Jan. 1811[2], which has come to light with the Mill-Ricardo papers, gives a summary of Ricardo's views on Bentham's work while he was reading it.

[1] Below, VI, 20.   [2] *ib.* 14–18.

CONTENTS

LIVRE I. PRÉLIMINAIRES.

DE LA RICHESSE CONSIDÉRÉE DANS SES MODIFICATIONS, SA VALEUR ET SES SOURCES.

INTRODUCTION.

La valeur de l'argent n'est à présent (en 1801) que la moitié de ce qu'elle etoit il y a 40 ans: elle ne sera dans 40 ans que la moitié de ce qu'elle est à présent. 1

Ces deux propositions servent de base à cet ouvrage et aux mesures qu'on indique pour prévenir ce mal....

---

1. As I attribute the fall in the value of money during the last 40 years to the increase of the metals from which money is made, I cannot anticipate a similar fall in the next 40 years unless we should discover new and abundant mines of the precious metals.

The argument in this chapter is that an increase of paper money has the same effects in increasing prices as an increase of metallic money. This is no doubt true, but we should recollect that paper money cannot be increased without causing a depreciation of such money as compared with the precious metals. It would therefore be true that the evils of an abundance of paper money would be visible by a rise in the prices of commodities,—but a paper money which should never be of less value than the coins which it represents can never be[1] in more abundance than those coins would have been if there had been no paper. The value of gold may be affected by the increase of paper but it will speedily regain

---

[1] 'permanently multiplied beyond the gold and silver which' was first written here, and then replaced by 'so multiplied as to be permanently', which was also deleted.

Augmentation des prix ou *dépréciation de l'argent* ne sont que
2 deux manieres differentes d'exprimer le même fait.

Il y a plusieurs hypotheses communes pour rendre compte de
l'augmentation des prix—on en accuse quelquefois les mauvaises
saisons, mais alors ce n'est qu'un effet passager—on l'impute plus
communément aux taxes, et l'opération de cette cause est incontestable, mais elle est bien loin de suffire pour expliquer l'effet
tout entier, et chacun peut observer que les articles de consommation les plus essentiels, le blé, le foin, le charbon, la viande
3 de boucherie ont augmenté de prix sans avoir été l'objet d'aucune
taxe directe. On l'attribue à l'augmentation du numéraire, à la
multiplication du papier, et c'est la, d'après toutes les recherches
que j'ai pu faire, qu'il faut chercher la grande cause, la veritable
cause qui explique cette depréciation passée du numéraire et qui
prépare la depréciation future.

D'un autre côté, s'il est une circonstance qui puisse servir
4 d'indice à la prospérité nationale, il semble que ce soit surtout
l'etat avantageux du crédit pécuniaire, tel qu'il se manifeste dans
l'accroissement du papier-monnoie.

La bonne-foi en est la base: la richesse réelle et substantielle
en est le résultat. C'est un sujet d'orgueil national soit qu'on
tourne ses regards sur son origine soit qu'on les porte sur ses
effets.

Mais ce n'est pas un bien sans mélange: il renferme un mal
actuel qui l'emporte peut être sur le bien et un danger qui, s'il
venoit à se réaliser, excederoit sans aucun doute tous ses avantages.

---

its value, as the mines would cease to supply the usual quantity owing to the diminished profits. No paper circulation
can therefore be permanently of less value than the coins
which they truly represent.

2. Is this passage quite correct? May there not be an
augmentation in the price of commodities whilst the value
of money continued absolutely stationary?

3. Commodities may rise from taxation tho' they are
not subject to any direct taxation themselves. If a tax were
laid on bread every commodity would rise, as there is no
commodity to the production of which the labour of man is
not necessary.

Le mal est celui d'une taxe indirecte qui affecte tous les revenus fixes, taxe en comparaison de laquelle toutes les autres ensemble, toutes celles qui portent ce nom, ne sont presque rien, ensorte que le fardeau qui résulte de la guerre s'evanouït presque quand on le compare à ce fardeau qui résulte de la paix.

Il est certain que cette dépréciation, si onéreuse pour une classe de la nation, est compensée pour d'autres classes qui s'elevent dans l'echelle de la fortune pendant que les autres descendent: mais cette compensation ne rétablit pas l'égalité entre le bien et le mal, parce qu'il paroit que le mal est vivement senti et que le bien est à peine apperçu.

Quant au *danger*, c'est le plus grand de tous les maux contingents, c'est une banqueroute universelle [*Dumont's note:* 'ceci sera-t-il prouvé?']: catastrophe dont il est impossible de calculer l'epoque avec précision, mais dont on peut demontrer la certi- 5 tude si on ne prend aucune mesure pour la prévenir....

Quoique ce mal considéré dans ses effets soit tel qu'il seroit difficile d'en faire un tableau trop effrayant, il presente deux circonstances qui doivent contribuer à tranquilliser les esprits et à prévenir les murmures.

La premiere, c'est que ce mal n'est fondé sur aucun acte d'injustice de la part de ses auteurs *immédiats*, les négociants et les 6 banquiers. Aucun blame *moral* ne peut s'attacher à leur conduite: ils agissent sous la protection des loix: il n'y a point de reproche à faire à leurs intentions....

La seconde circonstance, qui doit dissiper les alarmes, c'est

---

4. A rise of prices from depreciation of money is no proof of national prosperity.

5. The evils of depreciation have been fairly described in the last paragraph, and actually consist in defrauding creditors of their just demand. Bankruptcy may be said to commence with depreciation; it may be so gradual as to prevent all convulsion,—its ultimate effects is to enrich one class of the society at the expence of another.

6. Is it not an immoral act to take advantage of a law [1] the consequences of which the legislature had not in contemplation, to enrich yourself at the expense of your fellow citizens?

[1] 'in your fav' is del. here.

que la gravité de la maladie n'est pas plus certaine que l'efficace et l'innocence du remede. C'est dans l'emission illimitée du papier-monnoie et du numéraire qu'est le mal, c'est dans la limitation pure et simple que se trouve le remede.

Dans le cours de cette recherche, il sera prouvé en sus que l'augmentation des prix, entant qu'elle resulte de celle du numéraire métallique, n'a point été productive d'un accroissement de 7 richesse réelle—entant qu'elle resulte de l'augmentation du papier-monnoie, elle a été productive d'un accroissement de richesse réelle, mais d'un accroissement qui cessoit d'être un bien en résultant de cette cause, et qui auroit pu être produit avec moins d'inconvenient par des sommes d'argent que le gouvernement auroit levées par des taxes directes.

Une consideration qui devroit nous réconcilier avec un sacrifice aussi leger d'accroissement de richesse réelle que celui qui resulte du papier-monnoie illimité, c'est l'opération du fonds d'amortissement. Chaque million employé à payer la dette, c.a.d., à racheter les annuités du Gouvernem^t dans lesquelles consiste la dette, est autant d'ajouté au capital national. Cet argent levé par des taxes qui tombent principalement sur le revenu, passe dans les mains des ex-créanciers qui pour en tirer un revenu doivent l'employer en guise de capital ou le prêter à ceux qui le font valoir sous cette forme.

---

7. I wish the author had defined what he meant by *real wealth*. As I understand those words I can have no conception that a paper money can cause an increase of real wealth, whilst a metallic currency cannot.

If he applies his observation to the revenue of government only, there can be no doubt that taxes paid in a depreciated currency are of no more real value on account of the increase of their amount, whilst their standard is in the same degree depreciated.

8. The sinking fund is capital not money and therefore cannot raise prices.[1]

The Capital liberated by the sinking fund is not a creation of capital,—it is merely a transfer from the pockets of those who pay the necessary tax to create that fund, to the public

[1] This sentence is inserted.

L'effet de ce torrent de Capital sera d'avancer la production de la richesse réelle aussi longtemps qu'il restera une capacité de travail à mettre en œuvre et aussi rapidement que cette capacité peut être mise en action. 8

La classe des Capitalistes, riches ou peu riches, sera ainsi soumise à une double perte: l'une qui leur est commune avec toutes les personnes qui ont des revenus fixes et qui consiste dans la dépréciation de l'argent: l'autre qui leur est particulière et qui consiste dans une defalcation directe de cette quantité d'argent deprecié dont leur revenu se compose. [*Dumont's note:* ' Ceci ne me paroit pas intelligible—de quelle defalcation s'agitil?'] 9

L'emigration des Capitaux se presente comme une espece de remede: le capital qui emigre arrête l'augmentation des prix entant qu'il depend de celle du numéraire: et le Capital qui emigre soutient la valeur de celui qui reste. L'emigration du Capital est donc un bien si elle ne va pas jusqu'à augmenter le taux de l'intérêt: résultat qu'on ne doit pas craindre, parceque ce seroit un effet au delà de la cause, et *pro tanto* sans cause. 10

Si l'on considere encore l'accroissement rapide de la population, tel qu'il a été même durant la guerre, si l'on observe qu'il iroit bientôt par son cours naturel au point d'excéder les subsistences que les deux isles pourroient produire, on reconnoitra

---

creditor. The same effects would have followed if there had been no sinking fund, and the contributors had accumulated their portions of the tax into Capital.[2] Again its numerical amount is of no consequence we must judge of its real amount[3] by the quantity of industry which it can employ. The author argues as if it were a capital created.

9. The loss is here reckoned twice over.

10. What has the emigration of Capital to do with the depreciation of money. The depreciation of money neither promotes nor retards the accumulation of Capital. If Capital be transferred for advantageous employment to other countries it can arise only from its accumulation which is totally independent of the value of the circulating medium.

[2] This sentence is ins.
[3] 'its real amount' replaces 'it'.

que l'emigration des hommes et des Capitaux est un bien réel
11 dans l'etat présent de la grande-Bretagne.

En effet, s'il vaut mieux être dans une situation de prospérité
progressive que stationnaire ou retrograde, s'il est plus heureux
d'avancer que de reculer, de monter que de descendre, plus notre
marche est lente dans cette carrière de succès, plus elle est conforme à la saine raison. Ce ne sont pas là, j'en conviens, les vues
communes de nos spéculateurs et de nos Midas, mais plus on se
livre à un examen détaillé, plus on se confirme dans ces résultats.

Ces opinions se présentent d'abord sous un air de paradoxe—
avancer que le papier-monnoie, ce simulacre de l'argent, est
12 productif d'une richesse réelle—que l'argent métallique, cette
réalité substantielle, n'en produit point—et que les seules especes
de monnoie qui aient la faculté d'ajouter à la richesse réelle soient
précisement les seules qui puissent amener la catastrophè d'une
banqueroute—ce sont là des propositions qui ont un caractere
de nouveauté pour bien des lecteurs et qui m'auroient paru
etranges à moi-même, lorsque j'ai commencé à me livrer à ces
recherches....

Ch. i. DEFINITIONS ET DISTINCTIONS— ARGENT—RICHESSE, RÉELLE, PECUNIAIRE— NUMÉRAIRE—PAPIER-MONNOIE.

Le mot *Argent* a plusieurs acceptions qu'il est important de

---

11. It can never be allowed that the emigration of Capital
can be beneficial to a state. A loss of capital may immediately
change an increasing state to a stationary or retrograde state.
A nation is only advancing whilst it accumulates capital.
Great Britain is far distant from the point where capital can
no longer be advantageously accumulated. I do not mean to
deny that individual capitalists will be benefited by emigration in many cases,—but England even if [1] she received the
revenues from the Capital employed in other countries would
be a real sufferer.

12. I confess these opinions appear to me [2] paradoxical;

[1] 'even if' replaces 'unless'.
[2] 'sufficiently' is del. here.

bien distinguer. Il exprime le numéraire, le métal portant empreinte, et n'ayant d'autre fonction que de passer de main en main en échange de toutes sortes de choses.

Dans un autre sens qu'on peut appeller figuratif, il est employé pour toutes les choses mêmes, pour toutes les richesses. . . .

Cette malheureuse metonymie a occasionné des erreurs bien graves: Pour n'avoir pas distingué l'argent, le numéraire, d'avec la richesse, les hommes ont imaginé qu'accroître l'argent, le numéraire, c'etoit la même chose qu'accroître la richesse, et qu'on ne pouvoit accroître la richesse qu'en accroissant l'argent, le numéraire: tandis que l'accroissem.ᵗ de l'argent (excepté sous la forme de papier-monnoie) ne contribue point à l'accroissement de la richesse: et que passé certaines limites, cet accroissement devienne pernicieux.   14

Le mot de *richesse réelle* avertit assez de la distinction qui existe entr'elle et la *richesse pécuniaire*: mais il a l'inconvénient de donner à entendre que la richesse pécuniaire n'est pas une richesse réelle: idée qui n'est pas tout à fait juste: car quoique l'argent, sous la forme de monnoie, ne soit de lui-même bon à rien, excepté à l'echanger contre les choses utiles, il a outre cette grande utilité, la capacité de se convertir en une infinité d'usages, sous la forme d'ustensiles et d'ornements, capacité sans laquelle il n'eut jamais obtenu la valeur qu'il possede pour servir à l'echange.

   .   .   .   .

I will however endeavor to give to the authors views the most unprejudiced attention.

[13. I should find great difficulty to admit this proposition.][3]

14. Money cannot be increased if there have not been a previous increase of the precious metals. No advantage whatever attends the increase of money,—but as it must be preceded by an augmentation of the precious metals and as those precious metals are used to gratify the desires of man, by affording him plate &cᵃ,—their increase is an increase of the riches and enjoyments of man.

I perceive that this is admitted in the following paragraph.

[3] The Note is del. and no number corresponds to it on Dumont's MS.

Ch. 2. DE LA RICHESSE CONSIDÉRÉE PAR RAPPORT A SES MODIFICATIONS—A SA VALEUR—ET A SES SOURCES.

· · · · · · · · ·

La richesse nationale n'est susceptible d'un accroissement considerable que par rapport au fonds des articles de valeur d'imagination, du luxe des superfluités. Il n'est pas dans la nature de l'homme d'entasser le pur nécessaire au delà de ses besoins. Quand le paysan Irlandois a semé une quantité suffisante de pommes de terre pour son entretien annuel, se donneroit-il la
15 peine inutile d'en semer davantage? Non sans doute, à moins que par la vente de cette quantité superflue, il n'entrevoye qu'il pourra se procurer d'autres objets de desir qui ne sont pas pour lui du nécessaire absolu. C'est donc par l'addition à la masse des objets de luxe et non par l'addition à la masse du nécessaire, tant que ce nécessaire n'est pas un besoin, que la masse de la richesse nationale peut s'accroître.

Diminution de valeur par augmentation d'argent.

Chaque somme de numéraire, introduite dans la circulation, a deux effets opposés—elle ajoute à la richesse dans un sens et dans un autre, elle la diminue: elle ajoute à la richesse d'un

---

15. The national capital can never be augmented by an increase of the articles of luxury. The wages of labour are spent in the purchase of necessaries,—those necessaries must therefore be augmented before any increased industry can be called forth.

16. Altho' it were to be allowed that the commodities circulated were 100 times, in value, the money which circulates them, it would be equally certain that their rise or fall would[1] be in proportion to the increase or diminution of money; because it is the rapidity of the circulation of money which would cause any given portion to be 100 times opposed to the same description of goods. If goods of a million in value could be circulated by £10,000,—the million would

[1] 'depend on the' is del. here.

individu ou d'une classe d'individus, et tôt ou tard, elle diminue
la richesse d'un autre individu ou d'une autre classe d'individus.
Elle ajoute à la richesse, non seulement d'un individu, mais de
toute la Communauté, parce qu'étant donnée en échange soit
d'un travail productif soit d'un article déjà produit, elle fait
naître une portion de richesse qui autrement n'auroit pas existé.
Elle diminue la richesse, non de la Communauté en general, mais
de certaines classes de la Communauté, parce qu'en augmentant
la quantité du numéraire elle diminue sa valeur, comparée à la
valeur de tous les articles vénaux. La masse originale du numéraire
etoit avant l'addition égale en valeur à toute la masse des objets
à vendre. [*Dumont's note:* 'Cette proposition est-elle prouvée?
Ne peut-on pas concevoir que la masse des objets vénaux sur-
passeroit de beaucoup en valeur toute la masse du numéraire?
Il n'y a que 60 millions numéraire en Angleterre: n'y a-t-il pas   16
un capital réel pour une valeur triple, quadruple et peut être
decuple?'] Après l'addition, la valeur du numeraire augmenté
est encore egale à celle des objets à vendre, mais elle ne peut
pas être plus grande puisqu'il n'y a rien de plus à donner en
echange pour ce surplus—chaque piece de l'ancien numéraire
eprouve donc une diminution, exactement proportionnelle à la
quantité de nouveau numéraire....

Chaque personne qui introduit dans la circulation une nouvelle
somme de numéraire impose donc à l'ensemble total des pos-

---

not be less opposed to a million of money,—but the ten
thousand pounds by the rapidity of its circulation would be
100 times in that market. This is on the supposition that such
goods were only sold once but as they may be successively
sold,—the £10,000 if that sum were adequate would not
circulate only 100 times[2] but as much oftener as sales to that
amount should be effected.—

The manner in which money is depreciated by an increased
quantity is very clearly described,—the public require some
explanation on that subject.

We must not however forget that the precious metals are
used for other purposes besides money.

[2] Replaces 'the £10,000 would not represent only the million of goods
but 100 times'.

sesseurs du numéraire une taxe égale au montant de la somme nouvelle.

Ainsi la sûreté par rapport à la propriété est à peine etablie qu'il se manifeste un nouveau principe d'insecurité, qui semble en être inséparable.

Mais cette infraction de la sûrete est bien differente des autres: on peut la prévoir et la regler....

Il est remarquable que ce principe d'insecurité est né de la 17 sûreté perfectionnée. Il n'y a que la plus grande confiance dans l'administration de la justice qui ait pu accrediter ces émissions de papier-monnoie qui ont si fort degradé la valeur du numéraire.

Ch. 3. RICHESSE, SES MODIFICATIONS.

．　　　．　　　．　　　．　　　．　　　．　　　．　　　．

Ch. 4. DU REVENU EN GENERAL, ET DU REVENU PECUNIAIRE EN PARTICULIER.

On entend generalement par *Revenu* cette portion de bien qui arrive periodiquement dans la possession d'un individu, en sorte que quoiqu'il l'ait entierement consommée, il peut s'attendre à la voir remplacée en entier....

Le mot de *Capital* est employé pour exprimer les economies 18 faites sur le revenu passé: lesquelles economies sont des sources de revenu futur.

Dans nos climats Européens, chaque année a sa moisson et n'en a qu'une....

Avec nous par consequent le mot de revenu se rapporte

---

17. [1] Whilst Banks pay in specie there can be no additions to the circulation which can permanently lower the value of money,—because they cannot permanently lower the value of gold and silver. Those metals would not have been of greater value now if no bank had ever been heard of.

18. Articles of luxury which this author supposes to be the great object of increase cannot as I have already observed be the sources of future revenue.

19. The whole of the explanations following are very

[1] 'No other security' is del. here.

toujours à la periode d'une année. On entend le revenu annuel.
Par le revenu de la Communauté, c.a.d. son revenu réel, on
entend la portion de richesse renouvellée par la Communauté
dans le cours de l'année. Le mot *Capital* n'a rapport à rien de
périodique.

Par Revenu, on entend quelquefois ce qu'on peut appeller
revenu *réel*, et quelquefois revenu *pécuniaire*.

Par revenu *réel*, j'entends les *choses* elles-mêmes, les choses de
toute espece employées ou consommées par les individus pour
leur usage.

Par revenu *pécuniaire*, j'entends ce que tout le monde entend, —
l'argent employé par les individus à acheter les choses dont leur
revenu réel est composé....

Le revenu pecuniaire de la Communauté, excepté ce qui est
thésaurisé ou ce qui est employé sous la forme de Capital pécuniaire, sert aux differents achats et constitue les prix des articles 19
dont la plus grande partie du revenu réel est composé: l'autre
partie du revenu réel etant obtenue sans argent, soit par la production domestique, soit par echange, soit gratis.

La plus grande partie du revenu réel est consommée (c.a.d.
detruite) annuellement.

Le revenu pécuniaire ne se detruit point excepté par accident
et un peu par usure. Il passe de main en main, il va comme dans
un cercle.

Chez les nations les plus avancées dans la civilisation, la plus
grande partie du revenu réel de la Communauté est transmise aux
individus par le moyen (medium) du revenu pécuniaire: chacun
reçoit en argent sa portion du revenu réel.

---

satisfactory and give a very correct idea of the real source
of price.[2]

[2] Ricardo had first opened this
Note with: 'Does not all pecuniary revenue excepting'; then he
deleted it and started again: 'I feel
some difficulty in distinguishing
what the author means by "Capital Pecuniare", and as the same
sum of money forms successively
the pecuniary revenue of many
different people,—I cannot agree
that it is the pecuniary revenue
which constitutes the price of
those articles of which the real
revenue is composed. Suppose
the real revenue of a society
valued in money to be 100,000£,
and 1000£ to be sufficient to circulate that revenue, it will then
appear that the whole society will
have the £1000 go thro' their
hands so often as to constitute a
revenue of £100,000,—prices
then'. This was also del.

Un homme peut appliquer son revenu pécuniaire à cinq emplois differents 1º l'employer à l'achat du revenu réel 2º le thésauriser 3 le placer en forme de capital 4 le déposer chez un banquier qui le prête à intérêt, gardant par devers lui une partie pour son fonds de securité 5 le distribuer en dons gratuits ou conditionnels.

Par rapport à la portion de ce revenu pécuniaire qu'il employe à l'achat de revenu *réel*, à mesure qu'il obtient l'un, il se desaissit de l'autre : à mesure que le revenu réel vient, le revenu pecuniaire s'en va. Ce n'est qu'en donnant le shelling qu'il obtient la valeur du shelling : excepté les cas d'achat à crédit, dans lesquels la remise de l'argent est retardée plus ou moins jusqu'après la recette des marchandises achetées.

Tout cela paroit assez clair. Cependant Adam Smith n'a pas eu des idées suffisamment nettes sur le sujet. Il se demande à lui-même de quelle matiere un revenu ['est composé' is del. here by mistake], si c'est de l'*argent* ou des *choses* qu'on se procure pour de l'argent à mesure qu'on s'en défait : il s'embarrasse dans ce nœud et enfin se décide en faveur des *choses*—Selon cette decision, un homme n'a point de revenu quand il a reçu son argent, il ne l'a qu'au moment où il s'en désaissit. Si un
20 homme parvient à economiser son revenu tout entier, ce qui sûrement n'est pas un cas très rare, suivant Adam Smith, il n'aura point eu de revenu. D'où vient cette erreur ? C'est que sous le nom de *revenu*, il s'etoit fait une idée abstraite, une idée

---

20. Inasmuch as it would be impossible for[1] every man or a great portion to realise their pecuniary revenue Adam Smith was right. For example 10 men save out of their pecuniary revenue 1000£ each, which they lend at interest or deposit at their Bankers,—the society should therefore be richer by £10,000 money, but in all probability it is not £1000 richer in money the greatest part has realised itself in goods which are in hands of those who have borrowed the money saved. It makes no difference whether those who saved it lent it themselves or by depositing it with a banker enabled him to do it. In no case can a pecuniary revenue be realised in the form of money but by hoarding. "Si un homme parviene[2]

[1] 'any' is del. here.
[2] Ricardo had first written 'parvienne', but then altered it to
'parviene'. In Dumont's handwriting 'parvient' is hardly distinguishable from 'parviene'.

fantastique, sans réalité, au lieu de penser à son propre revenu, et de considerer l'usage qu'il en faisoit, sans subtilité et sans mystere. Adam Smith a converti en lumiere une grande masse de fumée: mais il y a aussi des cas où il a converti en fumée ce qui etoit auparavant lumiere.

Du revenu Naturel et Conventionnel.

Toute la masse du revenu réel de chaque année doit avoir été en premiere instance à son origine le revenu, la propriété des classes productives. Tant qu'il reste dans les mains de ceux qui   21 l'ont produit par leur travail et leur capital, on peut l'appeler le revenu *originaire et natif.*

C'est de leurs mains que ces differents articles du revenu réel doivent être sortis pour passer dans les mains des individus de la classe improductive.

La partie du revenu originaire qui passe ainsi dans d'autres mains que celles des producteurs peut s'appeler la *partie extraite* du revenu national....

Le revenu total avant qu'on en ait rien extrait, est aussi ce que j'appelle le *revenu naturel*: la partie extraite pour être distribuée aux classes improductives est ce que j'appelle *revenu conventionnel*: c'est en vertu d'une convention antérieure que les producteurs sont tenus de le livrer aux individus de ces classes.

à economiser son revenu tout entier, ce qui surement n'est pas un cas tres rare, suivant Adam Smith, il n'aura point eu de revenu." He would have a revenue but it would realise itself in the hands of him to whom he lent it in the shape of commodities. The money of the country would have been augmented in a very trifling degree,—and the remainder would be wholly commodities.

> The absolute revenue is produced by the labour of one man with the Capital of another, which shall be called the unproductive?[3]

21. The mass of real revenue is derived from Capital and Capital is derived from the savings of the productive class,

[3] This paragraph is ins. between Note 20 and the first Note 21: it seems to belong to the latter.

Sous d'autres points de vue, il convient de distinguer le revenu en revenu *absolu* et en revenu *rélatif*—J'appelle *absolu* le revenu réel, le revenu naturel celui qui ne pourroit être anéanti sans diminuer d'autant la masse de la richesse de la Communauté—J'appelle revenu *rélatif* celui qui pourroit être anéanti par rapport à ceux qui le reçoivent, sans que la richesse de la Communauté en fut diminuée....

Les sources du revenu absolu sont 1º le travail et le fonds (stock) employé dans l'agriculture 2 dans les mines 3 dans la pêche 4 dans les arts méchaniques et les beaux arts 5 dans les manufactures.

Les modifications ou sources du revenu rélatif ou conventionnel sont—

1º Obligations de payer des *rentes*—pour l'usage de la terre....

2º Obligations de payer un revenu à epoques fixes pour *intérêt d'argent prêté*....

3º *Annuités*....

---

the capital must therefore once have been revenue, but the produce of that capital could never have been revenue. If from my revenue I save 100£ which next year produces me £10– the £10– is new revenue never having existed in that state before.—If this again is employed as capital it will yield a new revenue which never existed in that or any other[1] shape before.

With this correction the argument founded on it appears to me perfectly correct.

22. [This remark would be just if in the real revenue the produce of the earth, of the seas, mines, and labour of man were not all included. It is taking from that real revenue to pay one sort of labour as much as another. The wages of the manufacturer as well as those of the cultivator of the earth no matter in what he is paid are derived from the same source.][2]

See Nº 44.[3]

[1] 'or any other' is ins.
[2] The whole paragraph is del.

[3] The cross-reference is obscure, there being no Note 44 on

4° Revenu consistant en *gages de travail*: sans aucune obligation antérieure, mais en vertu d'un choix libre de la part des individus et par une convention qui peut cesser et se renouveller à chaque service.—C'est à ce chef qu'appartiennent les revenus des medecins, des instituteurs, des avocats, et ceux des domestiques.

C'est encore à ce chef qu'il faut rapporter les gages du travail productif, de ce travail par lequel est produite la masse des choses qui constituent la matiere du revenu réel: car c'est par une convention, à parler en general, que chaque ouvrier individuellement reçoit sa part de revenu. [*Dumont's note:* 'Ceci me paroit contestable à certains égards et incontestable à d'autres. L'ouvrier en draps ne se nourrit pas de draps: mais l'agriculteur se nourrit en partie du produit de la terre; le pêcheur se nourrit en partie de sa pêche.—Ce qu'il a de plus que le nécessaire physique, il le 22 tire du revenu relatif. ?']

5°... Revenu *extrait par les impôts*....

21.⁴ This is rather mysterious. Does the author mean the net revenue of the⁵ productive classes of all sorts after paying themselves for their subsistence during the period of reproduction, or is it the gross produce. If whilst I am consuming a sack of wheat I can by my labour produce two would he call my revenue 2 sacks or one sack. If he answers one then the objection in the margin 22⁶ is well founded because the wages of labour have been already deducted.

[23. I cannot agree with this last remark.]⁷

Livre I, whilst Note 44 on Livre II deals with a different subject. Probably a mistake for 'N.° 4', meaning the second Note 21; see following footnote.

⁴ This note, which is misnumbered 21, presumably refers to Bentham's 4th form of relative revenue, that is to say, to what immediately precedes the passage marked 22. Bentham's grounds for including the wages of labour, or a part of them, in relative revenue are not given in Dumont's MS; Dumont in a subsequent passage here omitted says that the explanation is wanting in Bentham's original MSS and offers as his own conjecture: 'les *gages du travail* pourroient être anéantis—est-ce le cas que l'auteur entend quand on reduit l'ouvrier à l'esclavage?'

⁵ 'society' is del. here.

⁶ *i.e.*, Dumont's note.

⁷ The whole Note is del. No number to correspond with it is written on Dumont's MS.

Ch. 5. RICHESSE—CONSIDÉRÉE DANS SA VALEUR.

Les termes de *richesse* et de *valeur* s'expliquent l'un par l'autre. Pour pouvoir entrer dans la composition d'une masse de richesse, il faut qu'un article possede une valeur quelconque. C'est par les degrés de cette valeur que la richesse est mesurée.

24 Toute valeur est fondée sur l'utilité, sur l'usage qu'on peut faire de la chose. Point d'usage, point de valeur. Ainsi comme c'est toujours sous le rapport de subsistence, de defense ou de jouïssance qu'un article de la matiere de la richesse peut avoir son *usage*, c'est aussi sous ces mêmes points de vue qu'il a une *valeur*.

i. La premiere distinction qui se presente, est entre usage ou valeur *immédiate* ou *intrinseque*, et valeur *eloignée* ou *relative* (subservient)....

ii. La seconde distinction est entre les articles d'une valeur *essentielle* et *invariable*, et les articles d'une valeur *variable et de fantaisie*.

Les articles d'une valeur invariable sont les aliments, les vêtements, le chauffage, les logements, et surtout les moins dispendieux de chaque espece. Les articles d'une valeur variable et de fantaisie ne renferment que les objets de pure jouïssance....

Les valeurs de fantaisie sont le grand fonds de sécurité pour les valeurs essentielles. Tous les objets de luxe peuvent se convertir, au moyen de l'echange, en objets de subsistence et de défense....

Le luxe est l'emploi d'un revenu au delà du nécessaire. Un revenu considerable ne peut être depensé qu'en superfluïtés. Il y a une liaison inséparable entre la possession d'un revenu et l'emploi libre de ce revenu. La prodigalité est toujours blamable;

25 nuisible à l'individu, elle l'est dans sa personne à l'Etat: le luxe ne l'est jamais. Confondre le luxe avec la prodigalité, la depense dans les limites du revenu avec la dépense au delà de ces limites, regarder avec envie toutes les conditions supérieures à la sienne,

---

24. I like the distinction which Adam Smith makes between value in use and value in exchange.[1] According to that opinion utility is not the measure[2] of value.

25. Prodigality is positively injurious to a state as it diminishes the national capital and therefore its revenue and

[1] *Wealth of Nations*, Bk. i, ch. iv;   [2] Replaces 'source'.
Cannan's ed., vol. i, p. 30.

taxer de prodigalité dans les autres ce qui seroit prodigalité pour soi-même, se donner pour la regle de ce qu'on doit ou ne doit pas faire, c'est le procedé de l'ascetisme et de l'antipathie qui aboutiroient dans leurs conséquences à passer le niveau sur tous les rangs de la société et à detruire la propriété et l'industrie....

III. Une troisieme distinction, de grande importance, est celle entre valeur pour *usage* et valeur pour *échange*....

IV. Une quatrieme distinction est celle entre valeur *intrinseque* et valeur *conventionnelle*: *intrinseque*, quand la valeur de la chose depend de sa nature: *conventionnelle*, quand la valeur dépend d'une convention, soit tacite, soit expresse, à donner à la chose une valeur qu'elle n'a point par elle-même.

La monnoie métallique est du nombre des choses qui possedent une valeur intrinseque, parce que la matiere dont elle est composée, est éminemment propre à divers usages.

Le papier-monnoie est le principal article dont la valeur soit de l'espece conventionnelle....

Mais quelle est la source de cette valeur conventionnelle? Est-ce la convention toute seule?... Non. Ce qui n'a point de valeur intrinseque ne sera jamais la base d'aucune valeur conventionnelle. On ne fait rien de rien. *Ex nihilo nihil fit*....

Si un fragment de papier trop petit pour avoir une valeur d'usage s'est trouvé obtenir une grande valeur d'echange, c'est que ce papier a été considéré comme une *promesse* faite au porteur de lui delivrer la somme promise en argent. Une longue expérience a confirmé la foi de cette promesse: et le papier a été reçu comme l'equivalent du métal.

Dans le cas de la Banque d'Angleterre nous avons vu un exemple singulier où le papier a conservé sa valeur lors qu'il avoit cessé d'avoir la faculté de mettre le porteur en possession de sa valeur métallique.... La liaison entre les deux valeurs etoit interrompue. Dans cette conjoncture critique, une convention pour ainsi dire miraculeuse est venue lui donner un nouvel

---

resources;[3] A man who spends an ample revenue on objects of luxury is not a prodigal he does not diminish the resources of the state, but as far as he is concerned keeps them at a stationary point. The man who saves his income however ample and adds it to his capital increases the riches and resources of the country of which he is a citizen.

[3] 'But luxury if by that term we mean' is del. here.

appui. Mais quelle etoit la base de cette convention? la persuasion que cette liaison, suspendue pour un temps, seroit bientôt
rétablie.…

26 Le fait reduit à ses termes simples est donc que la valeur du
numéraire métallique, comme moyen d'echange, sa valeur conventionnelle, est fondée uniquement sur sa valeur usuelle, sur sa
valeur intrinseque—et que la valeur du papier-monnoie, quoiqu'elle puisse se soutenir pour un temps par la seule force d'une
convention, est fondée uniquement sur celle de la valeur métallique dont il renferme la promesse.

CH. 6. DE LA RICHESSE—SES SOURCES.

Toute richesse… est le produit combiné de la terre et du
travail—c.a.d., du travail humain.…

L'addition à la richesse par le moyen du travail est faite ou
par addition à la *quantité* du travail dans un temps donné, ou
à l'*effet* du travail, au degré d'effet dont il est susceptible dans le
même temps.…

L'addition faite à la quantité du travail ou à l'effet du travail
peut se rapporter au *capital*—à l'augmentation faite au capital
ou à l'effet du capital—à l'emploi d'un plus grand capital ou à la
meilleure direction du même capital.

Il est bon de montrer quelles sont les sources réelles de la

---

26. I much doubt whether this is the foundation of the
value of the precious metals,—I doubt rather whether the
assertion should not be somewhat qualified. If true whilst
we were secure of the ability of the Bank to pay, paper money
must retain its value,—but at the present moment we see the
contrary to be the fact,—as with the fullest confidence in the
stability of the issues of paper, that paper is at a considerable
discount proceeding from excess alone.

27. This objection does not appear well founded. No sum
of money carried into Switzerland would enable the possessor
to drain a marsh and render it productive. The money must
first be exchanged with some other country for those commodities which would increase the capital and revenue of the
country. The same observation is applicable to Scotland. It

richesse pour faire voir de plus en plus que le numéraire et par conséquent l'augmentation du numéraire n'est pas une de ces sources. C'est une confirmation de ce qui a été ci-dessus. [*Dumont's note:* 'Cela n'est pas clair. Je vais dans un pays pauvre, où il y a beaucoup de gens peu occupés—j'y porte une grande somme d'argent—je m'en sers à faire défricher un marais —à acheter du bétail—à payer le travail de bcp d'ouvriers—le numéraire n'est-il pas une des sources réelles de la richesse? L'Ecosse n'a-t-elle pas changé de face depuis que les Ecossois enrichis aux Indes y ont porté des capitaux pécuniaires. Il y a encore quelque mystere pour moi dans l'antipathie que l'auteur 27 a prise contre le numéraire.']

De l'accroissement de richesse.

.   .   .   .

Le travail en lui-même est incapable de rien produire sans la *terre*. Il faut qu'il opere ou directement sur la terre ou sur quelque chose qui originairement ait du son existence à la terre.

Abstraction faite du travail, la richesse ne reçoit aucun accroissement d'un simple accroissement dans la quantité de terre. Cet 28 accroissement de terre pourroit aller à l'infini sans produire aucun accroissement de richesse. En un mot la terre n'est source de richesse qu'à proportion du travail qu'on y applique. Sans cette proportion de travail, la possession de la terre ne pourroit con-

---

was not by money, but by capital that Scotland has been improved.

28. It appears to me that the possession of new Land would add to our sum of riches without additional labour, because the same labour employed on double the quantity of equally good[1] land now in cultivation in England would produce a greater return. This opinion is founded on the decreasing power of the land to produce in proportion to the labour and capital employed on it. The sentiment expressed is in the main undoubtedly true,—but I think it requires some qualification.

—I see this is admitted in the next paragraph.

[1] 'equally good' is ins.

tribuer à la richesse qu'autant qu'elle seroit transférée par maniere d'echange.

Cependant une nouvelle quantité (etendue) de terre pourroit devenir une source de richesse, sans augmentation de travail, si cette nouvelle quantité de terre à raison de sa fertilité naturelle ou du climat, ou de quelque autre circonstance, rendoit la même quantité de travail plus effective, ou en d'autres termes, donnoit plus de produit pour le même travail....

Ch. 7. NUMÉRAIRE, SES DIVERSES ESPECES.

.   .   .   .

Ch. 8. PAPIER-MONNOIE, SA VALEUR.

L'assurance d'obtenir l'argent (le numéraire) au moment de la demande remplit l'objet desiré aussi bien que sa possession actuelle....

29   C'est sur ce fondement que les *Banques* ont été etablies: institution qui a été mieux entendue dans presque tous les pays commerçants de l'Europe qu'en Angleterre. Ces banques supposent un *depôt*. L'argent y est reçu, non seulement compté, mais scrupuleusement examiné. Le papier qui repose sur un numéraire d'un bon titre doit etre plus estimé que celui qui n'a d'autre base que la masse miscellanée du numéraire courant dans la circulation.

---

29. The Bank of England is certainly not *quite* so secure as a bank of deposit such as at Amsterdam and Hamburgh,—but is infinitely more useful in making the whole capital of a country available. Paper in England performs the office of the precious metals,—and the precious metals are exported for those commodities which can be usefully and advantageously employed. In Holland and Hamburgh the advantages of the Banks is 1º in the use of paper instead of metals which has been admirably described by this author, and 2dly in having a uniform measure of value subject to no debasement or deterioration.

30. It was well observed by Mr. —— to the bullion Commeē [1] that he considered the agio on Bank money not

[1] 'Minutes of Evidence', 8vo ed., p. 81. On 'Mr. ——' see below, p. 427 ff.

Dans les places où ces Banques sont etablies, la quantité de papier qui represente l'argent deposé à la Banque, etant limité **30** par la quantité d'argent métallique représentée, se trouve susceptible d'une prime, laquelle prime varie selon la demande.

En Angleterre où la Banque n'est pas fondée sur un depôt, la certitude par rapport à la bonté du papier ne peut jamais être si entiere: cependant, deduction faite pour cette circonstance, la sûreté est assez grande pour donner lieu à l'existence d'une prime en faveur du papier, à raison de tous ses avantages.

Si cette prime n'a jamais existé, cela ne vient pas d'un sentiment d'insécurité, mais d'une toute autre cause. C'est que la somme du papier-monnoie n'a jamais été *limitée* comme elle l'est néces- **31** sairement dans les banques de depôt. Comme tout homme peut toujours se procurer contre de la monnoie métallique autant de papier-monnoie qu'il en demande et qu'il peut garantir, il ne peut en consequence exister aucune prime pour personne....

CH. 9. DES DEGRÉS D'APTITUDE A UNE PROMPTE CIRCULATION ENTRE TELLE MONNOIE ET TELLE AUTRE.

Les circonstances dont depend la facilité comparative à circuler entre telle espece de numéraire et telle autre peuvent se rapporter à 4 chefs.

---

as a prem^m for Bank money because that was invariable but as the measure of the value of the current money.

The nature of Bank money on the continent does not appear to me to be well understood by the author.

31. It is said that Bank paper cannot be sufficiently limited to be at a prem^m because any man possessing guineas may buy notes of the Bank at par. That these notes should be at par is sufficient security to the public,—would they had continued so till this time.—But the author is mistaken in supposing that Bank money cannot be bought at the banks of deposit,—for the most trifling prem^m 1 per mil I believe bank money may be bought with bullion at Hamburgh,—and bullion cannot be considered equally valuable with coin, weight and standard for weight and standard.

1º La petitesse de valeur, considerant à part la monnoie metallique et le papier monnoie.

2 La portabilité.

3 La certitude par rapport à la bonté, surtout dans le cas de papier monnoie: y compris la permanence de valeur des matériaux.

4 La promptitude de payement, dans le cas de papier monnoie.

1. De ces circonstances, celle qui exerce l'influence principale, c'est la *petitesse de valeur*. . . .

Il semble donc que si l'on avoit besoin d'augmenter la rapidité de la circulation, et par consequent le pouvoir effectif de la masse de numéraire d'un pays, il n'y auroit qu'à augmenter le nombre des pieces de petite valeur aux depends du nombre des pieces de plus grande valeur.

Mais cette operation n'auroit point l'effet desiré. [*Dumont's note:* 'pluribus omissis non intellectis']. . .

La multiplication de la petite monnoie au delà de la proportion absolument requise pour le *change* (c.a.d. pour changer un shilling en demi-sous et une guinée en shellings) seroit plutôt nuisible que favorable à la rapidité de la circulation, à raison de ce qu'elle est *moins portative*.

Aussi voit-on dans plusieurs pays que la monnoie métallique la plus précieuse porte une prime dans l'echange contre la monnoie d'une espece plus pesante. En France, au moins autre-
32 fois, l'or en grande quantité avoit plus de valeur que son equiva-

---

32. This may be accounted for from the relative value of the metals in the mints of France and Russia being incorrectly determined.

33. This does not appear to be necessary to a paper currency, witness the notes of the Bank of England for many years. They would even now preserve their value if they were not issued in excess, however distant might be the time of their final discharge.

34. Exchequer bills cannot be considered as paper money. They may be used as such on some occasions by Government but cease immediately to perform the functions of money. They can no more be considered as paper money than the funds. They never pass in payments from one individual to another. The possessor of an exchequer bill if he

lent légal en argent. En Russie, l'argent gagne habituellement contre le cuivre qui etant le produit des mines du pays est plus abondant que les métaux précieux.

．　　．　　．　　．　　．　　．　　．

IV. *Promptitude de payement*: derniere circonstance qui influe sur l'aptitude d'un papier-monnoie à une prompte circulation. **33** C'est par cette circonstance que la nature (l'effet—powers, properties) des papiers portant intérêt est plus ou moins affectée.

L'influence de cette cause n'est pas facile à démêler, par rapport aux prix, parce qu'elle est compliquée avec les autres causes mentionnées ci-dessus et diversifiée elle-même par un grand nombre de modifications. Dans le cas des lettres de change, la lenteur du payement, cause de retard dans la circulation, est combinée avec les degrés d'incertitude concernant la solvabilité des parties obligées au payement. Dans le cas des *bills de l'Echiquier*, le temps du payement quoiqu'eloigné en comparaison **34** avec les lettres de Change est communément à jour fixe. Dans le cas des *bills de marine*, heureusement hors d'usage aujourd'hui, l'incertitude par rapport au jour du payement les fit tomber dans cette dépréciation qui suffiroit seule pour en retarder la circulation de manière à les rendre peu propres au service du Gouvernement.

Dans le cas des *bills de l'Echiquier*, le principal et l'intérêt sont payés ensemble. Dans le cas des *billets de la Compagnie des Indes*,

---

has a payment to make must first dispose of his bill in the money market for bank notes,—and if there were a scarcity of money in the market an issue of exchequer bills would rather aggravate than supply such distress.

The navy bills were formerly at a great discount which arose from their being injudiciously pressed on the market for sale, rather than to the want of punctuality in their payment as they bore an interest till the day of payment and no one had doubts of their security.—

India Bonds for the payment of which no time is fixed are generally at a prem^m since a more judicious mode of sale has been adopted. And exchequer bills tho' paying less than 5 pc. for money are commonly at a prem^m of 5 or 6 shillings pc^t

quoique le payement de l'intérêt soit plus prompt et plus regulier que dans le cas des bills de l'Echiquier, cependant le payement du principal est reféré non seulement à un temps eloigné, mais à un temps incertain. C'est plutôt l'emprunteur qui peut exercer le droit de rembourser à son gré que le prêteur n'a celui de le forcer au payement.

Une autre circonstance de ces billets qui rend difficile de distinguer l'effet de la lenteur de payement sur leur circulation, c'est la grandeur des sommes: £100 au moins pour les billets des Indes: £500 et souvent £1000 pour ceux de l'Echiquier— cela suffiroit seul pour mettre cette espece de papier-monnoie hors de service dans les transactions communes des depenses.

Il ne faut pas croire toutefois que ces papiers n'exercent pas une influence indirecte sur la force totale du numéraire de toute espece et par conséquent sur l'ensemble des prix. Il y a beaucoup de transactions commerciales, entre les marchands en gros, où ces billets de £100, 500, et 1000 sont aussi applicables que les
35 billets de banque ordinaire le sont dans le cours des affaires communes: et en particulier les bills de l'Echiquier entrent dans la composition de cette espece de monnoie que les banquiers gardent par devers eux comme un fond de reserve pour subvenir à quelque demande extraordinaire d'argent de la part de ceux qui ont coutume de deposer une somme entre leurs mains pour la tirer en détail. La regulation de ces Bills est si bien etablie par l'expérience d'un siecle que quoiqu'ils ne soient pas payables à vue, on est toujours sûr de trouver un marché prêt pour eux dans la metropole, entre les négociants des premieres classes....

Ch. 10. DES FONDS DE SECURITÉ.

Toutes les especes de papier monnoie *payables a vue* exigent

---

35. This I am persuaded is a great mistake. Exchequer bills are never paid as money,—but are bought and held chiefly by bankers and monied men. No man becomes possessed of an exchequer bill without parting with an equal amount of money. If a contractor receives from Government a navy or ordnance bill he can do nothing with it till he has sold it in the market. Does not the whole transaction resolve itself into this? A has furnished government with

un fonds de *sécurité*: une masse d'argent toujours prête à remplir les engagements du papier-monnoie....

Observons d'abord qu'on peut appliquer à l'Arithmetique du commerce de banque ce mot de Swift sur les impôts, *Deux et deux ne font pas quatre*. Si le montant du numéraire métallique qui compose le fonds de securité est le tiers du montant du papier-monnoie, *trois et trois* de cette maniere ne seront pas égaux à *six*, mais seulement à *cinq*. [*Dumont's note:* 'non capio'.] 36

Fonds de securité de la banque d'Angleterre.

Le fonds de securité de la banque d'Angleterre est uniquement composé de métaux précieux, partie sous la forme de *numéraire anglois*, partie sous celle de *lingot*, ou d'argent monnoyé des autres nations....

Aussi longtemps que la Banque peut s'assurer de tirer de la Monnoie une quantité suffisante d'espèces pour la demande, il est de son intérêt de garder l'or en lingot autant qu'elle peut. Pour chaque once d'or, au même titre que celui des guinées, elle reçoit de la Monnoie le même poids, produisant en especes la valeur de £3: 17s: 10d$\frac{1}{2}$. Pour cette once d'or en lingot, le prix qu'elle donne au marchand est de £3: 17: 6d. Le profit qu'elle fait sur cette once, en l'envoyant à la Monnoie est de 4d$\frac{1}{2}$: un peu plus que 2 pour cent.... le profit qu'elle fait sur l'espece monnoiée, tout modéré qu'il est, est autant de gagné sans risque et sans peine, sur un capital qui ne leur rapporteroit rien. Il est vrai que si ce capital ne rapporte aucun intérêt, tant qu'il est stagnant, le papier qu'ils donnent en payement pour l'or, ne leur coûte non plus aucun intérêt. Ils en peuvent emettre sans crainte une quantité illimitée contre un tel gage. Si le papier emis en conséquence leur revient pour être échangé contre les especes,

---

stores for which government is enabled to pay by borrowing the money of B, which is effected by the sale of the debt by A to B.—They differ in no respect from the funds but by being less variable in price. The argument that a market is always to be found for them in the metropolis is equally true with respect to the funds. Money can be raised on the one with as much certainty as on the other.

36. I do not understand this passage.

ils n'ont qu'à faire frapper une portion égale des lingots qu'ils
37 ont acheté avec ce papier: et à mesure qu'ils se defont de leurs
especes, ils retirent la portion de papier qui etoit surabondante.
Bien loin de perdre par cette opération, elle constitue tout leur
profit: car ce n'est qu'à proportion du papier qui leur rentre
qu'ils font faire un nouveau monnoyage, et c'est à proportion
du monnoyage qu'ils gagnent la difference entre le prix d'achat
de l'or et le prix des guinées qu'ils reçoivent: c.a.d. les 2 pour
cent de profit....

Fonds de securité des banques (fragment).

Dans la proportion de l'edifice à la base, à mesure que la
quantité de papier jettée dans la circulation par chaque banquier
sur la force d'une quantité donnée de numéraire, la somme totale
du papier-monnoie et des moyens de circulation augmente.

Tout ce qui peut au jugement du banquier lui servir à obtenir
du numéraire en especes ou ce qui est reçu comme tel, sera pour
lui un moyen de garder moins d'especes, ou d'emettre une masse
proportionnelle de papier, toutes les fois qu'il le trouvera praticable
et profitable.

De cette maniere le papier d'une banque (supposé bon) formera
une base et même une base très commode, pour le papier d'une
38 autre banque et réciproquement: A prenant le papier de B,
B prenant le papier de A, et ainsi dans chaque cas l'edifice croît

---

37. This trade of buying gold at £3. 17. 6—and procuring it to be coined would be very unprofitable to the
bank, because as they would purchase the bullion with paper
they would cause an excess which would infallibly be returned to them for specie which they must provide immediately,—whereas they would not obtain the specie for their
bullion sent to the mint for some weeks amounting to a loss
of interest considerably more than the 4d.$\frac{1}{2}$ per oz.

The effects of an excessive issue of paper I have not yet
seen explained by this author.

4d.$\frac{1}{2}$ is not 2 pc^t on £3. 17. 10$\frac{1}{2}$ but less than $\frac{1}{2}$ pc^t

38. We are to suppose the author speaking of a paper
convertible at the will of the holder. If so his system is

en hauteur à une etendue indefinie, la base restant toujours la même....

Fonds de securité des banques Provinciales.

[*Dumont's note:* 'Chap. omis, fort long d^s les Mss.—je n'ai pas senti l'importance de traiter à fond ce sujet....']

Le fonds de securité des banques provinciales pour l'emission de leur papier-monnoie, est d'une espece toute differente.

On peut le diviser en deux portions, le fonds de securité *extraordinaire* comme on peut l'appeller et le fonds de securité *ordinaire*.

Chaque banque provinciale entretient une correspondance suivie avec une des banques de la Metropole: cette liaison à plusieurs egards a l'effet d'une association. Par le fonds de securité *extraordinaire* d'une banque provinciale, j'entends les secours de toute espece qu'elle peut recevoir et qu'elle reçoit de cette banque associée.

Par le fonds de securité ordinaire, j'entends la moyenne du surplus en numéraire qu'elle garde habituellement dans ses coffres, au delà de ce qu'elle est appellée à payer chaque jour.

On comprend que ce que j'ai appellé le fonds *extraordinaire* sera de la même nature que ce qui compose le fonds de securité du banquier de Londres....

Des bills de l'Echiquier, des billets des Indes, soit par leur 39

---

altogether erroneous. All the banks together can by no effort keep permanently more than a given sum in circulation.

39. It has lately appeared in evidence before the bullion Committee[1] that the Country Banks keep in London deposits of Exchequer bills, India Bonds &c^a, for which they can speedily obtain[2] Bank of England notes when necessary. It is also proved that their payments in return for the notes issued by themselves are frequently if not generally made by drafts on their London Agents. Country notes are seldom exchanged but for the purpose of obtaining London currency and this mode is convenient to both parties. To the country

[1] 'Minutes of Evidence', 8vo ed., pp. 162–3, 164, 212, etc.

[2] Last six words replace 'which they can speedily turn into'.

grandeur, soit par les variations de valeur auxquels ils sont sujets, ne seroient point propres à former le fonds de securité de ces banques provinciales.

Ce qui compose ce fonds, c'est d'abord une certaine quantité de numéraire effectif—des billets de la banque d'Angleterre depuis qu'on en a fait d'une et de deux livres St—et même du papier des banques rivales.. . .

---

banker as it prevents the necessity of keeping funds to any great amount unemployed.—To the holder of the country notes as they are chiefly exchanged for the purpose of making payments in London, it saves the risk which would attend sending the Bank notes to London.

The Bank of England deposits consist of bills of exchange government securities, besides coin and bullion. Those of the country Banks of government securities, bills of exchange coin and bank of England notes.

As all the banks together whilst they are bound to pay on demand in specie can only maintain a given amount of notes in circulation prices cannot be affected by any efforts of Banks.

LIVRE II.

DE LA HAUSSE DES PRIX ET DES EFFETS DU PAPIER-MONNOYE.

PRELIMINAIRES.

L'objet de cet essai est la partie permanente de l'augmentation qui s'est faite depuis quelques années relativement aux *prix*: par où je n'entends pas *tous les prix* sans distinction, mais seulement ceux par lesquels la valeur réelle des revenus a été affectée....

Les prix par lesquels la valeur du revenu est affectée ne sont pas les prix de tous les articles, mais de ceux qui servent à la consommation journaliere, les aliments, les vêtements, les combustibles &c.

Les articles par le prix desquels la valeur du revenu n'est pas affectée ou du moins pas immédiatement affectée sont les sources du revenu de toutes sortes, proprietés territoriales, maisons, mines, contrats, hypotheques, fonds publics, &c.

Que le prix de ces articles augmente ou diminue, la valeur d'un revenu n'en est pas affectée: si j'ai une annuité de £100, sa valeur est affectée par l'augmentation ou la diminution des denrées, mais aussi longtemps que je ne suis pas appellé à la vendre, la valeur du revenu n'est point augmentée ou diminuée par une augmentation ou une diminution dans le nombre des années d'achat que j'en recevrois si j'avois à la vendre.

Le prix d'une source de revenu est affecté par la même cause que la valeur du revenu lui-même, savoir, la quantité de numéraire: mais elle est de plus affectée par une autre circonstance, savoir, la proportion entre la valeur de la richesse presente et celle de la richesse future....   1

---

1. If money be depreciated, the value of an annuity payable in money must also be diminished. What other variation the author means is not clearly expressed.[1]

In this chapter the author does not clearly express to us

[1] This sentence replaces 'but as the augmentation of money adds nothing to the real riches of a country, the annuity cannot be subject to any further variation from this cause.'

DES PRIX.

.   .   .   .

Par le *premier coût* (prime cost) ou *prime-coût pécuniaire d'une production* j'entends la somme d'argent qui a été employée en differents prix, pour l'amener à son etat actuel, renfermant les prix des matériaux dont l'article est composé—celui des matieres consommées pour le travail, du combustible par exemple—celui du travail—celui qui a été payé pour l'usage de la terre, ou des maisons, des ustensiles, des outils, de tous les instruments en un mot qui ont servi à la faire ou à la transporter, ou à la conserver....

2 Comme le premier coût en argent donne la somme des prix elementaires qu'on ne peut parvenir à connoître separement avec certitude, il represente de même assez exactement la somme des portions de travail qui ont été employées pour amener l'article à son état actuel.

.   .   .   .

DES CAUSES DE HAUSSE ET DE BAISSE PAR RAPPORT AUX PRIX.

En considérant les causes de la hausse et de la baisse des prix, il est essentiel de commencer par faire une distinction entre les

---

what he means by money or circulating medium. Does he include checks on Bankers, Exchequer bills, India Bonds as well as Bank notes and metallic money. I consider the latter (Bank notes and metallic money) only, as circulating medium and I should think the mass of these changed hands much oftener than the author has supposed.

2. Provided no alteration has taken place in the value of money.

3. Why should the mere increase of money have any other effect than to lower its value? How would it cause any increase in the production of commodities?

4. This is true taking all commodities together,—but

causes *immédiates* et les causes plus ou moins *eloignées*: autrement des causes d'une tendance contraire seront rangées sur la même ligne, et l'on ne parviendra point à se faire des idées claires et nettes.

Je m'explique—Parmi les circonstances qui produisent une hausse en premiere instance, il en est plusieurs qui produisent une baisse en seconde instance. Un flux de nouveau numéraire 3 dans le marché rendra toutes les marchandises proportionnellement plus cheres: mais cette augmentation de prix, fournissant des moyens et des encouragements pour la production et l'introduction d'une extra-quantité de ces marchandises, a une tendance à les rendre proportionnellement moins cheres, dès que cette cause aura eu le *temps* d'operer.

Les causes qui influent sur la hausse des prix peuvent se distinguer en deux classes 1º celles qui affectent la masse du 4 numéraire 2º celles qui affectent la masse des objets venaux.

Par les causes qui affectent la masse du numéraire, j'entends toutes celles qui produisent une augmentation dans le total des sommes pécuniaires depensées pendant l'année en forme de revenu (on the score of revenue).

Ce total de depense peut être augmenté de deux manieres 1º par une augmentation de moyens pécuniaires, la proportion entre la recette et la dépense restant la même 2º par une augmenta- 5 tion dans la depense seule, le revenu restant sur le même pié qu'auparavant.

Cet accroissement de depense sans accroissement de revenu

---

fashion or other causes may create an increased demand for one article and consequently the demand for some one or more of others must diminish. Will not this operate on prices?

The author evidently means all commodities together or the mass of prices.[1]

5. Is not this assuming that what is not spent is hoarded. The revenue is in all cases spent, but in one case the objects on which it is expended are consumed, and nothing reproduced[2] in the other those objects form a new capital tending to increased production.

[1] This sentence is ins.   [2] 'and nothing reproduced' is ins.

n'est point une chose conforme aux dispositions habituelles des hommes: cela ne peut avoir lieu dans une Communauté que par des circonstances extraordinaires et temporaires, telles qu'un état de disette ou de guerre: la disette affectant principalement le prix des denrées: la guerre, indépendamment des dégâts locaux, affectant le prix des objets dont elle augmente la consommation, et de ceux dont elle rend l'importation plus dispendieuse.

6 Ces deux causes sont suffisantes pour operer, chacune dans la sphere de son action, une hausse des prix, et même une hausse considerable, sans qu'il y ait aucune addition faite à la masse du numéraire.

7 Ces deux cas exceptés, les prix ne peuvent s'elever qu'en raison d'une augmentation pécuniaire dans la masse du revenu national, c'est à dire, dans le total des revenus individuels: et cette augmentation ne peut avoir lieu que par l'addition d'une nouvelle quantité d'argent, ou par une plus grande rapidité dans la circulation.

En effet, le proprietaire ne peut faire une addition habituelle à sa depense de consommation qu'autant que son fermier lui paye une rente plus considerable: le fermier ne peut faire cette addition

---

6. If any rise in the price of commodities is caused in the way here supposed it must be by diminishing the amount of commodities, which will make the money which circulates them more relatively abundant. If the commodities remained the same and their price was increased, more money would be absolutely necessary to circulate them. But if it is the mass of prices of which the author speaks, he is mistaken because what one commodity rose in price another would fall.[1]

7. These arguments are all founded on the supposition of the country to which they are applied being insulated from all others. If not it is evident that the rapidity of the circulation would cause an exportation of money, and would not therefore raise prices at home.

8. If by increase of capital he could increase his productions the price of them or of some other commodities[2] must fall unless the money of the country has been also increased.

[1] This sentence is ins.   [2] The last five words are ins.

à la rente qu'autant que lui-même reçoit une plus grande somme des produits de sa ferme; et il ne peut recevoir cette plus grande somme habituelle qu'autant qu'il augmente la quantité de ces produits ou le prix qu'il en obtient: or il ne peut augmenter la quantité de ces produits que par une addition faite à la masse 8 de son capital productif; et le prix ne peut recevoir une addition habituelle à moins qu'il n'y ait eu une augmentation dans la quantité d'argent employée à ce genre de consommation par ses acheteurs: ce qui suppose de la part des acheteurs eux-mêmes un accroissement total dans la masse de leurs revenus.

Il s'ensuit donc qu'à prendre le tout ensemble nous ne devons chercher la cause de l'augmentation permanente des prix que 9 dans l'augmentation de la force effective, c.à.d. la quantité et la celerité de la masse de l'argent.

Ainsi la cause immediate de la hausse des prix est l'augmentation de la masse d'argent employée dans la depense de consommation: la cause immediate de cette augmentation est dans l'accroissement de la somme totale employée en forme de capital $9\frac{1}{2}$ productif. Mais de cette même cause il resulte un accroissement proportionnel dans la quantité des marchandises vénales. Si ces

---

9. In this conclusion I perfectly agree [3] if the author means the mass of prices, but a hundred articles might have risen, whilst another hundred might have fallen in consequence of increased or decreased demand, increased or decreased knowledge in the best means of producing them. Nay the mass of prices might remain the same tho' each individual article had risen in consequence of taxation.

[$9\frac{1}{2}$.] [4] Money cannot call forth goods,—but goods can call forth money.

The revenue of nations divided in two portions that

---

[3] The remainder of the Note replaces 'but I do not quite accord with the steps by which the author has arrived at it.'

[4] The number $9\frac{1}{2}$ appears on Dumont's MS, but not on Ricardo's. What is here assumed to be Note $9\frac{1}{2}$, is written in Ricardo's MS, upside down and without reference number, at the back of the page containing Notes 23 to 30 below: the assumption seems to be justified by the relevance of the comment to the text, as well as by the sequence implied in the opening of Note 10, 'Here again' etc.

deux accroissements se faisoient dans le même temps, s'ils etoient non seulement proportionnels mais égaux, il est evident que les prix resteroient toujours les mêmes. Le simple fait de la hausse des prix est une preuve, et une preuve concluante, que l'accroissement des marchandises vénales ne marche point du même pas que l'accroissement de la force effective de la masse d'argent, et ce même fait est l'indice de la difference entre ces deux accroissements.

10
Si cette conclusion paroit vraie d'après une vue generale du sujet, elle le paroit plus encore quand on l'examine en détail. Avant qu'un article de marchandise soit fini et prêt à être acheté par un consommateur, il a passé par le travail d'un grand nombre de mains, entre lesquelles le nouveau capital a été partagé: mais comme l'argent est payé aux ouvriers de semaine en semaine ou de jour en jour, et employé par eux aussitôt que reçu pour la depense de consommation, l'addition qui en resulte à la masse d'argent contribue immédiatement à hausser les prix, et produit cette hausse longtemps avant qu'elle ait pu produire l'effet opposé d'augmenter la quantité des marchandises vénales, qui doit amener la baisse. L'intervalle qui s'ecoule entre la production de ces deux effets opposés differe beaucoup selon la diversité des articles: mais il est clair que l'effet augmentatif par rapport aux prix precede toujours l'effet diminutif et il est prouvé par le dernier résultat qu'il le surpasse....

---

expended on consumable commodities, and that saved for future capital a source of great error as their effects on prices the same.

10. [1]Here again it is supposed that the augmentation of money precedes the augmentation of goods. I am of opinion however that it would seldom[2] cause any augmentation of goods, and if it did it would be before prices had found their new level.[3] It would be effected by turning a part of that fund destined for the wages of labour for a short time into capital.

[1] 'The augmentation' is del. in this place.
[2] Replaces 'never'.
[3] 'that the augmentation of goods is the only legitimate cause for an increase of money' is written above the latter part of this sentence in the MS, but it is not clear

MONTANT DE LA HAUSSE DES PRIX.

Un nouveau numéraire peut (comme nous l'avons déjà vû) être introduit par une voie commerciale ou par une voie non commerciale.

Celui qui est introduit par une voie non commerciale n'ajoute rien à la masse de la richesse: son seul effet est d'ajouter à la masse des prix. (c.a.d. des prix affectant le revenu) [*Dumont's note:* 'il est dit ailleurs qu'il ajoute à la richesse, par le profit des marchands &c.']

Celui qui est introduit par une voie commerciale augmente de tout son montant la masse des prix dans l'année, comme dans le premier cas: mais il faut deduire de cette augmentation des prix une somme proportionnelle à l'addition qu'il fait faire dans la masse des choses venales par laquelle les prix sont affectés. **11**

L'addition faite au total des prix par une introduction de nouveau numéraire par une voie non commerciale est donc sans deduction, comme la quantité de ce nouveau numéraire est au montant de la masse originaire dans laquelle il est introduit. Si par exemple le nouveau fonds est un $\frac{1}{10}$ du fonds ancien l'addition faite au prix sera comme $10+1$ à 10.

L'addition faite au total des prix par une quantité de nouveau numéraire introduit par une voie commerciale ne sera pas simplement comme le montant du nouveau fonds au fonds ancien, mais comme ce montant *moins* la partie qui a été employée à constituer

---

11. An increased capital[4] will maintain a greater amount of circulating medium without causing[5] any alteration in its value. But thro' commercial channels no money can be introduced into a country which shall affect prices, unless the mass of gold and silver have not only been increased in proportion to the increased demand, but much above it. It can be produced only by the discovery of new mines or the improvement in the mode of working the old. The question of the effect of machinery on prices is not once mentioned.

whether it was intended as a correction or as an addition.
[4] Replaces 'Is not this saying what has been before explained that an increased commerce and capital'.
[5] 'its depreciation' is del. here.

les prix des nouveaux articles venaux produits dans le même temps par l'emploi productif de ce nouveau numéraire.

12 Si l'addition faite à la masse des choses venales par l'emploi productif de ce nouveau capital, est supposée egale au profit ordinaire des capitaux, c.à.d. à 15 p^r cent,—c'est donc 15 p^r cent du montant de ce nouveau capital qu'il faut déduire du montant de ce qui auroit été ajouté à la masse des prix par l'introduction du nouveau capital.

13 Mais ce 15 p^r cent ne doit être compté que sur le premier emploi du nouveau capital: car après son premier deboursement qui va tout entier à la production, le nouveau fonds se partagera entre la depense productive et consommatrice, dans la proportion de ces deux depenses l'une par rapport à l'autre. [*Dumont's note:* 'mss fort obscur'.]

Si donc la proportion entre la quantité de numéraire et la quantité de revenu est comme 1 à 3, ou en d'autres termes, s'il falloit pour constituer tout le revenu que chaque pièce d'argent passât en trois differentes mains dans le cours de l'année,—ce n'est pas 15 p^r cent qu'il faudroit deduire de la masse du nouveau fonds mais seulement 5 p^r cent. [*Dumont's note:* 'Hébreu'.]

Si le nouveau fonds est comme $\frac{1}{10}$ du fonds originaire, le

---

12 & 13. This calculation does not appear to me correct, if correct it is very obscure.[1] If 15 pc^t be added to the amount of goods already in existence, there will be required 15 pc^t on the amount of money before employed to keep prices as heretofore[2] and this is in fact what this calculation asserts, but it is necessary to the authors conclusions that we should allow that an increase of money will call forth an additional amount of commodities,—but I do not see on what principle such a consequence can be expected.

Many pages appear to me very difficult to comprehend. The author in some places speaks of money as capital calling forth the production of commodities,—and in others as purely circulating medium raising prices in proportion to its abundance.[3]

[1] The last six words are ins.
[2] The remainder of this sentence replaces 'The calculation here requires 15 pc^t on the new capital.'
[3] 'I cannot allow that money can be augmented' is del. here.

nouveau total des prix sera non comme $10+1-1,5 = 10,85$ à 10, [*corrected by Ricardo:* '$10 + \overline{1 - \cdot 15} = 10,85$'] mais comme $10+1-0,5=10,95$ à 10.

La deduction ainsi faite la premiere année peut être considerée comme devant avoir lieu dans toutes les années suivantes, car aussi longtemps que le fonds additionnel est employé de la même maniere, il produit le même profit.

Si le total de l'argent etoit egal à la masse totale du revenu, la dépréciation de l'argent par une addition de nouveau numéraire seroit simplement comme l'argent ajouté. Cette dépréciation continueroit toujours tant qu'elle ne seroit pas compensée par une addition pour un montant égal à la masse des choses venales.

Mais si le total de l'argent, au lieu d'être egal au total du revenu, n'en etoit qu'un tiers, alors chaque £1 ajoutée à la masse du numéraire produiroit une hausse des prix de trois fois son montant: c.a.d. de £3 par année: tant qu'il n'y auroit pas une compensation proportionnelle à la masse des choses venales. &c. &c. &c. [*Dumont's note:* 'je n'y comprends plus rien du tout Voyez la masse de papiers Amount Profit Loss'.]

Cela etant ainsi, pour chaque million de nouveau numéraire ainsi introduit, une taxe annuelle de trois millions est imposée.   14

---

14. [4]In as much as the million could not be imported without a corresponding exportation of commodities, the country importing money would lose in consequence of the increased fertility of the mine.—This again would be a tax to that amount on one country in favor of another. It is precisely of the same nature though as that which would attend any improvement in a manufacture of England for example which should lower its value. In consequence of such decreased value a greater quantity would be imported into other countries. If the million had been at once introduced into England for example[5]

If in a foreign country new means of improving the pro-

[4] Four earlier attempts at opening this Note were del. in succession: 1, 'It would be a tax of'; 2, 'A tax of two'; 3, 'This tax would be'; 4, 'Can this be called a tax? It would be a tax to the former possessors of money only a great ['a great' replaces 'but the exact'] amount of which would be gained by other members of the society.'

[5] Left unfinished in MS.

Mais quoiqu'il y ait une taxe imposée au montant de trois millions, il ne faut pas croire que toute la Communauté souffrit une perte au montant de cette somme. Elle n'en est pas plus riche pour l'introduction de ce nouvel argent, mais elle n'en est pas plus pauvre. L'effet de l'opération est une revolution dans la propriété, mais non pas une destruction de propriété. Pour la Communauté prise ensemble, il n'y a pas plus de perte que si chaque année trois millions etoient levés en taxes et ajoutés à la liste des pensions....

PRIX—MESURE DU NUMÉRAIRE.

· · · · · · · ·

En prenant l'ensemble de tous les prix de deux années, si les prix de la seconde année sont plus grands que ceux de la premiere,
15 il faut que la quantité d'argent donné ou promis ait été plus grand la seconde année que la premiere.

· · · · · · · ·

EXPOSITION MATHEMATIQUE DE LA HAUSSE DES PRIX.

· · · · · · · ·

Si la masse du pouvoir pécuniaire a augmenté d'un 40eme et la masse des choses venales vendues a augmenté d'un 80eme, il y a eu accroissement d'argent et accroissement de richesse, en même temps—ce qui est le cours naturel des choses.

Quelque ait été l'accroissement de richesse, nous ne devons

---

duction of commodities be discovered it will be attended with real advantage to all countries which consume that commodity.—If the article were french cambrics for example England would import the quantity of cambrics she required at a less sacrifice of the produce of her own industry:—but when gold and silver are the commodities that become cheap in consequence of improved means of working the mine or the discovery of new mines no such advantage will accrue to England because the quantity of money she requires is not a fixed quantity but depends altogether on its value.

15. Or the quantity of goods less.

pas l'attribuer tout entier à l'accroissement du numéraire: sans accroissement d'argent, il y auroit toujours eu quelque accroissement de richesse. Dans les temps où le crédit pécuniaire etoit 16 inconnu, et où le numéraire a reçu très peu d'accroissement, la richesse réelle et la population ont avancé ensemble d'un pas assez rapide....

EFFETS DE LA GUERRE SUR LA BAISSE ET LA HAUSSE DES PRIX.

Nous avons dit que la guerre haussoit le prix des articles dont elle augmentoit la consommation et de ceux dont elle rendoit l'importation plus coûteuse.—Nous allons voir que la guerre a un effet plus general pour produire une baisse dans l'ensemble des prix.

Dans la situation de la Grande Bretagne, la guerre occasionne une addition continuelle tant qu'elle dure à la masse des annuités du gouvernement (ce qu'on appelle ordinairement mais improprement, les fonds publics). Cette addition ne peut se faire que par une soustraction d'une partie proportionnelle du capital employé dans les entreprises productives, les manufactures, les améliorations des terres, &c. Or cet emploi du capital dans les entreprises productives, tendant plus comme on l'a vu ci-dessus à augmenter 17 les prix en premiere instance qu'à les reduire en dernier résultat par l'augmentation des marchandises vénales, il s'ensuit que tout ce qui diminue ce capital productif a une tendance à faire baisser les prix. L'effet de la guerre sur les prix, au moins sous ce rap-

---

16. Is it not to be doubted whether the augmentation of[1] money in any way accelerates the prosperity of a country, for the reasons I have given I think it retards it.

17. I cannot comprehend how the increase of productions can cause commodities to rise in price, without any increase in the amount of money. War it would seem to me had rather the opposite tendency than what is here supposed, but the most correct opinion I think is that it has no effect on prices but thro' means of taxation.[2]

[1] 'the augmentation of' is ins.   should retain the same' is del.
[2] 'The author supposes that we   here.

port, n'est donc pas, comme on le croit generalement, de les hausser, mais plutôt de les reduire....

Les maux de la guerre sont si nombreux, si variés et si grands qu'il y doit se former naturellement une disposition à lui attribuer tous les inconvénients qui peuvent se faire sentir pendant sa durée, au moins tous ceux qu'on peut lui attribuer sans tomber dans une absurdité palpable. Mais quels que soient les maux qui en résultent, elle ne peut pas produire en même temps des effets 18 opposés et incompatibles—et des effets, tels que la hausse des prix et la diminution de la richesse, sont, dans un pays tel que l'Angleterre, opposés et incompatibles.

Diminution de richesse est un mal—hausse des prix est un autre mal—mais ces maux sont incompatibles.

La hausse des prix est un accompagnement inséparable de la 19 prosperité: mais la guerre ne peut pas produire deux effets opposés entr'eux, et si elle arrête le progrès de la prosperité, elle doit tout au moins ralentir la hausse des prix....

Dans le système des emprunts et du fonds d'amortissement, la depense de la guerre peut se distinguer en trois branches 1º le deboursement de l'argent levé par la vente des annuités du gouvernement: depense defrayée par les individus qui avancent l'argent à ces conditions 2º la depense qui consiste dans le paye-ment annuel de ces annuïtés possedées par les acheteurs, depense

---

18. What is there incompatible in a rise of prices and a diminution of wealth, if prices are regulated solely by the relative proportion of money. In a country insulated from all others such an effect would inevitably take place.

19. Is not this a very faulty opinion?

20. Not by a continuance of the same taxes but by an addition to them.

21. This does not appear clear to me. The tax for annuities is so much taken from the collective income of the nation, but it is not added to the revenue of a particular class of the same community. The capital which yielded me a revenue is annihilated by being lent to Government consequently the revenue which it produced is also lost, and tho' I may receive from the community the same income which I before enjoyed less my share of the tax,—to the community at large there is

defrayée par des taxes 3º la depense appliquée à la redemption de
ces annuïtés, depense defrayée par la continuation des mêmes taxes. 20

Cette soustraction des capitaux productifs, occasionnée par la
guerre, et leur application à des emplois improductifs (mais neces-
saires pour la protection du pays) est l'effet principal à considérer
sous le rapport de la richesse et des prix. Le montant des annuïtés,
etant levé par des taxes, est autant de retranché des revenus de
toutes les classes de la Communauté prises ensemble: mais c'est
autant d'ajouté aux revenus d'une classe particuliere de la même 21
Communauté, la classe des annuïtaires ou des propriétaires de
fonds.

La guerre a une influence qu'on ne niera pas sur la reduction
des prix de ce que j'ai appellé des *sources de revenu*. L'effet d'une
addition à la masse des annuïtés du gouvernement est de baisser
les prix non seulement de ces annuïtés, mais encore celui des
fonds de la compagnie des Indes, celui des maisons et des terres.
[*Dumont's note:* 'omissis non intellectis (in the article *War*)'.]

ACCROISSEMENT DES PRIX PAR DISETTE.

La disette accroit le montant total des prix pour un certain
temps sans qu'il y ait aucun accroissement dans la masse du
numeraire.

---

a loss to the amount of all that I receive, with my share of the
tax added to it.

The[1] effects of scarcity will be to raise prices, but whilst the
society does not expend more than its whole revenue it will
divert a portion of money from one employment rather than
another. If my revenue amounts to £1000– £800– of which
I spent in my family and 200 on those raw materials which
are imported from abroad it is evident that if I am constrained
by scarcity to spend 200 more on consumable commodities
some one else must go without those commodities. If each
member of the community consumed the same as before

---

[1] Although this paragraph appears in the MS as part of Note 21,
it was probably intended as a
separate Note, commenting on
the opening of the next Chapter
('Accroissement des prix par
disette').

Pour entendre comment cela se fait, il faut commencer par distinguer l'accroissement dans l'ensemble total des prix (des prix qui affectent le revenu) et l'accroissement dans tel ou tel prix particulier.

Un accroissement dans l'ensemble total des prix ne peut être produit, d'une maniere permanente, par aucune autre cause que par un accroissement de numéraire au delà de l'accroissement dans la masse des choses vénales.

Un accroissement temporaire dans l'ensemble total des prix peut resulter des saisons defavorables, dans lesquelles les produits 22 agriculturaux etant extraordinairement petits, les prix requis pour leur achat sont extraordinairement hauts: d'où il resulte que le total du numéraire employé à l'achat de ces produits augmente beaucoup proportionnellement au total du numéraire employé à constituer les prix de tous les autres articles.

· · · · · · · · · ·

CAUSES D'UNE TENDANCE AMBIGUE PAR RAPPORT A LA HAUSSE DES PRIX.

I. *Accroissement de frugalité nationale.*...

Supposez un accroissement dans les habitudes de frugalité....

Pour observer les effets de cette habitude dans une Communauté, voyons ce qui arriveroit dans le cas particulier d'un individu. Suivons les effets d'une guinée qu'il avoit coutume de debourser en dépense de consommation et qu'il applique maintenant à un emploi productif.

1. Il en fait lui-même l'emploi d'une maniere productive: par exemple, en payant à des ouvriers une heure de travail de plus tous les jours de la semaine.—Supposons qu'ils depensent en consommation ce surplus de gain à mesure qu'ils le reçoivent, et dans le même temps qu'il l'auroit fait lui-même.

---

there could be no scarcity because there would be the same consumption. I say this would be the case unless the 200 which I formerly employed on raw materials were now used in procuring from abroad an additional supply of consumable articles. The same effects would follow tho' I spent 1200 and were to encroach on my capital.

Dans cette supposition l'ensemble des prix ne sera point changé: mais ce qui peut arriver, c'est un changement dans le prix de certains articles: le maître eut depensé la guinée en vin ou en volaille; et auroit contribué *pro tanto* à elever ou à soutenir le prix de ces denrées: les ouvriers la dépenseront en viande de boucherie ou en biere, et il en resultera le même effet sur le prix de ces deux articles.

Mais d'un autre côté la difference sur l'ensemble des prix sera très sensible: le maître en bûvant son vin n'auroit rien produit, n'auroit contribué en rien à l'augmentation des articles vénaux: les ouvriers en bûvant leur biere, ont produit une addition à la masse des choses vénales, addition qui n'eut point existé si 23 l'argent en question n'eut pas été reçu et depensé par eux.

Si le produit de leur travail se trouvoit prêt à être vendu au moment même où ils ont depensé la guinée, il se trouveroit qu'il existe dans la Communauté pour une valeur au moins d'une guinée de plus de marchandise vénale: ce qui reduiroit *pro tanto* le prix de cette marchandise.

Il est vrai que cette supposition est presque idéale....

2. Supposons un second cas: celui où la guinée économisée est prêtée à quelque individu qui l'emprunte pour l'employer dans une depense productive.

Si l'emploi de cette guinée par l'emprunteur coïncide pour le temps, c'est à dire, se fait aussi promptement que dans le cas que nous venons de supposer, l'effet sur les prix sera exactement le même. Si l'emprunteur, comme c'est le cas le plus ordinaire, est obligé... d'attendre..., ces délais occasionnent un retard dans l'emploi de l'argent, une diminution temporaire de sa force effective.

3. Troisieme cas. Supposons que la guinée soit prêtée à quelque individu qui l'emprunte pour une depense de consommation.

Le résultat de cette recherche est curieux, instructif et digne d'attention. Dans les deux cas ci-dessus mentionnés, la masse

---

22. Is not the mass of prices the same after scarcity as before. May we not as before put the mass of commodities of all sorts on one side of the line,—and the amount of money multiplied by the rapidity of its circulation on the other. Is not this in all cases the regulator of prices?

23. Will not money increase in the same proportion?

des choses venales avoit reçu une augmentation manifeste, laquelle devoit au moins en premiere instance produire une réduction des prix. Dans ce troisieme cas, il semble au premier coup d'œil qu'il n'y ait rien de tel, mais en examinant la supposition de plus près, on s'apperçoit que c'est une méprise.

Pour placer l'erreur dans son jour le plus favorable, supposons que cette depense de consommation soit du genre le plus inutile, que ce soit celle d'un prodigue qui employant son capital en guise 23[*] de revenu, depense ainsi sa derniere guinée.—La somme d'argent qui dans une Communauté donnée, se depense annuellement en prodigalité, comparée à celle qui s'y depense d'une maniere pro- fitable, est une certaine proportion fixe, toujours très inférieure, et qui n'est point augmentée par l'accident d'une guinée employée à cet usage en preference à telle autre. Ce qui est emprunté d'un individu pour cet objet n'est point emprunté d'un autre. Ainsi cette guinée d'epargne, prêtée à un prodigue et employée en prodigalité, laisse une autre guinée libre, et disponible pour le service productif.

4. En quatrieme lieu, supposons la guinée envoyée par son proprietaire à un banquier pour quelque usage futur ou pour servir à l'achat de quelque source de revenu.

Dans cette supposition, l'effet de l'epargne peut paroître aussi avantageux que dans le premier cas ou au moins dans le second: En y regardant de plus près, on trouvera que son effet pour ajouter à la masse des choses venales, n'est pas tout à fait aussi grand. Il sera sujet à deux diminutions, l'une en fait de quantité, l'autre en fait de vîtesse.

1º En fait de quantité. Dans les deux premiers cas, la guinée entiere a été appliquée à un emploi productif. Dans le cas où elle est deposée chez le banquier, ce n'est qu'une partie de la 24 guinée qui sert à cet emploi. Le banquier ne peut pas disposer avec les emprunteurs de tout ce qu'il reçoit de la part des déposi- teurs: il peut disposer tout au plus des deux tiers: il est obligé de tenir l'autre tiers en reserve comme fonds de securité pour faire

---

23[*]. I can see no difference whether the owner of a guinea spends it himself on wine or in any other useless manner, or whether it be so spent by a prodigal to whom he may have unsuspectingly lent it.

24. It is a very doubtful point whether Banks keep a certain proportion of deposits. If their circulation be kept

face aux demandes journalieres de ceux qui ont deposé leur argent chez lui.

2º En fait de vîtesse... il peut y avoir un intervalle sujet à varier par mille causes depuis le moment où la guinée est déposée chez le banquier, et celui où elle passe de ses mains dans celles d'un emprunteur qui l'employe en depense productive.

5. Enfin supposons que la guinée, au lieu d'être mise en circulation, soit pour un temps indéfini mise et tenue en caisse.... L'effet de l'argent gardé en caisse, par comparaison avec un emploi productif, est de tenir les prix plus bas....

II. *Accroissement de la masse des produits domestiques qui n'entrent pas dans le commerce dans sa proportion avec la masse des produits achetés et vendus....*

III. *Décroissement de la masse des produits domestiques qui n'entrent pas dans le commerce dans sa proportion avec la masse des articles achetés et vendus....*

IV. *Accroissement dans la proportion des achats faits par échange sur celle des achats faits par argent....*

V. *Accroissement d'articles venaux, affectant le montant du revenu.*

Je donne pour exemple de ce genre d'accroissement les produits croissants d'une manufacture, et du sol.

Entant qu'un accroissement de ce genre a pour cause immédiate l'emploi d'un plus grand capital en depense productive, l'effet sur cette classe de prix est déjà connu. Quoiqu'il en resulte une addition à la quantité des articles venaux, cette addition n'est pas seulement accompagnée mais précédée d'une addition correspondente dans la quantité du numéraire, et même d'une addition plus qu'equivalente qui ne peut manquer de produire une hausse de prix. C'est dans le fait un accroissement dans la quantité d'argent deguisée sous l'apparence contraire et sous l'appellation d'un accroissement dans la quantité des articles venaux. [*Dumont's note:* 'Je ne comprends pas']... 25

VI. *Requisitions ou taxes en nature....*

VII. *Argent forcé....*

---

within due bounds their deposits need be very small,—on the contrary if the circulation be extensive they may be required to keep a large proportion.

25. How uniformly is the principle of the augmentation of money preceding the augmentation of commodities supported.

PROPOSITIONS SUR LA HAUSSE DES PRIX.

1. Position. Dans le cours du regne actuel, il y a eu une augmentation considerable de prix—augmentation dont la marche a été graduelle, quoiqu'accélérée dans les dernieres années.

2. Position. L'augmentation dont il s'agit ici est en sus de ce qui peut avoir été produit en certaines années par des causes occasionnelles, telles que les mauvaises saisons.

Obs. Dans l'estimation qui sera donnée ci-après, on aura soin de deduire de l'augmentation ce qui paroit avoir été le résultat de ces causes variables.

Sans une augmentation dans la quantité rélative de l'argent ou la vitesse de la circulation, aucune disette de grains ou d'autres denrées ne pourroit produire une hausse permanente dans l'ensemble des prix. Toutes les extra-sommes qui ont été employées à l'achat des articles devenus plus chers, doivent avoir été deduites soit des achats qui auroient été faits pour d'autres consommations, soit des divers emplois productifs qu'on eut fait avec les economies annuelles sur le revenu. S'il n'y a point eu de décroissement permanent dans la production des divers articles vénaux pour lesquels l'argent est nécessaire, il ne peut point y avoir eu d'accroissement permanent de prix, par où j'entends les 26 prix de toutes les marchandises venales dans leur ensemble, sans un accroissement correspondent dans la quantité de l'argent. Considerant le tout ensemble, on ne peut pas avoir donné plus d'argent pour les objets à vendre à moins qu'il n'y ait eu plus d'argent à donner.

III. Position. Durant la même periode, il y a eu une augmentation considerable dans la quantité de papier-monnoie en circulation....

IV. Position. Il y a eu néanmoins dans la même periode une augmentation considérable dans la masse de monnoie métallique.

Obs. Cette addition est un fait etabli sur des documents

---

26. Is not this principle to which I agree opposed by that which I have marked 22.[1]

27. This can by no means be admitted.

28. The same effects follow from a diminution in the amount of commodities as from an increase in the amount of currency so that an increase of prices is no more a

[1] Above, p. 310.

officiels. La quantité de monnoie d'or frappée dans ce regne 27 montoit en 1801 a £44.

C'est là le montant de ce qui doit exister aujourd'hui, *moins* la quantité qui a été fondue ou exportée sans retour.

Je ne connois aucune raison de présumer qu'il y ait eu une quantité un peu considérable fondue ou exportée sans retour....

v. Position. Quelle que ait été l'augmentation dans la masse de monnoie métallique, celle du papier-monnoie a été telle que des deux ensemble il en a resulté une addition considerable à la masse du numéraire.

Obs. Les prix n'etant ni plus ni moins que les sommes d'argent payées, affirmer qu'il y a eu augmentation dans l'ensemble des prix, pendant un certain temps, c'est affirmer en d'autres termes qu'il y a eu augmentation de numéraire. Or comme ce n'est pas 28 telle ou telle espece de numéraire, mais toutes les especes ensemble qui forment les prix, tout ce qui ne vient pas dans cette hausse de la monnoie métallique doit être attribué au papier-monnoie.

vi. Position. Dans les 40 dernieres années du siecle dernier, l'augmentation des prix a été telle qu'à la fin de ce terme ils etoient double de ce qu'ils étoient au commencement.

· · · · · · · · ·

ix. Position. L'effet de cette depreciation sur la valeur de cette classe de revenus qu'on peut appeller *revenus fixes* a été celui d'une taxe virtuelle quoique indirecte sur ces revenus....

x. Position. Cette taxe indirecte sur les possesseurs des revenus fixes ne produit aucun bénéfice au gouvernement ni sous 29 le rapport de la finance ni sous aucun autre.

· · · · · · · · ·

xii. Position. Durant la même periode de 40 ans, il s'est fait une addition très considerable à la masse de la richesse réelle; 30 entendant par richesse réelle toute espece de richesse autre que l'argent....

xiii. Position. L'augmentation permanente des prix a eu pour

---

proof of an increase of currency than a decrease of goods.

Ought the effects of taxation to be left out of the question?

29. If Government is indebted to the people it is so far benefited by a depreciation of money.

30. The author here asserts what I imagined he had before denied that an increase of prices may accompany increased wealth.

seule cause efficiente l'accroissement dans la quantité d'argent, au delà de ce qui a été balancé par l'accroissement de la richesse réelle....

XIV. Position. Toute augmentation dans la masse de l'argent par delà l'augmentation qui s'est faite dans la masse des articles vénaux, peut être considérée comme existant en *excès*: étant pro-
31 ductive de la hausse des prix, conséquemment d'une taxe indirecte sur les revenus fixes en proportion de cette hausse, et d'un surcroît de danger de la banqueroute....

PROPOSITIONS SUR LES EFFETS DU PAPIER-MONNOIE.

32   PREMIERE PROPOSITION. *L'accroissement du credit pecuniaire a produit un accroissement de richesse et par conséquent de population.*

Au premier coup d'œil, cette proposition paroit trop evidente pour avoir besoin de preuve. Quand on l'examine de plus près, il se presente des objections si fortes qu'elles semblent ne pas admettre de reponse: mais en approfondissant le sujet, ces mêmes objections s'evanouïssent et le premier apperçu se trouve confirmé par le dernier jugement.

.   .   .   .

La quantité de richesse d'un pays dependra donc à la fin d'une periode donnée des circonstances suivantes.

1. La capacité de travail employée durant cette periode.
2. L'emploi plus ou moins avantageux qu'on en a fait, c.a.d. les effets plus ou moins grands qu'on a su tirer de ce travail.
3. Le plus ou moins de durée des articles produits.
33   4. La proportion plus ou moins grande entre le travail productif et le travail improductif.

D'après cette analyse de la formation des richesses, le travail et l'efficacité du travail sont les seules causes productives: l'augmentation du numéraire n'y entre pour rien.

J'ai annoncé d'avance qu'un examen plus attentif résolvoit cette objection et replaçoit le numéraire parmi les causes de la richesse. La difficulté est levée par une distinction.

---

31. Why should we fix on a period 40 years back more than any other as the standard by which this excess is to be estimated.

Would it be desirable to have a money which was itself for ever invariable in its value?[1]

[1] 'I think the answer can not be doubtful.' is del. here.

Ce n'est pas la quantité d'argent introduite dans la Communauté, ce n'est pas cette quantité considérée *absolument*, qui peut augmenter la richesse. Cela dépend de la maniere dont elle est introduite et des mains dans lesquelles elle passe.

La richesse réelle de la Communauté n'augmente en effet que par les moyens enumérés ci-dessus: mais s'il est de la nature de l'argent, quand il est introduit d'une certaine maniere, de donner à ces moyens un developpement plus actif qu'ils n'auroient eu sans cela, l'argent, introduit de cette maniere devient source d'accroissement de richesse.

Dans un pays qui n'a point de mines d'or et d'argent, les métaux précieux ne s'augmentent que par une importation qui est le résultat de l'industrie et du commerce. Les hommes qui l'importent sont de la classe productive, et le premier emploi qu'ils en font est d'augmenter les productions, chacun dans le genre de leur commerce. Ceux qui emettent le papier-monnoie, ce papier représentatif de l'argent, sont de la même classe. Ce papier-monnoie n'est employé en première instance que pour des objets de production. Il n'est emprunté que par ceux qui veulent s'en servir en guise de capital productif dans des entreprises d'agriculture, de manufacture ou de commerce, dans lesquels il y a un profit, qui est autant d'ajouté à la masse de la richesse nationale.

Sans cette nouvelle introduction d'argent, il auroit manqué un moyen de faire naître cette nouvelle richesse. Les classes improductives qui vivent sur des revenus fixes les dépensent sans economiser: ces classes improductives pourroient avoir fait cette addition à la richesse, mais en general elles ne la font pas: les classes productives qui font cette addition, au moyen d'un nouveau Capital, auroient été assez disposées à la faire sans cela, mais elles ne l'auroient pas pû.

.   .   .   .

NOTE SUR I PROPOSITION.—*Effets d'une addition au numéraire selon son premier emploi.*

Pour placer cette vérite sous un nouveau jour par l'effet du contraste, prenons le cas où le numéraire (l'argent) est introduit

---

32. This chapter begins with what I consider a stumbling block,—I cannot agree that any addition to the money of a country produces riches, and population.

33. Do not all these points resolve themselves into the last?

par des non-commerçants. Nous verrons qu'il ne produit point
de nouvelle richesse, ou qu'il en produit moins que dans le cas
où il est introduit par le commerce.

Supposez que l'argent vienne sur le pied de rentes payées aux
proprietaires de mines d'or et d'argent; etant partie du produit
de ces mines.—Dans ce cas, il sera principalement employé dans
le premier progrès de sa circulation à l'achat des objets consom-
mables et improductifs qui constituent la depense de tout homme
vivant de ses rentes....

Au second pas, une portion de cet argent passera dans les
mains des classes productives, et aura l'effet d'ajouter à la somme
de la richesse réelle de la même maniere que le tout y auroit
contribué s'il eut été d'abord introduit par la classe productive.
Cette portion est celle qui compose le profit mercantile des classes
industrieuses sur les divers articles dans l'achat desquels ces rentes
ont été depensées. Ce profit, selon le calcul le plus ordinaire,
est de 15 p^r cent. De ces £15, £10 p^r cent seront depensées
sur des objets de consommation rapide pour l'entretien de ces
classes industrieuses, et pour le maintien de tout le capital fixe
en magazins, en outils, en machines &c. Les £5 restant seront
un profit net qui peut grossir leur capital productif et faire une
addition à la richesse réelle....

En un mot, le total des £15, soustraites des £100 depensées
en consommation par le riche rentier sur un revenu provenant
des mines d'or et d'argent et retenues comme profit par les classes
industrieuses sur la fourniture de ces valeurs, est employé exacte-

---

34. I wish this chapter had been introduced earlier, it
would have saved me much difficulty in endeavoring to
penetrate the views of the author. After the consideration
which he must have given to the subject it would appear
presumptuous in me to express myself so strongly as I feel
on what I consider the errors which this chapter contains.
That money is the causes of riches has been supported
throughout the work and has in my view entirely spoiled it.
There is but one way in which an increase of money no
matter how it be introduced into the society, can augment
riches, viz at the expence of the wages of labour; till the
wages of labour have found their level with the increased

ment de la même maniere et ajouté à la masse de la richesse nationale exactement dans la même proportion que le total des £100 l'eut été s'il eut été introduit par la classe industrieuse et appliqué à des emplois productifs....

En dernier résultat, il paroit donc qu'un nouveau numéraire produira une nouvelle richesse ou non, suivant le premier emploi auquel il est mis, et par consequent, selon l'espece de mains par lesquelles il est introduit et appliqué—qu'il produit une nouvelle richesse lorsqu'il est introduit par des classes industrieuses et appliqué à des emplois productifs—et qu'il n'en produit pas lorsqu'il est introduit par des rentiers qui depensent leurs revenus, comme on le fait communement dans cette classe, sur objets de consommation et de jouïssance.

Après tout ce qu'on vient de dire de l'argent métallique, il n'est pas besoin de nous arrêter longtemps sur le papier-monnoie. Le papier-monnoie a ce caractere qui le distingue, de n'être jamais introduit en premiere instance, que par des mains mercantiles pour être employé aux usages du commerce, à des emplois productifs, et toujours de maniere à faire une addition, dans son premier déboursement, à la richesse réelle.

Le seul cas où il n'ait pas été employé à l'enrichissement, c'est lorsqu'il a été emis en premiere instance par le souverain du pays pour fournir à des branches improductives de depense, nécessaires ou non nécessaires—à l'entretien des armées, à la fabrication des armes et à toutes les consommations qui constituent la splendeur 34 d'une Cour.

---

prices which the commodities will have experienced, there will be so much additional revenue to the manufacturer and farmer they will obtain an increased price for their commodities, and can whilst wages do not increase employ an additional number of hands, so that the real riches of the country will be somewhat augmented. A productive labourer will produce something more than before relatively to his consumption, but this can be only of momentary duration. I should endeavor further to prove what appears to me so obvious a principle was I not persuaded that you viewed it in the same light, and I should be therefore only repeating what had before suggested itself to you.

NOTE SUR I PROPOSITION.—*Vue hypothetique de l'accroissement de la richesse sans l'opération des mines
d'Amerique et du papier-monnoie.*

Ce seroit l'objet d'une spéculation assez curieuse que d'exa-
miner quel auroit été le progrès de la richesse, si plusieurs causes
modernes qui ont concouru à son accroissement n'avoient pas
existé: telles que l'augmentation des métaux metalliques par la
decouverte des mines du nouveau monde—l'etablissement des
banques—et le credit du papier-monnoie, émis par des banques
particulieres....

35   Quant aux prix ils auroient toujours été en diminuant: l'argent
devenant rare de plus en plus à proportion de l'accroissement
dans la population et dans les choses venales, les rentes en blé
eussent été etablies, non comme elles le sont quelquefois à présent
pour la protection des proprietaires, mais pour celle du fermier.

Les rentes fixes, comme les salaires, les pensions, les annuïtés,
les redevances pécuniaires, les hypothéques auroient été dans un
etat d'accroissement continuel. Dans le cours d'une longue vie
les annuïtés viageres auroient pu devenir un fardeau intolerable
pour le fond sur lequel elles auroient été assises.

Quant à la richesse réelle, son progrès n'eut pas été si rapide,
sans l'accession faite par ces divers moyens aux capitaux productifs. Mais on ne sauroit douter qu'elle n'eut été en croissant
chez les nations commerçantes et particulierement en Angleterre,
à proportion du degré de sûreté politique. Sans parler de l'ancienne
Grece et de l'ancienne Italie... l'exemple de la Chine est une
preuve suffisante qu'une nation peut arriver à un degré d'opulence
égal au nôtre sous un gouvernement moins favorable à la sûreté,
sans aucun de ces moyens d'accroissement dans la quantité ou
la force effective du numéraire.

---

35. Is it not probable that the old[1] mines would have
been productive of increase[2] in much the same proportion as the surface of the earth? Increased price must call
forth increased produce, unless the source of production
is exhausted.

If so pensions, and the div^d on the national debt would
not as here suppose have augmented in value.

[1] 'old' is ins.   [2] 'of increase' is ins.

D'un autre côté, si vous supposez que l'Europe n'eut pas eu par d'autres causes des guerres équivalentes à celles dont l'Amerique a été la source, et que vous déduisiez des profits du commerce avec le nouveau monde tout ce qu'il en a coûté pour ces guerres et pour l'etablissement des colonies,... il semble bien douteux que la non-existence du commerce Americain eut entraîné une diminution sensible dans la quantité de la richesse réelle. Sa 36 composition actuelle eut été un peu differente: mais je ne vois pas de raison decisive pour supposer qu'elle eut été moindre.

. . . .

. . . .

x. PROPOSITION. *Le papier des banques Provinciales est sujet à exister en excès.*

...Le papier-monnoie d'une banque donne au porteur le droit de demander au banquier une portion correspondente d'argent métallique.

La question est donc de savoir quelles circonstances—ordinaires ou extraordinaires—actuelles ou probables—peuvent occasionner une demande d'argent en lieu et place de ce papier.

Ce qu'on peut regarder comme les occasions extraordinaires sont:

1. Une defiance generale du papier-monnoie.
2. Une defiance particuliere du papier de telle banque.
3. Une demande extraordinaire sur la banque en question par une banque rivale ou hostile.

Je ne connois aucune autre cause appartenante à ce chef à 37 moins que ce ne soit une demande par un besoin de petite monnoie, pour servir aux transactions journalieres où les gros billets de banque ne s'appliquent pas. Ce cas a existé lors qu'il etoit defendu aux banques provinciales de faire des billets de banque au dessous de £5: il existeroit de nouveau si cette prohibition qui n'est que suspendue etoit retablie....

That the increase of money is[3] not been the cause of[4] increased riches the author himself gives us an example in China.

36. This is no doubt a correct opinion.

37. The greatest cause is here omitted and which forms

[3] Replaces 'That money has'. Ricardo obviously intended to delete 'been', two words below.

[4] 'necessary to' is written above 'the cause of', which however is not del.

Depuis 1797 où cette permission fut accordée, il s'est ecoulé un temps suffisant pour montrer que la demande d'argent qui
38 existoit alors n'etoit point fondée sur la défiance du papier, mais uniquement sur le besoin de petite monnoie pour les transactions journalieres....

La conclusion semble être qu'avec un fonds de securité suffisant pour reponde à ces demandes peu considérables d'argent, la nature de la chose ne fournit point de limite à l'emission du papier, aussi longtemps que le banquier peut y trouver l'expectative d'un profit.

La nécessité de reserver un fonds de sécurité proportionnel
39 à la quantité de papier qu'il emet peut sembler d'abord un contrôle qui opere pour moderer cette quantité. Mais nous venons de voir que la demande d'argent à laquelle il est exposé est bien peu considérable.

. . . .

x. PROPOSITION. Suite.... Le crédit du papier est une disposition de l'opinion publique qui s'affermit tellement par l'exemple general et par l'habitude qu'il arrive un temps où personne ne pense à le convertir en argent: abstraitement parlant, chacun peut savoir que la masse qui existe n'a point de base solide, mais cette reflexion spéculative ne se mêle point aux transactions ordinaires de la vie, et la defiance n'existe pas sur telle ou telle piece individuelle de ce papier. On le reçoit comme on le donne. Un autre s'y est fié, on peut s'y fier de même....

Que ce soient des *bulles d'air*, si l'on veut, ces bulles acquierent

---

the subject in dispute at the present day, the high price of bullion and low exchanges caused by excess of paper.

38. This has not been proved, on the contrary the fact of guineas having been hoarded in 1797 is well established.

39. It is evident that these principles are very defective. Bankers cannot safely emit paper in proportion to their deposits. A banker may with a million of deposit safely issue 3 but it does not follow that with a deposit of 10 million he may safely issue 30.

40. From what has been lately written on this subject the author's speculations in this chapter are founded in error.

41. By Negociable paper I conclude is meant bills of

par l'habitude une consistence qui suffit pour les rendre propres au service, jusqu'à ce qu'il arrive un choc imprevu et soudain auquel elles ne puissent pas résister. L'individu qui les prend ne les reçoit pas d'après l'opinion qu'il a lui-même de leur solidité, mais d'après l'opinion qu'il voit ou qu'il suppose dans les autres. Il en fut ainsi dans la spéculation du Mississipi—il en fut ainsi dans celle de la mer du Sud—Je puis croire qu'une note de £100 ne vaut pas un fétu—je n'en serois pas moins disposé à en donner £200 si je vois d'autres personnes disposées à la prendre de moi non seulement pour la même somme, mais pour une plus grande.   40

XI. Proposition. *Le papier négociable n'est pas susceptible du même excès que le papier-monnoie des banques Provinciales.*

.   .   .   .   41

XII. Proposition. *La Banqueroute est une conséquence nécessaire d'une augmentation de papier-monnoie, supposant qu'on ne lui mette aucune limite.*

Cette proposition est aussi importante que sa preuve est facile et certaine.

A mesure que le papier-monnoie s'accroit, les Banquiers reservent une quantité proportionnelle d'argent métallique pour *leur fonds de sécurité*, ou ils ne le font pas.—Dans le second cas, la banqueroute doit arriver par le déficit de ce fonds; dans le premier, par sa plénitude.

.   .   .   .   42

XII. Proposition. Suite—*Banqueroute.* J'entends par Ban-

---

exchange: These may be considered as the cause of the increase of paper issues, as it is on these securities that money is generally borrowed from Banks. It may therefore be affirmed that prices are raised in consequence of the increase of these bills, because the paper money would never be called into existence if bills did not precede them. The distinction in the effects of the two sorts of paper is not apparent to me.

This chapter is altogether objectionable.

42. This chapter very defective.—It is clear that the circulation cannot be indefinitely augmented in proportion to the increase of deposits—No notice taken of the effects of an excess of circulation in producing the export of gold.—The

queroute generale la destruction de la valeur de tout papier-
monnoie ainsi que du credit qui sert de base au commerce de
banque....

Une quantité de marchandises etant donnée, les prix sont en
proportion de la quantité d'argent qui est en circulation et de la
rapidité de cette circulation: l'anéantissement du papier-monnoie
et du commerce des banques aura donc pour effet nécessaire la
reduction de tous les prix, en supposant que la quantité des marchandises venales reste la même. Tous les prix tomberoient à peu
près au cinquieme de leur etat actuel et les gages du travail seroient
reduits dans la même proportion [*Dumont's note:* 'Je n'ai pas du
tout compris l'argument, et je l'ai supprimé:']. Les terres au lieu
de valoir 24 ou 30 années d'achat ne vaudroient plus que cinq
43 ou six années de leur rente actuelle. Une guinée alors vaudroit
autant que cinq à présent. L'heureux possesseur des especes
trouveroit sa propriété multipliée par *cinq*: tout autre proprietaire
trouveroit la sienne reduite dans la même proportion.

PROFITS ET AVANTAGES OPERANT EN COM-
PENSATION POUR LES MAUX DE L'EXCÈS.

1. Le premier avantage qui resulte d'une addition à la masse
du numéraire, faite par la voie commerciale, est une addition
44 correspondente faite à la masse de la richesse réelle: savoir, par

---

high price of bullion entirely owing to an excess of currency.
—General bankruptcy not to be occasioned by excessive
circulation whilst Banks pay in specie.

43. The utter discredit of all paper money would not be
attended with the effects here asserted,—Commodities would
no doubt fall very considerably but the fall would be temporary not permanent, provided the circulation of paper
before the annihilation of credit was exchangeable for the
precious metals at par.—We should very soon obtain such
a supply of gold in exchange for commodities that prices
would nearly regain their former level.

44. This principle has been repeatedly disputed.

The loss to individuals in consequence of additions to the

le premier emploi de ce nouveau capital en depenses productives....

S'il s'agissoit de mettre dans la balance le *bien* et le *mal* résultant de cette addition, il y auroit lieu à une grande diversité de sentiment. La même personne, selon que l'homme public ou l'homme privé prédomineroit dans la composition de ses sentiments, pourroit trouver des résultats bien differents....

AUGMENTATION DU PRIX DES TERRES ET DES FONDS PUBLICS ET AUTRES SOURCES PERMANENTES DE REVENU—MAL CONTREBALANCÉ PAR UN BIEN ÉGAL.

...A proportion que la masse des sources de revenu augmente en prix, la classe des capitalistes pécuniaires eprouve le sentiment d'une perte dans la même proportion, dans tous les cas où ils ont à faire l'achat de quelque source de revenu.

Cette perte en même temps est contrebalancée par le gain qui en résulte pour les possesseurs des terres ou des fonds de qui on achete.... 45

MONTANT DU PROFIT DES BANQUES COMPARÉ A LA PERTE.

.   .   .   .   46

---

circulating medium would not be compensated by any benefit to the public.

45. An augmentation of money in all cases operates to the disadvantage of some and the advantage of others,—[1] it will neither accelerate nor retard the growth of real[2] riches.

46. This would be the case if the Banks really added to the circulation by their issues,—but in the sound state of every currency no bank can add to the amount of the circulation they can only force the metallic circulation out of the country and replace it by paper. In which case the gains of the banker will be national gains, they will be made at the

[1] 'it destroys all security' is del. here.
[2] 'real' is ins.

EVALUATION DE LA PERTE SUR LES
REVENUS FIXES.

47   .   .   .   .

COMPARAISON AVEC LES FAUX-MONNOYEURS.

...D'après les lois d'Angleterre sur le monnoyage, lois qui pechent egalement par excès et par défaut, par severité et par négligence, le même individu qui met en circulation quelques pièces de métal de sa propre autorité, est puni ou par un leger 48 emprisonnement, ou par la transportation ou par la mort, selon le poids, la couleur ou les autres propriétés physiques du métal dont il s'est servi ou qu'il a pretendu imiter. Tel est le sort de ceux dont le profit derive d'une addition faite à la masse du numéraire sous la forme métallique: tandis que celui qui ajoute à la masse du numéraire sous la forme de papier jouït en pleine securité et avec honneur des benefices qu'il recueille sous la protection de la loi.

.   .   .   .

Singularité de cette taxe indirecte.

...Dans la banque d'Angleterre, l'exercice de ce droit de taxer est soumis à un certain contrôle.... Mais les banquiers privés, agissent chacun dans leur sphere, comme des Souverains indépendants, et ne sont responsables qu'à eux-mêmes de l'usage 49 qu'ils font de cette inestimable prérogative.... De simples individus, de simples marchands, avec la seule signature d'un Commis au bas de leurs billets de banque, levent chaque année un impôt indirect non seulement sur sa Majesté, mais sur tous les proprietaires, sur toute la masse du revenu national.

---

expence of the world at large,—in the first case they were made at the expence of the country only where the paper was issued.

47. The calculations here made are on a wrong basis,—they suppose a power in bankers to add at their pleasure [1] to the circulation,—whenever they can do this the circulation is diseased and cannot be exchangeable for specie.

48. No national advantage would attend the arts of the

[1] 'at their pleasure' is ins.

OPINION D'ADAM SMITH SUR LES PRIX.

Dès qu'il s'agit d'Economie politique, la pensée se porte d'abord vers Adam Smith. *Que dit ce grand maître sur le sujet de la hausse des prix, et du mal que vous lui attribuez? Que dit-il du papier-monnoie et de son influence sur les prix?*

...Quant au papier-monnoie, il en parle avec etendue: mais son influence sur les prix, il n'en dit rien. La raison de son silence est assez évidente. Dans sa maniere de voir, le papier monnoie n'a jamais fait et ne peut jamais faire aucune addition à la masse totale du numéraire en circulation. Comment cela?—C'est qu'il deplace toujours une quantité égale de monnoie métallique....

Examinons d'abord la verité du fait.

Voilà pour les faits. Par rapport à l'argument sur lequel Adam Smith s'appuye, il ne paroit pas d'une grande solidité.

. . . .

Il pose d'abord en principe qu'il y a dans tous les temps une certaine quantité d'argent qui n'est pas susceptible d'augmentation, à moins que la quantité des choses venales ne soit augmentée. Mais c'est affirmer la proposition même qui etoit à prouver: et au fond, c'est contredire un fait de notoriété publique et admis par lui-même: car à moins d'une diminution dans la quantité des choses vénales, comment les prix peuvent-ils avoir haussé sans une addition proportionnelle à la quantité du numéraire, lorsque la masse des choses venales restoit la même? **50**

La roue de la circulation, suivant son hypothese, est remplie avec du papier: par conséquent la monnoie métallique n'y sauroit entrer, il n'y a point de place pour elle. Mais ajoute-t-il *la monnoie metallique est trop précieuse pour rester oisive* (L.II. c.2.): il s'ensuit qu'elle est exportée.

---

coiner, but a real advantage would under proper circumstances attend the emission of paper.

49. This observation is applicable to the present state of our paper currency but not to the state in which it would be if our banks were not protected by a restriction bill.

50. The principle of Adam Smith is mistaken; he did not say that the[2] money of a country was not susceptible of increase, but that such increase depended on the diminished[3]

[2] 'quantity of the' is del. here.   [3] 'diminished' is ins.

Je conviens qu'elle est trop précieuse pour rester oisive: mais pour quoi sera-t-elle oisive en restant où elle est? Quel est le fondement de son assertion? Ce n'est qu'une simple metaphore, la métaphore de sa *roue* qui étant remplie rejette tout le surplus ou n'en admet point. Ce qui suppose que personne ne veut plus garder le numéraire métallique, que l'on n'en a plus besoin, qu'il n'est pas nécessaire pour servir de base au papier,—que la promesse est tout—que l'accomplissement n'est rien—et que l'or promis par le papier a moins de valeur que le papier qui le promet.

Tel est le danger de la rhétorique substituée à la logique. L'imagination est trompée par ces figures de roues, de circulation, d'ecluses, de torrents: et l'esprit laisse échapper le veritable rapport qui existe entre l'acheteur et le vendeur, entre le papier qui n'est qu'une promesse et l'or qui est la chose promise....

La facilité avec laquelle peut circuler une quantité de papier monnoie (promesses de payer) a ses limites parce que le crédit de ceux qui l'emettent est limité: il n'y en a pas d'autres....

---

value of the precious metals. He did not deny that the discovery of the mines of America augmented the circulation of all country but expressly affirmed it. It may be doubted whether any circumstances can raise prices generally but taxation, or a diminution in the real value of the precious metals in consequence of increased abundance.—The reason why gold was exported when paper was added to the circulation was not because both the paper and the gold could not be absorbed in the general mass of circulation but because the diminished value of the currency here, whilst it retained its value abroad made it a profitable article of exportation.

This is a consequence of which the author of the manuscript does not appear to have been aware, and is of great importance in all enquiries concerning money.

The reasoning in this chapter is excellent if applied to our present circulation but not[1] applied to that state of it when Adam Smith wrote. Dr. Smith was undoubtedly correct.

[1] 'when' is del. here.

POSITIONS RÉCAPITULÉES.   51

1. Mon opinion est que l'accroissement du numéraire [*Dumont's note:* 'métallique? je suppose'] a été productif d'un accroissement de richesse réelle, à raison de la maniere dont le numéraire additionnel a été introduit: c.à.d. par des mains commerciales qui l'ont employé en premiere instance en guise de capital productif, en travaux productifs &c.

2. Mon opinion en même temps est que cette addition au numéraire n'etoit pas une cause *sine quâ non* pour la production d'une même quantité donnée de richesse réelle: que si les mêmes valeurs qui ont été données pour obtenir du dehors ce numéraire additionnel avoient été employées à produire d'autres valeurs achetées par des consommateurs dans la grande Bretagne, et par conséquent achetées avec l'ancien fonds de numéraire, la même addition à la richesse réelle auroit pu avoir lieu, sans aucune addition à la richesse pécuniaire. (Ex. La Chine)

---

51. As this Chapter contains a recapitulation of the author's opinions it may require particular attention.

1. As the whole of the revenue of a country is spent either on productive or unproductive labourers, the prices of commodities for that year is not affected by the proportion, in which revenue may be actually consumed without reproduction,—or consumed and reproduced. It is difficult to comprehend why an increase of money should produce any other effect than to raise prices; and why the author should suppose that it will be the cause of the increased [2] production of commodities. Labour is paid not by money but by money's worth therefore if prices rise it will not occasion any increased production because more money must be given to the labourer to enable him to obtain the same amount of commodities.

2. If with the produce of the labour of England we purchase a quantity of gold from any other country which we

[2] 'increased' is ins.

3. Que par conséquent une augmentation dans la quantité de numéraire métallique est un accompagnement purement accidentel à l'augmentation de la richesse réelle—et n'a point de tendance à produire cette augmentation.

4. Que l'avantage d'operer sur une grande échelle, surtout dans les manufactures, a une tendance à produire un accroissement de richesse réelle—que l'exportation des articles manufacturés, donnant plus d'etendue à la fabrication, et faisant operer sur une plus grande échelle, a une tendance à augmenter la quantité de valeurs usuelles produites annuellement par l'emploi d'un capital réel donné: mais que c'est seulement dans cette supposition qu'un capital donné, réel ou pécuniaire, produit plus de richesse quand il est employé à produire des valeurs destinées à

---

add to our circulating medium, we in such proportion diminish our real capital and therefore the source of future riches. The additional money will yield no revenue whatever, the capital with which we should have parted would.

3. Consequently an addition to the quantity of metallic[1] money is not only of no advantage, but is a positive evil as it impoverishes the country which obtains it, or at least checks it in its progress towards wealth.

4. It is true that a capital employed in extending the manufacture of those commodities which may be advantageously exported is highly desireable, but an increase of[2] money will not enable us to add to the annual amount of the land and[3] labour of the country. The produce of[4] that labour will be measured only on a different scale. It can make no difference to the real wealth of the country whether the commodities produced be exported or consumed at home. If 100 pieces of cloth be consumed at home or whether they are exported to Portugal in exchange for wine and the wine be consumed at home can make no other difference but the profit.[5]—If they were exchanged for goods more durable the

[1] 'metallic' is ins.
[2] 'an increase of' is ins.
[3] 'land and' is ins.
[4] 'The produce of' is ins.
[5] Replaces 'can make no difference.'

l'exportation et exportées que quand il est employé à produire des valeurs destinées à la consommation du pays et consommées dans le pays. (Ex: brasserie)

5. Que quelque soit la proportion dans laquelle le commerce etranger peut contribuer à l'accroissement de la richesse au delà de ce qui auroit lieu sans ce commerce, cet accroissement ne depend en aucune maniere de l'addition à la quantité d'or et d'argent qui peut résulter de ce commerce etranger: l'accroissement en un mot seroit le même si le commerce se faisoit avec des nations qui ne donnassent point d'or et d'argent en retour, ou qui même n'en eussent point à donner.

6. Que par consequent l'effet d'un commerce etranger est plutôt de modifier la qualité et d'accroître la variété des in-

---

effects would be the same. If we imported Russias linen, and the consumers of the linen were to reproduce the value in some other commodity, it would be nearly[6] the same as if the consumers of the cloth at home were to reproduce the value of the cloth. I do not mean to depreciate the advantages of foreign commerce. If not beneficial we should not engage in it,—but it is not beneficial because we do engage in it.

By carrying on manufactures on a large scale you may undoubtedly increase the real riches of a country, and the exportation of manufactured commodities will encourage their production, and augment their quantity. It will do this in a greater degree than if the commodities were destined for home consumption. This is in other words saying that we engage in foreign commerce because it is advantageous to us.

5. This foreign commerce is not profitable because we import gold in return for our commodities, but would be equally if not more so if the nations with whom such commerce was carried on had neither gold or silver to give in return for the goods which we exported.

6. That therefore foreign commerce modifies the quality and increases the variety of productions which compose the

[6] 'nearly' is ins.

grédients dans la composition de la masse de la richesse que
d'ajouter à l'accroissement naturel de la quantité: et que l'importation d'or et d'argent, considérée à part des autres articles,
n'a point de tendance à ajouter à la richesse réelle.

7. Qu'entant que l'accroissement dans la masse d'or et d'argent
contribue à ajouter à la masse du numéraire, il n'a point de
tendance à augmenter la masse de la richesse réelle.

8. Que, entant que l'accroissement du commerce etranger
contribue à l'accroissement de la richesse, l'accroissement du
numéraire opere en sens contraire: parce que en augmentant le
prix pécuniaire des articles ainsi manufacturés, il diminue la
quantité que les nations etrangeres peuvent ou veulent acheter
de ces mêmes articles. [*Dumont's note:* '(Quære)'.]

9. Que quoiqu'une addition à la masse du numéraire métallique
n'ajoute rien à l'accroissement naturel de la richesse réelle, cependant une addition à la masse du numéraire représentatif ou papier-
monnoye contribue à l'accroissement de la richesse réelle: c'est
à dire, autant que cette addition se fait par des mains commerciales, qu'elle est appliquée en premiere instance à produire des

---

mass of wealth, and only adds to the natural growth of its
quantity by giving a more beneficial employment to labour;[1]
and that the importation of gold and silver has no tendency
more than other articles to increase the real wealth of
countries.

7. That because[2] the increase of the precious metals contribute to add to the circulating medium, it does not therefore
cause any[3] augmentation to the mass of real wealth.

8. It is not obvious that the rise of prices in consequence
of an increased circulating medium will check the growth of
wealth because it checks[4] the exportation of goods.—Such
an effect is generally counteracted[5] by the fall in the rate of
exchange.

9. If an increase of metallic money will not increase
national wealth,—why should an increase of paper money

[1] This sentence, first written as a literal translation of the French text, was subsequently altered as above.

[2] Replaces 'That inasmuch as'.

[3] Replaces 'it causes no'.

[4] 'foreign' is del. here.

[5] Replaces 'affected'.

valeurs usuelles; parce que l'addition faite par cette voie à la masse du travail productif n'auroit pu se faire par aucune autre, à moins de l'intervention coercitive du gouvernement—au lieu que l'addition faite au capital productif par une importation de numéraire auroit pu se faire egalement par le numéraire du fonds preexistent.

10. Que par conséquent des deux especes d'argent, le primaire et le secondaire, le réel et le représentatif, le métal et le papier, c'est le papier-monnoie seul qui est essentiellement productif d'une addition à l'accroissement de la richesse réelle: en augmentant la proportion du travail employé d'une maniere productive.

11. Que l'addition faite par cette voye à la richesse réelle, quoique plus grande qu'elle n'auroit pu se faire autrement, sans l'intervention coercitive du gouvernement, n'est ni plus grande ni même aussi grande que celle qui auroit pu se faire par cette intervention—que l'addition faite par cette voye a des desavantages particuliers qui ne se trouveroient point dans la même addition, résultant de l'intervention coercitive du gouvernement.

---

produce such effects. In what way can the increase of paper money operate on the production of commodities? Why should it increase productive labour more than an equal quantity of metallic money if obtained thro' the same channel and with equal facility.

10. It is difficult to comprehend how paper money should increase productive labour.

11. If the effects of an increase of paper money are the same as a coercive interference of government it must be because a portion of revenue will in consequence be employed in the maintenance of productive labour which but for that interference, or such addition of paper money[,] would not be so employed. But what proofs are there that additions to the paper currency would be the cause of accumulation of capital? What should give to one class a disposition to accumulate which is not possessed by another? This must be mere speculation—it might be so, but it is equally probable that it might be otherwise.

12. Que l'addition faite par l'introduction d'une nouvelle masse de papier-monnoie ne peut se faire sans imposer une taxe indirecte sur le revenu national, taxe infiniment plus forte et plus onéreuse que la taxe directe qui seroit levée par le gouvernement, pour être appliquée de la même maniere à des emplois productifs.

13. Que la tendance presque universelle à regarder l'accroissement du numéraire comme accroissement de richesse est le résultat (comme elle a peut être été originairement la cause) d'une impropriété dans le langage ordinaire, en conséquence de laquelle le mot *argent* (*richesse*) est indifféremment employé pour signifier des especes frappées et la richesse réelle,—l'argent, et tout ce qu'on peut avoir en echange pour de l'argent: c'est à dire, d'une part, tout ce qui est de l'argent, et de l'autre tout ce qui n'est pas de l'argent. [*Dumont's note:* 'En françois l'equivoque est plutôt sur le mot *richesse* que sur le mot *argent*—en anglois money and real wealth']...

RÉSULTATS OU PROPOSITIONS GENERALES.

52   1. Le haussement des prix et l'accroissement de la richesse sont des effets concomitants de la même cause.

2. Cette cause est l'extension du Credit, manifestée dans la
53 circulation du papier-monnoie et les opérations du commerce de Banque: toutes sommes ainsi prêtées etant employées en premiere instance à faire une addition au Capital productif et par conséquent à la masse de la richesse annuelle.

3. Quoique la masse de la richesse pût recevoir un accroisse-

---

12. The increase of paper money would operate as a tax on one part of the community in favor of the other part.

13. The disposition to consider an increase of money as an increase of riches arises out of the imperfection of language, which confounds the terms riches and money.

52. The rise of prices and the increase of riches have no necessary connection. Machinery adds to the real riches of a community at the same time that prices fall. An increased production of the mines will raise prices but will diminish the riches of the community who purchase

ment considerable du principe seul de l'Economie, sans aucune addition faite à la masse ou à l'efficacité du numéraire, par consequent sans aucune augmentation et même avec une diminution des prix,—cependant cet accroissement sera beaucoup plus considérable à l'aide de ces secours. 54

4. Comme il est de l'essence du papier-monnoie et autres opérations de banque, de créer une masse d'engagements qu'il seroit physiquement impossible d'acquitter tout à la fois si on venoit à en réclamer l'accomplissement, il s'ensuit que l'existence de ce papier-monnoie est accompagnée du continuel danger de la plus grande des calamités nationales—et qu'en un mot l'extrarichesse qui resulte de ce papier est achetée au prix du danger continuel d'une banqueroute. 55

5. Comme un Banquier qui emet du papier-monnoie risque son principal pour un profit qui n'excede pas l'intérêt, [*Dumont's note:* 'ai-je compris? texte obscur'] la présomption est qu'il n'existera de papier-monnoie que celui qui peut produire cet intérêt—mais comme le desir du gain peut l'emporter sur la prudence et que les calculs sont sujets à être déconcertés par une infinité d'accidents—le bien public semble exiger que les opérations des banques provinciales soient soumises au même contrôle que la banque d'Angleterre, par la connoissance qu'en prend le Gouvernement—d'autant plus que le Banquier ne hazarde pas sa propriété seulement, mais celle de la Communauté entiere, parce qu'une seule banqueroute affoiblit déjà le crédit et qu'un certain nombre de banqueroutes particulieres peuvent en amener une générale, genre de calamité qui surpasse infiniment toutes les autres. 56

6. Ce contrôle paroit d'autant moins sujet à objection, que

---

with commodities an additional amount of gold for money.

53. Denied.

54. D°

55. We should be exposed to this danger if we had nothing but the precious metals in circulation,—though certainly not in so great a degree.

56. The obligation to pay in specie will be a sufficient check against a too lavish issue of paper. It might be proper for government to take some precautions against adventurers entering into the Banking business.

chaque Banque est en effet une fabrique où l'on fait de l'argent
57 au profit du monnoyeur en égard à l'intérêt qu'il retire, et au
profit de l'emprunteur en égard à son gain sur le capital qui lui
est avancé—or indépendamment du danger exposé ci-dessus,
l'introduction de cette quantité d'argent agit plus promptement
pour hausser les prix qu'elle ne peut agir pour produire une
quantité proportionnelle d'articles à vendre.

.   .   .   .

8. Si l'on croit convenable de soumettre une Banque presque
Nationale, aussi anciennement etablie et qui jouït de plus d'un
58 siecle de confiance, au contrôle de la publicité, la même con-
venance s'applique encore plus fortement à des banques nom-
breuses et obscures qui n'ont point de corporation et qui se
multiplient de jour en jour.

.   .   .   .

10. A ces causes de danger pour le credit national déjà connues
du public, il faut en ajouter une autre qui l'est beaucoup moins:
et qui consiste dans le manque d'un petit papier monnoie
proportionné à la quantité toujours croissante du grand
59 papier: d'autant que les billets de banque de £5 et au delà
ne peuvent être adaptés aux objets de subsistence des classes
laborieuses.
11. Or ce defaut de petit papier, seul propre aux petits payements, dont la masse totale excede la masse totale des grands
payements, peut produire le même effet que le discredit du papier
en general, en donnant lieu à une demande proportionnelle pour
60 l'argent monnoié--or quoique cette demande des especes n'ait
lieu que par le besoin qu'on en sent pour les petits échanges, il est
presque impossible de la distinguer d'une demande qui seroit
fondée sur la défiance du grand-papier—et toute apparence de
defiance est accompagnée d'un danger proportionnel au credit.

---

57. Not a just comparison as the power of issuing paper
is limited.

58. The Bank of England was subject to no controul before
the restriction bill, and as they have of all other banks exclusively the power of forcing a circulation they ought to be submitted to a controul to which it is not necessary to submit the
other banks,—as they are subject to the controul of being obliged to pay their notes in the notes of the Bank of England.

. . . .

16. L'effet produit sur les prix, c.a.d. sur la valeur de l'argent, par l'extra-augmentation de richesse réelle qui a resulté de l'aug-mentation faite à la quantité et à l'efficacité du numéraire, est 61 tel que dans l'espace de 40 ans, l'argent ne vaut que la moitié de ce qu'il valoit, et que dans 40 ans, il est probable qu'il ne vaudra que la moitié de ce qu'il vaut à présent.

17. En conséquence tous les revenus fixes dans cet intervalle ont été réduits à la moitié de leur valeur, et dans un intervalle semblable, ils seront probablement reduits d'une autre moitié, c.a.d. qu'ils ne vaudront que le quart de ce qu'ils valoient au commencement du regne actuel.

18. De cette maniere, il y a une taxe progressive continuelle-ment imposée sur certaines classes de la société par l'opération et pour le benefice de quelques autres classes: taxe dont le montant 62 dans le cours de la vie d'un individu équivaut plusieurs fois à toutes les taxes levées sur la Communauté pour le benefice commun.

. . . .

Suite—Resultats.

1. Que la foiblesse radicale du papier-monnoie est con-tinuellement exposée à se manifester et se manifeste en effet de temps en temps dans ces demandes extraordinaires pour échanger le papier en argent—inconvénient qui jusqu'à présent a eu ses limites dans la pratique, mais n'a d'autres limites certaines que la destruction totale du credit pécuniaire.

2. Que dans les cas où ce discredit s'est manifesté, le remede s'est trouvé dans les associations qui se sont faites pour donner cours à ce papier par un commun consentement, chaque associé

---

59. As the large notes are exchangeable for small ones at the will of the holder there exists no danger of any un-equal proportion between notes above £5 and those under £5.

60. Answered by the last observation.

61. Depending altogether on the increase of the precious metals.

62. Denied.

fondant son acceptation sur l'assurance d'une acceptation pareille de la part de tous les autres.

3. Que pour la seconde fois depuis son institution le papier de la Banque d'Angleterre a été soutenu par la grande association 63 des Capitalistes de la Metropole—en conséquence de quoi il lui a été donné une valeur purement artificielle, quoique non moins effective, après que sa valeur intrinseque a été détruite par l'acte du Parlement qui rendoit non-exigible la promesse de payer d'ou dependoit sa valeur....

Suite—Resultats.

1. Que chaque nouvelle Banque provinciale qui s'etablit dans un lieu où elle peut ouvrir un depôt à des personnes qui jusques là avoient été dans l'habitude de laisser leur argent oisif, ajoute à la force effective et à la masse de l'argent, en proportion de l'etendue de ses transactions, c.à.d. dans la proportion de l'argent qu'elle tient en circulation par les mains de ceux à qui elle prête.

2. Qu'une nouvelle Banque dans ces circonstances en faisant 64 une addition à la masse de la richesse réelle en fait une aussi à l'inconvenient inséparablement attaché à cet avantage, la hausse des prix.

3. Qu'une banque qui s'etablit dans un lieu où il en existe déjà une semblable, ne fait aucune addition à la masse d'argent 65 en circulation, à moins que par des liaisons particulieres, elle n'obtienne des depôts d'argent de la part de personnes qui gardoient leur argent oisif, sans le prêter à la banque déjà etablie.

. . . .

AUGMENTATION DU NUMÉRAIRE MÉTALLIQUE.

[*Dumont's note:* 'je ne sais où placer cet article'.]
La quantité d'or et d'argent employée dans le Monnoyage est

---

63. The value of bank notes not dependent on the credit given to them by any association, but to the persuasion of the solidity of the Bank. No association of individuals can prevent Bank notes from being depreciated compared with the standard if their quantity is excessive.

64. If such effect takes place,—the bank of no advantage.

65. Not consistent with the principles before advanced.

le surplus de ce qui n'est pas demandé pour les diverses manu- 66
factures qui employent ces métaux ou pour l'exportation....

L'or en lingot est fourni à la Monnoie par la Banque d'Angleterre et rarement par des individus. La Banque est un marché
toujours ouvert pour l'achat du lingot, à un prix un peu inférieur
à celui de la Monnoie. L'individu trouve son compte à ce leger
sacrifice, parce que la valeur lui est payée immédiatement, au lieu
qu'en l'envoyant à la Monnoie, il faudroit attendre pour un temps
incertain jusqu'à ce que les especes fussent frappées et que tout
eut passé par les diverses formalités de l'office.

L'avantage pour la banque est non seulement dans ce petit
profit qu'elle fait sur le vendeur, mais encore dans l'emission d'une 67
somme égale de son papier qu'elle donne en payement, et pour
lequel elle reçoit un fonds de sûreté d'une valeur égale, et qui
n'est pas seulement en expectative comme dans le cas de l'escompte
des lettres de change, mais immédiatement dans sa possession....

QUE LE CRÉDIT PÉCUNIAIRE NE PRODUIT PAS UNE EXPORTATION DE MONNOYE METALLIQUE.

Un des mauvais effets qu'on attribue à l'abondance du papier-
monnoie, c'est de causer une grande et reguliere exportation du
numéraire métallique.... Je regarde cette opinion comme erronée
sous trois rapports.

1. Aucune exportation de numéraire n'a eu lieu dans la periode
de temps dont on parle, au moins aucune exportation considerable....

2. La cause alleguée, (l'accroissement du papier-monnoie) n'a
point de tendance à produire l'effet allegué, (l'exportation de la
monnoie métallique).

Dans le fait, elle a même une tendance opposée. Un fonds de

---

66. This is not correct because if half the money of the
world were annihilated a part of the plate of each country
would be coined into money.

67. If the bank have the gold coined which they purchase
as bullion they are losers for the same reason that the sellers
are gainers. They do not buy it sufficiently low to pay the
interest which they lose during the detention at the mint. It

securité est un accompagnement inseparable du papier-monnoie
68 en circulation. Ce fonds de securité est composé en grande partie
d'or et d'argent. Chaque addition faite au papier-monnoie produit non un décroissement mais un accroissement dans la demande
du numéraire métallique: ce numéraire est demandé non pour le
tenir en circulation, mais pour le garder en reserve, et constituer
le fonds de securité des banquiers.

3. Cette exportation est incompatible avec le fait universelle-
ment reconnu de l'augmentation des prix. Si chaque addition
faite au papier-monnoie avoit produit une diminution proportionnelle ou égale de monnoie métallique, les prix seroient restés
69 sur le même pié. La hausse des prix seroit dans cette supposition
un effet sans cause, à moins qu'il n'y eut une diminution dans la
masse des choses venales.

Si cette exportation du numéraire métallique etoit un résultat
70 de l'accroissement du papier-monnoie, ce mal prétendu seroit
plutôt un bien, sous le rapport que nous envisageons, c'est à dire,
qu'il auroit une tendance à prévenir la hausse des prix, et à com-
battre le mauvais effet du papier-monnoie.

Mais tout est l'ouvrage de l'imagination dans cette plainte:
le fait n'etant pas fondé, toutes les conséquences qu'on en deduit
tombent d'elles-mêmes.

---

is true they buy with their notes but inasmuch as they have
issued notes for such purpose they are precluded from making
interest on a like quantity which they might advance for
discounts. They cannot maintain both sums in circulation.

68. At the present time metallic money is not essential as
a deposit against the circulation of paper. The country banks
consider themselves as sufficiently secure if they have Bank
of England notes, and the Bank of England whilst the restriction bill is in force have no motive to keep metallic
money by them,—but every motive to get rid of it. There
can be no doubt that paper circulation forces the exportation
of the coins.

69. High prices might have been owing to the diminished

AUTRE AVANTAGE EN COMPENSATION DES [MAUX DE L'EXCÈS].

Une autre branche de profit est celle qui depend de la hausse dans le prix des fonds (c.a.d. des annuïtés du Gouvernement) et consiste à faire les emprunts publics à des termes moins desavantageux.

Le prix de ces annuïtés aura une tendance à baisser en pro- 71 portion de la quantité qui est mise en vente dans un temps donné et à hausser en proportion de la quantité d'argent qui peut être appliquée à leur achat.

Cet avantage se presente comme accompagné d'un desavantage proportionnel: savoir la hausse dans le prix des articles pour l'achat desquels cet argent a été levé par la vente de ces annuïtés du Gouvernement. L'avantage et le desavantage se presentent d'abord comme se détruisant l'un l'autre. [*Dumont's note:* 'Very long article, that I have not been able to understand, not even to catch the first meaning—partly for its being very obscure— partly being not legible—partly for want of marginals'].

value of gold as a commodity or of taxation: are not these adequate causes?

70. No doubt it is a good, not an evil.

71. An increase of money will raise the price of commodities but not of the funds or of annuities, because it will not affect the rate of interest, and the rate of interest is paid in the depreciated money. It is however neither of advantage or of disadvantage to Government as though they must raise more money in consequence of the rise of prices,—they pay less real interest though the same nominal amount. The advantage or disadvantage for the future must depend upon the increased or diminished value of the money in which the dividends will be paid.

NOTES ON THE BULLION REPORT
AND EVIDENCE
1810

THE Notes on The Bullion Report and Evidence printed below were written by Ricardo in October 1810 or shortly after.

The Report of the Bullion Committee had been issued on 12 August 1810[1] in the official folio edition. Ricardo's page-references, however, are to the octavo edition, which was published by Johnson and Ridgeway in September.[2] The MS is among Ricardo's Papers and has been published in *Minor Papers on the Currency Question, 1809–1823*, ed. by J. H. Hollander, Baltimore, The Johns Hopkins Press, 1932, pp. 45–59.

The MS consists of three parts:

(A) The Notes on the Report, which cover three octavo pages (these Notes begin on the last page of the MS denoted as (C));

(B) The rough Notes on the evidence of Goldsmid, Binns and Merle, which cover two quarto pages;

(C) The systematic Notes on the Minutes of Evidence, which cover twenty-five octavo pages.

While (A) and (C) were certainly written at the same period, (B) may have been written somewhat earlier.

Of the three MSS, (A) and (B) are merely jottings, but (C) forms a systematic commentary.

The reference numbers in the MS of the Notes on the Minutes of Evidence (described as (C) above) correspond to numbers written in pencil in Ricardo's hand on his working copy of the octavo edition of the Bullion Report which is in the Library at Gatcombe.[3]

---

[1] See above, p. 8, n. 3.

[2] Advt. in *The Times*, 23 Sept. 1810; and a new ed., *ib.* 13 Dec. 1810 [nos. 2 and 4 in F. W. Fetter's 'Editions of the Bullion Report', *Economica*, 1955, p. 153-4]. Ricardo's two copies are of the former edition. For dating the Notes see also the reference to Randle Jackson's speech of 20 Sept. 1810, below, p. 358, and the allusion to the table of discounts, which was first published in the *Morning Chronicle* of the 15 Oct., below, p. 358.

[3] There is another copy of the same edition of the Bullion Report that belonged to Ricardo in the Goldsmiths' Library of the University of London, but it bears no reference numbers.

Although the Notes (C) begin with a comment referring to p. 102 of the Minutes of Evidence, it is unlikely that any sheets containing comments on the earlier pages have been lost, since there are no numbers written on those pages in Ricardo's working copy of the Bullion Report.[1]

Ricardo, in the Notes (C), gives the page reference only for the first of his comments on each witness; subsequent comments, even if referring to later pages, have only a serial number which corresponds with the number pencilled on his copy of the Report.

The plan here adopted in printing the Notes (C) is the same as that used for the *Notes on Malthus* in Vol. II and for the *Notes on Bentham* in this volume. The relevant extracts from the Minutes of Evidence are printed in small type at the top of the page (with marginal numbers as marked by Ricardo in the Gatcombe copy) and the corresponding comments in larger type in the lower part. A number of exclamation marks written by Ricardo on the Gatcombe copy of the Report are also printed where he placed them.

To the Notes (A) quotations from the relevant passages of the Bullion Report have been prefixed.

---

[1] On the other hand, some later sheets of the MS may have been lost, since there are a few numbers written on pages *after* p. 102 which have no corresponding comment; see below, p. 360, n. 1 and p. 372, n. 1.

(A)

[NOTES ON THE REPORT OF THE BULLION COMMITTEE]

[p. 9.]   The Report points out that there have been considerable importations of gold into England from South-America.

Page 9.

The committee seem anxious to prove that there have been considerable importations as well as exportations of gold, but this fact is not in the least material to the principle which they are attempting to support.

[p. 21.]   The Report quotes from the evidence of the Continental Merchant: 'The Exchange against England fluctuating from 15 to 20 per cent. how much of that loss may be ascribed to the effect of the measures taken by the enemy in the North of Germany, and the interruption of intercourse which has been the result, and how much to the effect of the Bank of England paper not being convertible into cash, to which you have ascribed a part of that depreciation?—I ascribe the whole of the depreciation to have taken place originally in consequence of the measures of the enemy; and its not having recovered, to the circumstance of the paper of England not being exchangeable for cash.'

21   It is difficult to believe that the cause here assigned were adequate to produce such an unfavorable exchange as from 15 to 20 pc^t: much of it must in the first instance be attributed to the circumstance of Bank of England paper being excessive and not convertible into cash.

[pp. 55–56.]   The Report exposes the fallacy of 'not distinguishing between an advance of capital to Merchants, and an additional supply of currency to the general mass of circulating medium', under a system of paper currency: 'In the first instance, when the advance is made by notes paid in discount of a bill, it is undoubtedly so much capital, so much power of making purchases, placed in the hands of the Merchant who receives the notes; and if those hands are safe, the operation is so far, and in this its first step, useful and productive to the public. But as soon as the portion of circulating medium, in which the advance was thus made, performs in the hands of him to whom it was advanced this its first operation as capital, as soon as the notes are exchanged by him for some other article which is capital, they fall into the channel of circulation as so much circulating medium, and form an addition to the mass of currency.'

55   The advance is not useful even in the first instance if the amount of currency have already attained its natural limit. It can only be useful to one merchant in the same degree as it becomes hurtful to another. It enables one to make purchases, but, by the increase of prices, it deprives others of the ability of carrying on the same extent of trade.

[pp. 57–58.]   The Report reads: 'The suspension of Cash payments has had the effect of committing into the hands of the Directors of the Bank of England, to be exercised by their sole discretion, the important charge of supplying the Country with that quantity of circulating medium which is exactly proportioned to the wants and occasions of the Public. In the judgment of the Committee, that is a trust, which it is unreasonable to expect that the Directors of the Bank of England should ever be able to discharge. The most detailed knowledge of the actual trade of the Country, combined with the profound science in all the principles of Money and Circulation, would not enable any man or set of men to adjust, and keep always adjusted, the right proportions of circulating medium in a country to the wants of trade. When the currency consists entirely of the precious metals, or of paper convertible at will into the precious metals, the natural process of commerce, by establishing Exchanges among all the different countries of the world, adjusts, in every particular country, the proportion of circulating medium to its actual occasions, according to that supply of the precious metals which the mines furnish to the general market of the world. The proportion, which is thus adjusted and maintained by the natural operation of commerce, cannot be adjusted by any human wisdom or skill. If the natural system of currency and circulation be abandoned, and a discretionary issue of paper money substituted in its stead, it is vain to think that any rules can be devised for the exact exercise of such a discretion; though some cautions may be pointed out to check and control its consequences, such as are indicated by the effect of an excessive issue upon Exchanges and the price of Gold.'

58.   The proportion of currency which can conveniently be maintained in a country where a paper currency not convertible into specie exists can be adjusted by human wisdom and skill, as the Comm͠ee themselves assert in several parts of the report. It is precisely at its proper limit whilst gold does not rise above or fall below the mint price.

[p. 65.]   The Report refers to the crisis of 1793: 'In this crisis, Parliament applied a remedy, very similar, in its effect, to an enlargement of the advances and issues of the Bank; a loan of Exchequer Bills was authorized to be made to as many mercantile persons, giving good security, as should apply for them; and the confidence which this measure diffused, as well as the increased means which it afforded of obtaining Bank Notes through the sale of the Exchequer Bills, speedily relieved the distress both of London and of the country.'

65.   If the Bank had been more liberal in their discounts at that period, they would have produced the same effect on general credit as was afterwards done by the issues of Exch͟r bills. It would appear that the bank would buy the exch͟r bills but would not discount the merchants bills,—or rather they would not advance money to the merchants without the guarantee of Parliament. If the bank bought the bills it was then by an increase of circulating medium that public credit was ultimately relieved.[1] If the public and not the bank purchased the bills then was a portion of the circulating medium of the country which had been withdrawn from circulation again brought forth by the credit of government being pledged for the parties requiring relief.[2]

Perhaps after all that confidence was on the point of being restored at the very moment that recourse was had to this boasted measure.

[1] This sentence is ins.   [2] Replaces 'for the suspected parties.'

[ROUGH NOTES ON THE FIRST PART OF THE MINUTES OF EVIDENCE]

Aaron Asher Goldsmid.[1] This gentleman's evidence is very clear and explicit, both with regard to the price of gold, and the manner in which the bargains are executed. He stated, that, for these last 15 months, he had bought and sold more gold than on an average of years.

The chief imports of gold from the West Indies; principally from Jamaica. Spanish and Portugal coin have an extrinsic value as coin,—but French gold coin has not.

Does not this admission prove that it is not in consequence of our importations of corn from France that gold is greatly in demand, as if that were the case French gold coin would be particularly sought: of all gold that would be the best remittance. Yet Mr. G. believes that it is return for corn from France and Flanders that gold is[2] exported:—The largest quantity sent to Holland. Does not think that the quantity of gold exported considerably exceeded, in the last twelve months, the quantity imported. Has not any idea that the increase or decrease of Bank notes has any connection with the rise or fall of the price of gold,—but acknowledges that he has paid no attention to it. If a person were at liberty to export English Gold, he certainly would get 16 pc.t more than if he exported foreign gold.

Mr. Binns—[3] has frequently bought light guineas for which he has given not quite so much as 23 shillings

---

[1] The passages referred to are in *Bullion Report*, 'Minutes of Evidence', 8vo ed., pp. 4–18.

[2] 'chiefly' is del. here.

[3] *Bullion Report*, 'Minutes of Evidence', p. 23.

Mr. Merle—[1] has declined buying light guineas, as he thinks it contrary to law to give more than the coinage price for them; he has no doubt that the cause of the disappearance of guineas from circulation, [is][2] the high price of Gold Bullion and the temptation to export it on acc^t of the high price. He does not think that the increase of Bank notes has had any effect on the price of gold,—but confesses that he has never made any observation on it, nor considered the subject generally. He never thought of considering what effect a large issue of Bank notes might have on the price of gold. He allowed that if there were no legal restrictions against melting guineas, he should consider paper as of less value than specie,—it would make a difference of 10/- an ounce

[1] *ib*. pp. 26 and 37–8.   [2] Omitted in MS.

[NOTES ON THE MINUTES OF EVIDENCE]

MINUTES OF EVIDENCE

Taken before the Select Committee appointed to enquire into the Cause of the High Price of Gold Bullion, and to take into consideration the State of the Circulating Medium, and of the Exchanges between Great Britain and Foreign Parts.

. . . . . .

Jovis, 8° die Martii, 1810.

Mr. ——, a Continental Merchant, again called in, and Examined.

[pp. 102–103.] In what way do you think the present issue of bank notes and country bankers paper would operate to reduce the rate of exchange, supposing the balance of trade to be in favour of this Country?—The greater the issue, the more the exchange would be lowered; and supposing that a scarcity of the circulating medium of this Country existed, the higher the exchange would be. Independent of this direct effect, a reduction of the circulating medium would also have that of lowering the
1 prices of every article, and thus increase the facility and extent of their export.

That in consequence of an increase of bank notes in circulation, and articles of merchandize being raised in price, that the
2 exports are less than they otherwise would be, and in that way the operation on the exchanges is to our disadvantage?—Yes, in as far as there is any competition in trade between this and other countries.

Page 102

1. If the reduction of the circulating medium would raise the exchange, how could it cause the exportation of commodities seeing that any advantage from the reduction in their price will be precisely counteracted by the disadvantage from the rise in the exchange.

2 Is not the rise in the price of commodities, in consequence of an increase of bank notes, merely nominal to the foreigner, as whatever advance may take place in

Admitting that by an increase or decrease of the quantity of paper in circulation the prices of merchandize are increased and decreased, and the exportation greater or less, and that the exchange is of consequence indirectly affected; will you explain more particularly the direct operation of an excess of paper currency on the exchange?—An increase of the circulating medium enables persons to make greater advances to foreigners, and more 3 bills are thus brought into the foreign market; this must have the effect of lowering the exchange. Should, on the contrary, a scarcity of money exist here, it would become desirable to realize and accelerate the payment of debts due to this Country; advances now readily made to them would from necessity be curtailed, and the foreigner, who required a bill on this country, would be obliged to pay a higher price for that which was scarce than if it were abundant. The importations, from the same causes, would be curtailed; and the desire to raise money by sending a greater quantity of goods abroad, would be increased. However great the inconvenience to individuals, I conceive that a very material reduction of the circulating medium in this Country (by which I do not mean to make any distinction between coin and paper) would have the immediate effect of raising the exchange so far above par as to enable foreigners to send Bullion to this Country for the liquidation of their debt, provided this principle were carried to such an extremity.

· · · · · ·

[p. 103.] Supposing a diminution of the paper of Great Britain to take place, or an expectation of such diminution generally to prevail, would not the following effect follow; would not those English merchants who now trade on borrowed capital, and order goods from abroad on their own account, with a view

---

the price of goods, will, as just observed, be counteracted by the fall in the exchange, proceeding from the same cause.

3 The effects here stated could only take place when the currency was undepreciated. In raising the value of a depreciated currency to par, the effects on foreign trade would be purely nominal. If the value of the currency were raised above par by further curtailments of Bank notes, the effects, as stated in the latter part of this answer would follow.

to importation hither, or invite consignments from abroad by
4 offering to make large advances on the credit of them, curtail their
orders and limit the extent of their advances, in consequence of
their anticipating increasing difficulty in providing the means of
payment; would not this conduct on their part lessen the quantity
of drafts drawn upon them, and thus affect the balance of payments, and would not this alteration in the balance of payments
tend to improve the British exchange?—I perfectly agree in the
effect of the positions placed in the foregoing question, as I tried
to explain in my preceding answer.

. . . . . .

[p. 104.] In the case supposed [the circulating medium consisting almost exclusively of paper], will not the same general advance of prices in England, which you state an augmentation of
5 paper to produce, operate as a discouragement to the exportation
of English articles so long as the exchange shall remain the same,
which shall be assumed to be at par?—Yes, certainly; but it is an
assumption which, in my opinion, could never take place in fact.

. . . . . .

[p. 105.] Then if the exchange was affected solely by the
balance, the payments of exchanges with the North of Europe at
this moment ought, according to the information on which you
6 have formed your judgment, to have been in favour of England?
—If that were the only cause that influenced the exchange, it is
my opinion, that the exchange would have been in favour of
England for some time past.

. . . . . .

---

4. There would be no diminution of imports. Those
trading on borrowed capitals would cease to invite consignments from abroad, but as the value of the circulating medium
would be increased, those trading with their own capitals
would be enabled to import an increased quantity of commodities: The increase on one hand would be precisely equal
to the diminution on the other. The value of the currency
would not only be raised at home, but abroad also: the improvement of the exchange would enable the same sum of
english money to purchase a larger quantity of foreign commodities.

[p. 106.] Do you not conceive that without a free importation[1] of the coin of the country, a diminution in the amount of its
currency would produce a fall in the price of all commodities, and
a consequent rise of the exchange, in the same proportion as if
that diminution of currency had been effected by the export of a
part of our coin?—I should suppose it could only have one-half 7
the effect.

·   ·   ·   ·   ·   ·

[p. 107.] You have stated, that the exchange has been greatly
in our favour since the restriction on the Bank, and that the
balance of payments then due to England was in consequence
liquidated by great importations of Bullion into this Country;
you have also stated, that in your opinion, the balance of payments is now in our favour; explain to the Committee to what
cause you ascribe the difference in the exchange between those
two periods, in each of which you conceive the balance of payments to be in our favour?—At the period of the suspension, the
situation of the trade of this Country was very favourable to it:
the stock of goods on hand, and which were required by the
Continent, was very great; public opinion here in favour of the
measure empowering the Bank to withhold cash payments was
such, that for some time no traffic at home was carried on between this paper and coin: while the balance of trade therefore
continued in favour of this country, the foreigner could only

    [1] Corrected by Ricardo on his copy '[expo]rtation'.

───

5 Here the answer appears to recognize the principle
which I have stated above, and is at variance with the former
answer.

6. The exchange may be, and possibly is, really in our
favor, though nominally against us.

7 The effect of a diminution of the currency would be
precisely the same as the exportation of coin to the same
amount. If there be any difference it must be so small that
it can scarcely be estimated. The sum exported would be
divided amongst all nations and could not be permanently
retained in the importing country.

liquidate his debt by sending Bullion. Had the re-exportation
8 been allowed, a very small proportion of such exportation would
have been sufficient to keep the exchange at near par; or even the
public opinion would have fixed it at that rate, if it were ascertained that such operations could take place when required. This
not being the case, and some extraordinary causes (as explained)
having taken place, that depressed the exchange, and coin being
withheld both from internal circulation and from its operation
with foreign countries, I conceive this to be the cause of an unfavourable rate of exchange during a period of a favourable
balance of trade. In fact, the foundation by which what is called
a par of exchange is fixed, no longer exists as matter of fact.

.   .   .   .

Veneris, 9° *die Martii*, 1810.

John Whitmore, Esq. the Governor of the Bank of England,
   John Pearse, Esq. Deputy Governor of the Bank of England,
   called in together; and Examined.

.   .   .   .   .   .

[p. 112.] Let me suppose a case in which no demands were
made upon the Bank by Government for unusual accommodations, but an unusual demand was made by merchants for increased facilities of discount; would the Bank in such a case consider itself as bound, in order to support public credit, to grant
that increase of discounts, although there was a run upon it for
Gold, occasioned by the high price of Bullion and the unfavour-

---

8 The cause here mentioned could not have produced the
effect ascribed to it[1] if the circulating medium were not permanently excessive. The exchange may be completely con-
trolled by those who have now the power of issuing paper.
Whilst confidence is reposed in the Bank, the restriction might
continue and yet the exchange never deviate far from par.

Page 112.[2]
   1. If, during the Period that the exchange has improved

[1] Replaces 'produced any effect'.   [2] The exclamation marks on the
margins of this page are Ricardo's.

able state of the exchange?—I desire time to consider that question.   !!!

Supposing the Bank to be now paying in cash, and to experience a drain of Gold, as just mentioned; and supposing them also to afford precisely the same sum in the way of loan as before; would not a diminution of their paper take place, which would be proportionate to that diminution of their stock of guineas which the drain would occasion, inasmuch as every person coming to demand guineas would give in exchange for them an equal quantity of bank notes, which would be cancelled?—I would wish for time to consider that question.   !!!

Is there not reason to suspect that the present unfavourable state of the exchange may be in part owing to the want of that limitation of paper which used to take place before the suspension of the cash payments of the Bank, on the occasion of the exchanges becoming unfavourable?—My opinion is, I do not know whether it is that of the Bank, that the amount of our paper circulation has no reference at all to the state of the exchange.   !!!

Has that question ever been brought to a regular discussion and decision in the Court of Directors?—In the opinion of the Bank Directors, it had not sufficient bearing upon our concerns to make it more than a matter of conversation; it never was singly and separately a subject of discussion, though constantly in view with other circumstances.

Mr. Pearse.—The varying prices of the Hamburgh exchange compared with the varying amount of Bank notes at different periods, seem to prove that the amount of Bank notes in circula- 1 tion has not had an influence on the exchange.

. . . . . .

whilst the amount of Bank notes has increased, commerce and payments had not also increased, no such effects could have followed. An additional circulating medium, whilst it preserves the same value, will be required by an increased commerce and revenue, an augmentation of paper circulation may therefore take place at such time[3] without causing either

[3] First written 'An increased commerce and revenue *requires* an additional circulating medium, whilst it preserves the same value, it will therefore bear an *increase* of paper circulation', then altered as above. Ricardo omitted however to strike out '*requires* an' and '*increase*'.

[p. 114.]   Whether, since the suspension of the payments in cash down to the present time, there has been any material ex-
2 tension of commercial discounts?—I wish to have time to con-sider that question.

. . . . . .

Lunae, 12° die Martii, 1810.

Abraham Goldsmid, Esq. called in, and Examined.

. . . . . .

[p. 120.]   Does not the present low rate of exchange create
1 the demand and the high price of Bullion?—The present high price of Bullion is on account of the low rate of exchange.

. . . . . .

[p. 121.]   Is it your opinion that the circulating medium, as

---

the depreciation of paper, or of the foreign exchanges. Mr. Pearse does not prove,[1] even if the fact be as he stated, that the principle, "of the exchanges being affected by an excess of currency" is erroneous.

Page 114

2. Is it not surprising that the Governor of the Bank should require time to consider this question,—when it is (I am credibly informed) ascertained, that the discounts have increased in no less a proportion than[2]

Page 120

1. Mr. Randall Jackson said, in his speech at the Bank, that many respectable evidence had given it as their opinion to the committee that the high price of bullion had nothing to do with the fall of the exchange.[3] Mr. Goldsmid whom he

---

[1] 'therefore' was ins. and then del. here.
[2] Left blank in MS. The propor-tion was as 241 to 688, according to the 'Scale of Discounts' pre-sented by the Bank to the Bullion Committee with the request that

it should not be made public. It was however published in the *Morning Chronicle* of 15 Oct. 1810; see below, Appendix to Vol. IV.
[3] See *The Speech of Randle Jack-son, Esq. delivered at the General Court of the Bank of England, held*

entirely confined to paper in this country, produces any effect upon foreign exchanges?—I do not profess myself competent to give my opinion upon that.   2

.   .   .   .   .   .

Martis, 13° die Martii, 1810.

John Whitmore, Esq. the Governor, and *John Pearse,* Esq. the Deputy Governor of the Bank of England, called in together; and Examined.

.   .   .   .   .   .

[p. 124.] Supposing the currency of any country to consist altogether of specie, would that specie be affected in its value by its abundance or by its diminution, the same as copper, brass, cloth, or any other article of merchandize?—I have already said   1 that I decline answering questions as to opinion; I am very ready

---

often mentioned with great respect, is in this answer at variance with him. Indeed I can find no such opinion given by any evidence whatever

2. Mr. Goldsmid acknowledges that he is not competent to give an opinion upon the main point in dispute. It cannot, therefore, be on his authority that either Sir J. Sinclair[4] or Mr. Jackson so confidently rely, for the conclusions which they have formed "on the opinions[5] of the great practical authorities,"[6] examined by the committee.

Page 124

1. After this answer can the comm̃ee be blamed for not giving implicit assent to Mr. Whitmore's opinions? If he had answered this question, in the only way in which it could be answered, in the affirmative; he would have been obliged to

*on the 20th of September, 1810, respecting the Report of the Bullion Committee...*London, Butterworth, pp. 23–4; cp. above, p. 152.
[4] *Observations on the Report of the Bullion Committee.* By the Right Honourable Sir John Sinclair, Bart., M.P., London, Cadell and Davies, 1810.

[5] 'opinions' is written above 'evidence', which however is not del.

[6] Sinclair's words are 'Sanctioned by the authority of persons of practical detail' (*Observations,* p. 28)

to answer any questions as to matters of fact; I have not opinions formed upon the points stated in this and the preceding question sufficiently matured to offer them to the Committee.

.   .   .   .   .   .

[p. 125.]   You stated in a former examination, "Supposing the excess of the market price of Gold in Bank notes above the mint price to be 5 per cent. and that in consequence a drain of guineas takes place from the Bank, and the Bank, by diminishing the amount of its outstanding demands, raises the value of its paper 5 per cent.," in the manner described in a former answer of yours, would not the result be to bring the market and the mint price of Gold to a par, and consequently to put a stop to the demand for guineas?

Mr. Whitmore.—I believe my former answer did not go to the Bank raising the price of their notes, for in fact, if the Bank was to
2 raise the value of them, and give them for discounts, estimating them at such increased value, it would incur the penalty of usury. I therefore conceive this statement to suppose a case that cannot occur.

In taking into consideration the amount of your notes out in

---

admit that the issues of the Bank could be made to raise or fall the price of gold

2. He confounds price and value. How could the bank incur the penalty of usury whatever value a pound sterling might rise to. If £100—of our present currency, were so raised in value, by adding to the quantity of gold in a guinea, as to command double the quantity of commodities, which they can now purchase, and the Bank were to lend such £100—at 5 pc^t how could the increased value of the notes subject them to the penalties of usury?

130^1

1. Mr. Grefulhe seems to consider it as a possible case, that the balance of payments might be so much, and so

---

^{1} In Ricardo's copy of the Bullion Report, the figures 2, 3 and 4 are written against other questions to   Greffulhe (the first, fourth and fifth following the one reprinted above), but there are no corres-

circulation, and in limiting the extent of your discounts to merchants, do you advert to the difference, when such exists, between the market and the mint price of Gold?—We do advert to that, inasmuch as we do not discount, at any time, for those persons who we know or have good reason to suppose export the Gold. !

.   .   .   .   .   .

Mercurii, 14° *die Martii,* 1810.

John Louis Greffulhe, Esq. was Examined.

.   .   .   .   .

[p. 130.]   Is it not your opinion that, if no forced paper circulation existed in the Country, it would not be possible for the exchanges to fall materially below their par, or for the price of Bullion to rise materially above its standard price?—I conceive 1 that that would not prevent the exchange from falling very considerably under par, if the amount of Bullion in the Country were not sufficient to pay the balances.

.   .   .   .   .   .

---

permanently against a country that if there existed in that country a metallic circulation only, she might be exhausted of all her bullion and coin. He does not reflect that the want of a circulating medium is so urgent that we should cease to import commodities, after a considerable portion of our money had left us, if it can be supposed[2] foreign nations could be[3] so blind to their interest as to refuse to accept any thing else in exchange for them. Those who argue thus are always obliged to suppose that the balance of payments is accidentally and uncontrollably against us; they should go a little further in their examination of cause and effect, and they would discover that a balance of payments can never be[4] against any particular country, for any length of time, but

ponding notes in the MS. They may have been written on a sheet now lost.

[2] 'it can be supposed' is ins.

[3] 'could be' is written above 'were', which, however, is not del.

[4] Replaces 'is never'.

William Cecil Chambers, Esq. called in, and Examined.

.   .   .   .   .

1   [pp. 136–137.]   What do you say as to an excessive currency, though not forced?—I do not conceive the thing possible.

---

from a relative excess in the currency of that country.—It buys with money because money is too abundant:— diminish the quantity and it will cease buying altogether, unless it can buy with goods.

136

1. This seems to be the source of all the errors of these practical men. A paper currency cannot be excessive, according to them, if no one is obliged to take it against his will. They must be of opinion that a given quantity of currency can be employed by a given quantity of commerce and payments, and no more,—not reflecting that by depreciating its value the same commerce will employ an additional quantity. Did not the discovery of the American mines depreciate the value of money, and has not the consequences been an increased use of it. By constantly depreciating its value there is no quantity of money which the same state of commerce may not absorb; and it is of little importance whether the state forces a paper circulation, or whether it be issued by a company only when demanded by the public, in discounting good bills, the effects of an excessive issue will be the same.—

Suppose the paper in circulation not convertible into specie to be 20 millions, and I have credit sufficient with the bank to get a bill discounted at the Bank for £1000—wishing to extend my business to that amount. Suppose too that all the other trades possess equal facilities and that by these various bills being discounted a million is added to the circulation. Now the possessors of this additional million have

What do you mean by a forced paper currency?—A paper which I am obliged to take against my will for more than its value; it is not forced so long as people take it willingly, which they will naturally do whilst undepreciated.

·   ·   ·   ·   ·   ·   ·

not borrowed it to let it remain idle but for the purpose of extending their different trades. The distiller goes to the corn market with his portion; the cotton manufacturer, the sugar baker &c. with theirs; the quantity of corn, sugar, and cotton in the country remaining precisely the same as before. Will not the effect of this additional million be to raise the prices of all commodities $\frac{1}{20}$ or 5 pc^t that being the proportion in which the currency is increased. These borrowers of the Bank will succeed in their object of increasing their trade, but by rendering the 20 millions which was before in circulation less efficient there will be a corresponding loss in the trade of those who were before possessed of this sum. As no addition had been made to the quantity of the corn, the sugar or the cotton but only to the prices of those commodities there would be no increased trade but a different division of it. If another million were added to the circulation by new demands for discounts, the same effects would again follow. There can be no limits to the depreciation of money from[1] such repeated additions. The observations of Mr. Harman that the Bank never discount bills but for bona fide trans-actions[2] cannot limit the quantity,[3]—the same sum of money performs successively a great number of payments,— but a bill might be given for each of these payments for bona fide transactions and if the bank discounted them all we

[1] 'excessive' is del. here.
[2] See below, p. 375.
[3] 'because if all such bills were discounted we might have four times the amount of paper that is now actually in circulation' is del. here.

Veneris, 16° *die Martii,* 1810.

John Whitmore, Esq. the Governor, and *John Pearse,* Esq. the Deputy Governor of the Bank of England, called in together; and Examined.

[pp. 152–153.] Suppose a case in which no demands were made upon the Bank by Government for unusual accommodations, but an unusual demand was made by merchants for increased facilities of discount, would the Bank in such a case consider itself as bound, in order to support public credit, to grant that increase of discounts, although there was a run upon it for Gold occasioned by the high price of Bullion and the unfavourable state of the exchange?—I now consider my answer as my

---

might have four or ten times the amounts of paper that is now actually in circulation.

Page 135[1]

Mr. Chambers like those who have given their evidence before him ascribes the unfavorable exchange to the balance of payments being against us,—allows that a forced paper circulation would depress the exchange, but contends that the Bank of England cannot force a circulation; he does not conceive Gold to be a fairer standard for Bank of England notes than Indigo or broad cloth!!!

Page 152

It has been contended, by some intelligent men,[2] that in the year 1797 when there was a run upon the Bank for specie, —that the Directors would have upheld public credit and have put a stop to the demand for guineas by increasing their

---

[1] This note, which is a general comment on Chambers' evidence, pp. 135–7, follows in the MS the note to p. 136.

[2] See 'Report of the Lords' Committee of Secrecy. Order of Council 26th February 1797; Relating to the Bank', evidence of Henry Thornton, pp. 42–3, and of Walter Boyd, pp. 65–6; reprinted in *Parliamentary Papers,* 1810, vol. III. Cp. *Bullion Report,* 8vo ed., p. 65.

own opinion, not having the opportunity of consulting the Bank upon the question; in my opinion the Bank would not increase 1 their discounts, nor on the other hand would it, I think, after the experience of the years 1796 and 1797, do well materially to diminish them.

.   .   .   .   .   .

Veneris, 23° *die Martii,* 1810.

John Whitmore, Esq. the Governor, and *John Pearse,* Esq. the Deputy Governor of the Bank of England, called in together; and Examined.

.   .   .   .   .   .

[p. 176.] Taking the daily average amount [of payments

discounts, rather than by diminishing them. I am of opinion that the run upon the Bank in 1797 proceeded from political alarm, and a desire on the part of the people to hoard guineas. I was myself witness of many persons actually exchanging bank notes for guineas for such purpose,—therefore it is probable that the Bank could not have prevented the stoppage of payments to which they were obliged to have recourse. But a demand upon the bank for specie[3] from fears of the solidity of its resources, or from political alarm, are very different from a demand arising from a high price of bullion and a low rate of exchange and must be differently treated. In the latter case it can proceed only from an excessive issue of paper, if the gold coin is not debased and can only be checked by calling in the excess.[4] In 1797 the exchange was at 38 with Hamburgh and gold bullion at £3. 17. 6.—In 1810 the exchange is at 29 and gold bullion at £4. 13—

Page 176

If the notes of the Bank of England in circulation are em-

[3] Replaces 'But a run upon the bank'.

[4] Replaces 'checked by a diminu-

tion [replacing 'limitation'] of the amount of notes.'

made by all the London bankers put together] so low as five millions, does it not follow that in the course of the year the notes of the Bank of England in circulation are employed in making payments of above 1,500,000,000 sterling, on the counters of the London bankers alone?—According to the opinion that I entertain, it will amount to that.

Taking into consideration the quantity of Bank of England paper necessary for country bankers, and the various other uses and applications for which it is demanded, does it not follow that there is only a certain limited proportion of the total amount of Bank of England paper in circulation, available for effecting the payment of this 1,500 million?—It is only part of the circulation that is available for such purpose.

·   ·   ·   ·   ·   ·

Veneris, 30° *die Martii*, 1810.

John Whitmore, Esq. the Governor, and *John Pearse*, Esq. the Deputy Governor of the Bank of England, called in together; and Examined.

[pp. 184–185.] Does not the unfavourable course of exchange with foreign countries tend, even under the present

---

ployed in making payments of above 1500 millions, and only a part of the Bank of England paper is available for that purpose as a great proportion is wanted for deposits by the county bankers,—does it not follow that the proportion of Bank notes to actual payments is exceedingly[1] small?[2] If the daily and bona fide payments exceed 5 millions,—and if we suppose what is barely possible[3] such payments were made by bills of exchange payable at 60 days might not the bank contending as they do that by discounting bills given for real transactions they can never produce an[4] issue of notes be called upon to discount bills in 60 days to the enormous amount of 300 millions?[5]

[1] Written above 'very', which however is not del.
[2] 'If then every bona fide paymᵗ was made by a bill of exchange' is del. here.
[3] Last six words are ins.
[4] 'excessive' has probably been omitted here by an oversight.
[5] An earlier version does not contain the two lines, from 'con-

restriction, in some degree to render its continuance and prolongation necessary, in so far as that necessity may depend on the proportion of specie in the coffers of the Bank to the amount of its notes in circulation?

Mr. Whitmore.—In my opinion the high price of Gold bullion abroad, does make it necessary to continue the restriction; but I have already observed, that the low state of exchange has not operated before the restriction to drain us of our guineas to any 1 material extent.

Mr. Pearse.—Undoubtedly it does, as far as regards the supply of the public wants with a circulating medium, as it would not be possible for the Bank to continue that supply if the Restriction Bill were removed, whilst the foreign exchanges remain so unfavourable as at present; a profit of from ten to fifteen, to twenty per-cent. upon converting Guineas into bullion, would be too great a temptation to allow any to remain in the Bank, as long as a bank note remained in circulation. The Bank would therefore inevitably be driven to the necessity of calling in its notes, or in 2 other words of reducing its advances on bills, &c. which would produce that distress which the Restriction Bill was passed to prevent.

. . . .

[184]⁶

1 Before the restriction the exchange was never for any considerable time against this country. If such a state of the exchange had permanently existed,⁷ whilst the Bank paid in specie, the Bank might have been drained of every guinea.—

2 Mr. Pearse is no doubt correct in his answer as far as regards the necessity which the Bank would be under of reducing its advances on bills &cᵃ, but he is wrong in supposing that any distress similar to that in 1797 would ensue from the repeal of the restriction bill.

tending' to 'issue of notes', but it has in addition at the end of the paragraph: 'if they were to consider as they profess to do that they can never err in discounting bills for bona fide transactions'.

⁶ MS, by a mistake, has '181'.
⁷ 'had permanently existed' replaces 'were possible'; and, in the next line, 'might have been' replaces 'might be'.

[p. 186.]   Suppose the measure to be determined upon by Parliament, of the opening of the Bank at a distant period, should you think that in the event of the exchanges continuing the same or nearly the same, some restriction of the Bank issues ought to take place with a view to prepare for the opening?...

Mr. Pearse.—In the contemplation of the removal of the Restriction Bill at any definite period, it would become necessary for the Bank to regulate the amount of its issues, with a reference to the course of exchange with foreign countries; but while that 3 exchange continues unfavourable (an event as arising out of the balance of payments not within the control or influence of the Bank) I cannot see that any regulation within the means of the Bank, would in the event of an opening, effectually preclude the risk of a demand for specie being then made for the purpose of profit in exporting it to the Continent.

.   .   .   .   .   .

[pp. 187–188.]   Do you conceive that a very considerable reduction of the amount of the circulating medium, would not tend in any degree to increase its relative value compared with commodities, and that a considerable increase of it would have no tendency whatever to augment the price of commodities in ex- 4 change for such circulating medium?—It is a subject on which such a variety of opinions are entertained, I do not feel myself competent to give a decided answer.

In your examination of the 21st inst. you state, that an excess of country bank paper can only obtain when issued otherwise than as representing securities arising out of real transactions, and payable at fixed and not distant periods; and yet, in your examination of the 23d, you state, that this paper must always circulate at par, or it would return upon the parties that issue it; can there then be any permanent excess of country bank paper

---

3 The limitation of the Bank issues would certainly raise[1] the foreign exchange

4. Is not the affirmative to this question self evident?

188

5. Mr. Pearse must give up his accusation against the country banks of causing an excess of circulation, as he here admits that it is an evil which would correct itself.

[1] Replaces 'lower'.

while it is so exchangeable?—In my answer of the 21st of March,
I adverted to the causes which might be productive of an excess in
the issues of country bank paper: in my answer of the 23d, I
meant to allude to the consequences which must inevitably, in my
opinion, result from the existence of such an excess. It is certainly possible, were it important in amount, that the country
banks, by not regulating their issues on the principle of the Bank
of England, might send forth a superabundance of their notes;
but this excess, in my opinion, would no sooner exist in any
material degree, than it would be corrected by its own operation,
for the holders of such paper would immediately return it to the
issuers, when they found that in consequence of the over issue its
value was reduced or likely to be reduced below par: thus,   5
though the balance might be slightly and transiently disturbed,
no considerable or permanent over issue could possibly take place,
as from the nature of things the amount of Bank notes in circulation must always find its level in the public wants.

·   ·   ·   ·   ·   ·

[pp. 188–189.]   If, however, he [the foreigner] receives £.100
in Bank notes, and is under the necessity of going to market for
Bullion, will he the foreigner not rate his goods twenty per cent.
higher, the difference in the price between them; and will he not
invoice his goods twenty per cent. higher to his correspondent   6
accordingly? [*Mr. Whitmore*]—I cannot contemplate a trade
where the invoices are made out with reference to the price of
Bullion.

If this were the case, what prospect should we have of a rise in
the price of the exchange?—Never having weighed the subject   7
with any reference to the price of Bullion, I am not prepared with
an opinion how a merchant would act in such a case.

·   ·   ·   ·   ·   ·

189

6. Is it not self evident that the value of the money for
which the foreigner must sell his goods in this country must
enter into his calculation?

7. Is not this a confession that he has not considered a
most important question in political economy particularly
necessary to be well understood by a Bank director.

Lunae, 2° *die Aprilis*, 1810.

William Coningham, Esq. called in and Examined.

· · · · ·

[p. 190.]   It appears from your evidence before the Irish Exchange Committee in the year 1804, that you were of opinion that
the paper currency of Ireland was then depreciated, and that this
depreciation was the cause of the unfavourable state of the exchange between England and Ireland; are you of opinion that that
paper is still depreciated, and if so, to what circumstance do you
8 ascribe the improvement in the exchange between the two Countries?—I think it is still depreciated, but in a very inconsiderable
degree compared with what it was in the year 1804: and I am inclined to think, that the cause of the depreciation being so much
less now than it was at the period alluded to is, that there is
greater confidence in the paper than there was at that time; and
therefore the people take it with more freedom, and of course
consider it of more value.

· · · · ·

Mercurii, 4° *die Aprilis*, 1810.

Sir *Francis Baring*, Bart. called in, and Examined.

· · · · ·

[p. 195.]   Would not the removal of the restrictions upon
1 trade diminish the price of bullion?—The removal of the restric-

---

8 He does not consider it so much depreciated as formerly
because on a comparison with Bank of England paper it is
now nearly at par. which it was not then. To me it is evident
that the value of Bank of Ireland paper has not been raised
to the value which Bank of England paper then bore, but
that the value of Bank of England paper has been sunk to
that of Bank of Ireland paper, and that therefore they are now
both depreciated.

195
1. The removal of the restrictions on trade might undoubtedly facilitate the means of importing bullion, if circumstances were favorable to such an operation; but the ex-

tions upon trade would produce an exportation of merchandize, and facilitate the means of importing bullion.

. . . . .

[p. 196.] Are you not aware that the issuing of notes under five pounds has increased materially the whole amount of notes issued; and do you not believe that the amount of small notes should be left out of the account in comparing the present amount of notes in circulation with that existing at the period you have alluded to [previous to 1797]?—The small notes are equally paper, and they add to the mass of Bank notes before in circulation; they issue in the same manner in exchange for public or 2 private securities: Instead of being left out in a comparative view, I fear they rather tend to increase the difficulty more than their due proportion, because they cannot be withdrawn without an issue of specie to an equal amount, and therefore stand in the front of the battle.

. . . . .

[pp. 198–199.] Do you conceive that the Bank of England will effectually guard against the possibility of any excess in the circulation of the country (as well their own as the paper of country banks) if they regulate their issues by the demand for discounts of good bills founded on real mercantile transactions, as the occasions of the Public may appear to require?—It has been ascertained by long experience, that wherever paper has circulated under the power and influence of Government on the Continent, it has failed. The paper of the Bank of England has

---

portation or importation of bullion must be regulated by the relative value of bullion in the two countries, or which is the same by the rate of the real exchange between two countries.

2. This question is not fairly answered. It is certain that the small notes cannot be withdrawn without an issue of specie to an equal amount, as they are wanted for small payments and are therefore indispensible; but the question is whether in judging of an excessive issue by a comparison of the present amount of notes, and the amount in 1797, the amount of small notes should be taken into consideration.[1]

[1] 'As the guineas have been withdrawn and the small notes only substituted' is del. here.

stood firm for above a century, and flourishes at this moment with unabated confidence. The power reposed in the Bank is great; their paper is the basis on which the best interests of the Country rest; it is the seed which serves to produce the whole of its commerce, finance, agricultural improvements, &c. &c. Such a power may remain with safety, so long as the Bank is liable to discharge their notes in specie, because that circumstance constitutes a complete counteraction to any disposition (if it should be entertained) to increase the circulation beyond a reasonable and safe limit, and, under that circumstance, things (foreign exchanges, &c.) will find their proper level.... I consider the opinion entertained by some persons, that the Bank ought to regulate their issues by the public demand, as dangerous in the extreme, because I know by experience, that the demand for speculation can only be limited by a want of means; and I think the Bank would not be

3

If the small notes substituted have not exceeded the amount of guineas withdrawn, it is clear they should not be taken into the account.

3. Sir F. Baring is decidedly opposed to the opinion entertained by the Bank Directors, that they cannot produce an excess of circulation whilst they discount bills for real bona fide transactions.

217.

Mr. Tritton's evidence generally is very cautious,—he appears not to have paid much attention to the subject of currency, and the effects produced on it by London and country Banks.

Page 218, 219

Mr. Harman[1] thinks that the diminution of the paper of

[1] This note refers to the answer marked '2' in Ricardo's copy of the Bullion Report. Although the figure '1' is written against the first answer in Harman's evidence ('though the state of the exchanges is constantly watched, the amount of our discounts is not regulated with any reference to that circumstance'), there is no corresponding comment in Ricardo's MS.

disposed to extend their issues beyond three-fourth parts of its present amount, if the restriction was removed....

. . . . . .

Lunae, 9° die Aprilis, 1810.

[pp. 213–18.] *John Henton Tritton*, Esq. a Partner in the Banking-House of Barclay & Co., called in, and Examined.

. . . . .

[p. 218.] *Jeremiah Harman*, Esq. Director of the Bank of England and General Merchant, called in, and Examined.

. . . . .

[p. 219.] Do you conceive that the diminution of the paper of the Bank would, either immediately or remotely, tend to an 2 improvement of the exchange?—None whatever.

---

the Bank, would, neither immediately or remotely, tend to an improvement of the exchange.

In his answer to a subsequent question he allows that an augmentation of the quantity of Bank of England notes tends to raise the prices of commodities.

It therefore follows that a diminution of the quantity of Bank notes would lower the prices of commodities;—but if prices were considerably lowered and the exchange were not affected, this real fall in their price would not fail to encourage foreign purchasers. But such purchases[2] according to the principles of those who are for ascribing every effect on the exchange to the balance of trade, would speedily turn the balance in our favor or at least render the present balance less unfavorable and would therefore indirectly raise the exchange. It is to be regretted that the Committee did not press Mr. Harman for some explanation of these opinions which might have been proved so inconsistent.[3]

---

[2] The last two lines beginning 'this real fall' replace 'foreigners would be induced to purchase more of our commodities,—this' which however is not del.

[3] Replaces 'of these discordant opinions'.

Was it not the practice of the Bank, antecedently to the restriction of the cash payments, to lessen in some degree the amount of its issues, when a material demand for guineas was made upon
3 it?—It has been occasionally, and at one period in particular, according to my view of the subject, it accelerated very much the mischief which ensued.

. . . . . .

[pp. 219–220.] Supposing the Parliament to enact that the Bank of England should again pay in Gold at a distant period, say one, two or three years, would it be your opinion that the Bank ought to resort to the measure of restraining its issues, as a means of preparing itself to meet that event, supposing the exchanges and the price of Bullion to continue as they now are?—I conceive
4 that they must necessarily, if the exchanges were to continue as they now are, which, however, I deem barely within possibility.

. . . . . .

[p. 220.] Do you not apprehend that there is a disposition in persons keeping accounts at the Bank, to apply for a larger extent of discount than it is on the whole expedient for the Bank to grant?—Very many do, and we treat them accordingly.

---

3. But at the period here alluded to the exchange was considerably in our favor and therefore the present case and that case are totally dissimilar

4. That the exchanges should remain as they now are Mr. Harman thinks barely within possibility. Any material improvement of the exchange with the present amount of paper money I deem barely within possibility. Nothing can improve the exchange but some alteration in the relative state of the currency of this and the currencies of other countries

5 and 6. Are not the answers to 5 and 6 contradictory?

7. This opinion is built upon the idea that the interest of money rises or falls according to the abundance of money.— If the Bank Directors could be convinced that this is an erroneous principle we might expect to see them adopt a very different system. The interest which a man agrees to pay for the use of a sum of money is in reality a portion of the

Do you not think that the sum total applied for, even though the accommodation afforded should be on the security of good bills to safe persons, might be such as to produce some excess in the quantity of the Bank issues if fully complied with?—I think if we discount only for solid persons, and such paper as is for real *bonâ fide* transactions, we cannot materially err.

Supposing you were to afford your accommodation at four per cent. instead of five per cent. interest, the current interest being five per cent., would there not be danger of excess?—Perhaps so.   5

Does it not then follow, that, provided money is now worth something more than five per cent., and being in general difficult to be procured at that rate, you may fall into some excess by granting it at five per cent. on the principle which you have stated?—I think not, because we should discover the super-   6 abundance very soon.

What should you consider the test of that superabundance?—Money being more plentiful in the market.   7

.   .   .   .

[p. 221.] Supposing the exchange to continue long and

---

profits which he expects to derive from the employment of a capital which that sum of money will enable him to obtain. In the interest which he is willing to pay he is guided solely by the probable[1] extent of those profits. His profits are necessarily totally independent of the abundance or scarcity of the money which circulates commodities[2] in the country. If America had had no mines[3] but we had obtained by the discovery of that large portion of the world the same commerce which we now enjoy, the value of gold and silver would not have been depreciated, and no country would have had more than a third of the money which they now possess[4], but its greater value would have made it equally effectual for the commerce and payments of each. Profits

[1] 'probable' is ins.
[2] 'which circulates commodities' is ins.
[3] Replaces 'If the mines of

America had never been discovered'.
[4] Replaces 'she now possesses'.

greatly unfavourable, should you not be disposed to refer this circumstance in some measure to an excess of paper currency, or should you assume that the balance of trade had continued during 8 that long period unfavourable?—I must very materially alter my opinions, before I can suppose that the exchanges will be influenced by any modifications of our paper currency.

Have you ever known the exchange to fall to twelve or fifteen per cent. in any part of Europe, in which it was computed in coin 9 containing a fixed quantity of gold or silver, or in paper or bank money exchanged at a fixed agio, either for such gold or silver

---

would have been precisely the same as they now are though they would be expressed by a different amount of Pounds sterling. A man possessed of £500 year would then have been as rich as one possessed now of £1500. And a monied man with £5000—lent at 5 pc.[1] would[1] have had as abundant an income, as one under the present circumstances with £15000 lent at the same rate of interest. If gold were to become as abundant as lead it would make no permanent alteration in the rate of interest for money; the depreciation which money experiences renders the same nominal sum less effective in the precise degree of its depreciation. If then an abundance of paper circulation as allowed by Mr. Harman raises the prices of commodities or in other words depreciates the value of money, will not that circumstance alone be a cause for an increased demand for it? Will not the supply again depreciate it and the demand increase? And may not this continue ad infinitum. And as the larger quantity of depreciated money will be no more effective than the smaller quantity of undepreciated money was before who will be conscious of an excess?—who will find that the particular sum which he possesses is superfluous and endeavour to return it to the Bank in payment of a discounted bill. The bank during the suspension of Cash payments, with its present excessive issues produces the same effect as the dis-

[1] 'not envy' is del. here.

coin, or for gold or silver bullion of a definite amount?—I really
cannot from recollection answer that question.

.   .   .   .

Martis, 22° *die Maji,* 1810.

[pp. 228–31.]   *Thomas Richardson,* Esq. again called in, and
Examined.

.   .   .   .   .   .

---

covery of a new mine of gold which should materially depreciate the value of money. In the case of the mine, as the
currency of all countries would be equally depreciated its
effects would be visible only in the rise of prices of all commodities for which money is exchanged, and the exchange
which[2] expresses the relative value of the currencies of different countries would continue at par;—but in the case of
the augmentation of Bank notes not convertible into specie
at the will of the holder, the rise of the prices of commodities
is confined to the country where the notes are issued and
consequently the depreciation of money is local and not
general; and is made evident by the effect produced on the
exchange with foreign countries, which deviates from par
nearly in the same proportion as the money is depreciated

8 How unfit for a Bank Director, whilst the restriction
bill is in force, is that man who without qualification declares
"that he must very materially alter his opinions, before he
can suppose that the exchanges will be influenced by any
modifications of our paper currency.["]

9. This is the true test by which to try the soundness of
their principle. I defy them to answer it in the affirmative.

229

Mr. Richardson's evidence is full of information with re-

---

[2] 'only' is del. here.

spect to the details of money transactions in London as well as in the country. He proves most satisfactorily that there have been of late years great improvements in the way of economising the use of Bank notes which renders the same amount of notes effective for an enlarged commerce: He was asked whether he thought that ten millions of Bank notes would keep afloat the same quantity of business as fifteen millions would have done ten years ago. His answer was, "Not quite so much perhaps ten years ago". It must however be admitted that a considerable saving in the use of notes has been effected.[1]

---

[1] On the last sheet of the MS (B) there is written by Ricardo the following paragraph which appears to refer to Account No. XIX of the Appendix to the Bullion Report: 'What is the reason that gold monies in the years 1805, 6, 7, 8, 9 and 1810 should be coined at the mint from foreign gold, when by the evidence of the dealers in bullion English gold as it is called can be purchased cheaper?'

NOTES ON TROTTER'S 'PRINCIPLES OF CURRENCY AND EXCHANGES'
1810

NOTE ON 'NOTES ON TROTTER'

TROTTER's pamphlet attacking the Bullion Report appeared anonymously under the title *The Principles of Currency and Exchanges applied to the Report from the Select Committee of the House of Commons Appointed to Inquire into the High Price of Gold Bullion, &c. &c.*, London, 'Printed and sold by W. Winchester and Son', 79 pp., dated on the title-page 'Dec. 1, 1810'.[1] Coutts Trotter, the author, was a partner in the banking house of Thomas Coutts & Co.

Ricardo's comments were probably written in December 1810 or soon after.

The MS of Ricardo's Notes, which is among Ricardo's Papers, covers seventeen octavo pages.[2] Each comment begins with a page-reference to Trotter's pamphlet; when there are two or more comments referring to the same page, they are given progressive numbers. This suggests that (as in the case of his Notes on the Bullion Report and also of his Notes on Bentham) Ricardo wrote corresponding numbers on his working copy of the pamphlet; but no such copy has been found.[3]

In the text printed below quotations from, or summaries of, the relevant passages of Trotter's pamphlet have been prefixed to Ricardo's Notes.

---

[1] A 'Second Edition' of 80 pp. was published under the author's name and 'sold by Cadell and Davies, and W. Winchester and Son'; it is odd that it bears the same date, 'Dec. 1, 1810'. From the page references in Ricardo's Notes it is clear that he was using the first edition.

[2] The Notes have been published in *Minor Papers on the Currency Question*, ed. by J. H. Hollander, Baltimore, The Johns Hopkins Press, 1932, pp. 91–99.

[3] There is a copy of the first edition of Trotter's pamphlet which belonged to Ricardo in the Goldsmiths' Library of the University of London, but it bears no such numbers; 'by Coutts Trotter' is inscribed in Ricardo's hand on the title-page.

[NOTES ON TROTTER'S 'PRINCIPLES OF CURRENCY AND EXCHANGES']

[p. 7.]   In the course of a brief sketch of the origins of money Trotter says that in England the goldsmiths' notes were of the same value as the precious metals, so long as those who issued them were 'capable of fulfilling' their contracts.

Page 7.   And obliged

[p. 12.]   In the preceding pages Trotter has considered the functions of money.

12   Up to this page there is not a word with which I do not agree

[p. 13.]   There 'is a limitation and an insuperable one, to the quantity of money in any given state of society': 'the aggregate of the sum, in gold, in silver, and in paper engagements, in each person's pocket or house, will, in every state of such society, form the total of, and be the limit to, the currency of the country.'

13   Whilst money is not depreciated, and the nominal prices of commodities not raised. If with payments to the amount of 100 millions 10 millions be sufficient for circulation, no more than that sum will be used, unless the money be depreciated in value. The payments may by depreciation of money be increased to 200 millions nominally; in such case 20 millions of the depreciated money will be required for circulation.

[p. 14.]   There is, therefore, an absolute security against redundancy of currency, since in every case 'the check of a saturated circulation interposes; and the least excess beyond the wants of the public, estimated by each individual for himself, flows back upon the Bank of England or the country banker who occasions it.'

14   A circulation can never be so saturated as to [be][1]

[1] Omitted in MS.

incapable of admitting more. Before the discovery of America the same portion of commerce which now requires three millions of money was carried on (confidence[,] credit, and the economy introduced by banking being supposed the same) by one million. The currency is no more saturated with 3 millions now than it was with one then. It might as reasonably be contended that the two millions would flow back to the mine which produced it, as that the notes of the Bank of England, under the present system should flow back to the issuers.

[p. 15.] When a country banker increases his issues of notes 'the range of this bank...which is confined to the circle in which the partners are known, are observed, and are trusted, becomes filled with their notes to the extent of the former circulation of metals...; and gold, no longer wanted here, but still possessing qualities of universal attraction, finds its way to other districts, and finally to other countries. This done, the measure is full; the banker can, by no assiduity or skill, force upon his neighbourhood more of his notes than there was before of specie...; should he attempt to do so, they will return incessantly upon him, and he will be called upon for their value in what is of universal, not of local, request; that is, will be called upon for gold, or for Bank of England notes'.[1]

[p. 17.] There is consequently no need to feel anxious about the restriction of cash payments by the Bank of England, for 'the circulation even of this apparently unfettered establishment is limited: its managers cannot induce the population within their sphere to carry in their pockets, or hoard in their bureaus, more of bank-notes than each man anticipates the want of for his own purposes.'

17 This would be true if the notes retained their value, but when abundant their value sinks, and a greater amount becomes necessary for the same amount of trade and commerce.

[1] Ricardo refers to this passage in his comments on Trotter's pp. 19, 57, 59 and 71.

[p. 19.] In particular, the discount of bills, as one of the modes which the Bank employs for diffusing its notes, can never lead to an excessive issue, for 'it is evident that the whole of the bills so discounted and transferred into the hands of the Bank will become due in two months, that they will then be sent out for payment, and that as many notes will be received by the Bank in their discharge, and be thus withdrawn from circulation, as were issued by that body at the time of their discount.'

19 The correctness of these arguments depend entirely on the fact of the paper retaining its value,—they take for granted the subject in dispute. There is no question that the effects would be as here stated, if the paper did not whilst it was abundant cause depreciation. (See page 15)

[p. 21.] A paper currency is infinitely preferable to gold, 'which, depending on foreign influences, is liable to be often inconveniently reduced, and sometimes to be almost annihilated (as we now see it is) by our foreign exchanges turning against us.'

21 1. Impossible if not forced out by paper.

[pp. 20–21.] Whenever an unusual number of notes has been thrown into circulation, as it happens for instance at the quarterly payments of the public dividends, the immediate effect is to reduce the demand made to the Bank of England for issues upon discounting bills: 'At such times the depositories of mercantile men being overcharged with banknotes, the owners seek for productive employment of the excess in discounting bills;... Exactly, therefore, by so much as the excess of its notes in the hands of the public at any moment amounts to, the Bank will immediately be abridged of its usual power of diffusion.'

[21] 2. This is true if applied to a short period. Between the moment of the overissues of notes and their depreciation, there will necessarily be something like a glut of money in the market, but as soon as depreciation takes place, there is no longer a redundancy of money.

[pp. 23–24.] Trotter quotes the admission of the Bullion Report 'that a *part* [of the small notes issued since the restriction of cash payments] must be considered as being introduced to supply the place of the specie which was deficient at the period of suspending cash-payments'; to this he objects that 'this admission is evidently insufficient. In considering what void is filled up by small notes, our concern is not with the degree of deficiency of gold at the time of suspension, but with the actual amount of the void at this moment, after thirteen years of great waste by melting and exportation.'

24 1 This is perfectly a correct way of stating it, and should have been adhered to in Page 50.

[p. 24.] 'Now, so far from a *part* of this new description of notes being sufficient, the whole of it is unequal to supply the decrease of specie in the last thirteen years'.

[24] 2 May not small notes to any requisite amount be obtained at the Bank in exchange for large notes?

[p. 25.] Trotter's conclusion on this point is 'that the whole of the excess (if there be any) of Bank of England paper is to be found in the class of notes which are above the value of five pounds'.

25. 1. Perfectly correct

[p. 25.] Trotter then estimates that 'the mixed circulation of London before 1797, in gold and Bank of England notes, could not be less than sixteen millions and a half.'

[25] 2 Certainly not so much, or the present circulation could not be depreciated.

[pp. 25–26.] 'It is now twenty millions, exclusive of the small portion of gold which yet remains, being an increase of about one-fourth.

'But in the same period has there been no change whatever in the condition of society? has there been no addition to the population within the sphere of the Bank's circulation? has there been no greater number of commercial transactions to adjust, or larger public revenue to remit into the Exchequer? In each of these, singly, I think I see almost a sufficient demand to draw forth the additional sum in dispute'.

26   1. Has the trade increased a fourth as well as the money, if not the increase of money is excessive.

2   Taxation does not require any addition of money, or if any so little as not to be worth computing

[p. 26.]   Another circumstance involves an increased use for notes: 'Above seven hundred country banks, which formerly held in gold the sum which they deemed it prudent to keep as a deposit in their command, now retain that portion in Bank of England paper, thus attracting a great permanent issue of bank-notes to districts to which they never reached before.'

[26]   3   No; they have deposits of Exchequer bills in London, and have very few Bank of England notes. There is no temptation to exchange country bank notes for any thing but bills on London. See Mr. Stuckey's evidence Bullion Rep[t] [1]

[pp. 27–28.]   Trotter reverts to the increase of wealth during the period after the restriction of cash payments: 'Not only there are more considerable merchants, more bankers, more agents, more dealers in every species of property, in the period under consideration; but each man's transactions are numerically and actually increased.

'He has, in most instances, more rent to pay, more taxes, and more for the purchase of most articles of consumption; while, on the other hand, there is an equal increase in his receipts. In the upper ranks of society, except to those who unfortunately have only fixed incomes, there are every where increased rents of land, increased profits of trade; while, in the lower ranks, there are increased wages in every employment.'

27   1   Much is owing to depreciation
       2   D[o]

28   1   Caused by the depreciation of the currency. If money were depreciated 50 pc[t], the wages of labour would rise, and the same argument might be used. The point in dispute is constantly taken for granted.

[1] *Bullion Report*, 'Minutes of Evidence', 8vo ed., pp. 210–13.

[p. 28.] 'I think I have shown the existence of a restricting principle in our nature and habits, which, by limiting the quantity of money in every man's pocket or possession to the amount he finds necessary for his daily exchanges, limits, by consequence, the whole circulation of the realm.'

[28] 2   This principle limits the proportion of the value of money to the value of goods, but does not limit its absolute quantity.

[p. 29.]   Trotter objects to the assertion of Bullion Committee that the only adequate provision against an excess of paper-currency is the convertibility of all paper into specie, which he shows to be a practical impossibility: 'If, in times of the greatest abundance of specie, the public, from any cause, had called upon the Bank, and upon every country banker, for the sum declared in their notes to be held on the usual condition of repayment on demand, the Bank of England and the country banker must have been alike incapable of fulfilling the letter of their engagements.'

29 1 Of this the Committee were aware. The check against excess is convertibility of paper into gold whenever its value became less than gold coin. There never could be any temptation to demand gold coin for all the notes in circulation, unless the bank should lose all credit with the public.

This is not the case at present, and is a danger against which no human prudence can wholly guard us.

[pp. 29–30.] 'The actual degree of convertibility of paper before the Restriction Act' was excessive in ordinary times and insufficient in periods of popular alarm. 'The truth is, as the times become more secure, and more confidence prevails, there will always be a greater proportion of paper'.

30 1 This is no argument against the fact of an over-issue of paper.

[p. 30.] If paper 'is not convertible into gold, is it therefore of no value? is there nothing of intrinsic worth into which those

who are fearful of its security may convert it in the temporary
absence of this one article? Yes, into every thing that men desire,
or that gold can purchase'.

[30] 2 All this is allowed but it is contended that it cannot be exchanged for so much of those things which man
desires, or as gold can purchase, as it would do under a better
system. We do not say that paper currency is good for nothing but that it is not so good as it would and ought to be.

[pp. 31–32.] 'Why should we be thus tenacious of payment
in gold, which the next moment it would be our business not to
hoard or to enjoy, but again to send forth in purchase of some one
or other of these very objects we now so much set at nought?...
Although, in theoretical discussions, we are pleased with a supposed power of calling for our debts in the precious metals, it is
obviously impossible to exercise that power to any extent.'

31 It is not fair to charge us with wanting gold; we
contend that we should not want it nor take it, if we could
get it. We wish only to have the right to obtain it as an
effectual security against the depreciation of our property.

32 1 We have no childish affection for gold more than
for paper. Not a complaint would be heard if the paper was
not depreciated.

[p. 32.] 'Had the paper part of our currency retained its value
only by its convertibility into gold, it must have fallen gradually
for the last twenty years; during which time the proportion it
contains of the precious metals has been declining. In the last
ten years, it ought, by this rule, to have fallen above a half; and,
judging by the power of conversion it now possesses, a bank-note
of one pound ought not to be worth five shillings; yet we see our
notes retaining their original credit, commanding every article
at their original value, and exchanging for our coin itself in every
transaction in which they meet.'

[32] 2 We do not complain of any fall in the value of

paper which it suffers in common with gold, but of that fall over and above that which gold sustains.[1]

    3 It is not correct to say that they command every article at their original value. Our complaint is that they do not.

[pp. 32–33.] 'The truth appears to be, that all excess of paper-currency is restrained by the causes we have stated; and its convertibility into gold, in a very small degree, is sufficient for convenience, as well as for preserving it from depreciation.'

33.   1   This is our argument.

[p. 33.]   Trotter sums up the conclusions so far attained:
'That there is no excess in the paper circulation of the country;
'That there is a sufficient check and control over the issues of paper from the Bank of England and from country banks; and
'That the currency of the country is in no degree depreciated by the use of paper.'

[33]   2   All these conclusions are without proof.

[p. 34.]   It is true that the currency in England has lost some part of its value. This is due, *first* to gold itself having lost a part of its value, compared with commodities, throughout Europe: 'Let us put the saddle on the right horse, and not blame paper for a fault which is, in part, ascribable to gold itself.'

34   But let us fairly state how much is owing to one cause, how much to the other.

[p. 35.]   *Secondly*, to the increase of population: 'In a country insulated as ours now is, by political as well as natural circumstances, every increase of population must make an increase in

---

[1] This comment must refer to the first part of the quotation, although Ricardo appears to have overlooked the peculiar sense which Trotter attaches to 'convertibility'. Trotter says in effect: Had paper retained its value in terms of commodities in proportion to its gold cover only, it must have fallen in terms of commodities (as well as of gold). Ricardo's interpretation seems to be: Had paper retained its value in terms of gold by retaining its convertibility, it must have fallen in terms of commodities.

the demand for all the articles which land and industry produce. To raise the former, worse soils and more unfavourable situations must be taken into cultivation; and the produce therefore will be obtained, and must be sold, at an increased expense. To create the latter, men must be paid at a higher rate of wages, because in every state of society, and especially in one progressive, as that of England is, men must receive somewhat above what is necessary for their support; and the expense of that support will be regulated principally by the cheapness or dearness of food.'

35   Every increase of population must arise from an increase of capital, and has a tendency to lower the prices of commodities and therefore the wages of labour, not to raise them.

[p. 36.]   *Thirdly*, to the burden of taxation.

36   Taxation has some effect no doubt, but will not account for the rise in the price of gold.

[p. 37.]   Trotter denies that the rise in prices is due to the facility with which commercial men can procure notes from the Bank of England, and thus heighten the price of every article: 'An increase of capital (which this is to the small degree in which it exists) never raises the price of commodities, but has exactly the opposite effect'.

37   An increase of Capital never raises the prices of commodities, but an increase of money unaccompanied by an increase of Capital invariably does.   Can there be an increase of population without an increase of Capital having preceded it?, yet in Page 35 we are told that an increase of population will occasion a rise in the prices of commodities, and in the wages of labour.

[p. 38]   The competition of merchants, who buy to sell again, cannot heighten prices, since every merchant, in the offer he can afford to make, is limited 'by the price which he expects to obtain in selling again.   So far, indeed, from this increased capital being the occasion of high prices, it is one of the principal means of keeping them down;—a competition of capitalists, like a competition of manufacturers, restricts their respective profits....A great capital is the principal advantage which any country has in entering into a competition of sales with other nations; it makes roads, it erects machinery, it promotes canals....'

38. The same cause, namely, an increase of money which will induce him to give a higher price for goods, will secure him one proportionally higher when he sells again. A competition of Capitalists keeps down prices, but money is not Capital. An increase of Capital is attended with all the benefits enumerated; an increase of money to be retained in circulation is unattended with any benefit whatever.

[p. 39.]   Part II opens with a summary of the results reached so far:

'Having shewn that the amount of our currency is fixed by an impassable boundary, which precludes the possibility of excess; having shewn that the convertibility of the portion which is paper, into that which is of the precious metals, was always limited; having shewn that (except in times of alarm, when it might be better if there were none) a very moderate degree of convertibility is necessary for the common purposes of life; and appealing to every man's experience, that, in the small, indeed, but frequent exchanges in which gold and silver now mix, paper and these precious metals pass at a like value, thus establishing a standard for the former; it follows, that our currency is not now depressed by the use of paper.'

39.   1. This has not been shewn
       2. Not frequent exchanges.

[pp. 39–40.]   'But I am desired to take a guinea, and to melt it down; and I am shewn that the moment it is freed from the stamp of law,—as soon, in short, as it becomes bullion,—it rises in value; and that that portion of gold, which yesterday exchanged only for a one-pound note and one shilling, now exchanges for the same note, and four shillings and sixpence.

'This evidently must proceed from one of two causes; it must proceed from the currency of which it late made a part having fallen below its usual value, or from gold in the shape of bullion, which it has now become, having risen above it.'

It has been shown that it is not the former of these causes;

and therefore there can be no doubt that 'bullion has risen above its ordinary price to the whole extent of the disparity'.

40.   1   In either case the holder of bank notes has equal cause for complaint. Why should he not rise from the value[1] of bullion as well as lose from the fall. If bullion falls in value, the value of money, whilst the mint is open to every one falls in the same proportion. Why should not the owner of money be benefited by the rise of bullion? Did not the author say Page 35 that the cause of the rise of the prices of commodities was the decreasing value of gold generally, yet we are now told that bullion has risen. These opinions are directly at variance

[p. 40.]   It is an 'exploded belief, that gold is an unvarying standard.'

[40]   2. Who has asserted that gold is an unvarying standard of value? There is no unvarying standard in existence. Gold is however unvarying with regard to that money which is made of gold, and this proceeds from its being at all times convertible without expence into such money, and also from money being again convertible into gold bullion. If an ounce of gold bullion from being worth 15 ounces of silver rises to the value of 30 ounces of silver, an ounce of gold coin will do the same.

[p. 41.]   Gold is in fact subject to variations: 'Since the discovery of America, and the influx which the mines of that part of the world have poured upon Europe, its value has fallen in this country to one-third'.

41.   1. The discovery of the American mines though they had quadrupled the amount of gold would not have sunk its price, whilst the mint price has not altered, and whilst it was measured by gold coin.

[1] A slip, for 'why should he not gain from a rise in the value'.

[p. 41.]   Gold 'is also subject to some variation from locality: in America, where it is recently dug from the mine, it must necessarily be cheaper than in Europe, which it reaches with all the expenses of freight and hazard attending upon so long a conveyance.'

[41]   2   In America it is cheaper than in Europe but not cheaper measured in gold money. It is cheaper in labour,— cheaper in most goods or it would not be exported from thence.

[p. 42.]   But on the whole, gold is the 'best approximation to a perfect standard.... We have hitherto experienced very little inconvenience from such local and temporary alterations; nor shall we now from that we witness, if we do not create inconveniences by improper interference.'

42.   1.   We have unfortunately created inconveniences by improper interference already. A second interference is necessary in consequence of the first.

[p. 42.]   Without entering into the intricacies of foreign exchanges, it must be evident to every man, who will consider the subject, that when a country, like an individual, makes purchases more in value than it sells in return, that country must, for the moment, remain in debt to the extent of the difference'.

[42]   2.   A country generally speaking never does this,— and if it did so the exchange would not be affected till the debtor country was preparing to make the payment, and then it would not vary beyond the limits stated by the bullion Committee.

[p. 44.]   But there is a limit to the extent of the advances which England can obtain: something must therefore be remitted, and since the exportation of commodities from England is made impossible by political barriers, and gold is easily transported and concealed, 'the first thing that feels the impulse of an unfavourable exchange is this very gold, which the Committee would seem to think unsusceptible of influence.
'What then follows this demand for gold? All the train of

appearances which result from a demand for other articles: it becomes more and more scarce—it gets higher and higher in price.'

44   This is the fallacy. If the preceding position could be admitted gold might rise in *value*, but not in *price* whilst measured in gold coin or in bank notes accurately representing such coin,—particularly if one class of the community had no scruple to evade the law, and exported or melted the coin as best suited their convenience.

[p. 45.]   The 'scanty fund' of gold deposited in the Bank of England is ineffectual 'to settle the heavy balance of payments we are every day incurring'.

45.   This paragraph is indisputable.

[p. 46.]   Referring to the licences granted for the import of specie, Trotter asks: 'Could Government have found the precious metals as it could have done shoes, or clothing, or provisions, in England, would it have had recourse to such modes?'

46.   1. Yes if the trade were advantageous.

[p. 46.]   'Whenever the imports and the foreign expenses of this or any other country exceed its exports, its exchanges will be unfavourable, and gold dear; whenever the reverse is the case, when our exports exceed our imports and foreign charges, our exchanges must be favourable, and gold cheap. How then can that be considered as an undeviating measure, which is thus ever affected by circumstances so uncontrollable?'

[46]   2. True but within the limits specified by the committee.

3. Was it not allowed, Page 15, that the issues of paper forced the exportation of gold. Would not the reduction of their amount check exportation, and if carried sufficiently far produce importation

[p. 47.]   To the question, why during the long series of years when the balance of trade was favourable to England, the price of gold had not fallen, Trotter answers: 'When the balance of trade was against the Continent, it had always the option to pay its debts in whatever best suited our market, and, consequently, there never could be any redundancy of this, more than of any other article of commerce; as soon as the measure of our wants became full, the surplus would flow back to where it was more desired, and other articles would be selected, more suited to our market.'

47.   1. This is a just principle, but why does it not make gold revert back to us from the continent? The abundance of paper. For the same reasons that there could be no redundancy here, there could, under a sound system, be no deficiency.

[p. 47.]   'But it will be said this theory does not hold good at the present moment. The measure of the Continental market is admitted to be full: gold, therefore, not being dear there, there cannot be the usual attraction of a high price to excite exportation from England; yet the tendency of the current is strongly that way.'

[47]   2. This would be difficult to admit under any circumstances, but is wholly impossible whilst any commodities are imported. If commodities are imported for gold, the conclusion that gold is dearer abroad is inevitable.

[p. 48.]   'At this time, and in this country, gold is dear'.

48.   It is dearer compared with the depreciated currency, but cheaper compared with all other things.

[p. 49.]   During those periods between 1797 and 1810 in which the foreign exchanges were unfavourable, gold rose in price.

49.   It is not denied any where, that with a low exchange gold has a tendency, with the present legal restraint, to become more valuable than an equal weight of coin, and an opposite tendency with a high exchange; but the effects are very limited.

[p. 50.] By comparing the circulation of bank-paper with the price of gold, Trotter finds decisive proof that there is no correspondence between them. In the years 1797, 1798 and 1799, when there was an addition of 5½ millions to the circulation, 'gold never altered its price'. Further, in the years 1800–1802, the circulation increased 23 per cent., and gold rose in value only 4, 5 and 6 per cent. In the years 1803–1807, when 'a further increase of issues took place to the extent of a million and a half, gold bullion became cheaper'.

50. 1. How much of this was in small notes? It has been acknowledged, Page 24, that they should be left out of the account. Besides in the year 1797 the currency was much below its natural level as the exchange and the coinage will indicate.

2. The effects of the increased issues of the years 1800, 1, 2, 3, 4, 5, 6 and 7 were at length but not immediately counteracted by the exportation of bullion.

[p. 51.] Therefore the opinion held by some persons, that the 'currency is depreciated to the whole extent of the rise which bullion has experienced' leads to 'the most obvious absurdities.'

51. 1. I see no absurdity in such view.

[pp. 51–52.] From such an opinion, it would follow that in 1800 the currency of Great Britain became depreciated to the extent of 6 per cent., 'and that, in 1805, with a greater proportion of paper, with a larger public debt, and with an extended war, the same currency, in all these respects less secure, recovered all the value it had lost.'

52. 1 Not the same currency but one reduced by the exportation of the coin.

[p. 52.] 'Were such opinions just, it would follow also, that if Mr. Goldsmid, in executing any very urgent commission, should raise bullion two or three per cent. above the usual price, he would by such rash act strike off a million from the value of our currency: but the truth is, in all these instances it is only a few ounces of bullion that have got dearer or cheaper; our currency remains just the same.'

[52] 2. It is not the price given by Mr. Goldsmid "which will strike off a million from the value of our currency", any more than an extravagant price for coffee will add to the value of that commodity, unless in both instances the prices given is the fair, steady market price of the commodity. If so it is of little consequence whether one ounce or a thousand ounces be actually purchased. It is not the purchase but the price which proves depreciation.

[p. 53.] Trotter then replies to those who urge that the holder of a bank-note, by the letter of his contract, is entitled at all times to the same weight of gold: 'Independent of the injustice of placing the parties to any contract in a situation not in contemplation at the time of making such contract,...the very terms of the contract are against this reasoning. There is not in existence any note of the Bank of England, or of a country bank, engaging to pay a pound of bullion: the engagement such notes contain is to pay a certain portion of the coin of the realm; which coin, bereft as it is, and always has been, of exportability, is of the same value now that it was when it issued from the Mint; and never was intended to give to the possessor the fluctuating and now very unusual advantages of bullion, from which it is so distinctly separated by the law.'

53. 1. The Bank one of the parties have placed themselves there, and may extricate themselves from the consequences by diminishing the amount of their notes.

2. Whether intended or not the effect was such till the present period.

[p. 54.] A guinea, when melted into a small ingot, could be sold at £1. 4s. 6d.: 'Let this ingot again receive the unvarying character of coin which the law gave it, and meant it should always retain; let it once more be secured by the Tower stamp from those influences which its exportability subjects it to, and which now affect it so much...—then that ingot, that guinea, will be of the value of this note and this shilling'.

54   This is assuming the point in dispute. Coin is degraded in this case by the tower stamp, and no efforts of Government can or ought to keep it in that state. It is bad policy and at the same time contrary to every principle of equity. Bank notes can be kept in their degraded state and are therefore subject to a depreciation from which coin is exempted.

[p. 55.]   The Bullion Committee had shown that there was an exact correspondence between the price of bullion and the foreign exchanges. 'The natural inference' was 'that they were cause and effect'; but the Committee had formed a different conclusion and pointed to 'something in our domestic currency as the cause of both appearances.'

55.   Where do the Committee say that they are not cause and effect. The exchange is affected by the Bank issues, and becomes in its turn the cause of the high price of bullion.

[p. 56.]   'A high market-price of gold must continue just as long as the exchange is unfavourable, however long that may be: while we have an unfavourable balance to pay, we shall ever wish to pay it, amongst other things, in that article which is of cheapest conveyance; and that article will in consequence be dear'.

56.   A high price in paper does not enable us to obtain that article; it is only a nominally not a really high price.

[p. 57.]   'The exportable gold...has acquired a new power— that of paying at the cheapest rate a foreign debt—and consequently a new value;... That portion of our gold which is in coin, which we have barred from exportation, and, of course, from this accidental quality, remains as it was, at the Mint price'.

57.   The current gold coin possesses the same power, and is used for such purposes by many without scruple. The author Page 15 has himself told us so. Gold coin cannot therefore sink much beneath the value of gold bullion.

[pp. 57–58.]   The Bullion Committee have stated that the 'general rise of all prices, and in the market-price of gold, with a fall of foreign exchanges, will be the effect of an excessive quantity of circulating medium, not exportable to other countries, or convertible into a coin which is so.' To this Trotter replies: 'But, so long as the limitations I have explained exist, there can be no excess. Our circulating medium, when it was all of the precious metals, was never exportable,—consequently no change has taken place in this respect; and, in its present state, it is just as convertible into other coin, and into every thing that is valuable, as it ever was. One description of commodities alone have changed their relative price—those particularly fitted by their qualities for facility of transit; and surely it is not by comparing our currency with these only, that a fair test is offered of its deterioration.'

58.   This is the point in dispute. I deny it.

[p. 59.]   'Of what avail is it to us to know that gold would pay our Continental debt, at a loss of only 8 per cent. if we have not gold to the extent of that debt which we can export?'

59.   But why have we not gold? The author has himself, Page 15, answered. The issues of banks have forced it out of the country.

[pp. 60–61.]   The Bullion Committee, although they admit that there was an unfavourable balance of trade, state '—surely without cause—"that they find it difficult to resist an inference, that a portion, at least, of the late great fall in our exchanges, must have resulted, not from the state of trade, but from a change in the relative value of our domestic currency."'

60   The author forgets that the Committee are of opinion that a favourable or an unfavourable balance of trade is controuled by the Bank issues.

[p. 63.]   During the state of alarm in Ireland between 1799 and 1804, 'Irish individuals and Irish families gave more and more for bills upon England; the exchange on this country got higher and higher, and gold rose in Dublin to a corresponding premium. It was not that an Irish gentleman, so alarmed, thought the Bank of Ireland had issued too many notes that he wished to exchange them for those of England; but because he wished the whole or some part of his property to be out of the reach of risks then peculiar to that part of the empire.'

63   Not because he thought so, but that alive to his interest he felt that in twenty guineas he possessed a value superior to £21. in notes.

[p. 64.]   The alarm has been gradually subsiding, 'till now we see in Ireland, what we ought to anticipate seeing in this country, relatively with the Continent, the exchange restored to par, and that, too, with a circulation of notes in Ireland as unlimited and as great as it was in the deprecated year of 1804.'

64.   1. The fact is, we have degraded our currency equally to that of Ireland, instead of raising that of Ireland up to ours. Two blacks will not make a white.

[p. 64.]   'The case of the banking companies in Scotland seems at first view to be the most favourable to the arguments of the Committee; their fault was certainly in part that of over-issues'.

[64]   2. Over-issues are possible then! I wish the author had explained what in his opinion would be the effects of the over-issues of the Bank, *if the case were possible*. Would they be in any thing different from what we now see.

[p. 66.]   The year 1793 was one of singular distress. 'What was the real evil? It was not a want of the currency of the country then existing;…it was mutual confidence which was wanting, and the evil was cured by a restoration of that confidence.'

66   It was a want of currency which aggravated the evil arising from want of confidence. The issue of commercial Exchequer bills induced the Bank to advance money on them, which they would not have done on other securities.

[p. 70.]   In his 'Conclusion' Trotter reverts to the Report of the Bullion Committee: 'They recommend that, in two years, the Bank should resume its payments in gold, whether peace be restored or not. If peace shall then prevail, the order will have been superfluous, as the law unaltered already directs cash-payments in that event.'

70.   1. When peace comes we shall not want for advocates for a continuance of the restriction bill.

[p. 70.] 'Should peace not be restored, the Bank…must add to our unfavourable balance by increasing our imports: they must raise the difficult supplies, which they will be obliged to provide for their cash-payments, by the most ruinous means to themselves; for they must purchase abroad, to bring it home, that very commodity which the whole trading world are seeking at home to send abroad.'

[70]   2. There would be no such necessity. A contraction of their notes would make others import gold.

[p. 70.] 'Is it not apparent, that one supply, or one hundred supplies, will not suffice in the given state of exchanges?'

[70]   3. But the exchanges are controulable by the Bank issues

[pp. 70–71.] 'Have we not seen at least eight or ten millions of our specie melted down and sent away in the last fifteen years'?

71.   1. Yes; but caused by over-issues. Let paper be contracted and the inducement will cease. (See page 15)

[p. 71.] The regulations proposed in the Bullion Report, if 'carried to the extreme of possibility,…would produce the most inconvenient effects:—it is within possibility, that the Bank, constantly coining and constantly importing to supply a waste greater than it could replace, might be obliged to declare its inability to keep out its notes at this expense, and might find itself under the necessity (I put an extreme case) of withdrawing its paper from circulation altogether. What then would be the result?'

[71]   2 An unbounded importation of gold would be the result; a measure by no means desirable. Our adversaries charge us with being unfriendly to a paper circulation,—this is not just,—it is of its abuse that we complain

[pp. 71–72.] 'Either the public must be satisfied with a worse currency, and accept for their convenience the notes of private bankers to the extent of the void; or they must import twenty millions of the precious metals to perform the offices which bank-notes now execute so well.'

72. 1. Is not the principle of the Committee which is so often denied in this work acknowledged here. Viz that a reduction of notes, or rather their annihilation would cause the import of the precious metals, and consequently of a favourable exchange.

[p. 72.] 'In the former case our exchanges would remain exactly as they are now; in the latter almost inconceivable case… we should, at the expense of a million a year in interest for the use of this expensive instrument, and of two or three millions in unfavourable exchanges to acquire it, bring up our currency to the war-price of bullion, which price, obtained by such sacrifices, it would again lose the hour after peace and free intercourse were restored.'

[72] 2. What is meant by "bringing up our currency to the war price of bullion"? Would the price of gold under the circumstances supposed be above £3. 17. 10½ p^r oz? If it were who would take any part of the 20 millions imported to the mint to be coined? The bank it must be remembered is supposed to have ceased to exist.

3. The measure would be improvident and ruinous, because the same good might be obtained with a very small sacrifice.

[p. 73.] The restriction of cash payments has indeed prevented the Bank of England from paying its notes in coin, but 'it has left the law exactly as it stood before, with regard to the rest of the community: every individual stands precisely as he did before 1797, and is as liable to a settlement of his debt in the coin which the law alone acknowledges as he ever was.'

73 Can the consequences be contemplated, without the most fearful alarm, of every creditor insisting on payments

being made to him in coin, to which by law he is entitled?
Let them insist on this right and bank notes would be immediately at a great and acknowledged discount.

[p. 75.] The restriction has relieved the community 'from
the intolerable expense of purchasing gold only to coin, and of
coining gold only to be melted down.'

75 We might have been secured from all such consequences by a reduction in the amount of paper, at any time
since the alarm ceased in 1797.

[p. 76.] The restriction was 'an act of the Legislature, adopted
on public grounds, and in fulfilment of one of the duties of
Government—to prevent or lessen a public evil in the exportation
of our coin'.

76 But if those public grounds are proved to have
ceased, should not the measure itself?

[pp. 76–77.] The efficient state of the currency 'deserves our
peculiar care; but we ought to watch it without any of those
prejudices or alarms which we daily see in men otherwise intelligent, who impute our debts, our taxes, our commercial dis-
tresses, to some irregular action of this (to them) unintelligible
machine.'

77 They justly distinguish what is imputable to this
cause, and what to other causes. The machine is by no means
unintelligible to those against whom it is charged,—I suspect
the saddle is put on the wrong horse.

[p. 78.] The public ought to be unfettered in their choice
between a gold and a paper currency. 'That we have not now this
choice is the result of political circumstances entirely out of our
control.'

78. 1. Entirely within our control

[p. 78.] 'It is not to be anticipated that the Power which now
holds the Continent in bondage, and shuts its ports against our

commerce, will always be able to exercise the same injurious sway. Whenever that ceases, and with it ceases the necessity of our late foreign expenditure, we shall again see the precious metals at their Mint price'.

[78] 2 I doubt much whether bullion can ever fall to its mint price, whilst the present amount of paper continues in circulation. I should say decidedly it could not (unless our commerce was greatly to increase) if the value of gold and silver did not fall in Europe equal to the depreciation of our paper. This would have the effect of increasing the currencies of other countries in the same proportion in which ours has been increased.

OBSERVATIONS ON TROWER'S
NOTES ON TROTTER

1811

NOTE ON 'OBSERVATIONS ON TROWER'S NOTES ON TROTTER'

TROWER, like Ricardo, had written a commentary on Trotter's pamphlet. This commentary, extending to forty pages of MS, is headed 'Notes and Observations on a Pamphlet entitled The Principles of Currency and Exchanges...(Anonymous) by Coutts Trotter Esqr.' and is dated 'February 1811'. It is in reply to this paper that Ricardo wrote the Observations here printed.

Both MSS were found among Trower's papers. Trower's MS is unpublished and is in the possession of Dr Bonar. Ricardo's MS has been published in Appendix A (2) to *Letters of David Ricardo to Hutches Trower and Others 1811–1823*, ed. by J. Bonar and J. H. Hollander, Oxford, 1899,[1] from which it is here reprinted. The MS is in the possession of Professor Hollander.

[1] It is there prefixed to another paper, written by Ricardo in 1809, which in the present edition is printed above, p. 36 ff.; cp. p. 5.

[OBSERVATIONS ON TROWER'S NOTES ON TROTTER]

What does Mr. Trotter mean by saying that it may be more advantageous to discharge a foreign debt by the exportation of a dear than of a cheap article;—by the exportation of gold which is dearer than by commodities which are cheaper here than abroad?[1] This is evidently impossible;—it implies a contradiction and needs no argument to prove its absurdity. If he means that the exportation of all other commodities will be attended with so much expense as to make it more advantageous to export gold,—then gold cannot be said to be dearer here than abroad because it is under all circumstances the cheapest exportable commodity. When we say that gold is dearer here than abroad and that commodities are not, we must include the expences attending their transportation to the foreign market, otherwise they are not fair subjects of comparison. If Mr. Trotter means that nothing but gold will be accepted in payment of our debt notwithstanding its relative price,—then there is an end of all comparison between gold and other things,—we have contracted to pay gold and nothing but gold will absolve us from our engagements. But it is not with Trotter's; it is with Mr. Trower's observations that I have now to deal.

He observes that if it could be admitted that a foreign merchant would import gold at a loss, it would follow ["]that merchants were bartering two commodities *on one of which they both lose* (this one I suppose is bullion) [;] their profits then, he says, must be taken out of the other article. The seller must add to the price of the article (of wheat for example) the loss sustained upon the bullion he receives in

[1] See *Principles of Currency and Exchanges*, 1810, pp. 44–7.

payment; the buyer must afterwards add to the price of the article (wheat) over and above his profit the loss he sustains upon the bullion in which he pays for it. [”][1] In the first place this is not a fair answer to Mr. Trotter,—he supposes a debt already contracted and which can only be discharged by money;—his argument has no reference to any new contract which may take place between the exporter of wheat from the continent and the exporter of bullion or of money from England, and in which contract the consideration of the value of these articles must necessarily enter. His case is this, an importer of wheat into England has engaged to pay a sum of money, a certain weight of bullion, and the time is arrived at which his creditor will accept of nothing else.

Secondly, if we admit that the argument is fairly applied, we are not told on whose account the transaction took place; was it on account of the foreign or of the English merchant? We are led to suppose indeed that it is on account of both, and that they have both an interest in the value of bullion because they are both to add to the price of the wheat to compensate them for the loss on the Bullion,—one of them is to do so because bullion is cheap and the other because bullion is dear. If it be said that the importation of the wheat into England is on account of the English merchant only, then the transaction was complete as far as regarded the foreign merchant at the moment he sold the wheat. He bought it in France for a sum of French currency and sold it for a sum of French currency which was to be paid him either by means of a bill of exchange or by the actual transit of bullion of an equal value,—he has therefore no other interest but to take care to receive his payment, and his

[1] This passage is quoted from Trower's Notes on Trotter. As a result of Ricardo's criticism Trower crossed it out in his MS and replaced it with a new version.

profit if any should attach to it. It is probable that he might have only been an agent and have no other interest but his commission for his trouble. If then the transaction be on account of the English merchant what possible inducement will he have to import the wheat if the bullion which he has engaged to give in return for it, be dearer in England than in France, that is to say if he cannot sell it for more money than he has purchased it for.

If he can do so, does it not prove that bullion is cheaper in England than in France? that with the commodity wheat more bullion may be bought in England than in France? As far as those commodities are concerned, what greater evidence can we possess of bullion being dearer in France than in England? Is it a satisfactory answer to say, no; it is the wheat that is dearer in England;—dearer for what? why, for bullion. This I conceive is but another way of saying that bullion is cheaper in England and dearer in France. How are we to distinguish then whether the profit has been obtained by the sale of the money or by the purchase of the wheat, seeing that they precisely express the same thing?

In the supposed case then, of the exportation of bullion, notwithstanding its being dearer in the exporting country, in return for wheat, the fact that wheat is cheaper in the importing country is necessarily involved;—how then can there be any remedy against the disadvantage of exporting bullion by raising the price of the wheat? It is saying, because wheat is cheaper here than abroad,—I will add to the quantity by importing more and will at the same time increase its price. The same argument may be used if the whole transaction were on account of the foreign merchant.

OBSERVATIONS ON VANSITTART'S PROPOSITIONS RESPECTING MONEY, BULLION AND EXCHANGES

1811

NOTE TO 'OBSERVATIONS ON VANSITTART'

RICARDO'S Observations on Vansittart's Propositions on the Bullion Report appear to have been written between 26 April and 3 May 1811. The MS, which is among Ricardo's Papers, covers seven quarto pages. It has been printed in *Minor Papers on the Currency Question*, ed. by J. H. Hollander, Baltimore, The Johns Hopkins Press, 1932, pp. 111–17.

The Bullion Report, though published in August 1810, was not discussed in the House of Commons until the following year. On 5 April 1811 it was agreed, on Horner's proposal, that the debate on the Report should take place on 29 April; later, however, the debate was postponed to 6 May.

During the intervening weeks Resolutions were drawn up and circulated both by the supporters and by the opponents of the Report;[1] on 22 April Horner's sixteen Resolutions embodying the conclusions of the Report were printed,[2] and on 26 April Vansittart's seventeen Counter-Resolutions were printed under the title 'Propositions respecting Money, Bullion and Exchanges'.[3] On 3 May were printed Horner's Amendments to Vansittart's Propositions, and also a revised version of these Propositions.[4]

[1] Both sets of Resolutions are in *Parliamentary Papers*, 1810–11, vol. x.

[2] The Resolutions, like the Report, were drawn up by Horner, Huskisson and Thornton: 'I understand that the first ten or twelve were by Mr. Huskisson, and those which follow by Mr. Horner, except the resolution stating that "it is the duty of the Bank", et cetera, which is by Mr. Thornton.' (Letter of Lord Auckland to Lord Grenville, 25 April 1811, in *Historical MSS Commission, Report on the MSS of J. B. Fortescue at Dropmore*, 1927, vol. x, p. 131.)

[3] That Vansittart was 'the godfather, but not the father' of the famous third Resolution which equalizes Bank-notes with gold was disclosed by Canning in a speech in the debate on the Bank Charter, 13 Feb. 1826; but when challenged he declined to name the 'father' (*Hansard*, N.S., XIV, 331). According to the *Dictionary of National Biography*, article 'Vansittart', the Counter-Resolutions were 'drawn up by the request of Perceval'.

[4] A third version, only slightly differing from the second, was printed under the date 14–15 May 1811.

The debate on Horner's Resolutions began on 6 May and ended with the defeat of all his Resolutions on 9 May. That on Vansittart's Propositions began on 13 May and ended on 15 May with their adoption, after Horner's amendments had been negatived.

Ricardo's Observations refer to the first printed version of Vansittart's Propositions, dated 26 April 1811.[1] This establishes the earliest date for the writing of Ricardo's Observations and suggests as the latest date 3 May, when the revised version of Vansittart's Propositions was printed.[2]

The first ten of Vansittart's Propositions (which is as far as Ricardo's comments go), in their original version, are here printed in square brackets and in smaller type before the respective comments.

[1] In the second version, besides some alterations in the statistics, Resolutions 6 and 7 are transposed; Ricardo's comments follow the order of the first version.

[2] See also below, pp. 420, n. 2 and 421, n. 1.

OBSERVATIONS ON THE PROPOSITIONS RESPECTING MONEY, BULLION AND EXCHANGES

[Vansittart's Counter-Resolutions, dated 26 April 1811.][1]

[I. THAT the right of establishing and regulating the legal Money of this Kingdom hath at all times been a Royal Prerogative, vested in the Sovereigns thereof, who have from time to time exercised the same as they have seen fit, in changing such legal Money, or altering and varying the value, and enforcing or restraining the circulation thereof, by Proclamation, or in concurrence with the Estates of the Realm by Act of Parliament: and that such legal Money cannot lawfully be defaced, melted down or exported.

II.—THAT the Promissory Notes of the Governor and Company of the Bank of England are engagements to pay certain sums of Money in the legal Coin of this Kingdom; and that for more than a century past, the said Governor and Company were at all times ready to discharge such Promissory Notes in legal Coin of the Realm, until restrained from so doing on the 25th of February 1797, by His Majesty's Order in Council, confirmed by Act of Parliament.

III.—THAT the Promissory Notes of the said Company have hitherto been, and are at this time, held to be equivalent to the legal Coin of the Realm, in all pecuniary transactions to which such Coin is legally applicable.]

3ᵈ The Promissory Notes of the Bank of England cannot justly be said to be at "this time held to be equivalent to the legal coin of the Realm" when the coin is bought at a premᵐ of 6 and 7 pcᵗ,—and when it is prevented from openly rising to 15 or 18 pcᵗ (its real and intrinsic value above paper) by the terror of the law which deters all men of character from

[1] The first ten Propositions of Vansittart are here reproduced from the version of 26 April 1811, in *Parliamentary Papers*, 1810–1811, vol. x.

engaging in a traffic which is disreputable and illegal. Whilst the law can be enforced the currency may be depreciated 50 pc.ᵗ, and yet the coin and paper may preserve the same value as currency.

[IV.—THAT at various periods, as well before as since the said Restriction, the Exchanges between Great Britain and several other Countries have been unfavourable to Great Britain: and that during such periods, the prices of Gold and Silver Bullion, especially of such Gold Bullion as could be legally exported, have frequently risen above the Mint price; and the coinage of Money at the Mint has been either wholly suspended or greatly diminished in amount: and that such circumstances have usually occurred, when expensive Naval and Military operations have been carried on abroad, and in times of public danger or alarm, or when large importations of Grain from foreign parts have taken place.]

4ᵗʰ At no period have the exchanges before the restriction been more unfavourable to Great Britain than 5 or 7 pc.ᵗ or the expences attending the transportation of bullion. Neither did the price of gold bullion in bars, whilst the coin was undebased rise above the mint price excepting in the years 1783 and 4 when it exceeded the mint price about one penny halfpenny.

[V.—THAT such unfavourable Exchanges, and rise in the price of Bullion, occurred to a greater or less degree during the wars carried on by King William the 3d. and Queen Ann; and also during part of the Seven years war, and of the American war; and during the War and Scarcity of grain in 1795 and 1796, when the difficulty increased to such a degree, that on the 25th of February 1797, the Bank of England was restrained from making payments in Cash by His Majesty's Order in Council, confirmed and continued to the present time by divers Acts of Parliament; and the Exchanges became afterwards still more unfavourable, and the price of Bullion higher, during the scarcity which prevailed for two years previous to the Peace of Amiens.]

5ᵗʰ Though the exchanges were unfavourable and gold bullion rose above the mint price during the Wars of King

William and Queen Anne, this happened only[1] occasionally and in a moderate degree, all which occurrences may be satisfactorily explained—from the acknowledged state of the debasement of the coin. That this was the principal cause is abundantly proved by the fact of the price of gold falling below the mint price and the exchanges rising above par immediately on the reformation of the coin. During the seven years war the gold coin then the principal measure of value had become debased which will account for the price of gold having occasionally been as high as £4. 1. 6. The exchange was, though as low as 31.10 in 1760, never below the real par. The relative value of gold and silver was in the market at this time as 14 to 1. Gold was a legal tender in England and a pound sterling in gold was probably of less value in the market than the silver in 31/10 of Hamburgh. The real par of exchange between England and Hamburgh when the relative market value of gold and silver, agrees with the relative mint value viz as 1 to 15.07, is 35/1,—consequently when the relative value is as 1 to 14 the real par is 32/7. Now if we take into our consideration the debased state of the English coin in the year 1760 it is probable that the exchange when at 31/10 was really favourable to England.

At no period in the American War did the price of bar gold exceed the mint price excepting in 1783 when it was as high as £3. 18. p^r oz. 1½d. above the mint price. The exchanges were at this time never more than 3½ pc^t below par, the lowest exchange with Hamburgh being 31/5, whilst the relative value of gold and silver was as 1 to 14 and consequently the real par 32/7. In 1795 and 6 neither the price of bar gold nor of foreign coin exceeded £3. 17. 6 nor were the exchanges at any period lower than 32/4, the relative

---

[1] 'this happened only' is written above 'they were so', which however is not del.

value of gold and silver being as 1 to 14, and the real par 32/7. In 1797 when the Bank of England was restrained from making payments in Cash the exchanges were considerably in favour of England, and the price of gold 4½d. under the mint price.

In the beginning of 1799 the exchange was both nominally and really favourable to England, being at 37/7. In the latter end of that year the price of silver had risen 10 pc^t and then the currency of Hamburgh had risen relatively to that of England in the same proportion so that the exchange tho' nominally 10 pc^t unfavourable to England was really at par.— From this Period the exchange and price of bullion were operated on by the excessive issues of the Bank, which were after sufficient intervals corrected from time to time by the exportation of the coin.

[VI.—THAT during the period of 75 years, ending with the 1st of January 1796 and previous to the aforesaid restriction whereof, with the exception of some small intervals, Accounts are before the House, the price of Standard Gold in bars has been at or under the Mint price 34 years and 5 months; and above the said Mint price 39 years and 7 months; and that the price of Foreign Gold Coin has been at or under £3. 18. per oz. 31 years and 2 months, and above the said price 42 years and 10 months. And that during the same period of 75 years, the price of standard Silver appears to have been at or under the Mint price, 3 years and 2 months only.]

6th For a period of 22 years previous to 1st Jany 1796 that is to say from the recoinage in 1774, the price of gold in bars never exceeded the mint price excepting in the latter end of 1783 and beginning of 1784 when it rose to £3. 18—p^r oz. From 1717 when gold was declared a legal tender to 1774 it has generally been about £3. 18—p^r oz but occasionally rose to £4 and even to £4. 1 p^r oz.—This price is justly attributable to the debased state of the coinage. It is remarkable that the price of gold in coin seldom at these periods exceeded the price of gold in bars which I think is a satisfactory proof that the price of gold was occasioned by the state of the currency and not in consequence of a really unfavourable exchange and therefore any demand for gold abroad. Since the recoinage the price of gold in coin has frequently exceeded the price of gold in bars by 2 or 3/-. It would be a remarkable circumstance if one of the precious metals were not always above the mint price. In this country silver has been generally so circumstanced.

[VII.—THAT the unfavourable state of the Exchanges, and the high price of Bullion, do not, in any of the instances above referred to, appear to have been produced by the restriction upon Cash payments at the Bank of England, or by any excess in the issue of Bank Notes; inasmuch as all the said instances, except the last, occurred previously to any restriction on such Cash payments; and because, so far as appears by such information as has been procured, the price of Bullion has frequently been highest, and the Exchanges most unfavourable, at periods, when the issues of Bank Notes have been considerably diminished, and to have been afterwards restored to their ordinary rates, although those issues have been increased.]

7th The assertion in this resolution is by no means proved. If it is founded on Mr. Pearse's statement it must be given up as that gentleman's facts as well as his reasoning are incorrect.[1]

[VIII.—THAT during the latter part and for sometime after the close of the American war, during the years 1781, 1782 and 1783, the exchange with Hamburgh fell from 34.1 to 31.5, being about 8 per cent.; and the price of foreign gold rose from £3. 17. 6. to £4. 2. 3. per oz. and the price of Dollars from 5s. 4½. per oz. to 5s. 11¼. and that the Bank Notes in circulation were reduced between March 1782 and December 1782, from £9,160,000 to £5,995,000, being a diminution of above one third, and continued (with occasional variations) at such reduced rate until December

---

[1] See Pearse's evidence, above, p. 357.

1784: and that the exchange with Hamburgh rose to 34.6, and the price of Gold fell to £3. 17. 6. and Dollars to 5s. 1½. per oz. before the 25ᵗʰ February 1787, the amount of Bank Notes being then increased to £8,688,000.]

8. The price of foreign gold coin is frequently 2 or 3/- pʳ oz higher than bar gold being often wanted for particular markets. It appears that in the year 1781 the price of bar gold did not exceed £3. 17. 6 and gold in coin is once quoted £4. 0. 6. In 1782 bar gold did not exceed £3. 17. 9 and gold in coin is once quoted £4. 2.—In 1783 bar gold £3. 18— and foreign gold is in one month quoted as high as £4. 2. 3 and as low as[1] £3. 17. 9. The exchange in 1781—varied from 34/1 to 31/11 a fall of nearly 7 pcᵗ but during the same period silver rose 7 pcᵗ viz. from 5/5½ which was the price when the exchange was 34/1 to 5/10 its price when the exchange was 31/11. In 1782 the exchange fell to 31/8 and silver rose to 5/11½. In 1783 the exchange fell to 31/5 and 31/6 and silver to 5/8½. In neither of these years was the real exchange more unfavourable to England than 3½ pcᵗ—It should be remarked that the price of dollars was not 5/11¼ at the same period that the price of gold was £4. 2. 3. According to the wording of this resolution we should be induced to suppose that the fall of 8 pcᵗ in the exchange occasioned both the high price of gold and the high price of dollars. When dollars were at 5/11¼ gold in bars was at £3. 17. 9 and foreign gold in coin £4. —. 1 and the exchange 31/10—the relative value of gold and silver being as 1 to 13.1—so that the real par of exchange was 31/- and consequently the then exchange of 31/10 favourable to England.

I have no account of the Bank notes in circulation in the years 1781. 2. 3.[2]—Was the circulation in March 1782 of

[1] 'and as low as' is written above 'and varied from,' which however is not del.

[2] Figures for 1783 had already been published in February 1811 (see following note); figures for

9,160,000 a temporary or had it been a permanent amount?—what was the state of it in Jan.ʸ 1782, in Jan.ʸ 1783.[1] An increase of a month or two can produce no permanent nor even a temporary effect.—I should like to see the account of Bank notes in circulation up to 1790.[2]—Mr. Vansittart wishes his readers to suppose that the price of gold did not fall to £3. 17. 6; dollars to 5/1½; and the exchange did not rise to 34/6 till the increase of Bank notes in 1787 to 8,688,000,—but it appears that in Jan.ʸ 1784, bar gold and foreign gold were no higher than £3. 18— p.ʳ oz., from May 1784 to August 1785 neither of them were above £3. 17. 10½ and from that period till 1792 they were never higher than £3. 17. 6. In 1784 Dollars were at 5/1 and in 1785 as low as 5/- and the exchange was at 34/10 in 1784 and at 35/6 in 1785.

[IX.—THAT the Amount of Bank Notes in February 1787 was £8,688,000, and in February 1791 £11,699,000; and that during the same period, the sum of £10,704,000 was coined in Gold; and that the Exchange with Hamburgh rose about 3 per cent.]

9. Did the exchange during the periods alluded to in these resolutions vary beyond the limits laid down as the true principle by the Report,—this is the test by which they ought fairly to be tried. Who has denied that the exchange may be 1 or 2 pc.ᵗ or even more at one time in favour of Hamburgh, and at another 1 or 2 pc in favour of London. Who again has denied that during a period of successful

1781 and 1782, which had not been published when Ricardo was writing, were ordered to be printed on 3 May 1811 (*Parliamentary Papers*, 1810–11, vol. x, N°. 147).
[1] Ricardo adds in the margin:

'it was   6,354
July   6,392
Jan. 1784 6,074
July   6,504.'
These figures are from an Account ordered to be printed 22 Feb. 1811 (*Parliamentary Papers*, 1810–11, vol. x, N°. 22).
[2] Replaces '1787'.

commerce[1] an increase of 3 or 4 millions of circulating medium may not be wanted? This might have been occasioned too by a diminution generally in the market of the world of the value of the precious metals. The coinage from 1787 to 1791 inclusive from foreign gold did not exceed £4,000,000 that from light guineas cannot be considered as an augmentation to the currency. Mr. Vansittart states the whole at 10,704 millions[2].

[X.—That between the 25th of February 1795, and the 25th of February 1797, the amount of Bank Notes was reduced from £13,539,000 to £8,640,000, during which time the exchange with Hamburgh fell from 36 to 35, being about 3 per cent., and the said amount was increased to £11,855,000, exclusive of £1,542,000 in Notes of £1. and £2. each on the 1st of February 1798, during which time the Exchange rose to 38.2, being about 9 per cent.]

10. In January 1795 the circulation of Bank notes was from 10 to 12 millions[,] in March it was as high as 14 millions but was immediately reduced to about 10 millions, it continued during the whole year between 10 and 11 millions except for one fortnight when it exceeded it. It was not till after July 1796 that the amount of notes was lowered to below 9,500,000[,] for the rest of the year it varied from 9,500,000 to about 9,000,000. The exchange fell in 1795 from 36 at which it was in Feby to 32/10 in July. In the end of 1796 the exchange rose again to 34/7, the price of silver being at 5/4 and 5/6 and gold £3. 17. 6 the exchange was uniformly above par.

The average amount of notes in Jany 1795 was 11 millions[,] in Feby about 10 millions, in March 11,700, in April 11,100, in May 10.200, June 9,800, July 10,250, Aug 10600, —Sep 10,500, —Octr 10400, Nov 10750, Dcr 11,900, Jan 96

---

[1] 'that' is ins. here by mistake. [2] Replaces '10 millions'; an imperfect correction.

10300, Feb 10,350, Mar 9,800, Ap 10500, May 10,100, June 9,400, July 9,400 and continued about 9 millions till Feb 1797,—in which year the exchange rose to 38/2. It must be observed that the price of standard silver fell this year to 5/0$\frac{1}{2}$ so that the real par was perhaps not less than 36 or 37.

It appears then that it was between Ap! 1796 and Feb.ʸ 1797 that the amount of notes was reduced from 10,500 to 8,640, and that the exchange rose from 32/7 the price in Jan 1796 to 36/8 in April and 38/- in Sepʳ,[1] the earliest period perhaps at which the effects of the reduction of the amount of the circulation would be felt by the exchange.

[1] The last two rates refer to the year 1797.

APPENDIX

APPENDIX

APPENDIX

'*Mr. ——*' of the Bullion Report

In his *Notes on the Bullion Report* (above, p. 347 ff.) Ricardo comments extensively on the evidence of the anonymous Continental merchant who was a witness before the Bullion Committee, and refers to him several times in his *Reply to Bosanquet* (above, pp. 163, 168, 185) and once in his *Notes on Bentham* (above, p. 288).

This witness gave evidence on four days (2, 5, 7 and 8 March 1810), being described in the Minutes as 'Mr. ——, a Continental Merchant'; he is referred to in the Report as 'a very eminent Continental Merchant'[1] and again as 'the Merchant who has been already mentioned as being intimately acquainted with the trade between this Country and the Continent of Europe'.[2]

Professor Cannan, speaking of him in the Introduction to his reprint of the Bullion Report,[3] says 'An obvious conjecture is that this modest Mr. Blank was the great N. M. Rothschild.' Later writers have required no further proof and have taken this identification with Rothschild for granted.[4] This suggestion however can be dismissed, apart from the circumstances mentioned below, simply by comparing the evidence of Mr. —— with that given by Rothschild before the Secret Committees of 1819 (Resumption of Cash Payments) and 1832 (Renewal of the Bank Charter);[5] the differences in style and the contradiction between the opinions of Mr. —— in 1810 and of Rothschild in 1819 and 1832 are such as to rule out the hypothesis of their being the same person.

Besides, there is nothing that could be even remotely com-

---

[1] *Report*, 8vo ed., p. 19.
[2] *ib.* p. 26.
[3] *The Paper Pound of 1797–1821*, London, 1919, p. xlii.
[4] See A. Brady, *William Huskisson and Liberal Reform*, Oxford, 1928 ('The evidence of a few merchants, including N. M.

Rothschild', p. 25) and L. Stuart Sutherland, in *Economic History Review*, April 1932 ('Mr.——, to be identified in all probability, as has been suggested, with Nathan Rothschild', p. 378).
[5] I owe this comparison to Professor Hayek.

promising in Mr. ———'s evidence and it is difficult to imagine that anyone should feel so endangered by the acknowledgement of its authorship as to adopt the extraordinary expedient of being reported anonymously. The only possible reason for anonymity must have been to conceal the presence of the witness in London at the time. But there was no secret about Rothschild's residence in England, where he had been established for many years. Thus there could be no reason for his anonymity.[1]

As the anonymous merchant was the only witness, besides Sir Francis Baring, whose evidence on the whole supported the conclusions of the Committee, he was frequently referred to in the pamphlet literature and was singled out for attack by the Antibullionists; but none of these writers supplies any clue to his identity.[2] What was said in the Bullion debate in the House of

---

[1] Another false identification is suggested by the title of an anonymous pamphlet published many years later, at the time of the Bank Charter inquiry of 1832: *The Evidence that WOULD have been given by Mr. ———, Late a Continental Merchant, before the Committee of Secrecy Appointed to Inquire into the Expediency of Renewing the Bank Charter*, London, Pelham Richardson, 1832. A note on the author's own copy which is in the British Museum (8229. aaaa. 21/4) identifies him as John Cazenove (*ca.* 1788–1879), a member of the Political Economy Club and writer of several pamphlets on economic subjects, who was the son of a Geneva merchant migrated to London. Although the author describes himself in the same terms as the anonymous witness of 1810, they cannot be the same person, as they hold altogether different views on the subject; in any case Cazenove would have had no reasons for concealing his presence in London, and he could hardly have been 'a very eminent' merchant at 22 years of age.

[2] Sir John Sinclair, in his *Observations on the Report of the Bullion Committee*, 1810, p. 6, wrote: 'They have also reported the evidence of an anonymous witness, contrary to the usage of Parliament, unless special reasons can be, and actually are assigned, for the concealment; and they seem to have laid peculiar weight on the doctrines of this nameless individual. Yet this unknown individual may be a foreigner, or a person usually resident abroad, who may not be so anxious, as a British merchant would necessarily be, to deliver opinions favourable to the prosperity of this country.' On which the *Quarterly Review* for November 1810 (p. 524) observed: 'Now, for anything that Sir John has learned to the contrary, "this unknown individual *may* be a *foreigner*"; and yet the Committee have not, by printing his

Commons by critics of the Report is a little more informative. George Rose, Vice-President of the Board of Trade, said of him that 'though a most respectable man, [he] has more of Continental than of British interests'.[1] And Nicholas Vansittart, the leading opponent of the Report, referred to him as 'One gentleman...of whom (as he is not named) we know nothing more, than that he resides abroad, therefore has not had the means of forming his judgement on the spot'.[2]

That he was a resident abroad, and that he had more of Continental than of British interests is thus all the information that was disclosed at the time. Retaining this, we turn for further clues to his own evidence before the Committee.

Other Continental merchants[3] who were heard, under their names, by the Bullion Committee, were asked as one of the first questions: 'Are you acquainted with the subject of the exchanges between this Country and the Continent?'[4] Whilst merchants specialising in the trade with any one country were at once asked a question on the currency of that particular country.[5]

Now, the first question asked to the anonymous Continental merchant was the significant one: 'Are you acquainted with the subject of the exchange between this country and Hamburgh?'[6] And although he replied 'I am, and with other foreign Countries', his factual evidence on foreign countries refers largely to Hamburg or else to the other Northern countries. Indeed, when he is asked 'Can you state how much per cent. may be the present expence and risk of transporting Gold from London to Amsterdam or Hamburgh, or any other principal places of trade on the Continent?' he answers simply 'Independent of the premium of

---

evidence either in broken English, or in the *patois* of his country, thought fit to guard their readers against the poison of his representations.'

[1] 6 May 1811, *Hansard*, XIX, 836.
[2] 7 May 1811, *Hansard*, XIX, 931.
[3] These were, as the description usually implied, London merchants trading to the Continent.

[4] See the evidence of J. L. Greffulhe, 'Minutes of Evidence', p. 61 and of W. C. Chalmers, p. 135.
[5] See the evidence of T. Hughan, 'a merchant, trading to the West Indies', p. 55, and of S. Williams, 'a Merchant trading to the United States of America', p. 140.
[6] p. 77.

insurance, it would be from $1\frac{1}{2}$ to 2 per cent. from London to Hamburgh.'[1]

If therefore we assume that Mr. ——— was a resident of Hamburg, the reason for his wishing to remain anonymous and to conceal his presence in London becomes apparent. For Hamburg had been in French occupation since the end of 1806, and under the Berlin and Milan Decrees a visit to England constituted a serious offence.[2]

It is recorded that only seven British firms were able to continue their activity in Hamburg during the French occupation, as their partners had the Hamburg citizenship. The names of the firms in question are: Parish & Co.; Kirkpatrick & Co.; Humphrey Carvick & Co.; J. B. Smith, Barclay & Co.; Peacock & Co.; George Walker; Thomas Tattlock.[3]

Certain allusions in Mr. ———'s evidence, taken in conjunction with an entry in one of the accounts in the Appendix to the Bullion Report, indicate the firm among those listed with which he was probably connected.

Mr. ——— in his evidence mentions repeatedly 'foreign subsidies'[4] and 'the expenditures for the account of Government abroad'[5] among the 'extraordinary causes' which he regards as having operated on the exchange so as to depress it below par at times when the balance of trade was in favour of England.

Appendix LXX to the Bullion Report contains an account of the Bills of Exchange drawn on the Treasury for expenses abroad, from 1804 to 1809. One of the largest single items in this account is a payment for over £700,000, in the year 1806, to Edward

---

[1] pp. 83–4. Many others of his answers are equally significant as to his origin, *e.g.* (p. 78): 'Taking Gold...at Hamburgh at what we call its par, which is 96 stivers banco for a ducat....'

[2] As Mr.——— told the Committee, 'when the French got possession of the North of Germany [they] passed severe penal decrees against a communication with this Country' (p. 88).

[3] This list, from a document of August 1807, is given in H. Hitzigrath, *Die Kompagnie der Merchant Adventurers und die englische Kirchengemeinde in Hamburg 1611–1835*, Hamburg, 1904, p. 62.

[4] 'Minutes of Evidence', p. 97.

[5] *ib.* p. 105; see other allusions to these 'extraordinary causes', pp. 107 and 109.

Thornton, Minister at Hamburg, for 'Public services'; in connection with which, payments for over £5000 were made to each
of two firms of Hamburg merchants, Thornton and Power, and
Parish and Co., for 'Interest and commission on the negociation
of bills drawn by Mr. Thornton, &c.'[1]

It was the more likely that a Hamburg merchant would be
acquainted with the British Government's expenses abroad and
their subsidies to the Allies if he had been himself connected with
such transactions; now Thornton and Power had ceased activity
in Hamburg after the French occupation, so we may concentrate
our attention on Parish & Co.[2]

The firm, one of the largest merchant houses in Hamburg, had
been founded by John Parish, who had gone there as a boy from
Scotland in 1756. He retired from the business in 1796, entrusting
it to his sons, and fled from Hamburg when the city was occupied
by the French, settling at Bath in 1807, where he remained till his
death in 1829. In 1809 three of his sons, John, Richard and
Charles, were in charge of the firm. It appears that at this
time Richard conducted the ordinary commercial activity of
the firm, Charles was engaged in the dangerous business of
breaking through the Continental blockade, with bases at
Heligoland and the small ports of Holstein, and John, the eldest
brother, had undertaken the even more dangerous task of transmitting the British subsidies to Austria, then at war with Napoleon.

John Parish, junior describes his enterprise in a report to the
Emperor of Austria as follows. At the beginning of the year
1809, being in London, he was asked on behalf of the British
Government if he could devise means for transmitting to the
Austrian Government an instalment of the British subsidy. 'At
that moment this seemed almost impossible, as all communication

---

[1] 'Appendix of Accounts', p. 99;
similar entries, for much smaller
payments, in 1807, p. 101. In
both cases the dates are no doubt
those of the payment of the bills,
which may have been (in the case
of the 1807 bills, certainly had

been) drawn during the previous
year.
[2] The information in the following two paragraphs is derived
from R. Ehrenberg's monograph
Das Haus Parish in Hamburg,
Jena, 1905 (vol. II of the series
Grosse Vermögen).

with the Continent was so hindered by the French measures that there was danger of life even in receiving a simple letter.' He decided to hazard for the purpose his fortune and his person 'since no one else was then in a position to achieve the object desired.' In May he went from London to Hamburg to make arrangements for advancing the money from his own resources, as it was not possible to transfer it from England; and in June he proceeded, by way of Berlin, to the Austrian headquarters where he made the payment.[1]

This was not an isolated transaction, for in the autumn of 1810, a confidential British agent on the Continent, J. M. Johnson, wrote to the Under-Secretary of State at the Foreign Office that John Parish, junior 'has on various occasions rendered important services to the british government, and...it is thro' his house that most government payments have of late years been made on the continent', adding that Parish 'was frequently consulted by Mr. Canning and Mr. Hammond'.[2] Subsequently Parish went to London, with a letter of Johnson, dated 29 Nov. 1810, introducing him to the Under-Secretary as one 'who has rendered essential services to our government on many important occasions.'[3]

We know, therefore, that Parish was on secret visits to London both in the spring of 1809 and in the autumn of 1810. There is no direct evidence of his being there in March 1810, when Mr. —— was being examined by the Bullion Committee. But there is a circumstance which may have provided the occasion for a visit at that time. When Austria concluded her armistice with Napoleon (in July 1809), the monthly subsidy from the British Government

[1] From an address (in German) of John Parish, jun. to the Emperor Francis, published by Ehrenberg, op. cit., pp. 117–18. No date is given, but it was apparently written several years after the events described, probably in 1816.

[2] J. M. Johnson to C. C. Smith, from Gothenburg, 25 Nov. 1810.

(Public Record Office, F.O. 7/92, quoted by C. S. B. Buckland, *Metternich and the British Government from 1809 to 1813*, London, 1932, pp. 131–2.) George Hammond was the permanent head of the Foreign Office under Canning till 1809.

[3] F.O. 7/93, unpublished.

naturally came to an end. Metternich, however, requested J. M. Johnson, the British secret agent, to demand of the British Government that the subsidy be continued up to the ratification of the peace, on the ground that after the armistice 'the threatening attitude of the Austrian armies' continued to operate as a powerful diversion in favour of England. The message was to be delivered by the agent himself on his arrival in England; otherwise, as the agent reported, Metternich 'particularly requested that in case any unforeseen event prevented my immediate return to England I should not make the foregoing communication in writing untill a perfectly safe mode of conveyance presented itself'. In fact Johnson went only as far as Hamburg, where he wrote his report to the Foreign Office on 7 January 1810, and sent it to London where it did not arrive until 16 February.[1] It is probable that the transmission of the message would be entrusted to the house of Parish, which was the usual channel of communication;[2] and in connection with this negotiation (which does not appear to have achieved Metternich's object) John Parish, junior himself may have travelled to London just at the time when the Bullion Committee began its hearings.

Turning back to Mr. ⸻'s evidence we find one or two details which tally with events in the life of John Parish, junior as given by Ehrenberg. Mr. ⸻ in his evidence describes, as from first-hand knowledge, the state of public opinion and the general commercial conditions in England, following the suspension of cash payments in 1797, and refers to the commercial distress which existed in the year 1799;[3] now, in 1799 John Parish, junior made a prolonged visit to England.[4] Also, Mr. ⸻ alludes to the currency events in Austria in the summer of 1809,[5] when as we know Parish was on a mission to that country.

---

[1] This account of Johnson's mission is derived from Buckland, *Metternich and the British Government*, pp. 37–9.

[2] Buckland, *op. cit.*, pp. 128 and 131.

[3] 'Minutes of Evidence', pp. 101, 107 and 97.

[4] Ehrenberg, *op. cit.*, p. 92.

[5] Referring to the influence of the quantity of paper on its price: 'we have seen a strong instance of it last summer, when, from the extraordinary exertions of the Austrian Government....' ('Minutes of Evidence', p. 86.)

Apart from his evidence to the Bullion Committee (if it is admitted that he was the anonymous witness) John Parish, junior's only contribution to the subject appears to have been a paper on the Austrian Banking and Currency system, which he sent to Friedrich von Gentz in August 1816.[1] In that year, at the age of 42, he retired from business with a large fortune, bought the estate of Senftenberg in Bohemia and was made a baron by the Emperor of Austria in recognition of his services. He died in 1858.

The hypothesis here advanced as to the identity of Mr. —— has since been confirmed as a result of a search in the Hamburg Archives kindly undertaken by Dr Eduard Rosenbaum at my request. There is in the Archives, among the papers of Karl Sieveking (a contemporary of Parish) an unpublished 'History of the Pound Sterling from 25 February 1797 to the Second Peace of Paris'. Reviewing the evidence given before the Bullion Committee Sieveking writes: 'Particularly remarkable is the evidence of a Continental merchant, who is said to be Mr John Parish of Hamburg, at present owner of the estate of Senftenberg in Bohemia'.[2] Sieveking was in a position to know, for when writing his history in 1817 he was in touch with Parish who supplied him with a copy of the Bullion Report and a set of the *Edinburgh Review*.[3]

---

[1] Fr. v. Gentz, *Briefe*, 1913, vol. III, p. 336. Gentz, in October 1816, described Parish as 'unstreitig einer der ersten mercantilischen Köpfe unserer Zeit' (*Gentz und Wessenberg, Briefe*, ed. A. Fournier, 1907, quoted by Buckland, p. 132; see also Ehrenberg, p. 117, n.).

[2] Staatsarchiv der Freien und Hansestadt Hamburg; Aus dem Nachlass Karl Sieveking, Schachtel V, c: *Geschichte des Pfund Sterlings vom 25. Februar 1797 bis zum zweiten Frieden von Paris*, p. 28. 'Besonders merkwürdig ist das Verhör eines auf dem Continent ansässigen Kaufmanns, wie verlauten will des Hᵣ John Parish von Hamburg, jetzig. Besitzers der Herrschaft Senftenberg in Böhmen'.

[3] 'Von Parish erhielt ich den Report des Bullion-Committee und die Sammlung der Edinburgh Review'. Sieveking to his brother, 21 March 1817, in *Karl Sieveking, 1787–1847, Lebensbild eines hamburgischen Diplomaten aus dem Zeitalter der Romantik*, by Heinrich Sieveking, Hamburg, 1923, Part II, p. 211; cp. p. 226 ff. and Part III, p. 395.

Tables of corresponding pages

for Ricardo's Pamphlets in the original editions, *1811*,
McCulloch's edition (Works, *1846* etc.),
Gonner's edition (Economic Essays, *1923* etc.),
and the present edition.

THE HIGH PRICE OF BULLION

Edition 4 1811	McCulloch's edition	Gonner's edition	Present edition	Edition 4 1811	McCulloch's edition	Gonner's edition	Present edition
1–2	263	3	52	44–5	281	28–9	84
2–3	263–4	3–4	53	45–6	281–2	29–30	85
3–5	264	4–5	54	46–7	282	30–1	86
5–6	264–5	5–6	55	48–9	282–3	31–2	87
6–8	265–6	6–7	56	49–50	283–4	32	88
8–9	266	7–8	57	50–2	284	32–3	89
9–10	266–7	8	58	52–3	284–5	33–4	90
10–12	267	8–9	59	53–5	285	34–5	91
12–13	267–8	9–10	60	55–6	285–6	35–6	92
13–15	268	10–11	61	56–8	286–7	36–7	93
15–16	268–9	11–12	62	58–9	287	37–8	94
16–17	269–70	12–13	63	59–61	287–8	38–9	95
17–18	270	13	64	61–2	288	39–40	96
18–20	270–1	13–14	65	62–4	288–9	40	97
20–1	271	14–15	66	64–5	289–90	40–2	98
21–2	271	15	67	65–7	290–1	42–3	99
22–3	271–2	15–16	68	67–8	291	43	100
23–5	272–3	16–17	69	68–9	291–2	43–4	101
25–6	273	17–18	70	69–70	292	44–5	102
26–8	273–4	18–19	71	70–1	292	45	103
28–9	274–5	19–20	72	71–2	292–3	45–6	104
29–31	275	20–21	73	72–4	293	46–7	105
31	275–6	21	74	74–5	293	47	106
31–3	276	21–2	75	75–6	293–4	47–8	107
33–4	276–7	22–3	76	76–7	294	48	108
34–5	277	23–4	77	77–8	294–5	48–9	109
36–7	277–8	24	78	78–9	295	49–50	110
37–8	278	24–5	79	79–80	295	50	111
38–40	278–9	25–6	80	80–1	295–6	50–1	112
40–1	279–80	26–7	81	81–2	296	51	113
41–2	280	27–8	82	82–3	296	51–2	114
42–4	280–1	28	83	83–4	296–7	52–3	115

THE HIGH PRICE OF BULLION (*cont.*)

Edition 4 1811	McCulloch's edition	Gonner's edition	Present edition	Edition 4 1811	McCulloch's edition	Gonner's edition	Present edition
84–6	297	53	116	91–2	299–300	56–7	122
86–7	297–8	53–4	117	92–3	300	57–8	123
87–9	298	54–5	118	93–4	300	58	124
88	298	55	119	94–5	300–1	58–9	125
89–91	298–9	55–6	120	95–7	301	59–60	126
90	299	56	121	97	301	60	127

REPLY TO MR. BOSANQUET'S PRACTICAL OBSERVATIONS

Edition 1811	McCulloch's edition	Gonner's edition	Present edition	Edition 1811	McCulloch's edition	Gonner's edition	Present edition
1–2	305	63–4	159	41–2	323	88–9	187
2–3	305–6	64	160	42–3	323–4	89	188
3–5	306–7	64–5	161	43–5	324–5	89–90	189
5	307	65	162	45–6	325	90–1	190
6–7	308	66–7	163	46–7	325–6	91–2	191
7–8	308–9	67	164	47–9	326	92–3	192
8–10	309–10	68	165	49–50	326–7	93–4	193
10–11	310	68–9	166	50–2	327–8	94–5	194
11–13	310–11	69–70	167	52–3	328	95–6	195
13–14	311	70–1	168	53–5	328–9	96–7	196
14–15	311–12	71–2	169	55–6	329–30	97	197
15–17	312	72	170	56–8	330	97–8	198
17–18	312–13	72–3	171	58–9	330–1	98–9	199
18–19	313–14	73–4	172	59–60	331	99–100	200
19–21	314	74–5	173	60–2	331–2	100–1	201
21–2	314–15	75–6	174	62–3	332–3	101	202
22–4	315	76–7	175	63–5	333	101–2	203
24–5	315–16	77–8	176	65	333	102–3	204
25–7	316–17	78–9	177	66–7	334	104–5	205
27–8	317	79–80	178	67–9	334–5	105	206
28–30	317–18	80	179	69–70	335–6	105–6	207
30–1	318–19	80–1	180	70–2	336	106–7	208
31–3	319	81–2	181	72–3	336–7	107–8	209
33–4	319–20	82–3	182	73–5	337	108–9	210
34–6	320	83–4	183	75–6	337–8	109–10	211
36–8	320–1	84–5	184	76–8	338–9	110–11	212
38–9	321–2	85–6	185	78–9	339	111–12	213
39–40	322	86–7	186	80–1	340	113–14	214

REPLY TO MR. BOSANQUET (*cont.*)

Edition 1811	McCulloch's edition	Gonner's edition	Present edition	Edition 1811	McCulloch's edition	Gonner's edition	Present edition
81–2	340–1	114	215	109–10	354	132–3	236
82–4	341–2	114–15	216	110–12	354–5	133	237
84–5	342	115–16	217	112–13	355	133–4	238
85–7	342–3	116–17	218	113–15	356	134–5	239
87–8	343	117–18	219	115–16	356–7	135–6	240
88–90	343–4	118–19	220	116–18	357	136–7	241
90	344	119	221	118–19	357–8	137–8	242
91–2	345	120–1	222	119–21	358–9	138–9	243
92–4	345–6	121	223	121–2	359	139	244
94–5	346–7	121–2	224	122–4	360	140–1	245
95–7	347	122–3	225	124–5	360–1	141	246
97	347	123	226	127–8	363	143	247
97–8	348	124–5	227	128–9	363	143–4	248
98–100	348–9	125	228	129–31	363–4	144	249
100–1	349	125–6	229	131–2	364	144–5	250
101–3	349–50	126–7	230	132–4	364–5	145–6	251
103–4	350–1	127–8	231	134–5	365	146	252
104–5	351	128–9	232	135–7	365	146–7	253
106–7	351–2	129–30	233	137–8	365–6	147	254
107–8	352	130	234	138–40	366	147–8	255
108–9	352–3	130–1	235	140–1	366	148–9	256